ANGLO-SAXON(IST) PASTS, POSTSAXON FUTURES

Before you start to read this book, take this moment to think about making a donation to punctum books, an independent non-profit press,

@ https://punctumbooks.com/support/

If you're reading the e-book, you can click on the image below to go directly to our donations site. Any amount, no matter the size, is appreciated and will help us to keep our ship of fools afloat. Contributions from dedicated readers will also help us to keep our commons open and to cultivate new work that can't find a welcoming port elsewhere. Our adventure is not possible without your support.

Vive la Open Access.

Fig. 1. Hieronymus Bosch, *Ship of Fools* (1490–1500)

ANGLO-SAXON(IST) PASTS, POSTSAXON FUTURES. Copyright © 2019 by Donna Beth Ellard. This work carries a Creative Commons BY-NC-SA 4.0 International license, which means that you are free to copy and redistribute the material in any medium or format, and you may also remix, transform and build upon the material, as long as you clearly attribute the work to the authors (but not in a way that suggests the authors or punctum books endorses you and your work), you do not use this work for commercial gain in any form whatsoever, and that for any remixing and transformation, you distribute your rebuild under the same license. http://creativecommons.org/licenses/by-nc-sa/4.0/

First published in 2019 by punctum books, Earth, Milky Way.
https://punctumbooks.com

ISBN-13: 978-1-950192-39-7 (print)
ISBN-13: 978-1-950192-40-3 (ePDF)

DOI: 10.21983/P3.0262.1.00

LCCN: 2019947002
Library of Congress Cataloging Data is available from the Library of Congress

Book Design: Vincent W.J. van Gerven Oei
Cover Image based upon 'Tumulus 1' at Chatham, Kent, in James Douglas, *Nenia Britannica; or, A sepulchral history of Great Britain* (London: Printed by John Nichols; for George Nicol, in Pall-Mall, Bookseller to his Majesty, 1793). Image courtesy of The Newberry Library.

HIC SVNT MONSTRA

Donna Beth Ellard

Anglo-Saxon(ist) Pasts

postSaxon Futures

Contents

Foreword · 15

First Movement
Anglo-Saxon(ist) Pasts

1 · *OED*. 'Anglo-Saxonist, noun': Professional Scholar or Anonymous Person · 19
2 · *Krákumál,* Sharon Turner, and the Psychic Crypts of Anglo-Saxon History · 61
3 · *Beowulf,* James Douglas, and the Sepulchral Body of the Anglo-Saxonist · 101

Second Movement
Interlude—A Time for Mourning

4 · On Being an Anglo-Saxonist: Asser's *Life of King Alfred,* Benjamin Thorpe, and the Sovereign *Corpus* of a Profession · 175
5 · Becoming postSaxon, or, a Biochemical *Vita Ælfredi* · 239

Third Movement
postSaxon Futures

6 · Old/e English Poetics and 'Afro-Saxon' Intimacies · 283
7 · Becoming postSaxon · 337

Bibliography · 355

Index · 399

Acknowledgments

So many people have had a hand in making this book. I would like to thank Melissa Gniadek (who has been, throughout this process, the most generous reader and friend), Joe Campana, Claire Fanger, Helena Michie, Tim Morton, Judith Roof, Cary Wolfe, Diane Wolfthal, and the wonderful undergraduate students of Rice University, where the seeds of this project began to grow, while I was an ACLS New Faculty Fellow.

At the University of Denver, DU's First Book Group has been a sustaining force in transforming this project from several, loosely-conceived essays to a monograph in bloom. Thank you to Alejandro Cerón, Sarah Crockarell, Tayana Hardin, Sarah Hart-Micke, Chad Leahy, Ben Nourse, Juli Parrish, Orna Shaughnessy, Armond Towns, and Kristy Ulibarri. Elsewhere at DU, Bin Ramke and Selah Saterstrom have talked about family, writing, and the South with me; Tayana Hardin has lent her ears and given her emotional energy too many times to this project; and Chad Leahy has found precious hours to read, comment, and talk through several chapter drafts, despite his busy schedule.

Outside Rice and DU, Carol Pasternack, Aranye Fradenburg-Joy, and Alan Liu were extraordinary mentors at UCSB. Jessica Murphy, Megan Palmer, Maggie Sloan, and Mac Test were attentive interlocutors in graduate school, when this book was a misdirected dissertation. Alex Cook, Dorothy Kim, Clare Lees, Gillian Overing, Dan Remein, and Cord Whitaker have engaged in conversation and answered many questions from early to late stages of the project. Kathy Biddick, Mary Dockray-Miller, and

Robin Norris have graciously served as readers for this project and provided immensely helpful comments.

punctum books has magically transformed this manuscript into a book. Vincent W.J. van Gerven Oei has electrified the cover art in hot pink and made everything beautiful inside and out. Joyce King has done the all-important work of copy-editing the manuscript. Eileen Joy's unbelievable editorial comments and questions have challenged me to refine and make explicit the global arguments of this book. Her careful attention not only to the book's arguments but also to its prose are remarkable. I cannot thank punctum enough for taking a chance on it.

Portions of Chapters 1 and 2 were previously published as essays in postmedieval: a journal of medieval cultural studies and Rethinking History. I am grateful to the editors of these journals for believing in my work many years before issues of colonialism and race were topics of immediate concern in medieval studies.[1] Any errors and omissions in this book are strictly my own.

Outside academia, a very big thank you to my husband and girls, who continue to remind me what is really important in life.

---

[1] Donna Beth Ellard, 'Ella's Bloody Eagle: Sharon Turner's *History of the Anglo-Saxons* and Anglo-Saxon History,' *postmedieval: a journal of medieval cultural studies* 5, no. 2 (2013): 215–34 and '"Anglo-Saxonist, n.": Professional Scholar or Anonymous Person,' *Rethinking History* 23, no. 1 (2019): 16–33.

For Virginia Sugg, Virginia Dare, Virginia Anne, and Pressly Virginia—the Ellard women and girls.

For Brandon.

and

For Mississippi, whom I still love, despite it all.

Foreword

We are all, no matter how little we like it, the bearers of unwanted and often shunned memory, of a history whose infiltrations are at times so stealthy we can pretend otherwise, and at times so loud we can't hear much of anything else. We're still here — there differently than those before us, but there, otherwise known as here. And that matters for writers. That's the first intuition. The second one is that it seems a lot of us here when asked to talk about race are most comfortable, or least uncomfortable, talking about it in the language of scandal. It's so satisfying, so clear, so easy. The wronged. The evildoers. The undeserving. The shady. The good intentions and the cyclical manipulations. The righteous side taking, the head shaking. Scandal is such a helpful, such a relieving distraction. There are times when scandal feels like the sun that race revolves around. And it is so hard to reel conversations about race back from the heavy gravitational pull of where we so often prefer them to be.
— Beth Loffreda and Claudia Rankine[1]

The scandals of Anglo-Saxon studies do not need to be rehearsed here, although they do need to be worked through, in

---

1   Beth Loffreda and Claudia Rankine, 'Introduction,' in *The Racial Imaginary: Writers on Race in the Life of the Mind* (East Peoria: Versa Press, 2015), 13–14.

the sense that Freud gave to that phrase: the field needs better accounts of its intellectual history, as well as reconciliation and reparation, and that is a big part of what this book is about. These scandals continue to erupt, monthly — weekly — daily, in online platforms, professional conferences, and classrooms.[2] They are a repetition-compulsion, a symptom of our inability to work through 'a history...so loud we can't hear much of anything else.' But they are also an opportunity.

To my white colleagues: this book is an offering. It is the story of my family, myself, and a Mississippi world in desperate need of healing. As an offering, this book is written with the great hope that we might learn to speak about race in the profession and in our personal lives from outside the framework of scandal, and within the framework of decentering our whiteness in our scholarly work, and listening better to our colleagues of color.

To my colleagues of color: this book is also an offering. It is the story of my family, myself, and a Mississippi world in desperate need of healing. As an offering, this book is written with the great hope that (once, again) you will forgive the field previously known as Anglo-Saxon studies.

---

[2] I want to briefly express my gratitude as well to the early career, and also precarious, scholars in the field formerly known as 'Anglo-Saxon' studies who have been so brave, so smart, and so vigilant in exposing, confronting, and challenging the structural racism of our shared field, as well as urging others to commit to change, especially Mary Rambaran-Olm and Erik Wade. In the midst of the current 'scandals,' they shine a much-needed light on the past and show different, better paths forward.

First Movement

Anglo-Saxon(ist) Pasts

1

OED. 'Anglo-Saxonist, noun': Professional Scholar or Anonymous Person

In the 1990s, a wave of new forms of critique and critical theory broke over Anglo-Saxon studies, an interdisciplinary field that focuses on England's early medieval, 'Old English,' or 'Anglo-Saxon' period. Spurred by decades of European decolonization and American desegregation, Anglo-Saxonists reflected upon their field's nineteenth-century academic origins; its associations with nation, empire, and race; and the editorial and methodological practices that silently maintained these connections.[1]

---

1   See, among other representative works, Allen Frantzen, *Desire for Origins: New Languages, Old English, and Teaching Tradition* (New Jersey: Rutgers University Press, 1990); Allen Frantzen, ed., *Speaking Two Languages: Traditional Disciplines and Contemporary Theory in Medieval Studies* (Albany: State University of New York, 1991); Allen Frantzen and John Niles, eds., *Anglo-Saxonism and the Construction of Social Identity* (Gainesville: Florida University Press, 1997); John D. Niles, 'Locating *Beowulf* in Literary History,' *Exemplaria* 5, no. 1 (1993): 79–109; Katherine O'Brien O'Keeffe, ed., *Reading Old English Texts* (Cambridge: Cambridge University Press, 1997); Gillian Overing, *Language, Sign, and Gender in* Beowulf (Carbondale: Southern Illinois University Press, 1990); James W. Earl, *Thinking About 'Beowulf'* (Stanford: Stanford University Press, 1994); Roy Michael Liuzza, 'The Return of the Repressed: Old and New Theories in Old

These were important (if occasionally contentious) conversations within Anglo-Saxon studies, and when the twenty-first century began it appeared, to some, that the field had acknowledged the complex intellectual histories that belonged to its institutional past and had reckoned with them.

Yet, in 2008, while I was completing my Ph.D., the 3rd edition of the *Oxford English Dictionary* added a new entry, the proper noun 'Anglo-Saxonist,' which challenged the critical efficacy of the field's late-century self-examinations:

1. an expert in or student of Old English language, literature, and culture

> 1837 *Gentleman's Mag.* Nov. 493 Gibson edited that valuable and interesting historical document, the Saxon Chronicle; Rawlinson published Alfred's translation of Boethius....These names...belong to the school of the Anglo-Saxonists.

> 1896 S.H.V. Gurteen *Epic of Fall of Man* 21 There will arise many a fine Anglo-Saxonist to carry on the work begun by Turner, Thorpe, and Kemble.

> ...

> 1991 *Guardian* (Nexis) 18 July The Anglo-Saxonists...were defeated when they proposed that the Old English examination should be made harder.

2. a person who believes in the importance or superiority of Anglo-Saxon language, people, or culture (past or present)

English Literary Criticism,' in *Old English Shorter Poems: Basic Readings*, ed. Katherine O'Brien O'Keeffe (New York: Garland, 1994), 103–47; and John Hill, *The Cultural World in 'Beowulf'* (Toronto: University of Toronto Press, 1995).

1879 J.A. Weisse *Origin Eng. Lang. & Lit.* 672 In the face of this constant and steady increase, Anglo-Saxonists clamored in vain against the addition of foreign words.[2]

The OED's lexicographer presents, by way of the entry's definitions, a supposedly autonomous relationship between '1' and '2' of the headword, 'Anglo-Saxonist.' 'An expert in or student of Old English' is contrasted with 'a person' who has no academic intentions. Expertise and study are compared to the novice's 'belief.' 'Old English,' a contemporary linguistic term, is countered by its antiquated and ethnically charged precursor, 'Anglo-Saxon.' And the scholar's textual corpus and philological methods of 'language, literature, and culture' are set apart from the ethnic anthropology of 'language, people, or culture' that preoccupies the anonymous non-professional.

Although the two definitions of 'Anglo-Saxonist' are at pains to distance the academic from the anonymous enthusiast, the dictionary entry's nomenclature and its etymology point towards a deep history of semantic entanglement. Numbers 1 and 2 indicate that these definitions represent two 'senses, or meanings' of one word, which 'are ordered according to a structure resembling a family tree, so that the development of one meaning from another can be plotted.'[3] Anglo-Saxonist scholarship and Anglo-Saxonist ethno-nationalism are organized under the same headword. Likewise, the academic sense of the first definition, first attested in 1837, etymologically generates the nationalist sense of the second definition, which dates, in print, to 1879. The genealogical relationship between the two senses of 'Anglo-Saxonist' destines this word for semantic entanglement, and the OED's quotations bear silent witness to this process and its long-term effects. While the OED asserts, via its quotation of S. Humphreys Gurteen's 1896 *Epic of the Fall of the Man,* that

---

2 *Oxford English Dictionary,* s.v. 'Anglo-Saxonist,' http://www.oed.com/.
3 'Guide to the Third Edition of the OED, Sense Section,' *Oxford English Dictionary,* http://www.oed.com/public/oed3guide/guide-to-the-third-edition-of#sense.

Sharon Turner, Benjamin Thorpe, and John Mitchell Kemble are 'expert' Anglo-Saxonists in the first sense, when read in its original context, Gurteen's praise of these scholars also resonates with the political ideologies expressed in the second sense of the OED's definition.[4] Moreover (and more troublingly), the OED lifts its 1991 attestation of the first sense of 'Anglo-Saxon' from a Guardian article that traces lines of ideological descent between past and present Anglo-Saxonists. In a piece about Oxford's English department's curricular reforms, the British newspaper calls Anglo-Saxonist faculty members a 'very tight-knit cabal' set on 'keeping the degree well away from what the old guard regarded as the distractions of modern literature.'[5] Despite the

---

4 The OED's second quotation under sense 1 of the headword, 'Anglo-Saxonist,' is excerpted from a chapter in S. Humphreys Gurteen's *The Epic of the Fall of Man: A Comparative Study of Caedmon, Dante and Milton* (New York: G.P. Puntam's Sons, 1896), which surveys the current state of the field of Anglo-Saxon studies. In this chapter, Gurteen draws together Anglo-Saxon 'descendants' and Anglo-Saxon 'scholars' under the shared banner of 'the language and literature of their ancestors' (20); he warns against allowing 'foreigners' such as Erasmus Rask and G.R. Thorkelin to take pride of place in the study of Anglo-Saxon England (20); and then he appeals to 'many a fine Anglo-Saxonist to carry on the work begun by Turner, Thorpe, and Kemble' (21). When Gurteen's quote is read in context, it undermines the *OED*'s partitioning efforts. By attending, simultaneously, to senses 1 and 2 of the headword, this quote positions Turner, Thorpe, and Kemble as both Anglo-Saxon scholars and descendants of an Anglo-Saxon 'culture.'

5 Nicholas de Jongh, 'The Beowulf at Oxford's Door,' *The Guardian*, July 18, 1991, 23. Perhaps not unexpectedly, no curricular reform took place in 1991, and a decade later, in 2001, Oxford and *The Guardian* revisited the issue. Once again, Anglo-Saxonists were the focus of the story:

> Elaine Treharne insists that she would have specialised in [Thomas] Hardy if she hadn't been forced to apply herself to OE. 'I doubt that,' snorts David Lawton, director of graduate studies in English at Washington University in St Louis, and a keen advocate of the benefits of translation. 'I would be very surprised if her natural curiosity had not led her to it.'....Specialists in the language, he says, often feel that translation involves an 'improper sense of creativity. But I think we ought to be able to correct that,' he adds optimistically. (Ros Taylor, 'Valentine's Day of Reckoning,' *The Guardian*, March 20, 2001, https://www.theguardian.com/education/2001/mar/20/highereducation.english)

Another Anglo-Saxonist, Emily Thornbury, shared in the same article:

OED's partitioning efforts, its quotes not only trace hidden entanglements between academic and ideological Anglo-Saxonists but also hint at the presence of patronymic ghosts secreted within the ranks of contemporary scholars.

I spent eight years in graduate school becoming an Anglo-Saxonist, and I have since used this appellative to describe my scholarship in print, to colleagues, and, at times, to family and friends. Yet, when I read the *OED*'s headword, 'Anglo-Saxonist,' in 2008, and as I read it again now, I continue to ask myself: does my field's professional appellative locate me, a 'student of Old English,' in proximity to the unnamed 'person who believes' in Anglo-Saxon 'supremacy…(past or present)'? Does the academic process of becoming an Anglo-Saxonist somehow position me in an entangled relationship between senses 1 and 2 of the *OED*'s entry? No one in Anglo-Saxon studies would disavow the historical connections between academic and popular Anglo-Saxonisms (emphasis on the plural), and the field has engaged in field critiques that expose the nineteenth-century politics of nation, empire, and race that are co-terminous with the modern academic origins of Anglo-Saxon studies.[6] While the *OED*

'I think there's a personality factor involved in separation from the mainstream of English literature. Hard-core philology has hung on in Old English partly because of that. Anglo-Saxonists seem more positivistic than most literary scholars.' Thornbury, who studied astrophysics before moving to Cambridge for her Ph.D. studies, believes a desire to uncover the origins of English literature is what motivates many of her colleagues. (Ibid.)
'[N]atural curiosity' and 'an improper sense of creativity'; 'positivistic' thinking and a 'desire to uncover…[literary] origins' — as academics from outside and inside the field weigh in on what it means to be an Anglo-Saxonist, a portrait emerges that bears a distinct likeness to that of *The Guardian*'s 1991 reporting, which emphasized an anti-modernism that was attached to a silent but powerful 'old guard.' Moreover, these perceptions of Oxford's Anglo-Saxonists are directed across the Atlantic where, according to the *Guardian* reporter Ros Taylor, '[t]he peculiar combination of fear and reverence which Old English inspires has been a challenge in North American faculties, where the subject is widely taught but rarely compulsory for undergraduates' (ibid.).
6 See, for example, Susan Reynolds, 'What Do We Mean by "Anglo-Saxon" and "Anglo-Saxons"?' *Journal of British Studies* 24, no. 4 (1985): 395–414;

painstakingly separates the 'expert in or student of Old English' from the 'person who believes in the importance or superiority of Anglo-Saxon,' the shared interests and, moreover, sample quotations that it uses to attest these differences suggest that, despite my field's historiographic scholarship, *the signifier*, 'Anglo-Saxonist,' continues to locate me in the long shadow of an old guard, whose resistant anti-modernism undergirds an academic imperialism. The OED indicates an appellative that has, perhaps, outlasted its professional usefulness and points towards a professional dilemma.

This book takes as its subject the Anglo-Saxonist and the mysterious old guard that lies behind it. Despite the sensibility of the term, which identifies specialists of early medieval England, this book argues that 'Anglo-Saxonist' cul-de-sacs its scholars within Anglo-Saxon temporal, ethno-national, and methodological frameworks. As a signifier that nests Anglo-Saxon within itself, 'Anglo-Saxonist' calls us to claim a professional identity that is neither of the present tense nor necessarily grounded in our personal values, and it asks us to maintain the parameters of this identity by way of methodologies that do not sufficiently account for our personal affiliations or the embodied aspects of our and others' scholarship. These associations — with the past, with race, with methodological praxis (among other affiliations) — silently position the Anglo-Saxonist within a retrograde orbit of loss and desire. This is a state of being — not of *becoming* — and it is a static ontology that generates a melancholic scholarly position. Yet, being an Anglo-Saxonist is not simply a matter of locating ourselves in the orbit of a signifier that operates according to past-tense temporalities, value systems, and scholarly methods. 'Anglo-Saxonist' is likewise a term that engages a group of nineteenth-century scholars whose interdisciplinary research practices set the initial temporal boundaries

---

Frantzen, *Desire for Origins*; Frantzen and Niles, *Anglo-Saxonism and the Construction of Social Identity*; and John Niles, *The Idea of Anglo-Saxon England 1066–1901: Remembering, Forgetting, Deciphering, and Renewing the Past* (Malden: Wiley Blackwell, 2015).

and methods of our field. These first Anglo-Saxonists, whom the OED identifies as Sharon Turner, Benjamin Thorpe, and John Mitchell Kemble (and to whom this book adds James Douglas) made watershed contributions to the emerging disciplines of early medieval history, literature and philology, and archaeology. Moreover, their scholarship is set to the time of Britain's nineteenth-century empire and the racist systems that operated in tandem with it across Europe and America. Being an Anglo-Saxonist therefore invokes these so-called fathers of our interdisciplinary field *and* the imperial moment to which they belong. It acknowledges their haunting presence within our ranks as an old guard whose anti-modern stance is keyed to positions of nineteenth-century colonialism and racism. As the children of these spectral Anglo-Saxonist fathers, we are unknowingly (or, perhaps, more knowingly) melancholic — towards our professional ancestors, their empire, and the racial-colonial ideologies of Anglo-America.

In order to wrest the Anglo-Saxonist from a position of an over-determined ontological being, the ghosts of its interdisciplinary past, and the (repetitive) melancholia that attends these relationships, this book mourns our field's professional, imperial, and racial pasts. While mourning is emotional work, it is a labor enacted by reexamining, destabilizing, and reconfiguring the self's historical narrative. *Anglo-Saxon(ist) pasts, postSaxon futures* therefore begins by examining the historical figures, ideological freight, and scholarly processes — the colonial old guard — responsible for developing the signifiers, 'Anglo-Saxon' and 'Anglo-Saxonist.' The book's early chapters discuss intersections between certain medieval texts and their reception histories by historians, archaeologists, and philologists of the nineteenth century, revealing the mechanisms by which this old guard of Anglo-Saxon studies has become a ghostly presence secreted away within the field. These chapters likewise explore the ways in which this old guard keeps present-day scholars duty-bound to colonial figures of previous generations and to colonial ideologies and scholarly methodologies of the past that do not account nor suffice for the beliefs and bodies of our living, contemporary, and postcolonial world. By exposing the entanglement between living scholars and the dead, I want to reveal ghosts within Anglo-Saxon studies that have rendered the field overly (if sometimes collectively unconsciously) melancholic. Such an exposure opens a channel for critical reflection, exorcism, and grief: for Anglo-Saxon and Anglo-Saxonist, for the old guard which has not only haunted but, moreover, kept us from mourning, and for the static ontological state of being that we have inherited as a consequence of using these terms and keeping company with the unquiet (un)dead. The book's later chapters enter this open, affective channel, using creative nonfiction and speculative criticism to write alternative narratives of and about our profession. These prose narratives radically unsettle the identity positions maintained by 'Anglo-Saxon' and 'Anglo-Saxonist.' They create a space in which we can grieve, work through, and abandon Anglo-Saxon(ist) pasts and the shadows of their old guards. Further, these narratives open a horizon for imagining more capacious and critically generative postSaxon futures.

To return, again, to the 1980s and 1990s, if we look back on that period, one could say that a glimpse of these futures had already arrived. Almost thirty years ago, in 1990, Allen Frantzen's *Desire for Origins* sounded a clarion call. Frantzen's book argued that the politics of nation and empire are encoded within and maintained by the traditional 'academic' disciplines of philology and historicism. Further, he claimed that Anglo-Saxon studies's fidelity to these traditional field methodologies and its disdainful dismissal of postmodern critical theories unconsciously secured a national-imperial politics. While *Desire for Origins* was a lightning rod in the field during the 1990s, it succinctly articulated a sea change that was already in progress. Scholars before and after Frantzen were busy fruitfully coupling old-school philology and historicism with new-school postmodern approaches. Literary scholars, historians, art historians, and archaeologists, such as Patricia Dailey, James Earl, Shari Horner, Eileen Joy, Catherine Karkov, Susan Kim, Stacy Klein, Clare Lees, Mary Dockray-Miller, John Niles, Gillian Overing, Carol Braun

Pasternack, Alfred Siewers, Elaine Treharne, Janet Thormann, Renée Trilling, and Lisa Weston, were analyzing Anglo-Saxon texts according to post-structuralist methods and feminist theories, for example. The writings of these scholars proceeded apace with historicist discussions of the workings of nation and empire in Anglo-Saxon culture and history by Nicholas Brooks, Joshua Davies, Kathleen Davis, Irina Dumitrescu, Sarah Foot, Stephen Harris, Nick Howe, Chris Jones, Ananya Jahanara Kabir, Catherine Karkov, Janet Nelson, Larry Swain, and Howard Williams, among others. I pause here to express sincere gratitude for this remarkable body of knowledge.

The field's late-century embrace of post-structural methods and feminist (among other) theories, its discussions of premodern colonialism, and its participation in postcolonial and ethnic studies have all unsettled the narratives of nation, empire, and race that are sedimented within traditional Anglo-Saxon studies. Consequently, the inclusion of these theories within the field have challenged identity positions consonant with Anglo-Saxonist political ideologies. However, as the OED's 2008 edition suggests, the arrival of critical theory in Anglo-Saxon studies has not dislodged the anti-modern old guard of many years ago. This introductory chapter evaluates the assertion, championed by Allen Frantzen and long-held within Anglo-Saxon studies, that critical theory is a force that can disrupt and displace the nationalist, imperial, and racial politics embedded within the field's scholarly narratives. It examines and ruminates upon statements by prominent twenty-first-century scholars regarding the state of Anglo-Saxon studies, especially with respect to the place of theory within the discipline. These statements unconsciously trace the methodological, ideological, and affective shape of the old guard, outlined above, even when they advocate for theories of postcolonialism, race, and ethnic studies. Critical theory, I argue in this chapter, fails to render Anglo-Saxon studies postcolonial because it does not approach closely enough the secret sites of imperialist and racist ideologies: the often unthought, emotional positions that lie at the heart of scholarly attachments. In order to find the 'heart' of Anglo-Saxon studies,

I examine my own disciplinary attachments via an autoethnographic account of my Mississippi family, its inability to work through the loss of a post-Civil War South, and the ghostly, Confederate old guard that continues to haunt its identity politics and genealogical narratives. As I interrogate my own family biography, I find narrative parallels between my personal life and the state of Anglo-Saxon studies, and I delineate the affective relays between them. Autoethnography is a genre that helps me to disclose the very personal process of mourning the identities, narratives, and ghosts of my family, and this genre also enables me to do the grief work necessary to this book's project of mourning, and working through, the oppressive ghosts of the professional field of Anglo-Saxon studies.

In 2006 and 2007, Michael Drout, the anonymous 'Tiruncula,' Scott Nokes, Eileen Joy, and Larry Swain staged a critical debate in a series of blog posts regarding the state of Anglo-Saxon studies.[7] In 2008, the same year that the OED published its first entry for 'Anglo-Saxonist,' the field began to take more formal stock of its relationship to these critical perspectives. In

---

7 Michael Drout, 'State of the Field,' *Worm Talk and Slug Speak: My Life among the Invertebrates* [blog], December 29, 2006, http://wormtalk.blogspot.com/2006/12/; Michael Drout, 'Again with the State of the Field,' *Worm Talk and Slug Speak: My Life among the Invertebrates* [blog], January 7, 2007, http://wormtalk.blogspot.com/2007/01/again-with-state-of-field-tiruncula.html; Michael Drout, 'An Example,' *Worm Talk and Slug Speak: My Life among the Invertebrates* [blog], January 10, 2007, http://wormtalk.blogspot.com/2007/01/example-to-illustrate-point-i-was.html; Michael Drout, 'Gatekeeping?,' *Worm Talk and Slug Speak: My Life Among the Invertebrates* [blog], January 22, 2007, http://wormtalk.blogspot.com/2007/01/gatekeeping-while-back-i-p_116949841976709399.html; Tirincula, 'What does a healthy field look like from the inside?,' *Practica* [blog], January 7, 2007 [URL no longer active]; Scott Nokes, 'More on the State of the Field,' *Unlocked Wordhoard* [blog], January 10, 2007, http://unlocked-wordhoard.blogspot.com/2007/01/more-on-state-of-field.html; Eileen A. Joy, 'My Life Among the Anglo-Saxonists: More Anomie, Despair, and Self-Immolation,' *In the Middle* [blog], January 20, 2007, http://www.inthemedievalmiddle.com/2007/01/my-life-among-anglo-saxonists-more.html; and Larry Swain, 'State of the Field Repost,' *The Ruminate* [blog], March 11, 2007, http://theruminate.blogspot.com/2007/03/state-of-field-repost.html.

May 2008, a conference panel titled 'Is There a Theory in the House of Anglo-Saxon Studies?,' sponsored by the BABEL Working Group, was held at the International Medieval Congress in Kalamazoo, Michigan, and, in October 2008, Mary Dockray-Miller published 'Old English Literature and Feminist Theory: A State of the Field,' in which she interrogated the vibrancy of post-structuralist scholarship and feminist methods in Old English literary studies.[8] These online conversations and publications yielded productive fruit. Larry Swain invited his fellow bloggers to continue their conversation about the state of the field in a 2008 forum published in *The Heroic Age,* 'State of the Field in Anglo-Saxon Studies.'[9] Likewise, Eileen Joy invited interlocutors from the BABEL-sponsored panel, along with several other scholars, to express their thoughts on critical and feminist theories in the field of Old English studies in a 2010 essay cluster co-published across *postmedieval* and *The Heroic Age* called 'The State(s) of Early English Studies.'[10] In the titles of the above-mentioned blog posts, essays, forum, and essay cluster, 'state of the field' is used eight times to frame the discussions regarding Anglo-Saxon, Old English, and Early English studies. This phrase turns on the word, 'state,' a signifier that, according to Jacqueline Rose, connects one's mental condition to one's political investments.[11] In other words, psychological 'state' and

---

8 Mary Dockray-Miller, 'Old English Literature and Feminist Theory: A State of the Field,' *Literature Compass* 5, no. 6 (2008): 1049–59.
9 Michael Drout, Tom Shippey, Richard Scott Nokes, and Eileen A. Joy, 'State of the Field in Anglo-Saxon Studies' [forum discussion], *The Heroic Age: A Journal of Early Medieval Northwestern Europe* 11 (May 2008). https://www.heroicage.org/issues/11/foruma.php.
10 Eileen A. Joy, ed., 'The State(s) of Early English Studies' [special essay cluster], co-published across *postmedieval: a journal of medieval cultural studies* 1, no. 3 (2010) and *The Heroic Age: A Journal of Early Medieval Northwestern Europe* 14 (2010). In this essay cluster, many scholars exchange the compound, 'Anglo-Saxon,' for 'Old English' or 'Early English,' a move that, I suggest, gives contributors the disciplinary and semantic breathing room needed to take more theoretical stances.
11 Jacqueline Rose, *States of Fantasy* (New York: Clarendon Press, 1998). Note the OED's (2008) myriad definitions of the headword, 'state,' n.: I.2.b. 'A condition of mind or feeling'; I.3.a. 'Physical condition as regards internal

political 'state' work together to interleave the literary imagination with fantasies of nation and empire. Consequently, interrogating the S/states of Anglo-Saxon, Old English, and Early English studies is a process that, *pace* Rose, does not merely assess the critical condition of these literary, linguistic, and historical fields. It considers to what extent theories of embodied mind are welcome in them and, consequently, what political fantasies are harbored therein.

Among the most active contributors to the online debates in 2008 was Michael Drout, who first (and most frequently) used the phrase 'state of the field' to conceptually frame the 2006–2010 discussions. Drout's general assessment of Anglo-Saxon studies is that the field need not disavow postmodern theories but should reconfirm its commitments to philology. In 2007, and again in 2008, Drout writes:

> Anglo-Saxon studies and philology are a highly irritating rebuke to most of the rest of the sub-disciplines in English because our intellectual practices are a direct refutation of one of the current central dogmas of literary studies: that all 'knowledge is situated and contingent....'[12]
>
> I would submit that the 'something different' we should do is to focus on *language* and how it works in a historical sense rather than an abstract philosophical sense. Literary studies suffers from a continuous pull in two directions: towards solipsism and towards politics — you end up with 'that text means this *to me*' or 'that text illustrates this political/social phenomenon.'[13]

In positioning 'Anglo-Saxon studies and philology' as a 'highly irritating rebuke to most of the rest of the sub-disciplines in English,' Drout's statements recall the *The Guardian*'s Anglo-

---

constitution, nature, or structure'; III. 'A commonwealth or polity, and related senses.'

12 Drout, 'Again with the State of the Field.'
13 Drout, 'Anglo-Saxon Studies: The State of the Field?'

Saxonist cabal and its devotion to an old guard set against disciplinary change. Yet, Drout extends this old guard beyond the hedges of Oxford, and, in so doing, he rearticulates its form. This old guard does not bear likeness to disciplinary fathers such as Turner, Thorpe, or Kemble who were named in the OED's definition of Anglo-Saxonist but rather takes the shape of the partner fields of Anglo-Saxon studies and its primary methodology, philology. Regardless of these differences in place and form, the old guard of Anglo-Saxon studies and philology remains set upon disciplining the minds and bodies of those who claim affiliation with 'it.' As Drout avers, the supposed rebuke and refutation of philology's insights limit the influence of Anglo-Saxon studies and philology vis-à-vis the wider community of English disciplines, intellectually, and, by extension, socially. Such an antagonistic (and forbidding) intellectual and social posture is corollary to a stance towards 'knowledge' which denies that it could ever be 'situated' in the body or 'contingent' upon its affective displays. By setting itself apart from others and foreclosing scholarly consideration of embodiment and affect, the old guard of Anglo-Saxon studies and philology bars its devotees from expressing what the 'text means...*to me,*' as a person and as a political subject.

Drout's commentary on the state of Anglo-Saxon studies and the old guard which attends it exposes the state of its political fantasies. After emphasizing the important partnership between Anglo-Saxon studies and philology and its rebuke to other sub-disciplines of English studies, Drout discusses an unnamed essay that 'analyses novels which depict different kinds of immigrant and second-generation ethnic experience in America.'[14] While he concedes that the essay competently engages with critical theory and demonstrates 'some sensitivity to the literature,' Drout begins his assessment of it with the statement, 'there was, to my eye, an enormous, gaping, hideous lacuna right in the heart of it,' and concludes that absent a rigorous stake in second-language acquisition and linguistics, '[t]he paper is in-

---

14 Drout, 'An Example.'

stead 100% politics. Some of it sophisticated, some less so, but *everything* is taken as politics and nothing more.'[15] Previously, Anglo-Saxon studies and philology were removed from all other English sub-disciplines and the bodily aspects of language and literature. Yet, here, Drout summons an alliterative connection that is decidedly of the body. Drout's 'eye,' the organ of sight that generates the optics for his criticism, finds something 'enormous.' As he inspects it further, its enormity gives way to a 'gaping' and 'hideous lacuna,' a monstrous textual gap that is located right in the embodied and affective center — the 'heart' — of an essay that, according to Drout's summary description, gauges what it is like to be a non-Anglo body in America. An old guard moves and shutters. It shows itself in the poetics of this moment, which summons Drout's critical and therefore metaphorical eye, divested of its body, to look upon and find a body that is enormous, yet gaping. Its distended size is physically overgrown and therefore textually lacking. Consequently, for Drout, it is unbearable. Its immigrant, ethnic form, which Drout recognizes as all body and no text, is held in stark contrast to an Anglo-Saxonist position, which claims a superabundance of text in exchange for a non-body. Because the beating heart of the immigrant's politicized body possesses an affective vitality unpossessed by philology's textual, yet lifeless, *corpus*.

From the grave, this old guard sutures physical monstrosity and textual lack to the immigrant, ethnic, living body and its experiences. Yet, it tries to remedy such an unbearable embodied position by suggesting 'language acquisition, second language performance, the phonology of "accent," code switching or any of the multitude of analytical tools that could come from contemporary linguistics' that would rescue this critical essay from its stake in a non-Anglo body that is '100% politics.'[16] As 'An Example' of Drout's philological rebuke to contemporary ethnic literature, the poetics of his criticism reveal something else about this old guard, which exceeds its status as either, as the

---
15   Ibid.
16   Ibid.

OED suggests, the specter of previous scholarly generations or, as Drout's blog posts reveal, the conceptual figment of Anglo-Saxon studies and philology. This old guard is the racialized corpse of Empire long since buried in the grave. It is the ethnic subjectivity of a colonizer that maintains itself, undead, by way of the entangled, unconscious, and encrypted relationship between Anglo-Saxonist scholarship and Anglo-Saxonist nationalism.

While Drout's comments upon the state of Anglo-Saxon studies reveal fantasies of Empire and race buried within the discipline's methods, Eileen Joy, another contributor to the 2006–2010 conversations, articulates the field's state of mental health. In 'Goodbye to All That: My Personal State of Schizoid Anglo-Saxon Studies,' Joy references a neurological disorder called visual agnosia that is characterized by affects of coldness and detachment, emotional incapacity, failure to experience pleasure, an incapacity for erotics, and a preoccupation with fantasy, in order to describe the state of Old English scholarship.[17] Is this 'agnosia' one that is symptomized in Drout's blog posts and essays? Is the field mentally unhealthy? In order to maintain the graveyard politics of an old guard — one that this chapter has associated with genealogical fathers, a disembodied Anglo-Saxon philology, and the ethnopolitical fantasies of Empire — it has distanced itself from most other sub-fields of English, as well as from critical theory. Out of step with the rest of the discipline, the assessments of Drout and Joy suggest its states of social rank and mental health are in decline. While Joy goes on to reclaim the position of the schizoid by way of of Deleuze and Guattari,[18] her essay lands on a relationship, signaled across the discussions from 2006 to 2010, between an old guard that

---

17 Eileen A. Joy. 'Goodbye to All That: The State of My Own Personal Field of Schiziod Anglo-Saxon Studies' [forum post], in Drout et al., 'State of the Field of Anglo-Saxon Studies,' https://www.heroicage.org/issues/11/foruma.php.
18 According to Deleuzo-Guattarian philosophy, to be 'schizoid' in Old English studies would mean to undo its chief figures of 'Father' and 'Family' and 'Nation' and to seek more cross-disciplinary, theoretically informed, and even presentist approaches to the past.

disciplines the mind and body via its lifeless, encrypted corpse and a state of the field that suffers critically and politically, emotionally and affectively, from its overly rigid Anglo-Saxonist position.

Although, at times, these early twenty-first-century discussions pointed to dark clouds above,[19] they nonetheless also

---

19 Essays by Mary Dockray-Miller ('Old English Literature and Feminist Theory') and Clare A. Lees and Gillian R. Overing ('Still Theoretical After All These Years, Or, Whose Theory Do You Want, Or, Whose Theory Can We Have?', *The Heroic Age: A Journal of Early Medieval Northwestern Europe* 14 [2010]: https://www.heroicage.org/issues/14/lees&overing.php) underscore the relationship between the states of Old English and Anglo-Saxon studies and their relationships to feminist theory and feminist politics. As Lees and Overing write in their contribution to the *Heroic Age–postmedieval* essay cluster:
> *Anglo-Saxon England* has yet to publish a single feminist or gender-identified article (a record worse than even *Speculum* or PMLA). Second, the program committees for the bi-annual conferences of ISAS (International Society for Anglo-Saxonists) do not yet routinely offer a home for any theoretically oriented studies, although the International Medieval Congress at Kalamazoo offers a warm home to such organizations as the Medieval Feminist Forum (MFF) and the Society for the Study of Homosexuality in the Middle Ages (SSHMA), and the International Medieval Congress at Leeds devotes a strand of sessions annually to women's and gender studies.

As Lees and Overing point out, for an Anglo-Saxonist to think and write in modes other than historicism or philology is fraught with professional consequences. One can find ample homes for one's work within medieval journals; one can publish monographs and edited collections that are avowedly theoretical in method; one can find plenty of eager listeners and interlocutors at medieval conferences. But in order to publish, present, or otherwise gain access to the institutional venues of Anglo-Saxon studies that count, they suggest, one must alter, give up, or screen 'her' body by keeping, for example, 'feminist or gender-identified' theoretical methods from view. Joy levels a similar critique in 'Goodbye to All That':
> [E]ven a brief glance at the titles of papers presented at the biennial meetings of the International Society of Anglo-Saxonists — choose your year, any year, then look at them cumulatively if you have the time — reveals a lot about what the discipline of Anglo-Saxon studies would seem to either actively dismiss or set to the side or minimize: studies of gender, class, race, and sexuality; feminist and queer studies; Marxist and postcolonial studies; cultural studies (of the British or Benjaminian materialist type); post-processual archaeology;

forecasted sunshine. In 2012, Jacqueline Stodnick and Renée Trilling's *A Handbook of Anglo-Saxon Studies* was published. Stodnick and Trilling's *Handbook* is not, by any means, the first theoretically minded anthology of literary criticism published in Anglo-Saxon studies. Rather, it is a theoretical primer meant to introduce readers to a wide range of critical theories and methodologies already in use by Anglo-Saxonists. In their introduction, Stodnick and Trilling look back to Allen Frantzen, writing:

> [O]ur discussion of the word *handbook* has thus far been voiced in both of the 'two languages' that Allen Frantzen identified in his seminal 1991 collection *Speaking Two Languages* as a feature of the critical discourse employed by any Anglo-Saxonist interested in theory. In beginning with a historical analysis of a word [handbook], we are not far from the disciplinary 'comfort zone' for Anglo-Saxon studies, long dominated by textual study and specifically philological aims.[20]

In returning to Frantzen, whose scholarship in the early 1990s garnered much criticism as well as acclaim, Stodnick and Trilling negotiate a formal peace to longstanding debates regarding the appropriateness of postmodern theories within Anglo-Saxon studies, by emphasizing that their theoretical labors are 'not far from the disciplinary "comfort zone" for Anglo-Saxon stud-

---

media and textuality theory; new or post-philology; semiotics and deconstruction; Foucauldian genealogy; psychoanalytic and cognitive approaches; political and sociological theory; nonlinear dynamics and systems theory; the theoretically roguish thought and schizoid-rhizomatic theory of Deleuze and Guattari and their ilk; postmodern hermeneutics; and any other number of other schools of post-structural thought and analysis as well as their significant 'turns' — to language/discursivity, to the performative, to the body/embodiment, to space/habitus, to the Other/posthuman, to memory/spectrality, to reading/aesthetics, to ethics, to the animal, and to temporality.

20 Jacqueline Stodnick and Renée Trilling, 'Introduction,' in *A Handbook of Anglo-Saxon Studies* (Oxford: Wiley-Blackwell, 2012), 3.

ies, long dominated by textual study and philolog[y].' Theory is now practiced not only alongside historicism and philology but, moreover, from within the disciplinary frame of Anglo-Saxon studies. Consequently, it would seem that Frantzen's once-controversial arguments in *Desire for Origins,* which claimed that the active exclusion of critical theory from the field subtended its national-imperial politics, have finally been recognized and resolved. With a handbook of theory, Anglo-Saxonists must have settled the field's restless states and, *ipso facto,* become postcolonial.

In two consecutive chapters, 'Postcolonial' and 'Race and Ethnicity,' *Handbook* contributors Catherine Karkov and Stephen Harris signal the arrival of postcolonialism to a supposedly now-theoretical Anglo-Saxon studies. Karkov cites essays by Uppinder Mehan and David Townsend, Barbara Yorke, Kathleen Davis, and Elaine Trehane, which articulate 'postcolonial approaches to Anglo-Saxon England.'[21] However, when she turns to 'postcolonial medievalists,' she cites only two, Kathleen Davis and Ananya Jahanara Kabir, whose work has been positioned from within Old English and Anglo-Saxon studies.[22] What is the difference between a postcolonial approach and a postcolonial medievalist? Why a postcolonial medievalist rather than a postcolonial Anglo-Saxonist? Karkov's language suggests that one can employ postcolonial theories without occupying a postcolonial subjectivity, and it is worth noting that the recent publication histories of Davis and Kabir evidence a trajectory that moves further afield from (rather than closer towards) Anglo-Saxon studies.[23] Karkov's 'Postcolonial' chapter is followed by Harris's 'Race and Ethnicity,' an essay in which Harris does

---

21 Catherine Karkov, 'Postcolonial,' in *A Handbook of Anglo-Saxon Studies,* eds. Jacqueline Stodnick and Renée Trilling (Oxford: Wiley-Blackwell, 2012), 152.
22 Ibid.
23 It should be noted as well that Kabir eventually left Old English studies proper, and is now a scholar of the cultural and memory politics of contemporary South Asia and its diasporas (especially in Africa), medievalism and Empire, and postcolonial approaches to Philology.

not name other scholars within Anglo-Saxon studies who specialize in this area but rather repeatedly suggests that problems of race, ethnicity, and colonialism cultivated in nineteenth-century scholarship remain harbored within the field of Anglo-Saxon studies:

> Influential nineteenth-century scholars, whose interpretations and methods still powerfully inform our own, wrote studies of early English literature under a guiding presumption that a national literature somehow expressed the spiritual essence of a language group's founding race(s).
> ...
> The second supposition described above, that national habits of thought would be expressed in literature, follows from the first supposition. If race is a precondition of thought, it is certainly a precondition of literary art. This second presupposition has been a steady presence in OE criticism.... So we tend to teach OE poetry according to those purported racial characteristics: as more of a practical mirror for princes or a useful, historical record of a vanishing folk culture than as a site of philosophical speculation, for example.
> ...
> The *Rassenproblem* has left a rigid legacy. Assumptions about the racial limits of culture and nation still control our less considered approaches to OE poetry.[24]

While the *Handbook* announces that, as a field, Anglo-Saxon studies has finally caught up with the theoretical positions advocated by Frantzen and others during the 1980s, 1990s, and early 2000s, Karkov and Harris suggest that the embrace of critical theory does not render one postcolonial. For racism and colonialism are not always logical. They are systems of the conscious mind as well as of a whole host of affects. Consequently, cog-

---

24 Stephen Harris, 'Race and Ethnicity,' in *A Handbook of Anglo-Saxon Studies,* eds. Jacqueline Stodnick and Renée Trilling (Oxford: Wiley-Blackwell, 2012), 166, 169, 172.

nitive academic methods such as critical theory cannot reason colonialism out from under a field, nor can they excoriate the ghostly old guard that continues to haunt it from its unlocatable crypt. Thus, when Karkov and Harris are called on to explore and bear witness to theories of postcolonialism, race, and ethnicity in relation to Anglo-Saxon studies, Karkov can articulate the presence of postcolonial approaches but cannot name postcolonial Anglo-Saxonists, and Harris can talk about race and ethnicity but in the process must point out the ongoing relationship between nineteenth-century scholarship and our own. While the *Handbook* avows that Anglo-Saxon studies speaks two languages, the pursuit of Frantzen's argument reveals that attending to theory has not, in fact, decolonized the field nor quieted the old guard in its grave. For this can only happen, as this chapter will soon argue, at the interstices of both head and heart.

So, to start with the head: Kathleen Davis's work articulates cognitive steps that Anglo-Saxon studies must take in order to arrive at what Karkov might call a postcolonial medievalist subjectivity. In her essay, 'Periodization and the Matter of Precedent,' Davis articulates the legal concept of precedent as a discursive intervention that decides which elements of the past can 'serve as a rule for future guidance.'[25] She then discusses the Norman Conquest as the precedent that divides the English past into pre- and post-Conquest periods. The Conquest signals a precedent — a historical beginning and a future forward — that guides the Anglo-Norman period seamlessly towards the late-medieval period and Middle English. Conversely, the Anglo-Saxon period, which lies on the other side of Conquest, is a site where time flows backwards. Incompatible and therefore barred from a post-Conquest future, it is rendered obsolete, unhistorical, and primitive. Yet, in designating the early medieval period as that ethnically marked time zone from which a premodern England supposedly progresses, 'Anglo-Saxon' underscores

---

25 Kathleen Davis, 'Periodization and the Matter of Precedent,' *postmedieval: a journal of medieval cultural studies* 1, no. 3 (2010): 357.

an ethnic temporality from which all English legal, linguistic, and cultural histories have since been continuously, uninterruptedly, and progressively written. To route the arguments of Davis's 2007 book, *Periodization and Sovereignty*, in the direction of her 2010 essay, the Anglo-Saxon period functions as the untouchable point of origin for a sovereign medieval history that is written 'at the height of and in tandem with, colonialism, nationalism, imperialism, and orientalism.'[26] Its untouchability enables historians to simultaneously disavow and revere the Anglo-Saxon period so that it can maintain the machinery of an ethno-political progress narrative, in which an ever-unfolding imperial future extends into the so-called postcolonial moment in which we live.

Despite Davis's arguments that, in the name of postcolonialism, we must unmoor our field from the fastenings of traditional periodization, Anglo-Saxon studies remains attached to the Anglo-Saxon period and to the professional term 'Anglo-Saxonist' even as it tries to address the troubling problem of Anglo-Saxonism. Consequently, all intellectual histories and critiques of Anglo-Saxon studies, from Frantzen's 1990 *Desire for Origins* to John Niles's 2015 *The Idea of Anglo-Saxon England*, take as their *terminus ad quem* Queen Victoria's death or World War II, events that symbolically foreshadowed or materially triggered decades of world-wide European decolonization. These are critical years. For just as nineteenth-century politics coordinate with nineteenth-century scholarship, worldwide European decolonization and America's meteoric rise to power during the Cold War function as the political state during which contemporary Anglo-Saxon studies takes shape. When we leave the mid-century and what comes after undiscussed, we leave the project of decolonization unfinished. Instead, we spurn Anglo-Saxonism of the Victorian and pre-war years but can only

---

26 Kathleen Davis, *Periodization and Sovereignty: How Ideas of Feudalism and Secularization Govern the Politics of Time* (Philadelphia: Pennsylvania University Press, 2007), 5.

proceed forward under the banner of postcolonial approaches rather than as postcolonial medievalists.

As a case study, consider Helen Young's 'Whiteness and Time.' Young's essay argues that race, like the medieval period, generates and maintains a colonial progress narrative, a position that follows from and is corollary to Kathleen Davis's important work on sovereignty and periodization. Young uses Sharon Turner's *History of the Anglo-Saxons* as the example by which she articulates this position:

> Sharon Turner's *History of the Anglo-Saxons from the Earliest Period to the Norman Conquest* (1799–1805) was a core *popular text of Anglo-Saxonist thought* on both sides of the Atlantic *throughout the nineteenth century and into the twentieth century,* and helped shape widely held beliefs. Turner invoked *a progressivist model of race*…. In 1836, the preface to the sixth edition closed with an expanded version of this idea:
>
>> The Anglo-Saxons were deficient in the surprising improvements which their present descendants have attained: but unless they had acquired and exercised the valuable qualities, both moral and intellectual, which they progressively advanced to before their dynasty ceased, England would not have become that distinguished nation which, after the Norman graft on its original Saxon stock, it has gradually been led to.
>
> The Middle Ages, both before and after the Norman Conquest, are the key period in the progression of the Anglo-Saxon race according to his account; its history reaches back beyond them to the Classical era, but the Middle Ages make the transition from racial infancy to maturity possible.
>
> This *progressivist model of race* may have been shed in theoretical and academic writing *in the twenty-first century,*

but it remains very strong in the *medievalisms of popular culture*.²⁷

Young nests a quote from Turner's *History* at the center of three chiastic phrase pairs. An exterior chiasmus is constructed by a 'popular text of Anglo-Saxonist thought' and the 'medievalisms of popular culture.' A second, interior chiasmus circuits 'the nineteenth century and into the twentieth century' to 'the twenty-first century.' Young's chiastic structure first shields academics from implication as popular Anglo-Saxonists then excludes the decades of mid-to-late twentieth-century decolonization from purview. Upon figuring coloniality as a non-scholarly problem, then skipping from colonial to postcolonial moments, Young articulates the third, chiastic component formed by the repeated phrase, 'progressivist model of race,' which surrounds her quote from Turner's *History*. Young's cognitive argument works to expose the problem of coloniality, whiteness, and time, yet its unthought, chiastic form prohibits further redress. Consequently, when scholarly Anglo-Saxonists and the decades of the recent past are allowed obliquely into Young's passage, she can claim only that 'this progressivist model of race *may* have been shed in theoretical and academic writing.' Such a subjunctive, half-hearted faith keeps scholarly self-reflection at arm's length,²⁸ and it prohibits a postcolonial approach from generating a postcolonial medievalist.

As I read Karkov and Harris, Davis and Young, I began to recognize that, despite the field's best intentions, opening the crypt of the old guard, viewing its lifeless corpse, coming to terms with our academic S/states, and decolonizing the field of Anglo-Saxon studies, does not happen only by way of well-rea-

---

27 Helen Young, 'Whiteness and Time: The Once, Present, and Future Race,' in *Studies in Medievalism XXIV: Medievalism on the Margins* (Cambridge: D.S. Brewer, 2015), 44, my emphasis.
28 Note also that, throughout the essay, Young repeatedly uses 'Anglo-Saxonist' and 'medievalist' as adjectives for 'Anglo-Saxonism' and 'medievalism,' a move that conflates and confuses scholarly and popular uses of the terms.

soned arguments. Because this is a process of working through and letting go. This is a process of grieving. For all our love objects, once dead, must be mourned by way of some narrative framework lest we become trapped within the crypts of a corpse (or the rings of a chiasmus) and haunted by its ghostly presence. Consequently, my critical imperatives began to shift. I stopped focusing on the conversations of others so that I could pay attention to ones I was trying to have with myself. Why do I call myself an Anglo-Saxonist? How is my work in Anglo-Saxon studies perceived not only by my academic colleagues but also among those I live with and love? How does this professional identity penetrate the deepest quarters of my personal identity? These are questions about myself — about ourselves — that can never be known or understood completely. Yet it has been, at last, from this quiet place of self-critique, that I began to ask what devotional ties bind *me* to the signifiers 'Anglo-Saxon' and 'Anglo-Saxonist' and how might I let go of them in order to make not just my scholarship but moreover myself postcolonial. And so, I invite you, my reader, to stand with me, in vulnerability, and to listen to your own heart as I show you mine, in grief and mourning, in working through and letting go.

I was born and raised in Tuscaloosa, Alabama. I grew up, however, in Houston, Mississippi, where my grandmother, Virginia Ellard, lived. When I stayed with my grandmother on weekends, throughout the summer, and during holidays, I visited the cemeteries of my great-, great-great, and great-great-great grandparents. My cousins and I went off-roading in my dad's truck, looking for, but never finding, the old Ellard homestead that my Coz Vic could vaguely recall. I listened to my relatives talk. About the Depression. About the ill-timed death of my great-grandfather, a doctor who died while treating patients in the 1918 outbreak of the Spanish Flu. About relatives who survived the Delta floods of 1906. About my great-uncle's involvement in a lynching amid the 1915 revival of the Ku Klux Klan. About the War…the War…the War. As a child, I learned my family's history through narratives of loss, trauma, nostalgia, and elegy, all of it situated somewhere between the personal and the political. These acts of visiting and searching for others long since dead, and these stories of finding family in the deep and conflicted sadnesses of the post-War South, became my own. You could say that my family is as melancholic as it is Confederate. And you could say that this has been my only inheritance, a point to which I will return in a moment.

It's important to understand that I am the first in seven generations who was not born and raised somewhere between the adjacent counties of Calhoun and Chickasaw, Mississippi, and since leaving home for college, I have felt myself living as a Southerner in diaspora. First as a child, then as an adult, much of my personal life has been spent yearning for a place, a people, and a time to which I do not belong and can never return. To put it in terms that make me wonder with no small amount of chagrin about the stakes of my engagement with Anglo-Saxon studies, my family's grief for a 'Heroic Age' was passed on to me, and I have carried it as a silent, unspoken burden my entire life, as an old guard that was locked inside its crypt long before I was ever born. Although I would like to say with some certainty—though none of us knows the limits of our own desires—that my attraction to Old English is unrelated to my family's history, my professional interest in the intellectual history of Anglo-Saxon studies is undoubtedly and, at first, unconsciously personal.

Among scholars in the humanities, admitting the private stakes in one's academic projects can be forbidden (and forbidding) territory. It lays one vulnerable to charges of unprofessionalism, *ad hominem* attacks, and accusations of self-indulgence. Yet, in so many other disciplines, such as Sociology, Anthropology, Communication Studies, and Education, these admissions, frequently termed autoethnography, are methodological salvos by which an academic essay or book is meant to begin. In these fields, autoethnography 'refers to writing about the personal and its relationship to culture. It is an autobiographical genre of writing and research that displays multiple layers of consciousness.'[29] In connecting one's personal life to another's cultural experiences, autoethnography is writing 'the self as an evocative, unfolding, scenic, and dialogic plot.'[30] Yet, as Margaret Vickers argues, for the 'researcher' to become a 'storyteller' is to 'writ[e] on the edge — and there is no safety net' for this kind of work.[31] In other words, as she and others explain, when we allow 'life experiences to overlap into [our] intellectual work,' we make ourselves vulnerable and risk emotional exposure.[32] In the process, however, 'life becomes performance', and we 'writ[e] to make room, to create a space for what happens between note and line, emotion and intellect, thought and action.'[33] Such attention to the 'room' and 'space' between our personal experiences and our intellectual labors opens us up to what Stacy Holman Jones calls 'a lyrical place that gives *pause*…[f]or emotional space…for reciprocal conversations…to shift gears, to disengage and reengage standpoints, positions, and purposes.'[34] In this pause, we find an emotional and embodied research position. Autoethnography is 'thus a bodily, as well as [an] intellectual, production.'[35] Performative and often non-cognitive, it is the heart work from whence comes an argument. To put it simply, autoethnography 'do[es] not distinguish doing research from living life.'[36]

---

29 Carolyn Ellis, *The Ethnographic I: A Methodological Novel about Autoethnography* (Walnut Creek: AltaMira Press, 2004), 37.
30 Ibid., 32.
31 Ibid., 619.
32 Margaret Vickers, 'Researchers as Storytellers: Writing on the Edge — And Without a Safety Net,' *Qualitative Inquiry* 8, no. 5 (2002): 619.
33 Ellis, *The Ethnographic I*, 157; Stacy Holman Jones, 'Emotional Space: Performing the Resistive Possibilities of Torch Singing,' *Qualitative Inquiry* 8, no. 6 (2002): 753.
34 Jones, 'Emotional Space,' 754.
35 Sharlene Nagy Hesse-Biber and Patricia Leavy, 'Introduction: Emergent Methods in Social Research Within and Across Disciplines,' in *Emergent Methods in Social Research,* eds. Sharlene Nagy Hesse-Biber and Patricia Leavy (Thousand Oaks: SAGE Publications, 2006), xxiii.
36 Robin M. Boylorn and Mark P. Orbe, 'Introduction: Critical Autoethnography as Method of Choice,' in *Critical Autoethnography: Intersecting*

Among historians, similar projects, organized under the genres of autobiography and memoir, have become critical positions from which historical writing unfolds. As medievalist Gabrielle Spiegel discloses her childhood relationship to postwar loss, she writes that, '[i]t is my profound conviction that what we do as historians is to write, in highly displaced, usually unconscious, but nonetheless determined ways, our inner, personal obsessions.'[37] Put another way, as Rocío G. Davis notes, '[w]e comprehend that academics function not only as "scholars," committed to objective reality, but as "authors" who somehow project themselves in their texts which, in important ways, may become negotiations of their personalities and intellectual positions.'[38]

This book would not be possible if I could not look into the cryptic corners and gaze upon the Confederate corpses of my family; if I could not locate the old, Southern guard that has refused to let me mourn and find a space for grief; if I could not write myself in my scholarly project; if I could not, in the acts of working through and letting go of these specters, claim my body's affects — its physical and emotional engagement with grief — as the necessary means by which I have navigated my personal and professional self. For, once again, in 2008, as I had just started writing this book, my grandmother died. As many know, the death of a parent can be a devastating event, and my grandmother was not only my mother but, moreover, my first love. During the last three months of her life, my father, my aunt, my husband, and I cared for her, first at home, then in the hospital, and finally in hospice. Watching her die, all the while

---

Cultural Identities in Everyday Life, eds. Robin M. Boylorn and Mark P. Orbe (Walnut Creek: Left Coast Press, 2014), 15.

37 Gabrielle Spiegel, 'France for Belgium,' in *Why France? American Historians Reflect on an Enduring Fascination,* eds. Laura Lee Downs and Stéphane Gerson (Ithaca: Cornell University Press, 2007), 2.

38 See also Rocío G. Davis, ed., *Reading Academic Autobiographies* [special issue], *Prose Studies* 31, no. 3 (2009) and 'Introduction: Academic Autobiography and/in the Discourses of History,' *Rethinking History* 13, no. 1 (2009): 1–4.

trying to reassure her that she would recover, was the hardest thing I have ever done. And in the wake of her death, I did not know myself. As the voice of so many family stories, as the living image of so many dead relations, she was the narrator, matriarch, and the most beautiful piece of my melancholic Southern family: its seemingly timeless connection to the land and to unmournable, unbearable, unspeakable loss. A decade later, I still grieve her passing.

After my grandmother died, I continued to go home, to Houston, Mississippi, and to her house, which I had inherited. But absent my grandmother, I began to feel no longer comfortable there, and this gnawing feeling creeped inside me when I would visit Mississippi: that only ghosts were waiting for me there. Although my grandmother's house continued to remain a comfort, and her love encircled me when I walked through its rooms, going home was not a homecoming. Most of the people I grew up with — the relatives I once visited, accompanied on cemetery outings and other failed adventures, and listened to as they told their stories — were, like her, dead. In 2013, I had a daughter, and when she was six weeks old, I took her to my grandmother's house for a few weeks to meet my many extended family members, to meet my grandmother (for whom she was named), to be comforted in the rocking chair whose worn treads had put to sleep five generations of babies in my family. A week after I returned from my grandmother's house, my inheritance from her, it burned. To the ground. Not just the nineteenth-century furniture. Not just the daguerreotypes, the aquatints, the black and whites, the 1970s orange-smudged photos and boxes of Kodak slide carousels. Not just the walls, the bricks, the chimney, the surrounding flowers, the plants, the six-foot palm. Not just all the childhood possessions of my father and myself. Not just everything, but all of it. Burned. All of my family. Burned. All of myself. Burned. All that I imagined for my daughter. Burned.

Burned.

B

    u

        r

      n

          e

            d.

              ..

            .

       .

              .

Perhaps not unexpectedly, I began to feel without a place in Anglo-Saxon studies, and without knowing it at the time, I started to mourn what I believed to be the *in toto* loss of my personal self in intimate proximity to my professional one. In the drafting and redrafting of this book, I have mourned my losses and have been able to see, for the first time, the unmourned and unmournable intimacies of my own life that stretch towards my intellectual pursuits. I tell you these things as a matter of autoethnography, autobiography, memoir, confession, or penitential — whatever genre you find this narrative to belong — because not only are my personal stories instrumental to constructing my own identity, but they are acts of '*communication*' that 'hope for embodied and personally implicated understandings between writer and reader.'[39] To put it another way, it is in these written com-

---

[39] A.P. Bochner, 'On First-Person Narrative Scholarship: Autoethnography as Acts of Meaning,' *Narrative Inquiry* 22, no. 1 (2012): 158, author's emphasis, and Satoshi Toyosaki and Sandy L. Pensoneau-Conway, 'Autoethnography as a Praxis of Social Justice: Three Ontological Contexts,' in *Handbook of*

muniqués of my perceived life that we — you and me — can be together and believe together that there are histories as yet to be written because, to borrow from the conceptual framework of Kathleen Biddick, they do not exist in the archive but rather in the unsovereign and unspliced performances of my body, your body, our embodied minds.[40]

What's more, that grief, far from being a private and personal activity, is an intersubjective process. Counter to mid-century psychoanalytic literature, which emphasized the importance of decathexis, contemporary psychoanalysis finds that grief affects are efforts to communicate, to maintain relatedness, to engage other survivors in bereavement. Further, as George Hagman explains, 'many problems arising from bereavement are due to the failure of other survivors to engage the bereaved person in mourning together,'[41] and as Robert Neimeyer, Dennis Klass, and Michael Robert Dennis write, 'the meaning of loss as well as the meaning of the continued connection with the loved one are (literally) negotiated within families and communities, and not merely dealt with in the cognitive province of one or more isolated individuals.'[42] Consequently, this chapter is, in many ways, an act of engaging you so that I might narrate my way towards reconfiguring my relationship with personal losses and professional ones, for to say that these are separate, unrelated issues to be born alone and in silence is to deny on a fundamental level

---

Autoethnography, eds. Stacy Holman Jones, Tony E. Adams, and Carolyn Ellis (New York: Routledge, 2016), 565.

40 Kathleen Biddick, 'Doing Dead Time for the Sovereign: Archive, Abandonment, Performance,' *Rethinking History* 13, no. 2 (2009): 137–51.

41 George Hagman, 'Beyond Decathexis: Toward a Fresh Theory of Grieving,' in *Meaning Reconstruction and the Experience of Loss,* ed. Robert A. Neimeyer (Washington, DC: American Psychological Association, 2001), 25.

42 Robert A. Neimeyer, Dennis Klass, and Michael Robert Dennis, 'Mourning, Meaning, and Memory: Individual, Communal, and Cultural Narration of Grief,' in *Meaning in Positive and Existential Psychology,* eds. Alexander Batthyany and Pninit Russo-Netzer (New York: Springer, 2014), 329.

the twinning of one's personal and professional selves, one's individual and community relationships.

Finally, and most importantly, this book is an invitation for others in Anglo-Saxon studies to grieve. As an introductory chapter that locates my own subjectivity at a crossroads of my research field and my family, trespassing the boundaries between professional and personal identities, it serves as an intersubjective invitation. It invites others to recognize their own unacknowledged losses — whatever they may be — and mourn these losses alongside mine such that the field of Anglo-Saxon studies is reshaped and transformed through the transformative acts of its mourners. For it is an inability to grieve identity positions and love objects that are no longer tenable and no longer living that keeps us attached to professional signifiers like 'Anglo-Saxon' and 'Anglo-Saxonist' and the subterranean old guard that maintains them. In a certain, quiet stillness, we must ask ourselves what needs to be mourned in order for the states of our field to truly become postcolonial — to be radically changed by decolonial narratives, theories, and activisms[43] — and for the old guard that haunts it to be driven from its closeted S/states.

While such work is intimately personal, it is in the process of making oneself vulnerable that we can not only find collaboration but moreover underscore scholarship as ethical praxis. Eileen Joy elegantly explains the ways in which the process of grieving, or, as she terms it, 'revisiting,' long-held positions can be generative of collaborative and more ethical scholarship, as exemplified in the collaborative work of Gillian Overing, Clare Lees, and Diane Watt:

> There are certain debates that we need not to return to, for as Overing herself hopefully stated in 1993, 'we are changed by

---

43 See Walter D. Mignolo and Catherine E. Walsh, *On Decoloniality: Concepts, Analytics, Praxis* (Durham: Duke University Press, 2018); Walter D. Mignolo and Arturo Escobar, eds., *Globalization and the Decolonial Option* (New York: Routledge, 2010); and Bernd Reiter, ed., *Constructing the Pluriverse: The Geopolitics of Knowledge* (Durham: Duke University Press, 2018).

this new work' — i.e., we are already profoundly altered in our orientation toward our scholarship in Old English studies by the more 'new' critical methodologies, and in a sense, there is no going back, no slamming on of the brakes as regards new directions in the field. I would hold up Gillian Overing, however, as an exemplary model of how a scholar might be willing, nevertheless, to revisit *themselves* in the past and rethink everything all over again with even newer modes of thought....This risk-taking and willingness to become 'undone' that Overing exemplified, beautifully...was also on display in London in the collaborative presentation of Clare Lees and Diane Watt...where Lees and Watt are pushing and challenging each other past the usual terms of their scholarship...in order to consider newer, transgendered spaces within which their scholarship can be co-practiced, while also continuously argued and debated and struggled over, but *together,* even when in opposition. To me, this is such an exemplary model of scholarship, of scholarship, even, as an ethical life-practice, in which the *agon* of thought is not abandoned but reformulated along lines that are mutually sustaining while also productive of the types of difference [of thought, of methodologies, etc.] that are crucial to the progress of any discipline of knowledge. For while we will, of necessity, disagree with each other, we do not recognize enough the 'with,' the shared togetherness, of disagreement that holds us *in abeyance with,* and not against, each other. I wish we could see this better sometimes, as Lees and Watt obviously do.[44]

---

44 Eileen Joy, 'What Lies Before Us: Old English Studies, the Agon of Thought, and Our Moments of Unknowingness,' *In the Middle* [blog], August 21, 2008, http://www.inthemedievalmiddle.com/2008/08/what-lies-before-us-old-english-studies.html. Joy was commenting on scholarly work presented by Overing, and by Lees and Watts, at the 2nd International Workshop of the Anglo-Saxon Studies Colloquium, King's College London, May 23–24, 2008.

While Joy, Overing, Lees, and Watt challenge us to revisit, collaborate, and find in scholarship an 'ethical life-practice,' this is a monograph, and, consequently, there are no formal co-authors. Yet as an open invitation for some of us or, perhaps, all of us to grieve or revisit our relationships to Anglo-Saxon studies and our stakes in the terms 'Anglo-Saxon' and 'Anglo-Saxonist,' this book hopes that we might become collaborators, remembering that, as Joy makes clear, agreeing or disagreeing with its content is not the point of collaboration. For, as Spiegel and Rocío Davis have likewise said, all academic histories are, in some way, acts of writing the self, and as Joy reminds us, collaboration is 'the shared togetherness, of disagreement that holds us *in abeyance with*, and not *against*, each other.'

The need for such collaboration among scholars within Anglo-Saxon studies cannot be signaled more clearly than in this present moment. In 2016, the first waves of a new, rising tide of state of the field debates emerged. The New Chaucer Society's panel, 'Are We Dark Enough Yet?' articulated the enduring problem of race among medievalists in the weeks following the United Kingdom's Brexit decision.[45] Academic blog posts on sites such as *In the Middle*[46] and *The Public Medievalist*[47] continued this conversation though America's racially charged presidential election campaign, and, in May 2017, sessions at the 52nd

---

45 Jeffrey Jerome Cohen (organizer), 'Are We Dark Enough Yet? Pale Faces 2016,' 20th Biennial Congress of the New Chaucer Society, London, UK, July 11, 2016.

46 See Dorothy Kim, 'Antifeminism, Whiteness, and Medieval Studies,' *In the Middle* [blog], January 18, 2016, http://www.inthemedievalmiddle.com/2016/01/antifeminism-whiteness-and-medieval.html; Cord Whitaker, 'Pale Like Me: Resistance, Assimilation, and "Pale Faces" Sixteen Years On,' *In the Middle* [blog], July 20, 2016, http://www.inthemedievalmiddle.com/2016/07/pale-like-me-resistance-assimilation.html; Wan Chuan Kao, '#palefacesmatter?' *In the Middle* [blog], July 26, 2016, http://www.inthemedievalmiddle.com/2016/07/palefacesmatter-wan-chuan-kao.html; and Sierra Lomuto, 'White Nationalism and the Ethics of Medieval Studies,' *In the Middle* [blog], December 5, 2016, http://www.inthemedievalmiddle.com/2016/12/white-nationalism-and-ethics-of.html.

47 See 'Race, Racism, and the Middle Ages,' *The Public Medievalist* [blog], http://www.publicmedievalist.com/race-racism-middle-ages-toc/.

International Congress on Medieval Studies (ICMS) discussed troubling connections between racism, colonialism, and medieval studies.[48] During the summer of that year, an explosion of events happened that sharpened these connections. At the International Medieval Congress in Leeds (UK), a racist joke made by the moderator of the conference's keynote lecture prompted censure on Twitter, in online forums, and in *The Chronicle of Higher Education*.[49] The International Society of Anglo-Saxonists' biennial meeting in Honolulu was marked by accusations of native erasure.[50] Then, the white supremacist rallies, with resulting deadly violence, in Charlottesville, Virginia, happened,[51] and rifts that had been developing within medieval studies began to widen. In 2018, the Kalamazoo's Congress's leadership was unwilling to put in place measures to protect medievalists of color from harassment at the Congress, and, months later, the ICMS denied all Medievalist of Color-sponsored sessions for its 2019

---

48 See Sierra Lomuto, Shokoofeh Rajabzadeh, and Cord Whitaker (co-organizers), 'Medieval Race and the Modern Scholar,' 52nd International Congress on Medieval Studies, Kalamazoo, MI, May 11, 2017; Sierra Lomuto, Shokoofeh Rajabzadeh, and Dorothy Kim (co-organizers), 'Whiteness in Medieval Studies: A Workshop,' 52nd International Congress on Medieval Studies, Kalamazoo, MI, May 13, 2017. See also Matthew Hussey (organizer), '#ASESoWhite,' Modern Language Association Convention, New York City, NY, January 5, 2018.

49 @punctum_books, Twitter post, July 3, 2017, https://twitter.com/punctum_books/status/881788042507427840; 'On Race and Medieval Studies,' *Medievalists of Color*, August 1, 2017, http://medievalistsofcolor.com/statements/on-race-and-medieval-studies/; J. Clara Chan, 'Medievalists, Recoiling From White Supremacy, Try to Diversify the Field,' *The Chronicle of Higher Education*, July 16, 2017, https://www.chronicle.com/article/Medievalists-Recoiling-From/240666.

50 Adam Miyashiro, 'Decolonizing Anglo-Saxon Studies: A Response to ISAS in Honolulu,' *In The Middle* [blog], July 29, 2017, http://www.inthemedievalmiddle.com/2017/07/decolonizing-anglo-saxon-studies.html.

51 Dorothy Kim, 'Teaching Medieval Studies in a Time of White Supremacy,' *In The Middle* [blog], August 28, 2017, http://www.inthemedievalmiddle.com/2017/08/teaching-medieval-studies-in-time-of.html; Nell Gluckman, 'A Debate About White Supremacy and Medieval Studies Exposes Deep Rifts in the Field,' *The Chronicle of Higher Education*, September 18, 2017, https://www.chronicle.com/article/A-Debate-About-White-Supremacy/241234.

Congress. These (in)actions prompted open letters of dissent and concern from many within medieval studies and a boycott of Kalamazoo by many medievalists of color.[52]

As if to signal the failed promise of *Desire for Origins,* which advocated for critical theory as the antidote to methods of philology and historicism overdetermined by colonialist frames of thought, readers of this chapter may recall that Allen Frantzen's own fall from grace tipped off this list of events. In January 2016, medievalists responded to statements on Frantzen's personal website which decried feminism as 'a sour mix of victimization and privilege…use[d] to intimidate and exploit men.'[53] Scrutiny of Frantzen, who had, in the minds of some scholars, been an unflagging supporter of feminism and feminists in Anglo-Saxon studies, quickly turned to online discussions about the prevalence of misogyny and sexual harassment within the field. Yet Dorothy Kim deftly connects the 'femfog' of Frantzen to a 'credo and ethos…of white supremacy, white nationalism, and neo-Nazism,'[54] and, as the short list of events above indicates, it took only a few months for discussions regarding anti-feminism, misogyny, and sexual harassment in Anglo-Saxon studies to turn to issues of race and racism in the field as well.

---

52 Seeta Chaganti, 'Statement Regarding ICMS Kalamazoo,' *Medievalists of Color,* July 9, 2018, http://medievalistsofcolor.com/race-in-the-profession/statement-regarding-icms-kalamazoo/; BABEL Working Group, 'Letter of Concern, ICMS / Kalamazoo 2019,' https://docs.google.com/forms/d/e/1FAIpQLSdReGZAQJiSSDWTRV0kT2tO2b9LEaaPLTjDJGCeH6auDczBhA/viewform; Eileen A. Joy and Vincent W.J. van Gerven Oei, 'A Statement of Concern Regarding the Programming for the 2019 International Congress on Medieval Studies @Kalamazoo,' *punctum books* [blog], July 14, 2018, https://punctumbooks.com/blog/a-statement-of-concern/.
53 Allen J. Frantzen, 'How to Fight Your Way Out of the Feminist Fog,' *Allen J. Frantzen: Author. Boxer. Traditional Man* [URL no longer active], quoted from Cohen, 'On Calling Out Misogyny,' *In The Middle,* January 16, 2016, http://www.inthemedievalmiddle.com/2016/01/on-calling-out-misogyny.html.
54 Dorothy Kim, *Digital Whiteness and Medieval Studies* (upublished manuscript). My thanks to Prof. Kim for sharing her unpublished manuscript with me.

The past three years reveal a medieval studies that appears to be free-falling towards an uncertain future. Yet, amid so many problems, changes are being made that are cause for much optimism. In 2017, Medievalists of Color became a professional organization and has since become an integral voice in medieval studies, providing support for medievalists of color, organizing workshops and panels that address racial inequities and support inclusivity, and hosting an online forum that advocates for diversity in medieval studies. In 2018, the Medieval Academy created the Belle de la Costa Greene Award to support research and travel by scholars of color. In January 2019, the first 'Race-B4Race' symposium was held at Arizona State University, sponsored by the Arizona Center for Medieval and Early Modern Studies, and a second symposium was held at the Folger Shakespeare Library in September 2019. Also in 2019, important and highly anticipated books by Cord Whitaker and Dorothy Kim were published on race, whiteness, the middle ages, and medieval studies,[55] and in 2020 a special issue of *postmedieval* titled 'Race, Revulsion, and Revolution,' edited by Mary Rambaran-Olm, M. Breann Leake, and Micah Goodrich will add more voices to the mix.[56]

The tense proximity between events which signal disaster and developments which point towards hope indicates that some institutions and individuals within medieval studies are doing the difficult and painful work of mourning—and activism. As a result of these labors, old narratives that have structured these fields are slowly falling by the way, and new ones are supplanting them. Yet, despite many who have publicly and privately called for an end to the terms 'Anglo-Saxon' and 'Anglo-

---

55 Cord Whitaker, *Black Metaphors: How Modern Racism Emerged from Medieval Race-Thinking* (Philadelphia: University of Pennsylvania Press, 2019); Kim, *Digital Whiteness and Medieval Studies*.
56 Mary Rambaran-Olm, M. Breann Leake, and Micah Goodrich, eds., *Race, Revulsion, and Revolution* [special issue], *postmedieval: a journal of medieval cultural studies* 11, no. 3 (2020).

Saxonist,'[57] both are still in widespread circulation, intimating, as this chapter has argued, that the grief work by scholars who lay claim to these professional appellatives has yet to be done. This book engages in this work. As it moves from the tender spaces of personal grief towards grieving the field of Anglo-Saxon studies more broadly, it divides its chapters into three critical-emotional movements: 'Anglo-Saxon(ist) Pasts,' 'Interlude — A Time for Mourning,' and 'postSaxon Futures.'

The First Movement, 'Anglo-Saxon(ist) Pasts,' critically examines, exposes, and unearths the old guard of Anglo-Saxon studies that has lingered, silently, and for many centuries, within the unconscious quarters of the field. In chapters that place early medieval poetry in conversation with the historical, archaeological, and literary scholarship of Sharon Turner, James Douglas, and John Mitchell Kemble, three fathers of the interdisciplinary field of Anglo-Saxon studies, this Movement uncovers narratives of mourning and melancholy, colonial desire and ethnopolitics, that arc from Anglo-Saxon texts to Anglo-Saxon studies, impacting the minds and bodies of nineteenth-, twentieth-, and twenty-first-century Anglo-Saxonists.

Chapter 2 — '*Krákumál*, Sharon Turner, and the Psychic Crypts of Anglo-Saxon History' — works to rout the ghosts that linger, silently, within the unconscious quarters — the psychic crypts — of Anglo-Saxon studies and prohibit acts of mourning from unfolding. It begins by discussing the Old Norse poem, *Krákumál*, a crypt-making narrative of death and psychoanalytic incorporation that returns in Sharon Turner's *History of the Anglo-Saxons*. Turner, the first antiquarian historian of Anglo-Saxon history, is haunted by the medieval ghosts of Empire, and as this chapter traces his *History* from its publication during the rise of Britain's late-eighteenth-century empire to its disavowal

---

57 In addition to portions of this book, which were published in *postmedieval* and *Rethinking History*, Dan Remein's conference paper, 'ISAS Should Probably Change its Name,' International Congress on Medieval Studies, Kalamazoo, MI, May 2017 (https://www.academia.edu/34101681/_Isas_should_probably_change_its_name_ICMS_Kalamazoo_2017), makes the case for abandoning the term 'Anglo-Saxonist.'

amid twentieth-century decolonization, it locates the stirrings of Turner's encrypted ghosts in the narratives of Anglo-Saxon historians in criticism of the 1980s and 1990s. It then argues that the unacknowledged presence of Turner's ghosts maintains twenty-first-century Anglo-Saxon studies in a posture of unreflexiveness that prohibits the process of mourning from fully unfolding. Specifically, this chapter suggests that, in America, the field's inability to historicize the discipline has left room for popular historians to return Ragnar, the blood eagle, and medieval ghosts of Empire to television screens and American politics.

Chapter 3 — '*Beowulf,* James Douglas, and the Sepulchral Body of the Anglo-Saxonist' — which serves as a companion to Chapter 2, argues that in order to dislocate the field of Anglo-Saxon studies from a critical posture that prohibits mourning, we must discuss crypts not only of the mind but also for the body. In this chapter, I trace connections between early medieval funeral barrows, *Beowulf,* and James Douglas, the first antiquarian archaeologist of the Anglo-Saxon period. I argue that Beowulf and Douglas are barrow diggers, and in the process of opening another's grave, stepping into its mortuary interior, and retrieving the antiquities within, both become subject to the barrow's territory of dying and are reterritorialized as figures of interminable grief. Douglas's first barrow sketch in *Nenia Britannica* couples the affects of grief with those of British nationalism, and as his sketch is replicated in archaeological reports across the nineteenth century, a visual representation of the Anglo-Saxonist emerges as a grief-stricken, undead figure of racialized, national-imperial performance. The embodied representation and performance of the Anglo-Saxonist is encoded within *Beowulf* studies via John Mitchell Kemble, whose edition of the poem summarily precedes his barrow excavations in Hanover. Kemble's scholarship associates Beowulfian and Anglo-Saxon barrows, and it connects Beowulf's mortuary performances with those of the Anglo-Saxonist. In reading *Beowulf* we become the Anglo-Saxonists of Douglas and Kemble. We enter (and lead our students into) early medieval crypts and poetic graves. Yet we fail to attend to the affects, gestures, and movements of race and empire that accompany this funereal descent.

Together, the chapters of 'Anglo-Saxon(ist) Pasts' argue that Turner, Douglas, and Kemble form part of an old guard, the fathers of Anglo-Saxon studies. Their scholarship, which is driven by national-imperial sentiments and their associated ethnopolitics, recasts early medieval responses to death into those of interminable, colonial mourning. Turner, Douglas, and Kemble deposit, within the emerging scholarly narratives and methods of Anglo-Saxon studies, psychic crypts and material graves. From these funerary sites, the Anglo-Saxonist emerges, a professional who, in mind and in body, is not only raced and ethnically identified. Standing with one foot in the grave, his posture also takes on a colonial grief that has become, in the wake of twentieth-century decolonization, unconsciously melancholic. The Anglo-Saxonist is a racialized corpse of Empire that maintains itself, undead, by way of an entangled, unconscious, and encrypted relationship between Anglo-Saxonist scholarship and Anglo-Saxonist nationalism.

Once this corpse has been unearthed and its ghostly habitations have been located, the Second Movement, 'Interlude — A Time for Mourning,' enacts the process of working through and emotionally letting go of this Anglo-Saxonist and its old guard. Such grief work engages my professional and personal selves, and, in this section, I approach genealogical narratives of the field and my family in order to creatively rewrite them.

Chapter 4 — 'On Being an Anglo-Saxonist: Asser's *Life of King Alfred*, Benjamin Thorpe, and the Sovereign *Corpus* of a Profession' — turns to Alfred, King of the Anglo-Saxons, the sovereign father of the field who guards the professional signifiers, Anglo-Saxon and Anglo-Saxonist. It tracks the function of *rex Angulsaxonum* ('King of the Anglo-Saxons') in Asser's late ninth-century *Life of King Alfred*, a biography that establishes much of what we know about Alfred and the many Old English texts translated during his lifetime. Asser's *Life* uses the king's royal style to transform Alfred's chronically ill, ethnopolitical body into a sovereign, Anglo-Saxon signifier and a textual,

Anglo-Saxon *corpus*. The consequences of these actions become apparent centuries later in the writings of philologist Benjamin Thorpe, philological father of Anglo-Saxon studies and interdisciplinary companion to Turner, Douglas, and Kemble. By studying Thorpe's translation of Erasmus Rask's *Grammar of the Anglo-Saxon Tongue* and reading Thorpe's primer, *Analecta Anglo-Saxonica,* his reader plots a pedagogical path towards transitioning from a student of Anglo-Saxon into an Anglo-Saxonist: a professional and an ontological being who has positioned, within his body and mind, Alfred's sovereign, now-racialized corpse and its textual, Anglo-Saxon *corpus*.

For twenty-first-century Anglo-Saxonists, the ontological force of our professional appellative weighs heavily upon us. Yet, as Chapter Four discusses, the sovereign figure of Alfred, king of the Anglo-Saxons, which lies at the bedrock of our professional signifier not only keeps us in place as Anglo-Saxonists but also prohibits us from becoming something else. In order to emotionally give up, or at least loosen the ties that bind us to 'Anglo-Saxon' and 'Anglo-Saxonist,' Chapter Five — 'Becoming postSaxon, Or, a Biochemical *Vita Ælfredi*' — returns to the body and biography of King Alfred while contemplating my own family. It writes a micro-history of Alfred's body that tracks its purported engagements with hemorrhoids and Crohns disease, its eventual death and decay in the grave, and its supposed recovery in the 1999/2013 excavations of Hyde Abbey. This work of creative non-fiction attends to Alfred's body as a biochemical organism that, in life and in death, challenges and exceeds the Anglo-Saxon parameters and patriarchy that have been thrust upon him. Witnessing Alfred's decay enables me to supplant the settler colonialists and Confederates of my family and make room for a genealogy that runs counter to the Ellards' Anglo-Saxonist history. The process of making these new fictions circuits the personal back to the professional. By attending to Alfred's material corpse rather than his ethnopolitical and racialized *corpus,* Alfred is no longer (if ever he was) Anglo-Saxon, and I find myself no longer an Anglo-Saxon(ist) but a scholar of postSaxon becoming.

'Interlude — A Time for Mourning' enacts scholarly and creative means of rescripting, and thereby grieving, Alfred, the sovereign Anglo-Saxon father and primogenitor of Anglo-Saxon studies, even as it comes to terms with the fatherly old guard that lurks within my family. From here, the book turns to its Third, and final, Movement, 'postSaxon Futures.' As a placeholder, not a term, for what the field might become, 'postSaxon futures' serves as an invitation for a once-Anglo Saxon studies to reposition itself in relation to temporalities, bodies, and methods once excluded by its racial and ethnopolitical signifiers.

Chapter 6 — 'Old/e English Poetics and "Afro-Saxon" Intimacies' — explores one possible 'postSaxon' future by following the entangled histories of Olde English malt liquor and Old English language. The silent partnership between Olde and Old Englishes not only reveals that these terms are freighted (like Anglo-Saxon and Anglo-Saxonist) with the baggage of race and Empire. This chapter writes a narrative that sutures Olde English malt liquor to African American sociolinguistics and American rap music, impressing upon the scholarly community that it does not own Old English but is simply a user of a term that is unequivocally colonial. As African American linguistic and arts communities are drawn near to Anglo-Saxonist ones, this chapter leverages these intimacies in order to disinvent Old English and speculatively reinvent Olde English as a decolonial expression of 'becoming postSaxon.'

Chapter 7 — 'Becoming postSaxon' — returns to autoethnography, surveying changes afoot in Anglo-Saxon studies in relation to an account of how writing this book has changed me. It argues that narratives of open reflection and bereavement, which challenge the genre restrictions of academic writing, are critical to field change because they underscore scholarship and scholarly writing as processes of becoming rather than being. This chapter queries the possibility, set forth in the book's initial chapter, that postcolonialism is a possible future horizon, arguing that decolonization, like mourning, and like becoming, has no end. Further, it advocates, once again, that it is only in the collaborative performances of many scholars that once-called

Anglo-Saxonists can imagine new and more ethical postSaxon futures.

Anglo-Saxon(ist) Pasts, postSaxon Futures may seem, at a glance, to be a work of intellectual history that speaks exclusively to specialists in Anglo-Saxon studies. Yet medieval studies programs and English departments claim this historical period and academic sub-field as points of origin. Consequently, the arguments of this book gesture towards a much wider audience. Like Anglo-Saxonists, medievalists use a parallel nomenclature that locates them within a temporal and geographic past, and English departments, the institutional homes for many of these scholars, maintain ethno-political and racial affiliations by way of the discipline's attachments to Anglo-America. Indeed, despite the earnest efforts of medieval studies and English, the conversations that take place within these arenas remain largely tied to periodization, to Western canons, and to disciplinary methods that rarely consider one's personal identity or the embodied aspects of scholarship. *Anglo-Saxon(ist) Pasts, postSaxon Futures* is thus a test case for not only what our identity politics have been in the past but also what they could become in the future if we cease to point our fields in directions that harbor and maintain the ethno-political, racial, and methodological freight of previous academic generations.

2

Krákumál, Sharon Turner, and the Psychic Crypts of Anglo-Saxon History

From the Death of Egbert to the Death of Alfred[1] is the second volume of Sharon Turner's four-volume *History of the Anglo-Saxons*. Although a history of the eighth and ninth centuries, its narrative is crafted around a medieval Scandinavian poem that was quite popular during the eighteenth and nineteenth centuries called *Krákumál*. *Krákumál* was Turner's poetic inspiration while writing a history that entwines the arrival of the Vikings with the rise of Alfred. In *From the Death of Egbert*, Turner explains that the Viking hero Ragnar Lodbrog, on an ill-fated adventure to Northumbria, is captured by King Ella and

1   *From their First Appearance above the Elbe, to the Death of Egbert* and *From the Death of Egbert to the Death of Alfred* are the first two volumes of Turner's *History of the Anglo-Saxons*. They were printed in 1799 and 1801, respectively, with London printers, T. Cadell and W. Davies. In 1802 these volumes were reprinted by Longman and Rees, which likewise printed the last two volumes of the four-volume *History* (*From the Death of Alfred to the Norman Conquest* [1802] and *The History of the Manners, Landed Property, Government, Laws, Poetry, Literature, Religion, and Language, of the Anglo-Saxons* [1805]) and each successive edition (1807, 1820, 1823, 1828, 1836, 1852). Given the longevity of this relationship between Turner and Longman, I have chosen to cite the 1802 Longman edition in this chapter.

thrown into a pit of snakes.[2] In Ella's snake pit, Ragnar composes *Krákumál* before dying from the bites of venomous vipers. The sounds of *Krákumál* ring out across the open seas, and Ragnar's 'Death-song,' as Turner calls it, heralds the vengeful expedition of 'the Northmen' to Anglo-Saxon England.[3] Upon arrival in Northumbria, they 'inflicted a cruel and inhuman retaliation on Ella for their father's sufferings. They cut the figure of an eagle on his back…to tear out his lungs.'[4] Turner continues, explaining that Ella's 'blood eagle' is not simply a revenge act but a 'dismal sacrifice' that precipitates a Scandinavian politics of conquest and colonialism.[5] Once in Northumbria, 'the invaders did not depart' but extended their Viking vengeance across Anglo-Saxon England by conquering and colonizing its kingdoms.[6] If Ragnar's Death-song is Turner's poetic invocation, then Ella's death by blood eagle is the history called forth from it. This strange, singular, and likely apocryphal event sets in motion the coming of the Northmen and of Alfred. It serves as a fantastic trauma and a primal scene by which Turner's narrative of early English history arcs from Ragnar's colonial ambitions toward Alfred's Anglo-Saxon nation.

Could Ragnar and Ella be the mythical fathers of Anglo-Saxon history? I pose this question in relation to another: might Sharon Turner be a father of Anglo-Saxon historians? Allen Frantzen calls Turner the 'first modern historian of Anglo-Saxon England,' and Claire Simmons, in a statement echoed by Sarah Foot, goes so far as to rate his multi-volume *History of the Anglo-Saxons* as 'the most important single impetus to Anglo-

---

2   The stories of Ragnar and Ella are recounted in a number of texts from medieval Scandinavia and from eighteenth- and nineteenth-century England. The spelling of names and places varies in these texts, and, unless otherwise indicated, I use Turner's spellings for consistency.
3   Sharon Turner, *The History of the Anglo-Saxons, from Their Earliest Appearance above the Elbe, to the Norman Conquest*, vol. II (Paternoster-Row, London: T.N. Longman and O. Rees, Printed for the Author, 1802–1805), vii.
4   Ibid., 123.
5   Ibid.,124.
6   Ibid.

Saxon studies.'[7] Turner's *History* has been called 'pioneering' and 'immensely detailed and influential.'[8] Its historical breadth, archival research, and bibliographic citations signal milestones in the field's professional development. While Turner's importance to the history of Anglo-Saxon studies is well noted, Turner's scholarship is unequivocally disavowed. Written and revised as Britain sailed toward the national-imperial horizons of its Victorian Age, Turner's *History* envisions the Anglo-Saxon past as a romantic narrative that anticipates an English future. Consequently, as many scholars have explained, the historical integrity of Turner's labors in the British Museum is compromised by his Whiggish commitments, nationalist fervor, and imperialist beliefs. Likewise, the racist and colonialist uses to which later editions of his *History* were put in the post-Bellum American South and in settlement-period Australia have further jaundiced its academic legitimacy outside of England.[9]

Guided by the psychoanalytic research of Nicolas Abraham and Maria Torok and the sociopolitical implications of their work on transgenerational haunting, this chapter examines Sha-

---

7   Allen J. Frantzen, *Desire for Origins: New Languages, Old English, and Teaching the Tradition* (New Brunswick: Rutgers University Press, 1990), 33; Claire Simmons, *Reversing the Conquest: History and Myth in Nineteenth-Century British Literature* (New Brunswick: Rutgers University Press, 1990), 55; and Sarah Foot, *Æthelstan: The First King of England* (New Haven: Yale University Press, 2011), 237.

8   Jacqueline Pearson, 'Crushing the Convent and the Dread Bastille: The Anglo-Saxons, Revolution and Gender in Women's Plays of the 1790s,' in *Literary Appropriations of the Anglo-Saxons from the Thirteenth to the Twentieth Century*, eds. Donald Scragg and Carole Weinberg (Cambridge: Cambridge University Press, 2000), 123; Linda Pratt, 'Anglo-Saxon Attitudes? Alfred the Great and the Romantic National Epic,' in *Literary Appropriations of the Anglo-Saxons from the Thirteenth to the Twentieth Century*, eds. Donald Scragg and Carole Weinberg (Cambridge: Cambridge University Press, 2000) 144.

9   John Higham, *Strangers in the Land: Patterns of American Nativism, 1860–1925* (New Brunswick: Rutgers University Press, 2002), 10; Leigh Boucher, 'Trans/National History and Disciplinary Amnesia: Historicizing White Australia at Two *fins de siècles*,' in *Creating White Australia*, eds. Jane Carey and Claire McLisky (Sydney: Sydney University Press, 2009), 57–58.

ron Turner's *History of the Anglo-Saxons* as a crypt in which the unmourned losses and unacknowledged traumas of British colonialism are secreted. I argue that Turner, a historian inspired by the Old Norse poem *Krákumál* and driven by imperialist ideology, is haunted by a restless colonial other whose encrypted form stirs the pages of his *History* and makes 'incomprehensible signals.'[10] Turner narrativizes these signals as the blood-eagle, 'a cruel and inhuman retaliation' that rips apart Ella's body and tears out his lungs so that his Northumbrian kingdom might be conquered and colonized. Turner, moved by the ghostly sounds that emerge from his narrative voice, buries Ella's blood-eagled body within his *History*, which becomes a crypt across which Ella strays. This chapter suggests that Turner, an ambiguous father of Anglo-Saxon studies, has transmitted Ella's blood eagle, an encrypted specter of empire, to his children. I contextualize scholarly commentary on the blood eagle within late twentieth-century decolonization, arguing that scholars of the 1980s and 1990s return to the blood eagle and act out the trauma that Turner has passed on to them to try and heal (or re-inter) the hidden wounds of colonialism. This chapter analyzes Turner's historical work in order to ask what twenty-first-century future — what state of academic unmindfulness and unmourning — has been imagined for Anglo-Saxonists through over two centuries of wrestling with these encrypted ghosts of empire. It then turns to twenty-first-century visions of the blood eagle, the spectral presence of which has stirred, again, in the wake of 9/11 and also on the eve of Donald Trump's inauguration. While ghosts, as Stephen Frosh writes, may 'come from the future,' the blood eagle reminds Anglo-Saxon studies that it urgently needs to look more closely at how it minds its past.[11]

Although Turner cites an impressive breadth of medieval sources in his *History of the Anglo-Saxons,* his preface credits

---

10 Nicolas Abraham and Maria Torok, *The Shell and the Kernel: Renewals of Psychoanalysis,* ed. and trans. Nicholas T. Rand (Chicago: Chicago University Press, 1994), 130.

11 Stephen Frosh, *Hauntings: Psychoanalysis and Ghostly Transmissions* (London: Palgrave Macmillan, 2013), 11.

a popular poem as the primary impetus for the entire project. In Turner's 1802 Longman preface, he claims that the 'Deathsong of Ragnar Lodbrog' and Ragnar's death in Northumbria prompted his research for the *History*. Turner was not alone in finding inspiration in the Death-song. *Krákumál*, as it is known by contemporary academics, is a skaldic poem that dates from the late twelfth century. The poem's subject and speaker is Ragnar Lodbrog, a Volsung descendant and Viking king[12] who celebrates the bloody outcomes of past battles as he awaits death in the Northumbrian king Ella's snake pit. The poem's bellicose images collapse the ethical, physical, and temporal distance between Ragnar's body and that of cultural Others. In earlier stanzas, Ragnar claims, for example, that his skirmishes near Hjaðningavágr and Northumbria were neither 'like placing a fair maiden in a bed' nor like 'kissing a young widow.'[13] These remarks, which locate battle in negative proximity to sexual relations, loosen the ethical distinction between hostile and hospitable acts, and they lay the groundwork for subsequent, material elisions between enemies and allies. Ragnar contemplates the aftermath of battle in which men lay dead atop one another, and he considers single combat among unidentifiable warriors.[14] These remarks, which recognize no lexical difference between

---

12 According to *Ragnars saga* (*The Tale of Ragnar Loðbrok*), Ragnar marries into the Volsung line by wedding Áslaug, the daughter of Sigurd and Brynhild of the *Völsunga saga* (*The Tale of the Völsungs*). He inherits the throne of Denmark from his father, also named Sigurd.

13 'vasat sem bjarta brúði / í bing hjá sér leggja'...'vasat sem unga ekkju / í ǫndvegi kyssa' (Finnur Jónsson, ed., *Den norsk-islandske skjaldedigtning. B: Rettet tekst* [1912–1915; repr. Copenhagen: Villadsen & Christensen, Rosenkilde & Bagger, 1973], 652, stanza 13, ll. 9–10 and stanza 14, ll. 9–10). All translations of *Krákumál* are my own but lean upon Rory McTurk's prose translation, which follows, for the most part, Jónsson's edition. Rory McTurk, 'Samuel Ferguson's "Death-Song" (1833): An Anglo-Irish Response to *Krákumál*,' in *Constructing Nations, Reconstructing Myth: Essays in Honour of T.A. Shippey*, ed. Andrew Wawn (Turnhout, Belgium: Brepols, 2007), 167–92.

14 'Hverr lá þverr of annan'...'Hitt telk jafnt, at gangi / at samtogi sverða / sveinn í móti einum / hrøkkvit þegn fyr þegni' (*Den norsk-islandske skjaldedigtning*, 642, stanza 16, l. 2; 654, stanza 23, ll. 2–4).

mutually hostile warriors, anticipate Ragnar's own heroic celebrations in the dwellings of Óðinn. In death he will drink beer from 'the curved-tree of skulls.'[15] By way of an elaborate kenning that references a drinking horn, *Krákumál* emerges as an oral poem that locates future action in the present tense and transforms Ragnar's empty mouth into a site for poetic consumption. In ode to his own death, Ragnar drinks the dead.

Krákumál's emphasis on orality engages a rigorous discussion about the psychopolitics of incorporation, a concept that emerges in the psychoanalytic work of Abraham and Torok. As Abraham and Torok explain, when we do not mourn the death of a loved one — when we deny that we have lost an object of our affections — we refuse to abide the often painful and lengthy process of grieving. In a defensive act that violates the ethical, physical, and temporal constraints of mourning, we open our (psychic) mouth and fantastically 'swallow whole' their figure.[16] Through these illicit acts of 'eating' the dead, we magically incorporate their spirit, their drives, and their urges within our psyche as a self-preservative mechanism that shields us from the painful process of identity reconfiguration that is enacted across the time of mourning. As Ragnar lies dying in Ella's pit, his thoughts about the past relax the conceptual distance between war and love, foe and friend, self and other. Consequently, they prepare Ragnar for contemplating his future. As he envisions himself at Óðinn's banquet table, Ragnar fantasizes a scene of incorporation. He presses his open mouth upon the skull of an unidentifiable other, fantasizing an act of consumption that encodes a prohibition against mourning into the poetic fibers — its kennings — of *Krákumál*'s skaldic verses. Soon after, Ragnar predicts, 'Viðrir's switch [glossed frequently as Óðinn's spear] will stand fast in Ella. The slaying of their father will cause my

---

15 'Hitt lœgir mik, jafnan / at Baldrs fǫður bekki / búna veitk at sumblum; / drekkum bjór af bragði / ór bjúgviðum hausa' (*Den norsk–islandske skjaldedigtning*, 655, stanza 25, ll. 2–6).
16 Abraham and Torok, *The Shell and the Kernel*, 126, 128.

sons' hearts to swell with rage.'[17] Instead of grieving his death, Ragnar's sons will incorporate their father's libidinal energies: they will devour and ingest his Volsung-Viking spirit, and they will cleave their sense of self to the corpse of their Odinic father. As a consequence, 'Viðrir's switch will stand fast in Ella.' If *Krákumál* gestures toward the effects of incorporating Ragnar, then other medieval Scandinavian texts make these gestures clear. Ragnar's sons arrive in Northumbria, murder Ella by blood-eagling him, then conquer and colonize Anglo-Saxon England.[18] In *Krákumál*, psychological acts of incorporation hasten toward political acts of incorporation: in devouring, cannibalizing, and swallowing whole one's beloved father, one exacts a similar terror upon one's unloved enemy. In short, prohibitions against mourning become directed toward policies of colonialism.

As a poem that explores the psycho-politics of incorporation, it is not infelicitous that *Krákumál* is published first in English by Thomas Percy in 1763, a year that evidences the success of Britain's resounding colonial victories in both the Seven Years War and in the French and Indian War.[19] Percy's interests in translating *Krákumál* and other skaldic poems are underwritten by his investments in an English identity that is secured by association with 'a "Norse poetic" empire.'[20] As Robert Rix points out, Percy argued that 'a central feature of Norse poetics [was]…

---

17 '…Viðris / vǫndr í Ellu standi; / sonum mínum mun svella / sinn fǫður ráðinn verða' (*Den norsk–islandske skjaldedigtning*, 655, stanza 27, ll. 5–8).

18 See Saxo Grammaticus's Danish chronicle, *Gesta Danorum* (*Deeds of the Danes*), Book IX; the Icelandic prose works *Ragnars saga* (*The Tale of Ragnar Loðbrok*), Chapter 15; and *Þáttr af Ragnars sonum* (*The Tale of Ragnar's Sons*), Chapter 3.

19 While 'Indian' is an inappropriate term for the native and indigenous peoples of North America, I invoke this word, and repeat it throughout this chapter, within the context of eighteenth-century colonial history and according to its use by Percy and his contemporaries.

20 Robert Rix, 'The Afterlife of a Death Song: Reception of Ragnar Lodbrog's Poem in Britain Until the End of the Eighteenth Century,' *Studia Neophilologica: A Journal of Germanic and Romance Languages and Literature* 81, no. 1 (2009): 4, 13. Rix's quote derives from a statement made by Thomas Wharton, who was a co-collaborator (with Percy) of Runic theory. Here, I use Wharton's words in reference to Percy for the sake of expediency.

the inclination to make "poetical fiction" out of "poetical history"...[and] Percy believed this method of composition was embodied in Ragnar's epicedium.'[21] Ragnar's epicedium, which he titles 'The Dying Ode of Regner Lodbrok,' is the first among Percy's Old Norse translations. In selecting 'The Dying Ode,' Percy lays claim to his literary inheritance from 'the northern nations' and pronounces himself implicitly a son of Ragnar.[22] By making these genealogical claims, Percy finds himself entangled in the not-so-poetical history that follows from *Krákumál*'s poetical fiction. In his preface to 'The Dying Ode,' Percy writes, 'war in those rude ages was carried on with the same inhumanity, as it is now among the savages of North-America: their prisoners were only reserved to be put to death with torture. Ragner was accordingly thrown into a dungeon to be stung to death by serpents.'[23] Percy measures the 'inhumanity' of Ragnar's death by snake-bite against the 'savagery' of indigenous North Americans. He draws the medieval brutalities of Anglo-Scandinavia into dialogue with Britain's wars in North America. *Krákumál* acts according to what Gabrielle Schwab calls a screen memory, a story that 'focus[es] on histories of violence elsewhere in order to split them off from one's own violent histories…to cover up or work through another affectively closer history that would be more problematic to deal with.'[24] While Ragnar's death is a screen memory that shields Percy from the 'affectively closer history' of British colonialism, Ragnar's poetic legacy has directed him into ethically troubled waters. By way of poetry, have Ragnar's English descendants taken inside themselves Ragnar's Volsung-Viking spirit? Have they responded to their father's skaldic verses by incorporating his libidinal drives? In an act of gross unmourning, have they unleashed these Ragnarian energies upon North America in the vengeful-cum-colonial pursuit

---

21 Rix, 'The Afterlife of a Death Song,' 12.
22 Thomas Percy, *Five Pieces of Runic Poetry Translated from the Islandic Language* (London: R. and J. Dodsley, 1763), A3.
23 Ibid., 23–24.
24 Gabrielle Schwab, *Haunting Legacies: Violent Histories and Transgenerational Trauma* (New York: Columbia University Press, 2010), 23.

of their French and 'Indian' enemies? In 1763, Percy screens these questions but does not dare answer them.

In subsequent decades, *Krákumál*'s popularity keeps time with Britain's colonial actions in North America and elsewhere across the world,[25] and in 1782 Rev. Johnstone's *Lodbrokar Quida; or The Death-Song of Lodbroc* is published. In language that echoes Percy's preface, Johnstone explains the longevity of *Krákumál*:

> [D]uring the rude periods of society, the safety, both of nations and of individuals depends upon making themselves objects of terror. Hence, while the captive *Indian* mitigates his torments by the recollection of his exploits, he tramples, as it were, on the cruelty of his enemies... *The Lodbrokar-quida* shews, that a similarity of manners prevailed in the north; and, indeed, men, in the same degree of civilization, will act, and think, nearly in the same way.[26]

Johnstone's statements regarding the 'captive Indian' and the 'cruelty of his enemies' reverberate against Percy's prefatory rhetoric of the 'torture' of 'prisoners' and the 'inhumanity, as it is now among the savages of North-America.' Unlike Percy, however, Johnstone identifies the prisoner as an 'Indian' who is no longer destined for death but remains captive to a cruel enemy. Johnstone's revisions extend the horizons of colonization from North America to the Americas and to India. They implicate this 'Indian' as a hostage held for the unforeseeable future and imply, moreover, that an unspecified 'cruelty' locates the jailer in the same alliterative space as his 'captive.' Johnstone's prose keeps pace with Britain's imperial actions, tightening the bond between colonial subject and colonizer and entrapping Ragnar

---

25 For a list of available translations, see Frank Edgar Farley, *Scandinavian Influences in the English Romantic Movement* (Boston: Ginn & Co, 1903), 58 ff.

26 James Johnstone, *Lodbrokar Quida; or The Death Song of Lodbroc; now first correctly printed from various Manuscripts, with a free English translation* (Printed for the Author, 1782), 94, author's emphasis.

within his rhetoric: 'while the captive Indian mitigates *his* torments by the recollection of *his* exploits *he* tramples, as it were, on the cruelty of *his* enemies.' In the acoustical space between the 'captive Indian' and the 'cruelty of his enemy' — between the alliterative ties that link colonial subject and colonizer — Ragnar lies, silently, in the absence–presence of pronouns. Imprisoned together, Ragnar and the 'Indian' 'mitigate' their pain, 'recollect [their] exploits,' and 'trample upon' their jailers. In the same darkling pit, they stage a pyrrhic victory: because the sounds of Ragnar and the 'Indian' can be heard only within the confines of Johnstone's English prose. After two decades of simultaneous acts of translation and colonization, after two decades of employing an Old Norse poem that screens a modern English history too close to bear, *Krákumál*'s translators have held hostage, swallowed whole, and incorporated Ragnar and the 'Indian.' One a beloved father, one an unloved Other, Johnstone unknowingly ventriloquizes their defiant recollections.

Johnstone's comment appears in 'Notes to the English Reader,' the final appendix of *Lodbrokar Quida,* an edition that is not written for the casual reader. As Margaret Clunies Ross has explained, it is a collaboration between British diplomat James Johnstone and Danish scholar Grímur Jónsson Thorkelin.[27] A 'self-consciously accurate and scholarly production,' *Lodbrokar Quida* is meant for the aspiring scholar-translator of Old Norse.[28] Its bilingual text of 29 stanzas is preamble to a robust critical apparatus of 77 pages: (i) 'Epicedium,' a Latin translation of the poem; (ii) 'Glossarium,' an extensive Old Norse-Latin glossary of words, phrases, and figures; and (iii) 'Notes to the English Reader,' a description of places and events referenced in each stanza. In the last appendix of *Lodbrokar Quida* lie Rag-

---

27 Margaret Clunies Ross, *The Norse Muse in Britain 1750–1820* (Trieste: Parnaso, 1998), 173–75.
28 Thomas A. Shippey, '"The Death-Song of Ragnar Lodbrog": A Study in Sensibilities,' in *Medievalism in the Modern World: Essays in Honour of Leslie J. Workman,* eds. Richard Utz and Thomas Shippey (Turnhout: Brepols, 1998), 161.

nar and the 'Indian,' not simply held captive but buried alive together under a mountain of scholarly effects.

To return to the language of Abraham and Torok, Ragnar and the 'Indian' have been incorporated, entombed, and, moreover, encrypted within the final pages of *Lodbrokar Quida*:

> [When] this segment of an ever so painfully lived Reality… [is] untellable…[it] causes a genuinely covert shift in the entire psyche. This shift itself is covert, since both the fact that the idyll was real and that it was later lost must be disguised and denied. This leads to the establishment of a sealed-off psychic place, a crypt in the ego.[29]

A crypt emerges from incorporation. It is built when our grief and shame prohibit us from mourning our losses or grieving our traumas. Instead of giving voice to our pain, we 'disguise' and 'deny' it. We stage a psychic defense against suffering by depositing these secret losses, unshared traumas, and 'untellable' pains within ourselves. Trapped in 'a sealed-off psychic space,' they linger in deep and profound silence, inhabiting us as 'exquisite corpses' against which we unknowingly and unconsciously brace our subjectivity.[30] Ragnar and the 'Indian,' England's unmourned and unmournable relations, are corpses that disguise the losses and deny the traumas of British colonialism. Though hidden from view, their captive shapes sound out — in Johnstone's own words — the 'savage' violence, the 'inhuman' brutalities, the ceaseless 'torments,' and the constant state of incorporation that is necessary to build and sustain an empire. For all their noise, however, Ragnar and the 'Indian' cannot be found. '[S]ealed off' in the 'psychic place' of Johnstone's ego, they are 'inaccessible to [his] conscious self.' Consequently, as Johnstone ventriloquizes the sounds that come from within his psychic crypt, he misrecognizes them as scholarly artifacts and encodes them into his scholarly apparatus. *Lodbrokar Quida* becomes, as

---

29 Abraham and Torok, *The Shell and the Kernel*, 141.
30 Ibid., 120–23.

Esther Rashkin writes, a 'fictional saga' that is 'perturb[ed] and propel[led]' by 'unspeakable secrets.'[31] It is a literary work that is produced by 'subjects [who] deploy different practices and techniques to act on their world and themselves in their struggle to transcend psychic distress and create new paths for survival.'[32]

As these corpses make their way from Johnstone's unconscious to the final appendix of his scholarly edition, each section of the critical apparatus serves as a partition that erects the crypt of *Lodbrokar Quida* according to what Abraham calls anasemia, a process by which the meaning of signs is problematized through fracture: 'allophemic slippages, demetaphorization, spiraling language' — 'words buried alive' that are 'relieved of their communicative function' yet articulate 'that the desire was in a way satisfied, that the pleasurable fulfillment did take place.'[33] In anasemia, signifiers shatter into 'angular pieces... internal (intra-symbolic) partitions, cavities, corridors, niches, zigzag labyrinths, and craggy fortifications' as the semiotic effects of a refusal to mourn, to acknowledge, and to give voice to one's secret grief and shame. By way of anasemia, one incorporates these others in order to encrypt them within the unspoken, unsignified, and most unknown corridors of the unconscious.[34] Each scholarly appendix of *Lodbrokar Quida* functions as an anasemic partition that silences and fragments Ragnar's Old Norse voice and encrypts Ragnar and the 'Indian' within its pages. The Epicedium presents *Krákumál* first as a Latin text, a move that signals it as a learned poem written in a language worthy of extensive exegesis. To these ends, the Glossarium aids the aspiring reader's perusal of *Krákumál*'s Old Norse lexicon. It provides the Latin equivalents of difficult Old Norse grammar and vocabulary, and it glosses unfamiliar figures of Scandinavian mythology and saga with extended Latin explanation.

---

31 Esther Rashkin, *Unspeakable Secrets and the Psychoanalysis of Culture* (Albany: State University of New York Press, 2008), 16.
32 Ibid.
33 Jacques Derrida and Barbara Johnson, 'Fors,' *The Georgia Review* 31, no. 1 (1977): 99.
34 Ibid., 76.

While serving as helpful reading aids, the Epicedium tempers the Old Norse poem, and the Glossarium fractures the signifiers of its 29 verses across 42 pages of the edition. By way of anasemic gloss, the oral poetics of *Krákumál* are given a 'thorough dissection and explanation'.[35] Its kennings are demetaphorized, and its semantics are relieved of their communicative function, breaking *Krákumál*'s acoustical surfaces into a thousand irregular and angular pieces and cleaving them to Latin, a language meant to be studied but unspoken by the gentleman scholar. The Epicedium and Glossarium stage a rigorous defense that sets about to render the Old Norse sounds of *Krákumál* completely incomprehensible and entirely mute. Such a project is necessary to make ready the crypt for its occupants. 'Notes to the English Reader,' the last appendix, introduces the figure of Ragnar and his Scandinavian context in modern English prose. It assembles the angular pieces of Ragnar's shattered voice into English terms that misrecognize *Krákumál* as a pastime of scholars and poetic translators and therefore fail to take note of the bodies buried within.[36]

Lodbrokar Quida's illicit acts of entombment do not occur without consequence to Johnstone or to his 'English Reader.' As Schwab states, 'no one colonizes with impunity...histories of violence create psychic deformations not only in the victims but also in the perpetrators'.[37] As an English Reader pores over *Lodbrokar Quida*, Ragnar's Old Norse cries of unmourning shatter into silent Latin fragments, which are then reassembled into an English account of Ragnar. Once apprised of his dying body, this 'English Reader' approaches Ragnar's bilingual text,

---

35 Ross, *The Norse Muse in Britain*, 176.
36 Consider Shippey's remarks regarding the 'oddity' of *Lodbrokar Quida* as 'the most self-consciously accurate and scholarly production of [all translations of *Krákumál*]' and 'at the same time the most dictional and, in a sense, unfaithful' ('The Death-Song of Ragnar Lodbrog,' 169). Consider also Shippey's further comment regarding Johnstone's faithless English translations: 'For all his care Johnstone seems almost afraid of his subject, or at least exposing it to English-speaking readers' (169).
37 Schwab, *Haunting Legacies*, 48.

fashioning her scholarly self by vocalizing and ventriloquizing a poem, the acoustics of which are shaped according to the encrypted outlines of its captive corpses. The 'English Reader' of *Krákumál* is inhabited by the dead. She suffers from the effects of extreme psychic splitting but cannot perform the painful and conscious work of self-analysis. After poring over its multiple critical partitions and multi-lingual chambers, the 'English Reader' becomes, like the poem itself, a 'subject particularly resistant to analysis,' a subject carrying within herself a 'puzzle of shards about which we would know nothing: neither how to put it together nor how to recognize the pieces.'[38] From *Lodbrokar Quida* emerges an English scholar-translator of Old Norse poetry who is so terrified, so guilty, and so ashamed of England's ceaseless colonial pursuit of incorporation that she has encrypted its effects within herself. She has constructed her subjectivity against the voices of Ragnar and the 'Indian,' and she ventriloquizes from the crypt of *Krákumál* their captive cries.

Krákumál achieves a 'paradigmatic status' in the eighteenth century.[39] Its 'extraordinarily high evaluations' among antiquarians and poets anticipate the twenty-one English translations, partial 'paraphrases,' and 'elaborate [literary] creations' that emerge during the eighteenth and nineteenth centuries.[40] As Peter Mortensen quips, 'Regner's death-defying laugh could be heard throughout the period' as the most popular medieval Scandinavian text in England.[41] Among *Krákumál*'s most devoted English Readers is Sharon Turner, who not only references Percy's translation and cites Johnstone's edition but, moreover, frames *From the Death of Egbert to the Death of Alfred*—the second volume of his *History of the Anglo-Saxons*—according to the encrypted acoustics of its anasemic translations. *From*

---

38 Derrida and Johnson, 'Fors,' 76–77.
39 Ross, *The Norse Muse in Britain*, 91.
40 Shippey, 'The Death-Song of Ragnar Lodbrog,' 157; Ross, *The Norse Muse in Britain*, 168.
41 Peter Mortensen, '"The Descent of Odin": Wordsworth, Scott and Southey among the Norsemen,' *Romanticism* 6, no. 2 (2000): 211; Ross, *The Norse Muse in Britain*, 231.

the Death of Egbert begins in Denmark, where Ragnar Lodbrog, an undefeatable sea king, builds 'two ships of a size which the North had never beheld before,' loads them with soldiers, and sails toward England.[42] Turner explains that the unwieldy size of these ships makes them unnavigable, and they run aground off the Northumbrian coast. Ragnar is captured by the Anglo-Saxon king, Ella of Northumbria, and thrown into a pit of snakes, where he composes *Krákumál* before dying from their poisonous venom. Turner describes the enraged responses of Ragnar's sons, his Danish kin, and 'all the fury, and all the valour of the North' who set out to redress Ragnar's murder and colonize Anglo-Saxon England.[43] No kingdom is safe from 'the Northmen,' Turner explains, and in a final battle against Ragnar's relations, King Ethelred of Wessex is killed.[44]

From the ashes of complete defeat, Alfred emerges as its new leader, fighting the Northmen continuously across Anglo-Saxon England and meeting them, finally, at sea. In a statement that resolves the two ships of an unprecedented size by which Ragnar sailed to Northumbria, Turner argues that Alfred builds 'vessels...full-twice as long as theirs,' which are 'swifter, higher, and less unsteady' than those of his enemy.[45] Alfred's ship design and naval strategy acoustically and martially outperform those of Ragnar. Once his enemies have departed, Alfred extends his Wessex 'sovereignty,' first, over all Anglo-Saxons, then over the Welsh.[46] By way of sustained engagement with Ragnar's Northern ilk, Alfred has incorporated Ragnar's military drives, his seafaring spirit, and his colonial urges. By modeling his *History* upon *Krákumál*'s psycho-politics of incorporation, Turner explains that Alfred wrests power from his colonial oppressors and fashions an English nation.

Upon declaring Alfred an English sovereign, Turner announces Alfred's death, concludes his historical narrative, and

---

42 Turner, *The History of the Anglo-Saxons*, 2:115.
43 Ibid., 2:118.
44 Ibid., 2:153.
45 Ibid., 2:240.
46 Ibid., 2:246.

begins an epicedium, a Death-song, to Alfred. From an early age, Turner explains, Alfred 'was an eager auditor, and was industrious to commit them ["Saxon" poems] to memory.... It was always one of his principle pleasures to learn Saxon poems, and to teach them to others.'[47] As a king, Alfred's literary pursuits turn towards Latin. Alfred learns by keeping a 'little book' of devotions close to his 'bosom' and by gathering together and inscribing 'diversified extracts' of Latin conversation and scripture within it.[48] Turner does not narrate the time Alfred spends in Latin study or labors in his Latin translations because Alfred learns instead by incorporation. By keeping a little book close to his heart, Turner explains that Alfred magically swallows whole these Latin fragments, and, after a time, writes his Preface to *Pastoral Care* and translates Orosius, Bede, and Boetheius into the vernacular language. Braced against *Krákumál*'s psycho-politics of incorporation, Turner's Epicedium reveals that Alfred's political projects — his armed resistance to Ragnar's Northmen — have occurred simultaneous to his personal projects of translation. With the eighth and ninth centuries as a colonial backdrop, Turner fashions a posthumous account of the process by which Alfred becomes a scholar, a translator, and an 'English Reader.' To wit, as Turner translates the Preface to *Pastoral Care*, he encounters Alfred's statements regarding the state of Latin learning in Anglo-Saxon England and introjects, 'this statement would tempt us to imagine that the Anglo-Saxons had been a learned people before the days of Alfred; but the discriminating king prevents the delusion by his subsequent paragraphs. They had the means of knowledge, not its possession.'[49] Although Turner recognized initially the 'Saxon' poets that Alfred enjoyed as a child and recited as an adult, here Turner elides the 'Saxon' voices of the hall and instead hails Alfred — a Latin scholar and translator — as the first learned 'English Reader.' While Turner's Epicedium locates the voices of England's earliest vernacular

---

47 Ibid., 2:252.
48 Ibid., 2:267.
49 Ibid., 2:278.

poetry, such a reference tells the lie that Turner's *History*, which gives voice to Alfred, pivots upon the muted sounds of another.

Although Turner avows his relationship to *Krákumál* and pursues vigorously its paths of incorporation, he does not know that his is an anasemic *History* and therefore shaped in relation to a crypt. As Abraham and Torok explain, when we encrypt a loss or a trauma, we do so as a self-preservative action. In cleaving our self to a corpse, however, we leave ourselves vulnerable to its haunting maneuvers. They write, 'the "shadow of the object" strays endlessly about in the crypt' and 'sometimes in the dead of night, when libidinal fulfillments have their way, the ghost of the crypt comes back to haunt the cemetery guard, giving him strange and incomprehensible signals, making him perform bizarre acts, or subjecting him to unexpected sensations.'[50] Turner explains that when Ragnar's sons arrive in Northumbria, they 'inflicted a cruel and inhuman retaliation on Ella for their father's sufferings. They cut the figure of an eagle on his back, divided his ribs, to tear out his lungs, and agonized his lacerated flesh by the addition of a saline stimulant.'[51] Strange and incomprehensible in its logic. Bizarre in its performance. Unexpected in sense and in sensation. This elaborate act breaks apart Ella's ribs and turns his body inside out to render him without air or breath, effectively mute, and suffering in silence. It is a torture of surgical precision that, despite its deliberate method, makes little sense: it disables Ella's Anglo-Saxon body violently in order to steal his Old English voice. In a footnote at the bottom of the page, Turner, the dutiful historian, cites his sources: 'Frag. Isl. 2 Lang. 279. Ragnar Saga, ib. The Scalld Sigvatr. ib. Saxo Gram. 177. This punishment was often inflicted by these savage conquerors on their enemies. See some instances in Stephanius, 193.'[52]

---

50 Abraham and Torok, *The Shell and the Kernel*, 141, 130.
51 Turner, *The History of the Anglo-Saxons*, 2:123.
52 Interestingly, while Ella's death by blood eagle is accounted for in the *Ragnars saga* (*The Tale of Ragnar Loðbrok*) and Saxo Grammaticus's *Gesta Danorum* (*Deeds of the Danes*), the only Scandinavian text that includes the 'lung-ripping' component is the *Þáttr af Ragnars sonum* (*The Tale of Ragnar's Sons*), which Turner does not mention here.

In these marginal, academic quarters, Turner draws the blood eagle from the hazy reaches of an Icelandic fragment to a saga narrative in prose, from the voice of a skald to that of an historian, from Saxo's medieval history to Stephanius's early modern commentary.[53] Turner's footnote genealogically excavates the blood eagle from the sedimented layers of Scandinavia's past. Suspended, however, in between the medieval and early modern citations of Turner's footnote is his own commentary — 'this punishment was often inflicted by these savage conquerors on their enemies' — which does not hearken back to the rhetoric of Scandinavia but to that of Percy and Johnstone. In the dead of night, when libidinal fulfillments have their way, Turner's prose butchers Ella's body and voice. In the light of day, when these pleasures are restrained, Turner's notes legitimate these actions under the aegis of scholarship and translation. Turner, the cemetery guard, has unearthed a ghost of the crypt. Like Percy's North American 'savages' and Johnstone's 'Indian,' Ella stages a colonial resistance against Ragnar and his Northern relations that takes place at home, in England, not abroad, in English colonies. Ella, not Alfred, is the real figure of Anglo-Saxon sovereignty and 'Saxon' poetry, but his body has been broken, and his voice has been rendered mute by Turner's *History*.

---

53 Turner, *The History of the Anglo-Saxons*, 2:123n9. Stephanus Stephanius is an early modern commentator. In 1645, he published *Notæ Uberiores in Historiam Danicam Saxonis Grammatici* (Sørø: Crusius, 1645), an edition and exegetical commentary of Saxo's *Gesta*. Stephanius expands Saxo's mention of the 'aquilam figurante' by explaining that it was a practice common to the 'Angles, Danes, and other Northern nations' ['Anglos, Danos, and aliasq[ue] nationes Boreales'], in which 'the victor, about to inflict his defeated adversary with the greatest dishonor, drives a sword into the spine in the back near the shoulder blades, and, with a massive incision having been cut along the length of the body, he separates the ribs from the spine, both of which [the ribs], having been drawn out to the sides, represent the wings of an Eagle' ['victor ignominia summa debellatum adversarium affecturus, gladium circa scapulas ad spinam dorsi adigebat, costasqu[e]amplissimo per corporis longitudinem facto vulnere, utrinque a spina separabat: quae ad latera deductae alas repraesentabant Aquilinas'] (193). My translation.

It takes Turner two subsequent paragraphs to give direction to the ceaseless straying of Ragnar's sons and to make comprehensible the incomprehensible signals of Ella's death. Immediately after describing the blood eagle, Turner explains that, 'after this battle, decisive of the fate of Northumbria, it appeared no more as an Anglo-Saxon kingdom.'[54] Then he narrates briefly the ascension and expulsion of several of Ella's successors. Amid these internal politics, which span an uncertain length of time, Ivar, one of Ragnar's sons, remains, quietly 'usurp[ing] the scepter of Northumbria from the Humber to the Tyne.'[55] Turner, unable to understand the sequence of events or the timeline of his own narrative, returns to the scene of Ella's death and revises the history he has just written. He begins a new paragraph that recodes the 'cruel and inhuman retaliation' of Ragnar's relations as 'a dismal sacrifice [that] had been offered up to the manes of Ragnar, yet the invaders did not depart.'[56] Turner then narrates the complete destruction of Northumbria and Mercia by the 'manes of Ragnar,' concluding with the fall of Wessex and the death of Athelred. Upon Ella's broken body, silenced voice, and conquered kingdom Turner's historical arc pivots: from the death of Ragnar to that of Alfred, from colonial invasion to national unification, from an Anglo-Saxon past that is trampled and silenced to an English future that will be forever incorporating the bodies, voices, and territories of others. Turner arranges the strange stirrings and haunted visions that emerge jointly from his scholarly sources and from his psyche into a primal scene. The murder of Ella, a mythical father, is enacted by all of Scandinavia's sons: poets and saga writers; skalds and chroniclers; translators and scholars; Sigvatr, Saxo, and Stephanius; Percy, Johnstone, and Turner. This traumatic fantasy shapes a nation's history. The 'dismal sacrifice' of one Anglo-Saxon king's sovereignty allows Alfred to claim a greater reward for all of England.

---

54 Turner, *The History of the Anglo-Saxons*, 2:124.
55 Ibid.
56 Ibid.

While Turner arranges his *History* to make sense of something incomprehensible, he remains horrified by these stirrings and signals that come from without and within. Consequently, as Turner reflects upon his *History,* he buries Ella's blood eagle within its Preface:

> On comparing their documents with our own, he [self-referentially, Turner] was struck with the resulting fact, that the great Danish invasion, by which Alfred and his brother were so afflicted, was not a casual depredation, but a deliberate attack to revenge the death of the celebrated Ragnar Lodbrog. The circumstance, which gave system and meaning to what appeared before to be incoherent and unconnected, occasioned further researches, and it at last became apparent, that the inattention of our writers, to the Northern documents, had filled their histories with obscurity and mistake.[57]

One event, which Turner concedes as 'the circumstance,' not only explains 'the great Danish invasion' but also 'gives system and meaning' to the 'incoherent and unconnected' events of Anglo-Saxon history. This circumstance, upon which Turner previously elaborated in his narrative but does not name in his Preface, is the torture by blood eagle of Ella of Northumbria. Turner's elusive and obscurantist lexical choice denies Ella's presence. Likewise, Turner's syntax, which locates 'the circumstance' as the subject of a new sentence that succeeds 'the great Danish invasion' that 'afflicted Alfred,' confuses the sequencing of these events. Turner obfuscates, obstructs, and renders inaccessible the scene of Ella's death. He anasemically disables Ella's bloody shape. These processes of encryption shield Turner from recognizing that he is inhabited and haunted by restless specters that have caused him to tear apart the body, render the mouth voiceless, and ravage the territory of an Anglo-Saxon sovereign, while writing an Anglo-Saxon history. Consequently, Turner cannot mourn Ella. He can neither speak his grief for the death

---

57 Ibid., 2:vii.

of this Northumbrian king nor express his shame in causing it. So Turner hides Ella. He locks his blood-eagled body away where no one will find it with language that disregards Ella's death as merely 'the circumstance,' thus dislocating it from its place in the narrative. In an act of double encryption, Turner installs Ella's captive body and his muted voice with those of Ragnar and the 'Indian.' To the unspeakable traumas of colonialism, he adds the unvoiced shame of nation-building, a fantasy of incorporation that is as inhuman, savage, and tortuous as that of Empire.

From the Death of Egbert and its companion volumes initially received mixed reviews,[58] and despite Turner's continuous revision and republication (he revised the *History* until this death in 1849[59]) it took almost 70 years for its seven editions to sell about 4500 copies, the last of which were purchased by scriveners and shipped to America in the 1870s.[60] Nonetheless, Turner's *History* was highly influential during the first half of the nineteenth century. Longman ledgers record that Turner's 1820 third edition — its most popular and fastest-selling *History* — was purchased by romantic writers Sir Walter Scott and Robert Southey, popular historian Charles Mills, and former Bombay judge, Whig MP, and professor at East India Bombay College, Sir James MacKintosh.[61] Shortly thereafter, the 1824 edition of *The Library-Companion* recognizes Turner alongside John Lingard as 'among the most eminent of those of our living historians,' and, much later, Turner's biographer for the *Oxford Dictionary of National Biography* recognizes the *History* as 'a work which

---

58 For example, Anonymous, 'The Second Part of the History of the Anglo-Saxons: From the Death of Egbert to the Norman Conquest,' in *The Edinburgh Review* 4, no. 6, ed. Francis Jeffrey (London: T.N. Longman and O. Rees, 1804), 360–74.

59 In a telling move, the posthumously published seventh edition (1852) removes all of Turner's Prefaces, the content of which had, over the course of revision and republication, replaced *Krákumál* and Ragnar's death with the British empire as the inspiration for his *History*.

60 Longman Manuscript, Records of the Longman Group, University of Reading, MS 1393/I/A7/164, 623.

61 Ibid.

was to have a powerful influence on historical thought for the succeeding half-[of the nineteenth]century.'[62]

Perhaps because of its celebrity status as a popular rather than a scholarly text, Turner's *History* was discarded in favor of other narratives of the Anglo-Saxon period written by Stubbs, Green, and Freeman. As these nineteenth-century historians were replaced by a new generation of twentieth-century scholars, Turner's *History* became not simply old-fashioned but untenable, and Ella's blood eagle, encrypted long ago within the tomb of the *History*, was an entirely forgotten sacrifice. Yet, as Abraham and Torok explain, while 'the dead do not return to join the living,' they 'lead them into some dreadful snare, entrapping them with disastrous consequences. To be sure, all the departed may return, but some are destined to haunt.'[63] From the mid-1940s through the mid-twentieth century, the blood eagle begins to stir, appearing first in the dismissive comments of Frank Stenton's monumental *Anglo-Saxon England*. First published in 1943 amid World War II, Stenton returns Ragnar to the spoken shores of Anglo-Saxon history in chapter eight, 'The Age of Alfred':

> At the end of the eighth century each of the three Scandinavian peoples of historic times formed a nation.... The invasions which deflected the course of English history in the ninth century arose from internal movements among the peoples who commanded the entry to the Baltic Sea, and at the court of Charlemagne were regarded as forming a single kingdom of the Danes.[64]

---

62 T.F. Dibdin, *The Library-Companion: Or the Young Man's Guide and the Old Man's Comfort in the Choice of a Library* (London: Harding, Triphook, and Lepard, 1824), 237.
63 Abraham and Torok, *The Shell and the Kernel*, 171.
64 Frank M. Stenton, *Anglo-Saxon England* (New York: Oxford University Press, 1971), 239.

From Denmark, the Great Army descends upon East Anglia, and, after a year in England, it turns towards Northumbria, where it encounters Ælla:

> The contemporary account of these events in the *Chronicle* shows that he [Ælla] had barely come into power before the Danes were on him, and, if disproof were necessary, would disprove the famous Scandinavian legend that as king in York he had killed Ragnar Lothbrok, the father of Ivar and Halfdan, by throwing him into a pit infested with snakes.[65]

After almost a century of Anglo-Saxon histories that have left Ragnar and his sons unmentioned, Stenton's *Anglo-Saxon History*, written and published during England's darkest hours of war, turns to the myth and poetry of Ragnar and his Death Song as a means of explaining historical threats to English sovereignty by outsiders. In the 1940s, England's national other is no longer Napoleonic France or Britain's own imperial self, but Nazi Germany. Amid English wartime propaganda and Churchill's statements about 'Hunnish' barbarians, Ragnar's name and the 'Scandinavian legend' of simple 'disproof' rise to Stenton's historical consciousness with ironic force as couched signifiers of German invasion and the threat of Nazi empire. To combat such a mythic threat, Stenton turns to Alfred's defenses, arguing that Alfred's fleet of ships mark the beginnings of the English navy, and he concludes the chapter, '[i]t thus becomes important evidence of the new political unity forced upon the various English peoples by the struggle against the Danes.'[66]

In the wake of World War II, interest in the blood eagle was rekindled by a group of Stenton's fellow Oxford academics. Its inarticulate signals grow louder in the prose of Gabriel Turville-Petre and Gwyn Jones.[67] A few years later, as Roberta Frank ob-

---

65 Ibid., 247.
66 Ibid., 276.
67 E.O.G. Turville-Petre, *Myth and Religion of the North: The Religion of Ancient Scandinavia* (London: Weidenfeld and Nicolson, 1964), 254–55; Gwyn

serves, 'the significance of the blood-eagle was heralded in the 1974 Stenton Lecture when J.M. Wallace-Hadrill made available the then-unpublished observations of Alfred Smyth':[68]

> What happened to Duke Seguin in 845, when he was captured and put to death? *Occisus est.* Or Archbishop Madalbert of Bourges in 910? Dr. Alfred Smyth has advanced some reasons for holding that as late as the eleventh century the Vikings practiced ritual sacrifice of important victims of Odin, in the form of the blood-eagle. That is, the victim, after being a target for javelins or arrows, was stretched face-downwards over a stone, so that his ribs could be torn upwards from the spine in a shape suggestive of an eagle's wings. Finally he was beheaded. Examples of this practice may have included: King Ella of Northumbria, Halfdan son of King Haraldr Harfagri of Norway, King Edmund (a victim, like Ella, of the great Danish Viking Ivar), King Maelgualai of Munster, and just possibly Archbishop Ælfheah if Thietmar is to be trusted. It may also be noted that where one source will report little more than *occisus est,* or will concentrate on some aspect of the torture reminiscent of earlier Christian martyrdom (as, use of arrows,) another will betray the essentially complex procedure of the sacrifice. It happened in Scandinavia, in Ireland and in England. I am presuming Francia was not exempt.[69]

As if to acknowledge what Stenton only dared to allude,[70] Wallace-Hadrill's Stenton Lecture describes an intricate ritual that

---

Jones, *A History of the Vikings* (1968; repr. New York: Oxford University Press, 2001), 219n2.

68 Roberta Frank, 'Viking Atrocity and Skaldic Verse: The Rite of the Blood-Eagle,' *The English Historical Review* 99, no. 391 (1984): 332.
69 J.M. Wallace-Hadrill, *Early Medieval History* (Oxford: Basil Blackwell, 1974), 224–25.
70 Note that Wallace-Hadrill's lecture begins, 'It seems fitting that a lecture bearing the name of the man who, more than any other historian, has enabled us to understand the English Danelaw...Sir Frank Stenton was wonderfully at home with Danish settlers and their problems while at

adds javelins, arrows, body-stretching, and decapitation to the blood-eagling process. He explains this 'ritual sacrifice' as a practice that punctures and hacks away at all material surfaces, rendering a person without recognizable voice, physical form, or identity. Yet Wallace-Hadrill can correctly identify the blood eagle torture and name its victims by bracketing his own statements with the italicized Latin verb phrase, 'occicus est.' From this untranslated, undisclosed, and, moreover, encrypted expression — a passive construction that allows for all kinds of terrible deaths[71] — Wallace-Hadrill identifies the blood eagle, explains its procedures, and turns to Ella as its first unquestioned victim. *Occisus est* is rhetoric fraught with equivocation. Consequently, Wallace-Hadrill begins with a question: What happened to Duke Seguin and Archbishop Madalbert? *Occisus est*. And he ends with a statement: the precise and 'essentially complex' descriptions of the blood eagle are *occisus est*.

Wallace-Hadrill delivers his 1974 Stenton Lecture in the wake of three decades of intensive decolonization. Beginning with India, which won independence in 1947, Britain's empire had fallen apart. It lost Asian, Middle Eastern, and African territories in the late 1940s and 1950s, and these conflicts were followed by the abrogation of its remaining African lands in the 1960s. The changes taking place within Britain's empire reflect those elsewhere in Europe during the post-war period, and Michael Wintle explains this worldwide decolonization process as 'symptomatic and emblematic of Europeans having to accept that their role in the world had changed radically, and then for the worse in terms of power politics.'[72] As the British empire contracts and

---

the same time recognizing the full extent of the terror they inspired and the destruction they caused in the earlier phases of their English career' (Wallace-Hadrill, *Early Medieval History*, 215).

71 Wallace-Hadrill quotes here from Adémar de Chabannes, an eleventh-century French monk and historian. Note that as the passive, indicative, active conjugation of 'occido,' *occisus est* is an expression that implicates any number of deaths by beating, smashing, crushing, slaughtering, and torturing, to name a few variations.

72 Michael Wintle, 'Editor's Introduction: Ideals, Identity and War: The Idea of Europe, 1939– 1970,' in *European Identity and the Second World War*,

its identity adjusts 'for the worse,' mid-century historians reconsider and fiercely debate the impact of the Vikings on medieval Europe.[73] They begin to challenge (or defend) the predatory image of the Vikings, the violence of their conquests, and the lasting impact of their engagements with other European peoples. Amid these discussions, the blood eagle begins to stir. Its phantom presence, encrypted within Turner's colonial *History*, can be felt in the scholarly conversations that circulate around the Vikings. The blood eagle locates what Abraham and Torok call a 'gap' in narrative that points toward an unspeakable secret.[74] As Abraham and Torok explain, these gaps and secrets — these phantoms that arise within a subject's memory — are not generated by her own traumas. They are skeletons in the closet, 'postmemories' that are not experienced by the children of parents who have been traumatized but come secondhand 'as full and as empty, certainly as constructed, as memory itself.'[75] As Schwab writes:

> it is almost as if these children become the recipients not only of their parents' lived memories but also of their somatic memories. Children of a traumatized parental generation, I argue, become avid readers of silences and memory traces hidden in a face that is frozen in grief…without being fully aware of it, they become skilled readers of the optical un-

---

eds. Menno Spiering and Michael Wintle (New York: Palgrave Macmillan, 2011), 4.

73 Peter Sawyer's *The Age of the Vikings* (London: Edward Arnold, 1962) and the contentious debates that surround it (Peter Sawyer, 'The Two Viking Ages of Britain: A Discussion,' *Mediaeval Scandinavia: A Journal Devoted to the Study of Mediaeval Civilization in Scandinavia and Iceland* 2 [1969]: 196) are exhibits that reflect the relationships between mid-century academic historicism and European cultural unconscious. For a brief discussion of the impact of decolonization on English Studies in general, see Bart Moore-Gilbert, 'Anglo-Saxon Attitudes: Empire, Race and English Studies in Contemporary University Fiction,' *Wasafiri* 13, no. 26 (1997): 3–8.
74 Abraham and Torok, *The Shell and the Kernel*, 171.
75 Marianne Hirsch, *Family Frames: Photography, Narrative, and Postmemory* (Cambridge: Harvard University Press, 1997), 22.

conscious revealed in their parents' body language.... The second generation thus receives violent histories not only through the actual memories or stories of parents (postmemory) but also through the traces of affect, particularly affect that remains unintegrated and inassimilable.[76]

Wallace-Hadrill, a 'child' of an imperial generation of nineteenth-century scholars, has become the 'recipient' of his 'parents" lived and somatic memories: their silenced and encrypted colonial losses and traumas. He bears no responsibility, no guilt, and no shame in this but has been, nonetheless, affected by it. Consequently, Wallace-Hadrill, like many other medievalists of his generation, has become a 'skilled reader' of his parents' 'optical unconscious,' the 'traces of [scholarly] affect,' and the parts of an 'unintegrated and inassimilable [history].' Like others who bear witness to the blood eagle, he recognizes that some unspeakable secret — some gap, some *occisus est* — has been passed down from another's historical memory to his own. A century later, however, as Wallace-Hadrill eyes Ella's encrypted body, voice, and Northumbrian territory, these bloody outlines do not form the sacrificial shape of a nation but map the entirety of northern Europe: 'it happened in Scandinavia, in Ireland and in England. I am presuming Francia was not exempt.'[77] In the post-war twentieth century, an era during which Europe's nations have given up the majority of their empires, an era in which their political futures are uncertain, Wallace-Hadrill finds the unspeakable gaps and secrets of the ninth century and arranges them the best way he can: in the shape of a Viking empire marked by blood-eagle butchery.

Wallace-Hadrill's Stenton Lecture and Smyth's 1977 monograph, *Scandinavian Kings in the British Isles 850–880,* signal a hotly contested but fleeting revival of the blood eagle in terms

---

76 Schwab, *Haunting Legacies,* 14.
77 Wallace-Hadrill, *Early Medieval History,* 225.

that offer an eerie acoustical echo of Turner's narrative voice.[78] While James Campbell, Eric John, and Patrick Wormald write that its 'particularly gruesome' operations 'involved ripping a victim's lungs out of his rib-cage' in a sacrificial ritual that dedicates the bodies of Ella and other victims 'to Othinn (the Scandinavian Woden),'[79] Roberta Frank and Bjarni Einarsson dispute whether or not the practice was 'a conspiracy of romantic hopes' or a 'refined method of execution [that] seems thus to have been reserved for royals.'[80] Despite two rounds of arguments between Frank and Einarsson, neither side reached consensus.[81] *Saga Book,* the journal in which the concluding exchanges were published, however, did: it placed the debate's final episode under one heading, 'The Blood-Eagle Once More: Two Notes,' and featured Frank's and Einarsson's comments side-by-side.[82] *Saga Book*'s flagging editorial interest and historical equivocation foreshadow the blood eagle's reception history from the 1990s forward. Aside from another round of debate between Smyth and Frank,[83] the blood eagle no longer makes headlines.

---

78 See Nicholas P. Brooks, 'England in the Ninth Century: The Crucible of Defeat,' *Transactions of the Royal Historical Society,* Fifth Series 29 (1979): 13; James Campbell, Eric John, and Patrick Wormald, eds., *The Anglo-Saxons* (Ithaca: Cornell University Press, 1982), 148–49.

79 Campbell and Wormald, *The Anglo-Saxons,* 148.

80 Roberta Frank, 'Viking Atrocity and Skaldic Verse: The Rite of the Blood Eagle,' *The English Historical Review* 99, no. 391 (1984): 337. Bjarni Einarsson, '*De Normannorum Atrocitate,* or on the Execution of Royalty by the Aquiline Method,' *Saga Book* 22, no. 1 (1986): 79.

81 For the first volley of debate, see Roberta Frank, 'Viking Atrocity and Skaldic Verse,' which was countered by Einarsson, '*De Normannorum Atrocitate,*' to which Frank responded in 'The Blood-Eagle Again,' *Saga Book* 22, no. 5 (1988): 287–89.

82 Bjarni Einarsson and Roberta Frank, 'The Blood-Eagle Once More: Two Notes; A. Blóðörn — An Observation on the Ornithological Aspect; B. Ornithology and the Interpretation of Skaldic Verse,' *Saga Book* 23, no. 2 (1990): 80–83.

83 See Alfred Smyth, 'The Effect of Scandinavian Raiders on the English and Irish Churches: A Preliminary Reassessment,' in *Britain and Ireland, 900–1300: Insular Responses to Medieval European Change,* ed. Brendan Smith (Cambridge: Cambridge University Press, 2004), 19, and Roberta Frank, 'Skaldic Poetry,' in *Old Norse-Icelandic Literature: A Critical Guide,*

In discussions and debates among Stenton, Wallace-Hadrill, and Smyth, as well as Frank and Einarsson, along with other mid-to-late-century historians, the blood eagle functions as an effect of secondhand trauma. One might argue that, as scholars turned to the blood eagle, they compulsively acted out hidden wounds as a means of healing — that they exorcised encrypted ghosts of empire by speaking a heretofore silenced shame. But did they? In the 1990s, as the nations of post-imperial Europe began to imagine transnational and global futures, interest in the blood eagle faded. It has been over a decade since scholars have weighed in on the ritual, and most have edged away from wholehearted belief in the practice.[84] Yet, the blood eagle consistently finds its way into the passing comments, footnotes, and bibliographies of contemporary scholarship. It lingers quietly in the academic margins as a figment, a specter, a ghost. Its restless figure, an unmourned and unmournable body of Empire, is a long-term effect of nineteenth-century colonization and twentieth-century decolonization.

In 'The Underdeveloped Image: Anglo-Saxon in Popular Consciousness from Turner to Tolkien,' Tom Shippey asks why, despite nineteenth-century England's power as a global empire and Western hegemony, its Anglo-Saxon history has been all but forgotten and left in the medieval shadows of Arthurian and Viking worlds. Shippey proffers: 'I suggest that the developing and potentially powerful image of Anglo-Saxon origins was *sacrificed* during the nineteenth century to the needs of an Imperial and a British, not an English ideology.'[85] Shippey speaks here of a

---

eds. Carol J. Clover and John Lindlow (1985; repr. Toronto: Toronto University Press, 2005), 170.

84 See, for example, Gareth Williams, 'Raiding and Warfare,' in *The Viking World*, ed. Stefan Brink, in collaboration with Neil Price (New York: Routledge, 2008), 196, and Anders Winwroth, *The Age of the Vikings* (Princeton: Princeton University Press, 2014), 36–39.

85 Thomas A. Shippey, 'The Underdeveloped Image: Anglo-Saxon in Popular Consciousness from Turner to Tolkien,' in *Literary Appropriations of the Anglo-Saxons from the Thirteenth to the Twentieth Century*, eds. Donald Scragg and Carole Weinberg (Cambridge: Cambridge University Press, 2000), 225, my emphasis.

metaphorical sacrifice, and he explains its genesis as a response to pressures within and upon the British empire. Over the course of the nineteenth century, he argues, Anglo-Saxon cultural identity was not expansive enough to manage non-English nationalist traditions developing within the British archipelago. Yet, as a host of Western European countries clamored to claim their Germanic origins, a Saxon identity was too non-specific to be the exclusive property of Britain. England, Shippey suggests, ceded memory of 'the developing and potentially powerful image of Anglo-Saxon origins' in exchange for greater, immediate goods, some of which endure into the twenty-first century: the wealth of its remaining colonies, a global *lingua franca,* and a position of international cultural and political prestige. In its 'post-Imperial situation,' however, Shippey points out that these Anglo-Saxon sacrifices have left England 'suffering from an identity crisis caused by the retreat from Empire.'[86] Shippey's comments[87] speak of a future for England at the turn of the twenty-first century that is, arguably, shared by its Anglo-Sax-

---

86 Ibid., 235.
87 As a counterpoint to his 2000 article, I mention briefly a subsequent essay by Thomas A. Shippey, 'Tolkien, Medievalism, and the Philological Tradition,' in *Bells Chiming from the Past: Cultural and Linguistic Studies on Early English,* eds. Isabel Moskowich-Spiegel and Begoña Crespo García (New York: Rodopi, 2007), 265–79, that, perhaps unwittingly, revises his response to the question of why Anglo-Saxon studies is in decline: 'Tolkien's professional speciality continues its long decline. Compulsory Anglo-Saxon has lost its long struggle for survival at Oxford, the same has just been decided at University College London, and my successor at Leeds (also, of course, Tolkien's successor) tells me heart-rending stories about the trouble he has had to keep Anglo-Saxon on the curriculum even as a minor option — the situation is even worse in most American university departments of English. People love Middle-earth. They have no time for the Middle Ages. Why this enormous contrast?' (265–66). Shippey responds to his own question with a statement that is, itself, a response to the stirrings of an old guard discussed at length in this book's introductory chapter. He points to Tolkien, the Grimm brothers, and nineteenth-century philological traditions in which 'the study of literature should never be separated from the study of language, and the history of language. The refusal to see this by departments of English, in Britain and America, has been a disaster for the subject' (274).

onists, who find themselves struggling to maintain a toehold in English Studies. While Shippey's language of sacrifice reverberates acoustically against Turner's 'dismal sacrifice' and Wallace-Hadrill's 'ritual sacrifice,' his is not an encrypted rhetoric, but a mourning call—a cry to look to the past without nostalgia and to acknowledge a history that is no longer tenable. Shippey's own contributions to nineteenth-century Anglo-Saxon historiography and literary appropriation, along with those of many others,[88] could be perceived as similar modes of mourning and, possibly, of exorcism. In recognizing the ties that have bound Anglo-Saxon studies to Anglo-Saxonism, medieval studies to medievalism, the identity politics of nations and empires to those of their academies, Shippey seems to desire a scholarly self-awareness that would loosen the knot between narratives of early medieval history and of national-imperial ideologies.

Is this time of mourning over, though? Or has it yet arrived? The postcolonial 'turn' has come to Anglo-Saxon studies[89] and with it an archipelagic view of the field. But how sharp is its arc if, as Aranye Fradenburg argues, we are located and write within an 'ambivalent, indeed melancholic, relation to modernity' that has not, as of yet, mourned its 'archaic signifiers'?[90] As an oblique response to these questions and Fradenburg's cautionary words, this chapter now turns to popular culture, where, in

---

88 See Frantzen, *Desire for Origins*; Allen Frantzen and John D. Niles, eds., *Anglo-Saxonism and the Construction of Social Identity* (Gainesville: Florida University Press, 1997); Scragg and Weinberg, eds., *Literary Appropriations of the Anglo-Saxons*; Ross, *The Norse Muse in Britain*; Margaret Clunies Ross, *The Old Norse Poetic Translations of Thomas Percy* (Turnhout: Brepols, 2001); Andrew Wawn, *The Vikings and the Victorians: Inventing the Old North in Nineteenth-Century Britain* (Woodbridge: Boydell and Brewer, 2000); Andrew Wawn, ed., *Constructing Nations, Reconstructing Myth: Essays in Honour of T.A. Shippey* (Turnhout: Brepols, 2007).

89 For example, see Catherine Karkov, 'Postcolonial,' in *A Handbook of Anglo-Saxon Studies*, eds. Jacqueline Stodnick and Renee Trilling (Malden: Wiley, 2012), 149–63.

90 L.O.A. Fradenburg, '(Dis)Continuity: A History of Dreaming,' in *The Post-Historical Middle Ages*, eds. Elizabeth Scala and Sylvia Federico (New York: Palgrave Macmillan, 2009), 89.

the post-9/11 decades, the blood eagle's notoriety has soared. It is defined by online sources such as *Wikipedia* and *Urban Dictionary*. It is the name for online gaming groups,[91] pagan religious organizations,[92] and heavy metal bands.[93] It has been the subject of various internet discussion boards, some of which advocate

---

[91] Warhammer, Planet Tribe, and the no longer available BattleField 2 have co-opted it as a name for online gaming clans. Brakus D'Vehne, a member of Blood Eagle Talon Prime Tribe, states, 'They call us butchers, murderers, and worse, as if pretty rules govern war. Heh. There's only one rule: win! Whatever the cost! If the other tribes are too soft, we'll carve the blood eagle on their sorry carcasses and carry the remains as banners into battle. It's simple: Win and live. Lose and die' (Sons of Ma'as, *Tribes Webring*, http://som.iwarp.com/main.html). On a smaller scale, the recently created role-playing game, 'Blood Eagle: Skirmish Warfare in the Legendary Dark Ages,' asks, 'Have you ever wanted to replicate the bloody feats of heroism you see in The Thirteenth Warrior movie and the *Vikings!* TV series?' ('North Star Military Figures').

[92] Blood Eagle Kindred is a New England chapter of the Ásatrú Alliance, a religion that practitioners claim is descended from Northern Europeans.

[93] A short list of songs include 'The Sons of the Dragon Slayer (Blood Eagle)' by Rebellion; 'Blood Eagle' by Ritual In Death; 'Blood Eagle Sacrifice' by Cobalt; 'Blood Eagle' by The Wound Man; 'The Blood Eagle' by Vreid; 'Blood Eagle' by Amon Amarth; 'Blood Eagle Wings' by Anthrax; and 'Blood Eagle' by Firespawn. The lyrics of these songs emphasize overwhelmingly the story of Ælla and Ivar, Ælla's tortured body, and Viking conquest of England. A handful of bands likewise have adopted the Vikings as figures of racist agendas, and several have chosen the blood eagle as a signifier of these politics. Blood Red Eagle, an Australian RAC / Viking Rock band of the early 2000s, describes its music as 'heavily influenced by the traditional Scandinavian Viking Rock style before it was pacified by many of the weak politically correct "acts" of today, Viking Metal, Folk metal, while still retaining their roots as a skinhead band with an aggression to match.' The now-defunct website, BloodRedEagle.com, had weblinks to the white power organizations, Blood & Honour, Volksfront International, and Hammerskin Nation, all sites now discontinued.

neo-Nazi activity,[94] others which denounce Al-Qaeda.[95] In the

---

[94] Connections between Nazism and neo-Nazism, Odin, and, by proxy, the blood eagle, run deep. In the 'Culture and Customs' segment of *Stormfront.org*, the discussion board of the Stormfront White Nationalist Community, many of its threads concern Scandinavia and the Vikings. One entitled 'viking blood eagle' addresses the veracity of the practice. Discussants differ in their historical opinions, but all are fascinated. One writes, '[m]ost of us here are pissed off that it appears to be a myth.' Another *Stormfront.org* thread begins with the comment, '[w]ell im looking for a good looking tattoo, that dont just blatently stand out and scream "im a racist" but also want something some may notice every now and then,' [sic] see 'help me with a tattoo, please.' Among the suggestions, panzerjeagar responds: 'I would recommend the "Blood Eagle." This is the one with wings swept down and head to the left. Often it is clutching a reath [sic] in its claws. It is also known as the "Sentries Eagle." If you ever see a ring of this sort, chances are the wearer is involved with law enforcement, especially amongst the military types. In the graphics gallery it is featured with a swazi in a wreath, but there are version [sic] with claws outstretched w/o the swazi. I have had this tatt for a while and when people see it they usually associate it with european [sic] flags of various sorts, but racially aware usually associate it with white pride. Also Thor's hammer (Mjolnir) is a good one, especially with runes on the head.' These posts extend the reach of the blood eagle further into the company of white supremacists as a stand-alone symbol of racism. Likewise, pangerjeager's suggestion of a tattoo with a graphic that is 'associate[d]…with European flags of various sorts' displaces further the rite from its Scandinavian origins by conflating the Viking blood eagle with German nationalism and Nazism. In this context, the blood eagle becomes a frightening code for State-sponsored racial violence and torture.

[95] While contemporary fictions most often associate the blood eagle with Nazi and neo-Nazi movements, the blood eagle has leached into post-9/11 on-line conversations about America's relations with the Islamic Arab world. In a posting about Al-Qaeda member Zacarias Moussaoui's 2006 testimony, one participant, Othala, writes, 'Give him a blood eagle and cover him in pig grease and bury him facing south. :beer: / and tell all of the terrorists this is what is awaiting you if you attack us. :yes:' Email to a thread, 'Moussaoui Says He Was to Hijack 5th Plane,' in *CurEvents.com* discussion forum, site now discontinued.

In the discussion topic entitled, 'How Do You Think Saddam Should Be Punished?,' respondent Evil Engineer writes, 'give him a blood eagle and fly him from the witehouse [sic] flagstand, to show other countries not to fuck with america. [sic] Or give him a sex change operation and force him to live with the Taliban': email to a thread, 'How Do you Think Saddam Should Be Punished?,' in Tribal War discussion forum. In another

wake of 9/11 attacks that remind America of its identity politics as both a nation and an empire under threat, the blood eagle makes its restless presence felt. It is no surprise, then, that in popular fiction and television, the relationship between Nazi movements, Al-Quaeda, and the blood eagle is revealed by way of medieval history.[96]

In Craig Russell's 2005 novel *Blood Eagle,* Jan Fabel is Chief Commissioner of Hamburg, Germany's murder unit. He begins to investigate the deaths of two women killed within a twenty-four-hour time-span. Their bodies are mutilated, but it is not until he visits his former medieval history professor that he learns of the blood eagle and begins to put together clues that link a former SS officer, the Hamburg Cell (the al-Qaeda group that masterminded the 9/11 airline attacks), and a shadowy arch-criminal who operates with tacit protection by anti-terror departments of the American CIA and Germany's Bundesnach-

---

thread, 'Who's Afraid of Islam?,' Fletcher Christian responds, '"Muslims have somehow have failed to convey to the world that they are good." Perhaps because they're not? And also perhaps, it's time to start reviving some old traditions, such as hanging drawing and quartering, the blood eagle, and burning at the stake–for use on violent nutcases who plan to kill and maim numbers of people they don't even know': email to a thread, 'Who's Afraid of Islam?,' in Winds of Change discussion forum.

The blood eagle is only one of many death fantasies that are suggested for Al-Qaeda members, Saddam, and the Muslim community. While other suggested forms of torture appear once or twice on different message board sites, the blood eagle recurs with startling frequency.

96 Note that fictional works that reference the blood eagle have been popular since the mid-1980s: Andrew J. Offut and Keith Taylor, *When Death Birds Fly* (New York: Ace Books, 1984); R.A. MacAvoy, *Book of Kells* (New York: Spectra, 1985); Edward Rutherfurd, *Sarum: The History of England* (New York: Ballantine Books, 1987); Philip Pullman, *The Golden Compass* (New York: Random House, 1995); Thomas Harris, *Hannibal* (New York: Random House, 1999); Alan Moore, *Voice of the Fire* (Atlanta: Top Shelf Productions, 2003); Guy Gavriel Kay, *The Last Light of the Sun* (New York: New American Library, 2004); Alfred Duggan, *Conscience of the King* (1951; repr. London: Phoenix Press, 2005); Craig Russell, *Blood Eagle* (London: Hutchinson, 2005); David Gibbins, *Crusader Gold* (London: Headline, 2006); Robert Barr Smith, *Blood Eagle* (Palm Beach: Medallion Press, 2007); and *Bones* (2009) episode: 'Mayhem on the Cross,' 4 (20), dir. Jeff Woolnough.

richtendienst because his military experience in Afghanistan makes him a valuable 'source of information on al-Qaeda and other Islamic terrorist organizations.'[97] In the following year, David Gibbins's novel, *Crusader Gold,* signals more clearly the integral and dangerous role that medieval historians play in tracking down the blood eagle. During archaeologist Jack Howard's search for the lost Golden Menorah of Jerusalem, he discovers that Viking armies plundered the menorah during their raids on Constantinople. Nazis attempt an excavation in Greenland to find it, and, in the process, a group of Nazi archaeologists recreates the 'félag,' a Viking secret society that tortures errant members with the blood eagle. When Maria de Montijo, a medieval historian from Oxford, and Father O'Connor, a Catholic priest and medievalist by training, hear about the Nazi félag, they engage in the following exchange:

> 'The outline of an eagle was carved on the back of the victim, while he was still alive,' Maria said quietly. 'Then they cut away the ribs and ripped out the lungs.'
> 'God almighty.' Even Costas was at a loss for words.
> 'They haven't used it yet on one of their own,' O'Connor said. 'But at the Einsatzgruppen trial one of the Jewish survivors spoke of a rumor that ss officers had carried out something like this on a group of prisoners, using his ceremonial dagger.[98]

Gibbins enmeshes Viking lore with Nazi history, and the blood eagle is registered as a Viking signifier for Nazi barbarisms. Yet, at the moment at which it is introduced into the plot, it is linked to unspeakability. Maria, whose mother is a Holocaust survivor, 'quietly' explains the procedure, to which 'Even Costas was at a loss for words.' O'Connor references the 'rumored' possibility that 'something like this' may have been carried out by the Einstazgruppen, and Gibbin's turn to the Einsatzgruppen trials

---

97 Russell, *Blood Eagle,* 393.
98 Gibbins, *Crusader Gold,* 224–25.

echoes the unsayable and therefore cryptic nature of the blood eagle.[99] Late in the novel, we learn that the blood eagle is not a figment of history but a murderous agent against its medieval historians, when Maria finds the body of Father O'Connor, who has been blood eagled by the neo-Nazi Pieter Reksnys.

In the post-9/11 world of crime fiction and historical fantasy, only medieval historians have the capacity to locate the blood eagle. Yet the ambivalence and, moreover, the silence of 'real' medievalists towards the blood eagle's ghostly presence has left popular culture to its imagination. Likewise, this silence by medievalists has given agents of popular culture permission to act as though they were medieval historians. Most notably is the History Channel's television series, *Vikings,* the narrative of which follows the figure of Ragnar Lothbrok. From its first season in 2013 to its fourth season, which spanned 2016–2017, the death of Ragnar in King Ælla's snake pit and the subsequent blood-eagling of Ælla by Ragnar's sons has been a narrative through-line of the series. After a glimpse of Ælla's snake pit in Season 1, in Season 2 Ragnar describes the blood eagle before enacting it upon fellow Viking Jarl Borg:[100]

> The offender gets down on his knees and his back is opened with knives. And then, with axes, his ribs are chopped away from his spine. And then his lungs are pulled out of these

---

99 The Einsatzgruppen were a special unit of the ss, which operated as death squads in Eastern Europe, killing over a million Jews between 1941 and 1943. Their commanders were tried in post-Nuremberg military tribunals held by the U.S. Government. As part of the Court's opinion and judgement, it wrote: 'a crime of such unprecedented brutality and of such inconceivable savagery that the mind rebels against its own thought image and the imagination staggers in the contemplation of a human degradation beyond the power of language to adequately portray' ('Nuremberg Military Tribunal,' Vol. IV, 412,' The Mazal Library: A Holocaust Resource,' http://www.mazal.org; 'Nuremberg Military Tribunal,' Volume IV, Page 413,' The Mazal Library: A Holocaust Resource,' http://www.mazal.org).

100 *Vikings,* 'Burial of the Dead,' 1 (6), dir. Ciarán Donnelly, *The History Channel,* April 7, 2013, and *Vikings,* 'Blood Eagle,' 2 (7), dir. Jeff Woolnough, *The History Channel,* April 3, 2014.

huge, bleeding wounds and laid upon his shoulders, so they look like the folded wings of a great eagle. And he must stay like that, suffering, until he dies. If he suffers in silence, he may enter Valhalla. But if he screams, he can never enter its portals.[101]

As Ragnar describes the practice, his hands slide forward and grip the front of a bathtub in which he is soaking so that they are parallel with his shoulders. As 'his ribs are chopped away from his spine,' Ragnar lifts his hands, drawing them around his own back in order to show the site of 'these huge, bleeding wounds.' Recounting its steps not only draws Ragnar forward in the bath, as if in anticipation of the event, but also engages his own body as locus of the blood eagle. Likewise, the *lentissimo* with which Ragnar explains the process — each step joined by an 'and' as the slow, but eerie strand of a violin begins to accompany his words — implicates a sensual intimacy with the practice, one that is accented by his place in the warm water of a bath.

When the torture is finally enacted, Ragnar appears dressed as a priest, and the blood eagle is staged as a night-time ritual sacrifice. Although it is introduced by the close-up shot of a snake, which recalls Ælla's snake pit of Season 1, and also foreshadows Ragnar's own death in the distant future, on this night, Ragnar is not the victim, but the executioner. The camera moves from the snake to Jarl Borg, the intended victim. As Borg is taken from his cell, the snake retrenches, and when Borg steps outside, he is met by Ragnar, who is dressed in a long, white robe and standing barefoot on a wooden dais, surrounded by his entire community. Torches light the night; drums beat in unison; spears, skulls, stones, and shells hung from twine decorate the space. The camera slows down the pace of the action, and the only sound that can be heard is the unrecognizable voice of a man, whose chant is accompanied by a bell and other ambient sounds. As Borg approaches the dais, he makes eye contact with many of Ragnar's Vikings, all of whom look silently and

---

101 Ibid.

unflinchingly back at him and at the elevated platform where he will be blood-eagled. This, the viewers of The History Channel are to understand, is not revenge but a serious and meaningful act, and they are asked to participate in it, watching, for over three protracted minutes—from Ragnar's initial cut on Borg's back to the final extraction of his lungs. As all eyes silently gaze on Ragnar's bloody but unseen operations, and Borg remains open-eyed, unspeaking, and unflinching despite his immense pain, viewers are asked to mimic the behaviors of the characters on screen: to watch, open-mouthed but silent, at the ritual severity of its practice and to acknowledge Ragnar's priestly status.

Again, absent the voices of 'real' medievalists, The History Channel takes on this role, supported by the *Viking*'s creator and writer, Michael Hirst. In an interview with Curt Wagner of the Chicago Tribune's *redeye,* Hirst articulates his own faith in the practice:[102]

> It [the 'Blood Eagle' episode] is a totally extraordinary TV event, I think. And one of the things I'm proudest of…it's a profound experience of suffering and spirituality in the Viking context. And if it wasn't in a Viking context it would be like watching, I guess, the crucifixion of Christ….It is a very profound and a very real experience. In other words, it actually happened to people. It's not fancy. It's not made up. It's not for show. It's a profound spiritual experience.
>
> For me this is what Vikings is [sic] all about. This is where we are. This is real; it's honest. It's about spirituality. It's about profound things. It's not a joke.
>
> …
>
> It was like being present at some extremely wonderful, sacrificial, frightening event. And I just wanted the opportunity to say that. For me, it's a very, very important moment in television history.

---

102 '*Vikings* Creator on Frightening, Spiritual Death,' *Chicago Tribune,* April 10, 2014, http://www.chicagotribune.com/redeye/redeye-vikings-post-mortem-ragnar-kills-borg-20140410-story.html.

Hirst expresses a terrifying romance with the blood eagle and, upon waxing poetical with respect to its 'profound spiritual experience,' states that 'this is what Vikings is all about.' Is Hirst referring to the historical Vikings or to the *Vikings* of The History Channel? Does he consider himself a Viking? While Hirst's interview statement is ambiguous, his words not only point back to the sensuality of Ragnar's description and the reverential silence of the Viking community in the recently aired 'Blood Eagle' episode. Moreover, they foreshadow the events of Season 4, in which the long-awaited blood-eagling of Ælla takes place. In an episode titled 'Revenge,' Ragnar's sons nail Ælla's hands to a horizontal beam, and as a hot blade is inserted into his back, Ælla's cries are heard by King Ecbert of Wessex, who sits up in his bed, looks up, and calls out 'Christ.'[103] Unlike Ragnar's priestly performance, in which the camera showed only the bloody evidence of the blood eagle, this time Ælla's back, pieces of bone, and finally his entire blood-eagled body are on display. After four seasons of preparation, the *Vikings,* the Vikings, and their American viewers are ready for the intense scopophilia of this event. When Ælla's blood-eagled body is hoisted, with outstretched arms, into the air, everyone is asked to believe, with Christian faith, in the 'profound spiritual experience' of Ælla's blood-eagling.

In the world of network television, the dates of TV shows are plotted months, if not seasons, in advance. Yet 'Revenge' aired two days before Donald Trump's 2017 presidential inauguration, a temporal proximity that is uncanny, if not down-right chilling. As Stephen Frosh argues, ghosts signal the future as well as the past, and Ella's blood eagle is that spectral haunting which, in the decades since 9/11, has increased the frequency of its signals as American politics take up the banner of ethno-nationalism. Yet the failure or, rather, the inability of early medieval historians to contemplate and speak openly about the blood eagle marks its cryptic presence in the field. As Kath-

---

103 *Vikings,* 'Revenge,' 4 (18), dir. Jeff Woolnough, *The History Channel,* January 18, 2017.

leen Biddick cautions, when 'the consequences of the fathers' work still elude acknowledgement,' a discipline's 'disavowal of them[, its 'excluded objects,'] actually reflects an inability to historicize the discipline' and therefore to mourn the objects and narratives which have created it.[104]

The blood eagle is that encrypted specter — that excluded object — passed down from Sharon Turner's imperial psyche to those of his children, a post-imperial generation of Anglo-Saxon historians. As a ghost of Empire, it haunts the unconscious quarters of the discipline, keeping the field of Anglo-Saxon history unmindful of its presence and therefore unable to engage fully in the process of mourning. Yet psychic crypts are often positioned next to material ones, and, consequently, while cryptic hauntings impact the mind, they likewise impact the body. The next chapter searches out these material crypts by examining the writings of another father of the interdisciplinary field of Anglo-Saxon studies, eighteenth-century barrow digger and early medieval archaeologist James Douglas. Douglas spends his life stepping into and out of Anglo-Saxon graves, and his archaeological report, *Nenia Britannica,* bears witness to the affective displays of interminable grief that arise from standing too close to the skeletons of the racialized, Anglo-Saxon dead.

---

[104] Kathleen Biddick, *The Shock of Medievalism* (Durham: Duke University Press, 1998), 1.

3

Beowulf, James Douglas, and the Sepulchral Body of the Anglo-Saxonist

Just a few years before Sharon Turner's *History of the Anglo Saxons* appeared in print, James Douglas published *Nenia Britannica: or, a sepulchral history of Great Britain; from the earliest period to its general conversion to Christianity*.¹ Printed initially in twelve parts, then as a monograph in 1793,² *Nenia Britannica* is an archaeological report and a general history of pre-Christian funerary practices in Britain. Its material is not organized into chapters but into tumuli, or barrows, each of which contains

---

1 For a biography on Douglas, see Ronald Jessup, *Man of Many Talents: An Informal Biography of James Douglas 1753–1819* (London: Phillmore, 1975).
2 Several different printings of *Nenia* were made in 1793, one of which is for Benjamin and John White: James Douglas, *Nenia Britannica; or, A Sepulchral History of Great Britain* (London: Printed by John Nichols; for Benjamin and John White, 1793). Another copy was made for George Nichol: *Nenia Britannica; or, A sepulchral history of Great Britain* (London: Printed by John Nichols; for George Nicol, in Pall-Mall, Bookseller to his Majesty, 1793). These two printings have different images on page 3. One (Benjamin and White) depicts a draped urn on page 3 while another (Nicol) depicts the Grim Reaper sitting on a tumulus. This chapter references the Nicol edition throughout.

an aquatint plate of numbered artifact illustrations followed by short artifact descriptions.

'Tumulus I,' the first of *Nenia Britannica*'s tumuli, opens with an illustration numbered '1,' which depicts the cross-section of an excavated barrow. Inside a thickly inked circle, which represents the barrow's ring ditch, a skeleton stands with one foot turned outward in a gentlemanly stance. One hand grasps a sword, the other holds the decayed shaft of a spear, and a knife and shield boss are positioned within easy reach. Although dead, the body inside Tumulus 1 seems to be alive, and its connection to the living is strengthened when Douglas explains that the barrow depicted in Figure 1 was opened by soldiers at work outside the naval town of Chatham, Kent. The identity of the skeleton, and its relationship to Chatham's soldiers, comes into focus when Douglas cross-references the sword in the skeleton's left hand with illustrations of 'a Saxon foot-soldier's dress' that appear in a manuscript copy of Prudentius's *Psychomachia*.[3] Douglas's assessment of the weapons in Tumulus 1 suggests that the skeleton in this barrow is a Saxon. Furthermore, Douglas's visual and narrative accounts of the excavation suggest that Chatham's soldier-excavators are also Saxons. The first tumulus and figure of *Nenia Britannica* underscore barrow digging as an activity that draws living bodies into the graves of the dead, creating physical, cultural, and racial connections between generations of 'Saxon foot-soldiers.'

The previous chapter employed the psychoanalytic concepts of mourning, incorporation, and transgenerational haunting in order to consider the role of Sharon Turner as a father of Anglo-Saxon history.[4] In tracing a genealogical relationship between Turner and contemporary historians, it uncovered a psychic

---

3 Douglas, *Nenia Britannica*, 128, 128n1, 128n3.
4 Briefly summarized, mourning is a process of coming to terms with the death of a loved one (whether a person, thing, or idea). This process involves constructing a new narrative of the future self that is no longer inclusive of the beloved. Incorporation is the fantasmatic act of taking into one's body the dead love object as a mechanism for avoiding the pain of losing it. It is a prohibition against mourning that installs the love object

crypt of Empire located within Turner's imperial unconscious, deposited within his *History,* and passed on to the minds of his 'children,' the post-imperial generation of twentieth–century Anglo-Saxon historians. This chapter, which complements the previous one, examines James Douglas as a father of Anglo-Saxon archaeology. By tracking Douglas's excavation of British barrows, it draws the psychic crypts and psychoanalytic theory of Chapter 2 into conversation with material crypts and two relational modes of embodied identity-making: the Deleuzoguattarian concept of territory and the rhetorical practice of ekphrasis. In so doing, this chapter examines the mental state of Anglo-Saxon historians alongside the bodily state of Anglo-Saxon archaeologists and, by extension, literary scholars. Together, Chapters 2 and 3 articulate the embodied psychic-social profile of the interdisciplinary Anglo-Saxonist scholar.

Nenia Britannica has been acknowledged as a 'notable milestone' and a 'turning point' in Anglo-Saxon archaeology, and Douglas has been called a 'pioneer in the field' who established 'standards of accuracy and observation' in antiquarian excavation and analysis.[5] Using the illustrations and descriptions of *Nenia Britannica*'s twenty-six *tumuli* as visual data, Douglas compares and distinguishes, for the first time, Anglo-Saxon burial mounds and funerary objects. *Nenia Britannica* and Figure 1 become critical references during the mid-nineteenth century. Victorian antiquarians consult *Nenia Britannica* when assessing Anglo-Saxon artifacts recovered from their own bar-

---

within the self. For a more extensive explanation of these two interrelated concepts, see Chapter 2 of this book.

5 Rosemary Sweet, *Antiquaries: The Discovery of the Past in Eighteenth–Century Britain* (New York: Hambledon and London, 2004), 211, 345; C.J. Arnold, *An Archaeology of the Early Anglo-Saxon Kingdoms* (New York: Routledge, 1997), 3; and Gale R. Owen-Crocker, *Dress in Anglo-Saxon England* (Woodbridge: The Boydell Press, 2004), 2. See also Kelley M. Wickham-Crowley, 'Looking Forward, Looking Back: Excavating the Field of Anglo-Saxon Archaeology,' in *The Archaeology of Anglo-Saxon England: Basic Readings,* ed. Catherine E. Karkov (New York: Garland Publishing, Inc., 1999), 2, and Lesley Adkins and Roy Adkins, *Archaeological Illustration* (Cambridge: Cambridge University Press, 1989), 4, 9.

row excavations, and they use Figure 1 as a template when drawing their own barrow illustrations. Yet Douglas's report and his barrow sketch, especially, are not simply reference materials for the emerging field of Anglo-Saxon archaeology. As Douglas arranges Saxon bone and artifacts according to the postures and gestures of Chatham's living soldiers, Figure 1 becomes ekphrastic. In other words, its visual rhetoric transforms Douglas's two-dimensional Saxon skeleton into a performative figure that reaches out from its ink-drawn barrow and phenomenologically impacts the viewer. The ekphrastic performance of Figure 1 prompts antiquarians to respond *affectively* to this Saxon. They interpret barrow excavation as an act of mourning and construe bone-artifact collection as a mechanism for incorporating the dead within the self. As these Victorian antiquarians are drawn into the ekphrastic orbit of Figure 1, they imagine themselves to have psychically incorporated a Saxon soldier, and, consequently, they fantasize an embodied physical, cultural, and racial association with it. Douglas's Victorians continue to use Figure 1 as a model for the barrow illustrations of other Saxon skeletons, and, in the process, they generate the archaeological portrait of an 'Anglo-Saxon.' As a figure that is positioned inside psychic *and* material crypts, the 'Anglo-Saxon' is simultaneously within and exterior to its antiquarian excavators. Consequently, its military artifacts, skeletal height, and cranial shape and size articulate a racial-cultural body that refracts the bodies of a growing community of professional Anglo-Saxon antiquarians. The skeletonized, undead, yet performatively embodied 'Anglo-Saxon' is characterized by an insatiable appetite for destruction, but possesses mental faculties that are marked by balance and reason.

Although James Douglas is a 'father' of Anglo-Saxon archaeology, he has been most influential among scholars specializing in the disciplinary sub-field of mortuary archaeology. In *Death and Memory in Early Medieval Britain,* Howard Williams explains that 'early and mid-twentieth-century approaches' to early Anglo-Saxon archaeology, which 'develop[ed] upon… precedents' set by Douglas and the Victorians, 'took the form of "culture-history": charting the history of tribes and ideas, and their origins, movements and evolution through burial rites and the artefacts contained within graves.'⁶ Over the past forty years, however, the field has moved away from these interests. Although archaeologists continue to recognize Douglas's pioneering work and disciplinary milestones, mortuary archaeologists have replaced the term 'Anglo-Saxon' with 'early medieval' when referencing their scope of study. Likewise, Williams continues, 'the influence of new theoretical paradigms employed throughout archaeology' has led early medieval mortuary archaeologists to 'adop[t] alternative perspectives from traditional culture-history.'⁷ Such changes within the field have had a consequential

---

6 Howard Williams, *Death and Memory in Early Medieval Britain* (Cambridge: Cambridge University Press, 2006), 6.
7 Ibid. For example, much work over the past twenty years has focused on the metaphorical and symbolic use of grave goods. For a recent survey, see Heinrich Härke, 'Grave Goods in Early Medieval Burials: Messages and Meanings,' *Mortality: Promoting the Interdisciplinary Study of Death and Dying* 19, no. 1 (2014): 41–60. On the the social agency and social identity of the dead and their communities, see, for example, Nick Stoodley, 'Age Organization and the Early Anglo-Saxon Burial Rite,' *World Archaeology* 31, no. 3 (2000): 456–72; Howard Williams, 'Death Warmed Up: The Agency of Bodies and Bones in Early Anglo-Saxon Cremation Rites,' *Journal of Material Culture* 9, no. 3 (2004): 263–91 and 'Assembling the Dead,' in *Assembly Places and Practices in Medieval Europe*, eds. Aliki Pantos and Sarah Semple (Dublin: Four Courts Press, 2004), 109–34; Kirsty E. Squires, 'Piecing Together Identity: A Social Investigation of Early Anglo-Saxon Cremation Practices,' *Archaeological Journal* 170, no. 1 (2013): 154–200; and Zoë L. Devlin, '"(Un)touched by Decay": Anglo-Saxon Encounters with Dead Bodies,' in *Death Embodied: Archaeological Approaches to the Treatment of the Corpse*, eds. Zoë L. Devlin and Emma-Jayne Graham (Oxford: Oxbow Books, 2015), 63–85. On emotional expressions in funerals, see Howard Williams, 'The Emotive Force of Early Medieval Mortuary Practices,' *Archaeological Review from Cambridge* 22, no. 1 (2007): 107–23. On mortuary practices and social memory, see Williams, *Death and Memory in Early Medieval Britain*, 2006. On landscape and monumental contexts of commemoration, see Howard Williams, 'Ancient Landscapes and the Dead: The Reuse of Prehistoric and Roman Monuments as Early Anglo-Saxon Burial Sites,' *Medieval Archaeology* 41, no. 1 (1997): 1–32; and 'Monuments and the Past in Early Anglo-Saxon England,' *World Archaeology* 30, no. 1 (1998): 90–108; and Sarah Semple, *Perceptions of the Prehistoric in Anglo-Saxon England: Religion, Ritual, and Rulership in the Landscape* (Oxford: Oxford University Press, 2013).

impact on the study of barrow burials. Howard Williams has employed the methods of comparative anthropology and ethnography. Sarah Semple and Andrew Reynolds have used charters, historical documents, early medieval poetry, boundary markers, and place names to reconfigure the barrow from a funereal site to a dynamic landscape of ritual, movement, community activity, and monument re-use.[8] Heinrich Härke has assessed grave goods from multiple excavation sites in relation to the *Anglo-Saxon Chronicle,* reinterpreting the function of weapons burials from a reflection of warrior status to a strategy for constructing identity.[9] Martin Carver has appropriated the language of metaphor and symbolism to reframe the grave's funeral tableau from a material reality to a material poetics.[10] These examples not only reflect the influence of theoretical approaches within mortuary archaeology but also evidence methodological changes to a field that was once tied exclusively to excavation and archaeological reports. Contemporary studies in early medieval mortuary archaeology have taken Saxon skeletons and artifacts from the hands of Douglas and his Victorian

---

8 See Williams, 'Death Warmed Up,' 'Assembling the Dead,' *Death and Memory in Early Medieval Britain,* and 'The Emotive Force of Early Medieval Mortuary Practices'; Sarah Semple, 'A Fear of the Past: The Place of the Prehistoric Burial Mound in the Ideology of Middle and Later Anglo-Saxon England,' *World Archaeology* 30, no. 1 (1998): 109–26, 'Burials and Political Boundaries in the Avebury Region, North Wiltshire,' *Anglo-Saxon Studies in Archaeology and History* 12 (2003): 72–91, and *Perceptions of the Prehistoric in Anglo-Saxon England*; and Andrew Reynolds, 'The Definition and Ideology of Anglo-Saxon Execution Sites and Cemeteries,' in *Death and Burial in Medieval Europe: Papers of the 'Medieval Europe Brugge 1997' Conference,* Vol. 2, eds. Guy De Boe and Frans Verhaeghe (Zellik: Instituut voor het Archeologisch Patrimonium, 1997), 33–41.
9 Heinrich Härke, '"Warrior Graves"? The Background of the Anglo-Saxon Weapon Burial Rite,' *Past & Present* 126, no. 1 (1990): 22–43, and 'Material Culture as Myth: Weapons in Anglo-Saxon Graves,' in *Burial and Society: The Chronological and Social Analysis of Archaeological Burial Data,* eds. Claus Kjeld Jensen and Karen Hoilund Nielsen (Aarhus: University of Aarhus, 1997), 119–27.
10 Martin Carver, 'Burial as Poetry: The Context of Treasure in Anglo-Saxon Graves,' in *Treasure in the Medieval West,* ed. Elizabeth M. Tyler (York: York Medieval Press, 2000), 25–48.

antiquarians and thereby worked towards unknotting the racial and cultural ties between dead and living 'Saxon' bodies.

Despite these changes in the theories, methods, and perspectives of early medieval mortuary archaeology, one connection remains between James Douglas, barrow diggers of the nineteenth-century past, and archaeologists of the twenty-first–century present, a connection that persistently ties the larger field of Anglo-Saxon archaeology to Anglo-Saxon literature: *Beowulf*. In this chapter, I first argue that *Beowulf*'s formal architecture — specifically, its chiasmus and interlace — constructs a poetic barrow, and the circulation of Danes and Geats around this poetic barrow engages a conversation about how these early medieval funerary structures facilitate identity-making as an embodied and performative act. *Beowulf*'s association with early medieval barrows positions the poem in relation to sites excavated by Douglas and claimed by his Victorian acolytes to contain Anglo-Saxon graves. Likewise, *Beowulf*'s investment in expressing identity through physical performance anticipates the work of these antiquarians. When interest in the poem is rekindled in the nineteenth century (and early medieval barrows and bodies have been claimed as Anglo-Saxon), *Beowulf* enables archaeologists and literary scholars to construct and maintain an interdisciplinary relationship as Anglo-Saxonists.

Digging *Beowulf*'s Grave: Mortuaries, Territory, Ekphrasis

Early medieval barrow burial is one of the many ways that communities of eastern England commemorated their dead during the pre-Christian, or final-phase, period, which dates from the mid-fifth to the early eighth century. Some barrows are affiliated with a single grave, while others are part of a regional cemetery. Some contain inhumed bodies, and others contain cremated ones. While many of these barrows were built by Anglo-Saxons as a means of honoring their own dead, others — erected by neolithic, British, and Roman peoples — were re-used, enlarged, or supplemented with new mounds by Anglo-Saxon communities in what is known as secondary or associative burials.[11] Whether a primary, secondary, or associative grave site, barrows are placed in meaningful proximity to other landscape features. Often near waterways, on hilltops or promontories, or adjacent to active or unused structures, barrows command a panoramic view of an area. Among the most visually distinct and prolific manmade landscape features of eastern England, barrows remained visible for over a thousand years until industrializing efforts of the eighteenth and nineteenth centuries razed many to the ground.

Although these earthworks were built for the dead, they were continuously reused by the communities that lived near them. For example, Howard Williams considers the early medieval cremation cemetery of Lovedon Hill, Lincolnshire, a prominent hill and 'one of the most striking and easily recognized landmarks in the vicinity' that 'Anglo-Saxons may well have regarded…as an ancient burial mound.'[12] Given the size of Lovedon Hill (the second largest early medieval cemetery found in England, with 1,800 excavated graves), it is regarded as a 'central burial plac[e] serving many settlements and farms and perhaps related to a defined "tribal" territory.'[13] Williams argues that its size and central location suggest Lovedon Hill as an assembly place where large numbers of people — not only the dead but also 'close kin,' 'friends of the deceased,' 'other individuals owing allegiance,' 'as well as those with more specific duties, roles and obligations to enact' — from small, dispersed communities met and interacted.[14] Consequently, the funerals enacted here may have been large events where 'a wide range of social activities' took place, 'including feasting, settling disputes and forming alliances through gift giving.'[15] When Williams assesses the topography, archaeological evidence, and geography of Lovedon Hill in relation to other Anglo-Saxon cremation sites, he hypothesizes that cremation cemeteries like Lovedon Hill were

---

11 Williams, 'Ancient Landscapes and the Dead.'
12 Williams, 'Assembling the Dead,' 123.
13 Ibid., 113.
14 Ibid., 115.
15 Ibid.

encircled by a network of places in which people lived, worked, and worshipped, making them sites of assembly or 'central places' for both the dead and the living.[16] Even after barrows were abandoned as places for burying the dead, onomastic, historical, and archaeological evidence reveals their continued function throughout the Anglo-Saxon period as sites for community assembly, administration, judicial activities, and execution.[17] Despite their central placement in early Anglo-Saxon geographies, barrows likewise are found along the boundaries of villas

---

16 Ibid., 124–26, especially Figs 5.6 and 5.7; Howard Williams, 'Cemeteries as Central Places: Place and Identity in Migration Period Eastern England,' in *Central Places in the Migration and Merovingian Periods,* eds. Birgitta Hårdh and Lars Larsson (Stockholm: Almqvist and Wiksell International, 2002), 341–62.

17 Aliki Pantos identifies barrows and mounds (OE *hlæw* and *beorg*; ON *haugr*) as the most common 'physical feature' referenced in the names of meeting places ('Assembly Places in the Anglo-Saxon Period: Aspects of Form and Location,' PhD diss., University of Oxford, 2002, 69–70, cited in Semple, *Perceptions of the Prehistoric in Anglo-Saxon England,* 217). See also Alexandra Sanmark and Sarah J. Semple, 'Places of Assembly: New Discoveries in Sweden and England,' *Fornvännen* 103, no. 4 (2008): 245–59.

and estates,[18] hundreds,[19] parishes,[20] and wapentakes.[21] As sites located at the outermost edges of these land divisions, barrows are borderlands. Their position on the margins of later medieval geographies is reflected in both Old English poetry, where they are depicted as evil, monstrous, and haunted 'pagan' spaces,

---

18   Peter Sawyer, *From Roman Britain to Norman England,* 2nd edn. (New York: Routledge, 1998), 147–48, and Martin Welch, 'Rural Settlement Patterns in the Early and Middle Anglo-Saxon Periods,' *Landscape History* 7 (1985): 19–21. D.M. Hadley cites, as an example, the barrow burial at Caenby, which is close to the junction between Hemswell, Harpswell, Glentham, and Caenby vill boundaries, and she writes that 'presumably such burials either were located on existing boundaries, or were used to mark out new boundaries; either way it suggests that such boundaries existed in the early Anglo-Saxon period' (*The Northern Danelaw: Its Social Structure, c.800–1100* [London: Leicester University Press, Continuum, 2000], 98).
19   The Hundred is an administrative division of land. Dating to about the mid-tenth century, it subsumed a large amount of land under juridical and fiduciary control. Each Hundred, scholars assume, had an open-air meeting place, where trials, disputes, etc. would take place. Wenslow (Bedfordshire) and Thunderlow (Essex), for example, contain elements of the word hlæw, one of several Old English words that can mean 'mound,' 'cairn,' 'hill,' 'mountain,' 'grave-yard,' or 'barrow' (Audrey Meaney, 'Pagan English Sanctuaries, Place-Names and Hundred Meeting-Places,' *Anglo-Saxon Studies in Archaeology and History* 8 [1995]: 36).
20   Ann Goodier, 'The Formation of Boundaries in Anglo-Saxon England: A Statistical Study,' *Medieval Archaeology* 28 (1984): 1–21. For an analysis of Goodier, see Welch, 'Rural Settlement Patterns,' 19. For cautionary statements regarding barrows and boundaries, see Andrew Reynolds, 'Burials, Boundaries, and Charters in Anglo-Saxon England: A Reassessment,' in *Burial in Early Medieval England and Wales,* eds. Sam Lucy and Andrew Reynolds (London: Society for Medieval Archaeology Monograph 17, 2002), 173–74. For initial, but now disproven assessments of barrows and boundaries, see Desmond Bonney, 'Early Boundaries and Estates in Southern England,' in *Medieval Settlement: Continuity and Change,* ed. Peter H. Sawyer (New York: Edward Arnold, 1976), 72–82.
21   Alexis Tudor Skinner and Sarah Semple, 'Assembly Mounds in the Danelaw: Place-name and Archaeological Evidence in the Historic Landscape,' *Journal of the North Atlantic* 8 (2016): 115–33.

and in real life, where they become gallows sites[22] and staging grounds for battle.[23]

As a topography that marks the center of a settlement or the borderlands of a region, barrows make territory, in the geopolitical sense, by parceling land into districts.[24] In addition, their enduring material participation in a network of ever-shifting cultural practices points towards an engagement with a different kind of territory. Borrowing from the methodology of Deleuze and Guattari,[25] territory is not simply a material place that is claimed (and reclaimed). It is a concept that sees identity as an ever-shifting process that is assembled, disassembled, and

---

22 Semple, 'A Fear of the Past,' 123, and Andrew Reynolds, *Anglo-Saxon Deviant Burial Customs* (New York: Oxford University Press, 2009), 248–50. Reynolds's survey of *cwealmstowe* (execution places) reveals that the great majority were located on barrows on boundaries, especially hundred boundaries ('The Definition and Ideology of Anglo-Saxon Execution Sites and Cemeteries,' 37). Martin Carver points out that Mound 5 of Sutton Hoo has around it the remains of hanged or beheaded bodies, and on the eastern periphery of the cemetery, another group of burials lies amid the postholes attributed to a gallows site (*Sutton Hoo: Burial Ground of Kings?* [Philadelphia: Pennsylvania University Press, 1998], 137–43). On the placement of gallows on barrows in the medieval period, more generally, see Nicola Whyte, 'The Deviant Dead in the Norfolk Landscape,' *Landscapes* 4, no. 1 (2003): 33.

23 Recently, Sarah Semple and Alexandra Sanmark articulated an example that highlights both the 'real significance' and *longue durée* of the barrow's power when they discuss *Cwichelmeshlæwe*, an Iron Age round barrow in Northumbria. Purportedly named to commemorate Edwin of Northumbria's killing of Cwichelm of Wessex in 636 CE, the homicidal power of the 'Mound of Cwichelm' is invoked and challenged four hundred years later when a troop of Danes camped near the barrow and then marched around it, 'boast[ing] threats, because it had often been said that if they sought out Cwichelm's Barrow, they [the Danes] would never get to the sea' (Sample and Sanmark, 'Assembly in North West Europe,' 1).

24 For a discussion of the role of barrows in the contested territorial frontier of Wessex-Mercia, see Sarah Semple, 'Burials and Political Boundaries in the Avebury Region, North Wiltshire.'

25 While Deleuze and Guattari are discussed infrequently in relation to early medieval studies, Manish Sharma's recent essay on Old English formulaic theory offers an exciting engagement with these philosophers ('Beyond Nostalgia: Formula and Novelty in Old English Literature,' *Exemplaria* 26, no. 4 [2014]: 303–27).

reassembled by means of our affective performances. We make signs and sounds; we hold postures; we gesture, display, and advertise. We demonstrate via our bodies how we feel and who we are, in a given moment, at a given location. We communicate an identity that is assembled in performance. Consequently, it is always changing, never the same, and always attached to the place where we are standing. And we respond to these behaviors in others. To use the language of Deleuze and Guattari, our identities are de- and re-territorialized with each shift in sign, sound, and movement; and the 'territory' is the locus 'where' all these re-codings of identity take 'place.' Thus, geopolitical territory and expressive territory are intertwined, and when we stand in a particular place, we express an assemblage of identities that are always on the move.

As sites for celebrating alliances and making war, for managing community affairs and executing criminals, for mourning one's dead and being terrified by them, barrows are, to reemphasize, geopolitical territories — they mark the most central and peripheral boundaries of a socio-cultural community. Here, people gather and display signs, sounds, and movements that are keyed to the barrow's particular territorial function: Who belongs and who does not? How should we (and others) live and die? How can we account for others' relationships to this place and, nonetheless, make it our own?[26] As communities assemble and performatively negotiate answers to these questions, over and over again, early medieval barrows come to function as liminal zones striated by vectors of deep power. They draw together,

---

26 Alfred Siewer's essay, 'Guthlac's Mound and Grendel's Mere as Expressions of Anglo-Saxon Nation Building,' *Viator* 34 (2003): 1–39, considers how early medieval poetry engages barrow landscapes and identity formation and as such is an important precursor to the arguments of this chapter.

by material means, human acts of intimacy and extimacy,[27] ways of dying and living.[28]

As burial sites, the surfaces, soil, geography, and climate of barrows make possible and prohibit certain kinds of funeral activities, mourning rituals, and monumental construction. Their abiotic features shape 'dying practices' that (re)assemble, or re-territorialize, a community's sense of self while doing the same for the dead. Yet once these dying practices are complete, the grave is covered up. A barrow is erected over its mortuary interior, and the exterior surface of this new landscape becomes the site of ever-expanding networks of 'living practices': how to call into being and confirm alliances, how to make and re-make culture, and how to distinguish self from other. Barrows shuttle death towards life by enjoining the force of the earth to that of human movement. With each new community re-use, postholes are dug, surfaces are worn down, and materials are left standing or forgotten. These changes code and re-code, and re- and de-territorialize, barrows that record old and new identity assemblages and the relationship between them. As a recording, barrows broadcast this range of assemblages between and among communities over long stretches of time. Consequently, to extend our understanding of the barrow by invoking one other Deleuzoguatterain term, barrows are a geophilosophical

---

27 'Extimacy' (in French, *extimité*) is a term coined by Jacques Lacan, who adds the prefix ex- to 'intimacy' [*intimité*] and writes, 'this central place, this intimate exteriority, this extimacy, which is the Thing' (Jacques Lacan, *The Seminar of Jacques Lacan, Book VII: The Ethics of Psychoanalysis 1959–1960*, ed. Jacques-Alain Miller, trans. Dennis Porter [New York: W.W. Norton & Company, 1992], 167). As a word that yokes 'inside' to 'outside,' extimacy reveals the relationship between interior and exterior domains.

28 Giles Deleuze and Felix Guattari, *A Thousand Plateaus*, trans. Brian Massumi (Minneapolis: University of Minnesota Press, 1987), 325–26. For a recent discussion and overview of cemetery — in particular, barrow — re-use, see Sarah Semple and Howard Williams, 'Landmarks of the Dead: Exploring Anglo-Saxon Mortuary Geographies,' in *The Material Culture of the Built Environment in the Anglo-Saxon World*, eds. Maren Clegg Hyer and Gale Owen-Crocker (Liverpool: Liverpool University Press, 2015), 137–61.

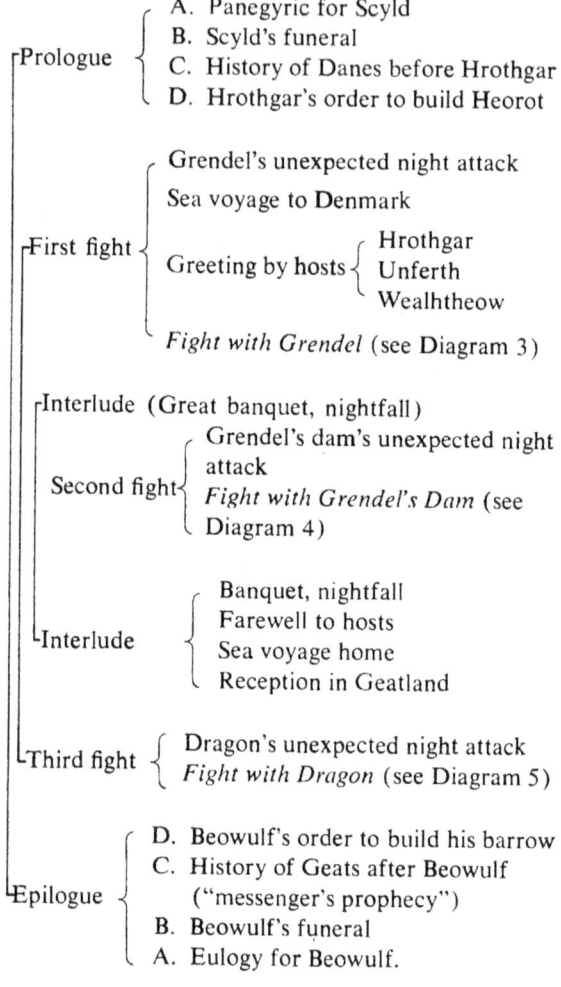

Figure 1. John Niles's 'Diagram 6' of the 'chief correspondences that knit the poem [*Beowulf*] together.' John D. Niles, 'Ring Composition and the Structure of *Beowulf*,' PMLA 94, no. 5 (1979): 930. Image courtesy of PMLA.

territory and moreover its Natal, the territory's 'intense center' and the 'extra-territorial convergence of different and distant territories.'[29] Put another way, barrows are homing sites. They point the way towards a forever-becoming entity that we currently call 'Anglo-Saxon,' a multiplicity of identity assemblages that are always in motion, never stable, and perpetually unmaking and remaking themselves.

Beowulf is a poem that is deeply concerned with practices of living and dying. The funerary rituals of Scyld Scefing and Beowulf, which bookend the poem, call into question and confirm what it means to be Danish or Geatish. Toward the poem's narrative interior, the attacks of Grendelkin and the dragon upon Heorot and Daneland challenge these identity positions and prompt their reorientation. Amid these many and varied dying practices, the construction of Heorot and the celebrations that take place therein express living through performances, gestures, conversations, and stories that further adjust and reconfirm 'Dane' and 'Geat' as highly mobile assemblages. *Beowulf* is also a poem that constructs, by way of these dying and living practices, the three-dimensional outline of a barrow.

As John Niles argues,[30] *Beowulf*'s key episodes generate three nested ring structures: Prologue and Epilogue, First Fight and Third Fight, Interlude and Interlude (see Figure 1). For Niles, ring structure provides the poem with a circular frame, which, this chapter argues, is given height, depth, and dimension in its coupling with interlace patterning. Moreover, the interplay of ring structure and interlace — *Beowulf*'s overarching poetic modes — articulates a calculus of dying and living strategies that

---

29 Consider Sarah Semple's article, 'Recycling the Past: Ancient Monuments and Changing Meanings in Early Medieval Britain,' in *Antiquaries and Archaists: The Past in the Past, The Past in the Present*, eds. Megan Brewster Aldrich and Robert J. Wallis (Reading: Spire, 2009), 29–45, as an alternative mode of expressing the openness of funerary territory.

30 See also Gale Owen-Crocker, *The Four Funerals in Beowulf and the Structure of the Poem* (Manchester: Manchester University Press, 2000).

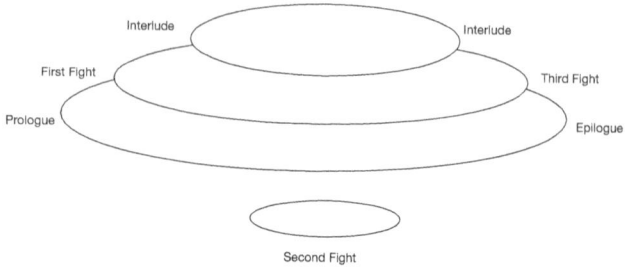

Figure 2. Author's visual remapping of John D. Niles's diagram (see Fig. 1).

Figure 3. Stephen Plunkett, photograph of reconstructed Mound 2 at Sutton Hoo (S2007). Image courtesy of Dr. Stephen Plunkett.

narratively erects a three-dimensional barrow (see Figures 2 and 3).[31]

In the Prologue, Scyld's boat funeral turns to Hrothgar's hall building, and the boat's wooden hull and funereal gold are transformed into Heorot's wide-gabled roof and gilded lintels. As Niles's diagram makes clear, these narrative activities and architectural spaces anticipate those of the Epilogue, and the Prologue opens a circuit that will be closed when Scyld's death is revisited in Beowulf's death. Yet as an episode that likewise summons the activities of Hrothgar and the hall of Heorot, it interlaces the Prologue and the First Fight. Together, ring structure and interlace give the narrative material dimension. The poem fastens together two kingly deaths and their burial structures in order to assume an emergent sense of circular depth and width, and it also weaves together the passing of Scyld with the ascent of Hrothgar's reign, and Heorot's hall, to add height to these dimensions. From dying to living, from royal death to a bare life, *Beowulf* traces the outline of a barrow's foundation.[32]

Beowulf's First Fight with Grendel makes these outlines more materially present, as Hrothgar's rule and Heorot's hall are refigured into even more capacious 'living structures,' and in the subsequent Interlude, Danes and Geats feast in celebration of a community that does not merely survive, but now thrives. These two episodes, which pivot jointly upon chiasmus and interlace, plot the upward slope and outer curvature of a barrow as they angle towards modes of vibrant living — towards a more robust assemblage that articulates what it means to be a Dane or a Geat now that Grendel has been defeated. Moreover, as the Interlude that occurs after Beowulf's fight with Grendel is circuited to the Interlude that follows his victory against Grendel's mother, this ring structure doubles as a poetic and a material plateau, a

---

31 For a discussion of the narrative functions of ring structure in *Beowulf*, see H. Ward Tonsfeldt, 'Ring Structure in *Beowulf*,' *Neophilologus* 61, no. 3 (1977): 443–52.

32 Note also that Robert Boenig argues that Scyld's boat burial represents 'a burial in a grave mound like those found in East Anglia and Scandinavia' ('Scyld's Burial Mound,' *English Language Notes* 40, no. 1 [2002]: 3).

'place' where Danes and Geats gather and feast, tell stories and give gifts. At the poem's 'highest' point — as if sitting atop a barrow — these two communities meet and take part in an array of social activities that, as Howard Williams has explained, are associated with this funerary structure.

From these celebratory Interludes, the poem begins to calculate the downward slope and curve of a barrow. Upon Beowulf's homecoming to Geatland, stories of intra- and inter-community hostility, warfare, and execution descend towards Beowulf's Third Fight with the dragon. This episode closes the chiastic loop opened by his battle with Grendel even as it interlaces Heorot's wooden hall, golden gift exchanges, and practices of sociability with the dragon's *stan-beorh,* treasure hoard, and lost community. As ring structures that were opened in the first half of the poem are now closed, narratives of living give way to stories of dying even as architectures of hospitality are refigured as places of interment. Beowulf dies from wounds sustained in his Third Fight, and the Epilogue depicts his funeral rituals. This final episode returns the poem to its chiastic beginnings: the wealth brought from the dragon's cave echoes Scyld's golden treasure, the war-gear in which Beowulf is posthumously dressed is reminiscent of Scyld's funerary battle-dress, and the Geatish woman who mourns during Beowulf's cremation recalls the grieving community of the Danes who watch Scyld's boat launch. Likewise, even as the wooden hull of Scyld's boat returns as kindling for Beowulf's funeral pyre, the architecture of the dragon's barrow cave produces Beowulf's barrow. In an energetic display of interlace and chiasmus, the Epilogue employs building materials from its earliest and most recent episodes in order to complete the double construction of *Beowulf*'s poetic barrow, an aesthetic form that has been materially finished.

Beowulf's poetic barrow does not simply reflect historical engagements between land and people. To borrow the language of Aranye Fradenburg, it is a 'representatio[n]' that 'show[s] us where we might or might not live.'[33] It shows us who we might or might not (want to) be. It is a material territory and an expressive one. As a form that is continuously produced and refigured by means of chiasmus and interlace, *Beowulf*'s barrow is, as Fradenburg writes, 'always, already multiply transformed,' estranged, and 'elsewhere.'[34] Like the material earthworks and the dying and living practices that it replicates, *Beowulf* is a territory that is open and forever becoming, 'for the meaning of territory is mobility and expressivity.'[35] Its barrow does not direct 'us' towards a particular place or people in northern Europe[36] but towards a 'home' that abides in its poetic form.[37]

---

33 L.O. Aranye Fradenburg, 'Life's Reach: Territory, Display, Ekphrasis,' in *Staying Alive: A Survival Manual for the Liberal Arts,* ed. Eileen A. Joy (Brooklyn: punctum books, 2013), 227.
34 Ibid., 228.
35 Ibid., 229.
36 For recent attempts at locating the poem in the landscape and in specific geographies, see Sam Newton, *The Origins of* Beowulf *and the Pre-Viking Kingdom of East Anglia* (Cambridge: D.S. Brewer, 1993); John D. Niles, Beowulf *and Lejre* (Tempe: Arizona Center for Medieval and Renaissance Studies, 2007); and Leonard Niedorf, ed., *The Dating of Beowulf: A Reassessment* (Suffolk: D.S. Brewer, 2014). Assigning a composition date and location to this poem has, historically, been one of the most contentious areas of *Beowulf* scholarship. While the motives and emotions that surround arguments about the poem's provenance remain undiscussed by the scholarly community, a recent review of Leonard Niedorf's *The Transmission of Beowulf: Language, Culture, and Scribal Behavior* (Ithaca: Cornell University Press, 2017), suggests that identity politics underwrite these, at times uncivil, debates. Reviewer Craig Davis, for example, points to Niedorf's 'unusual devotion…for an early *Beowulf* that is written by 'Anglian peoples' who replicate the poetic forms and narratives of 'Germanic-speaking migrants to Britain' who come from 'the ancestral homeland of the Angles in Schleswig' ('The Transmission of "Beowulf"', *The Medieval Review,* September 30, 2018, https://scholarworks.iu.edu/journals/index.php/tmr/article/view/25665). Niedorf's 'devotion' to and his arguments for a Migration-Era *Beowulf* sound very much like those of John Mitchell Kemble, whose racial ideologies, this chapter will argue much later, position *Beowulf* on the Anglo-Saxon branch of the Teutonic family tree.
37 Mary Kate Hurley, 'Ruins of the Past: Beowulf and Bethlehem Steel,' *The Heroic Age: A Journal of Early Medieval Northwestern Europe* 13 (August 2010), https://www.heroicage.org/issues/13/ba.php.

For Beowulf, however, the poem's barrow-shaped home becomes an increasingly complicated place in which to live. On the outer perimeters of Prologue and Epilogue, Danes and Geats point the rituals commemorating the deaths of Scyld and Beowulf in the direction of community survival. In other words, the dying practices that take place at the beginning and end of the poem are circuited to and woven into living strategies that take place during the poem's Interludes. Danes and Geats circulate across the narrative surfaces of *Beowulf*'s barrow, moving always towards the post-war celebrations that take place atop its plateaued surfaces. Unlike the communities with which he is associated, Beowulf repeatedly finds himself engaged in combat within the poem's architectures. As he fights to protect Danish and Geatish communities — to maintain living practices that not only negotiate relationships between these two peoples but also distinguish humans from monsters — he discovers the mortuary interior of *Beowulf*'s poetic barrow.

Nested within the poem's Interlude ring structure is *Beowulf*'s Second Fight with Grendel's mother. Described by Niles as the poem's 'single [chiastic] kernel,' this episode takes Beowulf to the poem's narrative epicenter and to the impossibly deep 'grundwong,' or 'bottom [of the mere]' of Grendelkin.[38] Yet, archaeological assessments of this underwater cave and Beowulf's fight inside it reframe this space as a barrow's mortuary interior. The chiastic kernel of the poem, in association with the arguments of mortuary archaeology, reveals the home of Grendelkin as the deep, funerary center of *Beowulf*'s barrow territory.

As Patrick Geary and Howard Williams have remarked, the cave of Grendelkin is described like a barrow, a place that during the later Anglo-Saxon period was believed to be haunted by monsters and revenants.[39] Beowulf enters, fights Grendel's mother, and mutilates Grendel in a supernatural battle that ech-

---

38 Niles, 'Ring Composition and the Structure of *Beowulf*,' 924.
39 Patrick J. Geary, *Living with the Dead in the Middle Ages* (Ithaca: Cornell University Press, 1994), 67; Williams, *Death and Memory in Early Medieval Britain*, 172; and Semple, 'A Fear of the Past,' 109–36.

oes the practice of early medieval 'mound-breaking': 'dramatic, staged events' in which individuals tunnel into and destroy the skeletons, grave goods, and burial tableau within a barrow.[40] Mound-breaking can serve a variety of functions that range from 'punishment/revenge, neutralization of the dead, humiliation of a defeated enemy, trophy hunting or destruction of memory,' but upon killing Grendel's mother and decapitating Grendel with a sword that he has found inside this barrow, Beowulf discovers that neither is its rightful occupant.[41] As the sword's blade melts in the monster's hot blood, the poem remarks that Beowulf did not take from this underwater 'wic' ['habitation'],[42] 'many treasures, although he saw many there, except the head and hilt, together, shining treasures' ['maðmæhta ma, þeh he þær monige geseah, / buton þone hafelan ond þa hilt somod / since fage,' ll. 1558a, 1562b].[43] In calling this a *wic* in which Grendelkin dwell, the poem casually marks this place as a temporary home and implicates these monsters as barrow squatters. Moreover, it suggests that the treasures sighted by Beowulf are funerary objects belonging to others. While no physical remains are mentioned that would identify the barrow's rightful occupant, the 'giant's old sword...a work of giants' ['ealdsweord eotenisc... giganta geweorc,' ll. 1558a, 1562b] that he has just used to kill and mutilate Grendelkin suggests that this is a giant's burial chamber. Upon making this discovery, Beowulf takes Grendel's head and the sword's remaining hilt, then leaves the barrow. In these actions, his acts of mound-breaking become acts of grave-rob-

---

40 Jan Bill and Aoife Daly, 'The Plundering of the Ship Graves from Osenberg and Gokstad: An Example of Power Politics?' *Antiquity* 86, no. 333 (2012): 818.
41 Christoph Kümmel, quoted in Bill and Daly, 'The Plundering of the Ship Graves from Osenberg and Gokstad,' 818.
42 In addition to its primary definition as 'a dwelling-place, abode, habitation, residence, lodging, quarters,' *wic* can also reference 'a temporary abode, a camp, place where one stops,' or more suggestively, 'a place where a thing remains' (*Bosworth-Toller Dictionary*).
43 All citations are by line number to R.D. Fulk, Robert E. Bjork, and John D. Niles, eds., *Klaeber's* Beowulf: *Fourth Edition* (Toronto: University of Toronto, 2008). All translations from Old English are my own.

bing, an early medieval practice in which the deceased's body and grave goods were subject to intentional disturbance, mutilation, and looting.[44]

Whether an act of mound-breaking or of grave-robbing, archaeologists Hella Eckardt and Howard Williams point to this particular moment in *Beowulf* as one that 'illustrate[s] the importance attached to entering into ancient tombs to retrieve old objects...usually swords,' and they explain that although a trespass, this action was 'an important social process by which [early medieval] communities *physically* reordered their histories and memories.'[45] Eckardt and Williams's comments ring true for the Danish and Geatish communities that celebrate during the poem's Interludes. Beowulf's triumphs over Grendel and his mother allow Heorot's denizens to live without fear of future attack, to celebrate together in the hall, and subsequently to enable Hrothgar and Hygelac to reestablish a *comitatus* broken by Hrethel. Further still, Beowulf's encounter with the giant's sword enables him to eradicate and mutilate the monsters that have intruded upon Heorot's peace and God's cosmology. For Danes and Geats, Beowulf's physical actions reorder community history and memory. In the process, they disassemble and reassemble what it means not only to be Danish and Geatish, but moreover to be human.

Yet barrows are not made to be penetrated, disturbed, or looted. Their mortuary interiors, which harbor a decomposing body and grave goods, are intentionally arranged into a burial tableau.

---

44 For discussions of early medieval grave robbing and reopening, see Bill and Daly, 'The Plundering of the Ship Graves from Osenberg and Gokstad'; Edeltraud Aspöck, 'Past "Disturbances" of Graves as a Source: Taphonomy and Interpretation of Reopened Early Medieval Inhumation Graves at Brunn am Gebirge (Austria) and Winnall II (England),' *Oxford Journal of Archaeology* 30, no. 3 (2011): 299–324; and Sean Lafferty, 'Ad sanctitatem mortuorum: Tomb Raiders, Body Snatchers and Relic Hunters in Late Antiquity,' *Early Medieval Europe* 22, no. 3 (2014): 249–79.

45 Hella Eckardt and Howard Williams, 'Objects Without a Past? The Use of Roman Objects in Anglo-Saxon Graves,' in *Archaeologies of Remembrance: Death and Memory in Past Societies*, ed. Howard Williams (New York: Springer, 2003), 145, 144, my emphasis.

This 'poetic' scene, Martin Carver explains, is composed ritually and according to a particular temporal sequence by those who survive and mourn the deceased.[46] Consequently, Carver, with Howard Williams, explains that it refracts the 'emotive force' of a funeral. It visualizes a dynamic network of death, loss, and grief; reverence, honor, and love; and anger, shame, and relief. The emotional constellation that is created by those who shape the funeral tableau is expressed by the choice, arrangement, and order in which grave goods are placed. Together, these material artifacts transform the barrow's mortuary interior into a territory of dying, which is then covered up with dirt and screened from view so that it might become the invisible foundation upon which a barrow is built and living takes place. To enter a barrow is, consequently, to encounter a territory that, subsequent to the rituals of a funeral, is meant only for the dead because it expresses an identity assemblage that was organized in response to death. For the Danes and Geats, communities that benefit *in absentia* from Beowulf's Second Fight, mound-breaking and grave-robbing are productive strategies. To return to Eckardt and Williams's language, the traumatic 'histories and memories' of Grendelkin's predations upon Heorot are 'physically reordered' by another, whose violent acts make life more livable. For Beowulf, however, opening *Beowulf*'s barrow and robbing the giant's grave (performances enacted by descending into the underwater cave and grundwong of Grendelkin) draw him into its territory of dying. Here, he encounters a sword, part of a funeral tableau that materially broadcasts practices enacted long ago to commemorate an unknown deceased. He activates these identity-oriented practices when he uses the giant's sword to kill and physically mutilate Grendel's mother and her son. However, it is not until Beowulf brings the remaining hilt back to Heorot that these dying practices physically reorder — they disassemble and reassemble; they de- and re-territorialize — him.

---

46 As Carver writes, 'A grave is not simply a text, but a text with attitude, a text inflated with emotion…like poetry it is a palimpsest of allusions, constructed within a certain time and place' ('Burial as Poetry,' 37).

The physical effects of entering and exiting *Beowulf*'s barrow become apparent upon the hero's return to Heorot. Specifically, they extend from a discussion of the sword hilt, the only piece of loot that Beowulf has brought back from the grave:

> Hroðgar maðelode,   hylt sceawode,
> ealde lafe.   On ðæm wæs or writen
> fyrngewinnes: syðþan flod ofsloh,
> gifen geotende   giganta cyn,
> frecne geferdon;   Þæt wæs fremde þeod
> ecean dryhtne;   him þæs endelean
> þurh wæteres wylm   waldend sealde.
> Swa wæs on ðæm scennum   sciran goldes
> þurh runstafas   rihte gemearcod,
> geseted ond gesæd,   hwam þæt sweord geworht,
> irena cyst   ærest wære,
> wreoþenhilt   ond wyrmfah. (ll. 1687–98a)

[Hrothgar spoke, he looked at the hilt, the old heirloom, on which was written the origins of former strife, when the flood — the rushing ocean — destroyed the community of giants. They fared terribly. That was a people estranged from the eternal Lord; the Ruler gave them a final retribution for that by means of the surging of water. So it was on that metal plate of shining gold marked, set down, and said in runic [or secret] letters, correctly, for whom [or by whom] that sword was made, the best of swords [that] was first made with a twisted hilt and serpentine patterning.]

As he looks upon the hilt's engraved surfaces, Hrothgar explains that, once upon a time, God sent a flood to destroy a community of giants. Despite their terrible suffering and estrangement from God, some of them seem to have survived. The inclusion of this hilt in a giant's funeral tableau shapes a territory of dying according to expressions of emotional duress and physical survival in the face of total community destruction. Hrothgar's narrative emerges from looking and touching the secret letters [*runstafas*], metal plate [*ðæm scennum sciran goldes*], twisted sides [*wreoþenhilt*], and serpentine pattern [*wyrmfah*] of the hilt. His statements are prompted by an object that does not document the past but materially displays and gestures towards the identity assemblages of those who have been affected by it.

Hrothgar's words and the hilt's visual imagery collaborate to produce an ekphrasis that draws forth a previously unknown territory of dying from the mortuary *wic* of Grendelkin into Heorot. A term of literary criticism and art history, ekphrasis has been understood traditionally as the detailed description of an object. Over the past two decades, however, it has undergone extensive redefinition.[47] No longer considered to be a mimetic form, and no longer defined in relation to the exclusive pairing of verbal text with visual image,[48] ekphrasis can be understood simply as the imagistic 'response' in one medium to an image that is presented in another medium.[49] As a response rather than as a representation, ekphrasis not only enacts a non-hierarchical intermingling between media but also functions as a performative agent. For some scholars, the performative agency

---

47 See Renate Brosch, ed., *Contemporary Exphrasis,* a special issue a special issue of *Poetics Today* 39, no. 2 (2018), for a survey of past understandings of ekphrasis and current reconsiderations of the concept.
48 Beginning in the late 1990s, scholars began to challenge the twentieth-century definition of ekphrasis as a specifically verbal representation of a visual representation. See, especially, Claus Clüver, 'Ekphrasis Reconsidered: On Verbal Representations of Non-Verbal Texts,' in *Interart Poetics: Essays on the Interrelations of the Arts and Media,* eds. Ulla-Britta Lagerroth, Hans Lund, and Erik Hedling (Amsterdam: Rodopi, 1997), 19–33, and 'Quotation, Enargeia, and the Function of Ekphrasis,' in *Pictures into Words: Theoretical and Descriptive Approaches to Ekphrasis,* eds. Valerie Robillard and Els Jongeneel (Amsterdam: VU University Press, 1998), 21–34. In 2000, Siglind Bruhn radically redefined the concept as 'representation in one medium of a real or fictitious text composed in another medium' (*Musical Ekphrasis: Composers Responding to Poetry and Painting* [Hillsdale: Pendragon Press, 2000], 8). Ekphrasis has since been used in discussions of theatricalization, film, *tableau vivant*, and digital works, to name a few, all of which rhetorically expound upon the text of a different medium.
49 Renate Brosch, 'Ekphrasis in the Digital Age: Responses to Image,' *Poetics Today* 39, no. 2 (2018): 227.

of ekphrasis gives it material depth and dimensionality. Timothy Morton explains that vivid, often dramatic and imaginative, statements descriptively generate an object, the expressive 'spaciousness' and enduring 'nowness' of which exceed the borders of its narrative frame.[50] Fradenburg refines this position when she explains that 'the ekphrastic object is nearly always a relic, living on, undead.'[51] Morton's and Fradenburg's thinking allows us to explore the hilt as a reliquary object of the barrow that gathers material 'spaciousness,' temporal 'nowness,' and 'undead' animation via Hrothgar's description. Suspended in space, time, and movement as a thing undead, the hilt does not simply represent a diluvian story or the funerary world of giants. Via ekphrasis, its engravings of past war, flood, destruction, duress, and survival acquire dimensionality and performative agency. They objectively display and gesture, extending an assembly of identity-making forces in space and in time. The hilt's ekphrasis reaches out beyond the barrow's mortuary interior and beyond the time of the giant's funeral. In Heorot, *ekphrasis shows us a territory that once was lost and enables us to find it over and over.*

As an object that performs outside and beyond its spatiotemporal origins, the hilt's ekphrastic displays seek interactions and generate a response. Unwittingly, when Beowulf uses the hilt to kill Grendel's mother and decapitate Grendel, he activates the full force of the hilt's dying practices and wipes out the suffering and estranged community of Grendelkin. Consequently, Hrothgar's meditation upon the hilt proceeds to a meditation upon Beowulf's fate, and the hilt's territory of dying exacts its territorializing forces upon Beowulf's living body. Hrothgar warns:

Nu is þines   mægnes blæd
ane hwile;   eft sona bið,
þæt þec adl   oððe ecg eafoþes getwæfeð,
oððe fyres feng,   oððe flodes wylm,

---

50 Timothy Morton, 'An Object-Oriented Defense of Poetry,' *New Literary History* 43, no. 2 (2012): 222.
51 Fradenburg, 'Life's Reach,' 265.

oððe gripe meces,   oððe gares fliht,
oððe atol yldo;   oððe eagena bearhtm
forsiteð ond forsworceð;   semninga bið,
þæt ðec, dryhtguma,   deað oferswyðeð. (ll. 1761b–67a)

[Now is the glory of your power but a little while; presently, in turn, it will be that disease or the sword will deprive you of strength, or the grip of the fire or the surging of a wave, or attack of a sword or the flight of a spear, or terrible old age; or the brightness of your eyes will fail and become dim. Suddenly, death will overpower you, warrior.]

Hostile enemies, sickness, and infirmity encroach upon the safe borders of Beowulf's body, serially, simultaneously, and crossmodally. The fire's grip, the wave's surge, the sword's attack, and the spear's flight enact a catalogue of protracted physical traumas that are stretched across an unending temporal moment that is 'now' ['nu'], for 'a little while' ['ane while'], 'presently, in turn' ['eft sona'], and 'all of a sudden' ['semninga']. Like the material spaciousness of the hilt and the nowness of its temporality, Beowulf is caught up in the de- and re-territorializing forces that once physically reordered Grendelkin and now physically reorder him. Yet, unlike Grendel and his mother, who are killed by a blade, the hilt's ekphrasis transforms Beowulf into a rhetorical canvas upon which disasters sequentially and simultaneously erupt. Amidst total ruin, he survives. Beowulf lives on, suspended between the forces of fire and wave, sword and spear, old age and infirmity. He acquires dimension with each poetic turn. The words 'oððe…oððe…oððe' become a delicate refrain that not only invites tragedy but also animates his form with descriptive texture and drama. Like the hilt, Beowulf is transformed into a reliquary object that has been totally ruined in its production process; his warrior's body has been unforged and made undead. To return again to Fradenburg, Beowulf, like the hilt, is a relic that has become ekphrastic: 'embellish[ed]' and 'art[ful],' restively alive, even in death.⁵²

As an ekphrastic object, Beowulf exceeds his status as a human participant in the world of the poem and is now a communicative form. He is a zone of contact between the living practices of Geats and Danes who circulate across the barrow's exterior surfaces and the dying practices of an unnamed community of giants that has been buried and hidden within the barrow's funerary interior. In drawing together *Beowulf*'s barrow territories of life and death, Beowulf functions as an undead, liminal zone that stretches across the poem's territorial strata. Is he a monster or a hero? An adopted Dane or a Geat? Beowulf's ekphrasis prompts us to ask not only who he is but moreover who we are. These communicative aspects are a crucial part of ekphrasis. As Liliane Louvel argues, 'the performative aspect of visually imbued texts' phenomenologically affects the reader, 'work[ing] on our senses, on our percepts, emotions, and bodies.'⁵³ While the readers of Beowulf (and the hilt) are communities within the poem, for Louvel, the reader is extra-textual — a point to which this chapter will return. As 'word and image…time and space' are 'blend[ed]' together, the reader's body is 'moved, "seized" by ekphrasis, she — the reader — "is activated".'⁵⁴ She 'reach[es] unheard-of or unspoken truths' and links 'memory and imagination' across time and space.⁵⁵ *Ekphrasis prompts emotional and embodied responses that reassemble identity in relation to the territory from which it emerges.*

It is important to note that this is not the first time that Beowulf has entered and emerged from a barrow. From Heorot to the Grendelkin's mere, from the dragon's *beorg* to his own *biorh,* Beowulf constantly enters and exits each of the poem's increasingly barrow-shaped structures, the last of which circuits back, via chiasmus, to Scyld's funeral. Indeed, as Niles's

---

52 Ibid., 109.
53 Liliane Louvel, 'Types of Ekphrasis: An Attempt at Classification,' *Poetics Today* 39, no. 2 (2018): 247, 259.
54 Ibid., 259.
55 Ibid.

diagram (see Figure 1 above) and his essay make clear, each of these episodes is organized according to its own internal ring structure (and interlace patterns). *Beowulf* therefore reveals itself to be internally populated with barrows. As Beowulf moves in and out of this virtual barrow cemetery, he becomes more like to the dead than to the living with each entrance and exit (see Figures 4 and 5), and he prompts ever more complex questions about Danes, Geats, and ourselves. Thus, *Beowulf* is not a single or a singular barrow territory that, all at once, transforms dying practices into living practices. Rather, it is an expanding network of mortuary 'homes' to which Beowulf returns 'again and again' in order to navigate the ever-becoming but never-the-same process of identity making that phenomenologically impacts the emotions and bodies of many different communities across many different times.[56]

Tumuli, Antiquarian Mourners, and Undead Saxons

Throughout the early modern period, barrows remained dynamic sites of community activity and continued to function as landscapes engaged with a variety of living practices.[57] However, as Nicola Whyte explains, the rapid enclosure of open fields

---

56 Fradenburg, 'Life's Reach,' 265.
57 For example, as Nicola Whyte explains, early modern communities continued to recognize the boundary-making function of barrows. Barrows were 'key focal points along customary routes' that separated parishes and estates and were used by seigniorial lords to designate the boundaries of fold-course territories as late as the mid-eighteenth century. Likewise, the early medieval function of barrows as meeting places 'continued to structure territorial jurisdictions into the post-medieval period,' and Whyte cites examples from early modern court cases that evidence that the annual leet courts of Great Fransham, Great Dunham, Kempstone, and Beeston took place at barrows. In addition, Whyte suggests the ongoing connection between barrows and early modern gallows sites, and, as an example, she references an eighteenth-century map of South Acre, 'which depicts a number of apparently extant barrows on "Gallow Hill Heath," possibly the remains of the Anglo-Saxon *cwealmstow*' (*Inhabiting the Landscape: Place, Custom and Memory, 1500–1800* [Oxford: Windgather Press at Oxbow, 2009], 146–54).

Figure 4. Cliff Hoppitt, aerial photograph of Sutton Hoo. Image courtesy of Cliff Hoppitt.

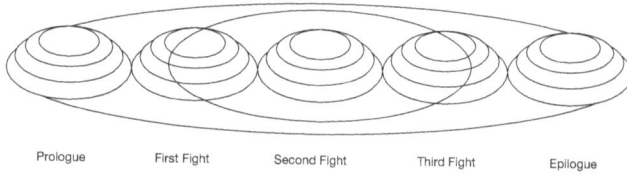

Figure 5. Author's diagram, inspired by Sutton Hoo aerial photo, which maps how the internal and overarching ring structures of the poem work together.

during the eighteenth and nineteenth centuries rendered them unavailable as area landmarks and for public use.[58] No longer territories on the landscape or territorial expressions of local peoples, barrows were rapidly destroyed.[59] For antiquarian James Douglas, however, barrows are exciting places that warehouse Britain's ancestors, material culture, and history. When he excavates their mortuary interiors, Douglas engages early medieval barrows once again as geopolitical and expressive territories, arranging fragments of bone and artifacts into complete historical portraits that he describes and illustrates in his archaeological report, *Nenia Britannica*. In the process, Douglas is emotionally and physically reordered by their ekphrastic displays. His embodied emotions, affects, and performances are re-figured, and his identity assemblage is de- and re-territorialized. While Douglas is a respondent to the ekphrasis of grave goods and human remains, his embodied and emotional performances have a transformative effect on the medieval barrows from which they emerge. As Douglas interprets its funerary contents, the barrow becomes a new kind of territory—an antiquarian one—and Douglas comes to identify the early medieval peoples interred within these barrows as Saxons.

In his preface to *Nenia Britannica*, James Douglas touches upon changes in British barrows. According to Douglas, barrows have now become remote places. On 'barren ground; on commons, moors…[and]…near villages, of no great name or importance in history…it is only by a casual discovery with the plow, or the accidental use of the spade and pick-axe, that the contents of these interments have been found.'[60] No longer a site around which communities settle and assemble, and also stake

---

58 Ibid., 163.
59 Graeme Kirkham, '"Rip it up, and spread it over the field": Post-Medieval Agriculture and the Destruction of Monuments; A Case Study from Cornwall,' *Landscapes* 13, no. 2 (2012): 1–20.
60 Douglas, *Nenia Britannica*, 1. Douglas's assessment contradicts extensive evidence by Nicola Whyte that points towards the continued relevance of barrows to communities living in the later medieval and early modern periods (*Inhabiting the Landscape*, 146–54).

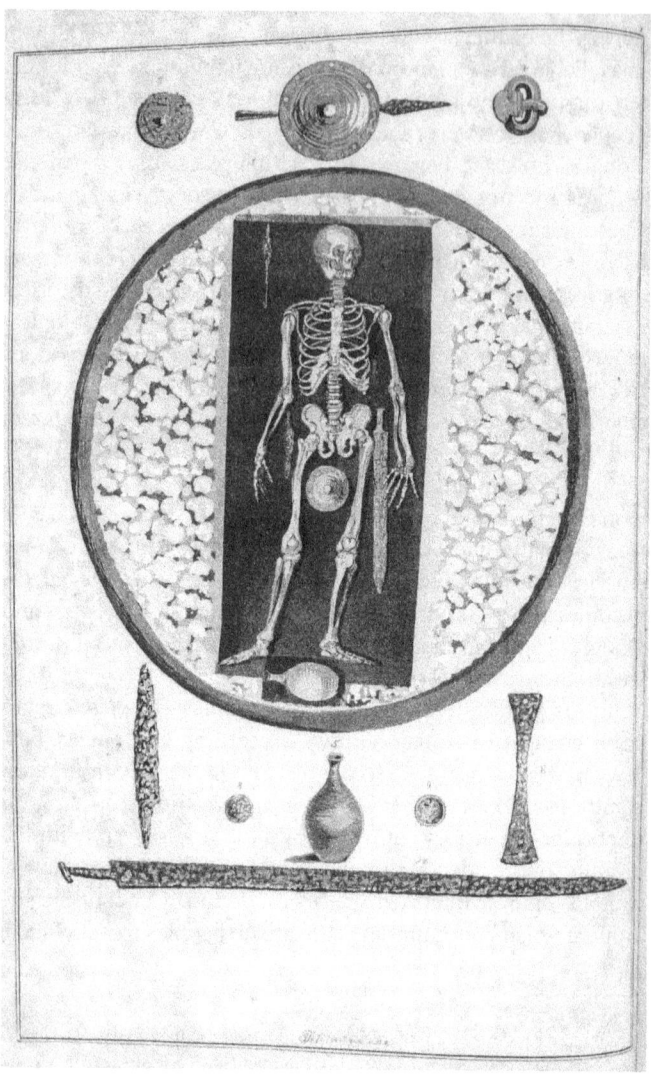

Figure 6a. Aquatint of numbered artifacts from 'Tumulus 1' at Chatham, Kent, in James Douglas, *Nenia Britannica; or, A sepulchral history of Great Britain* (London: Printed by John Nichols; for George Nicol, in Pall-Mall, Bookseller to his Majesty, 1793), 2. Image courtesy of The Newberry Library.

Figure 6b. Tumulus I in James Douglas, *Nenia Britannica; or, A sepulchral history of Great Britain* (London: Printed by John Nichols; for George Nicol, in Pall-Mall, Bookseller to his Majesty, 1793), 2. Image courtesy of The Newberry Library.

out their borders and do battle, Britain's barrows are incompatible with and incidental to contemporary agricultural and industrial modes of living. For the antiquarian, however, the opening up of a barrow with a 'spade and pick-axe' is not a 'casual' or 'accidental…discovery,' but an intentional activity.

On the first page of *Nenia Britannica*'s archaeological report, in the middle of a plate of artifact illustrations, is a figure numbered '1.' 'Figure 1' presents the outline of a ring ditch, sedimentary fill, and a rectangular coffin (see Figure 6a). In its center, accompanied by a variety of weapons, stands a skeleton that is remarkably intact and strangely vibrant. Its skull is in slight profile, its right hand leans upon its spear and touches a seax, its left hand reaches for its sword, and its right foot is out-turned in a gentlemanly stance. Armed and at the ready, this skeleton is stylized according to late-eighteenth century portraiture, impressing upon the viewer that these bones need only a little flesh on them in order for this long-dead 'warrior' to come alive. Figure 1 turns his head and casts his eyes across the page towards 'TUMULUS I.,' 'Fig. 1' (see Figure 6b).

The page-long description that accompanies and contextualizes the illustration states that 'Fig[ure] 1. represents the horizontal section of a tumulus opened on the Chatham Lines*.'[61] The asterisk that marks the end of this clause draws the reader's eye towards a lengthy footnote, which explains that when 'labourers and soldiers…travers[ed] a range of these small *tumuli*' in order to dig out the defensive earthworks — the Lines — that surround the military town of Chatham, Kent, they dig up 'some spear-heads, umbos of shields, and a few other fragments of arms.'[62] For Douglas, 'opening' the barrows at Chatham is a productive activity. In the physical motion of carving out earth, new earthworks are built, and old ones are disturbed. Military men of the present tense encounter military artifacts of the past.

Douglas seems to sense the de- and re-territorializing stakes of excavation, and upon drawing together Chatham's Lines and

---

61 Douglas, *Nenia Britannica*, 3.
62 Ibid.

barrows, its martial bodies and artifacts, he imagines a similar bridge between military and mortuary geographies. Positioned on 'the western slope of the steep hill,' which 'descend[s] to the barrack gate' of the Kentish militia, Douglas explains that Chatham's barrows are 'bounded' and 'enclose[d]' on the 'extremity' and 'interior' by the militia's barrack-wall and the Lines's retaining wall.[63] Douglas's cartography redistricts the landscape. Clustered together on a hilltop slope and routed towards the entryway of a soldier's living quarters, Douglas's language transforms Chatham's barrows into a military territory that 'descends' to and is surrounded by a military settlement.[64] These geopolitical acts have a transformative effect on Chatham's soldiers. When Douglas begins to recount their excavations a second time, the unnamed assemblage of 'labourers and soldiers' that once 'traversed' a 'range of...*tumuli*' is replaced by a 'Hanoverian encampment' that is 'situated on them.'[65] This Germanic military body no longer freely crosses the landscapes of the dead but temporarily settles on them. As they dwell here, they sink into the grave, becoming secondary inhabitants that Douglas himself now claims to excavate. He identifies Chatham's 'Hanoverian encampment' only by way of 'the remains of the[ir]...kitchens,' which 'were to be seen on the centre of the burial ground.'[66]

Although Douglas was a member of the Kentish militia, an engineer on the Chatham Lines, and a supervisor of its earthworks, he did not physically engage in the labor of barrow excavation. The artifacts dug up by soldiers and recovered from Chatham's barrows found their way to Douglas's office,[67] where he collected and then examined, sketched, and engraved them, arranging his representations of bone and funerary objects onto lithographic plates. In his office, not in the field, Douglas excavates from his armchair. As he handles materials that have been

---

63 Douglas, *Nenia Britannica*, 3n*.
64 Ibid.
65 Ibid.
66 Ibid.
67 Jessup, *Man of Many Talents*, 25.

brought out of Tumulus I, Douglas (re)arranges them. He positions bones and artifacts such that a dead Saxon and its funeral tableau suggest the posture and stance of Chatham's living soldiers.

Within the first pages of *Nenia Britannica*, Douglas refigures Chatham's barrows—remote places of little interest to nearby communities—into what appears to be a military territory. Then he fills this territory with soldier occupants. While Douglas identifies the soldiers who excavate Tumulus I as Hanoverian (an adjective that references the Germanic origins of Britain's current monarch), he says nothing about the skeleton's identity. Towards the end of *Nenia Britannica*, however, Douglas makes historical assessments about British *tumuli* and barrow artifacts that draw Chatham's military territory and the living practices of its Hanoverian soldiers towards a Germanic past. In a lengthy 'OBSERVATIONS' section, Douglas rightly notes that Anglo-Saxon barrows are small, round, and often appear in clusters. Likewise, he dates them to the pre-Christian period, which extends from 'the year 429 [when] the Saxons arrived' to 'the admission of cemeteries within the walls and near to churches anno 742.'[68] Douglas further connects these Saxon barrows by evaluating their grave goods. Specifically, he focuses on 'the nature of the arms, the most convincing proof of a parity of custom,' and he cross-references the illustration of a Saxon soldier in a manuscript copy of Prudentius's *Psychomachia* with a sword from Tumulus I, the shield boss of Tumulus VII, and '[s]pears, knives, and axes,' which Douglas claims to have 'in great numbers.'[69] Douglas further surmises that these weapons burials identify Saxons who were either not 'peasantry' or 'under military enrolment.'[70] Douglas's observations bear heavily upon the grave plan of Tumulus I. The circular ditch, which is drawn tightly around a skeleton's coffin, resembles Douglas's statements regarding the size and shape of Saxon barrows. The

---

68 Douglas, *Nenia Britannica*, 127, 128.
69 Ibid., 128, 128n1, 128n3.
70 Ibid., 128n4.

weaponry inside the grave suggests the identity of a pre-Christian, migration-period Saxon male who is either of high rank or enrolled as a foot soldier.

The barrows at Chatham seem to be a military territory shaped by its Lines and barracks and the activities of its soldiers. However, when Douglas makes assessments regarding the funerary aspects of these barrows, they become, first and foremost, an antiquarian territory. It is constructed from Douglas's office, rather than from the excavation site, and according to his semi-professional assessments of barrow landscape features and grave goods. Douglas directs the living places and practices of Chatham's Germanic (Hanoverian) community towards the dying places and practices of another Germanic (Saxon) community. He positions a military territory within an antiquarian one and, in so doing, reassembles — de- and re-territorializes — the identity assemblages of Britain's present and past Germanic soldiers.

Douglas presents this re- and de-territorialized Saxon soldier visually in Tumulus I. Its skeletal body and the military grave goods that surround it represent the bone and artifacts that were excavated from a Chatham barrow, sent to Douglas's militia office, then arranged according to *Nenia Britannica*'s antiquarian assessments. As a consequence, this skeleton seems to move and to step out of its grave, such that Figure 1 becomes an object. Its physical body and material grave goods extend the intertwined identity-making performances of two different groups of Germanic soldiers from their spatiotemporal domains in Chatham's barrows towards the new domain of Tumulus I. As an object that not only provides access to barrow territories that have been destroyed through excavation but, moreover, enables the viewer to re-find these territories over and over, again, each time she looks at its illustrated grave plan, Figure 1 of Tumulus I reveals itself to be ekphrastic. It is a warrior-relic that 'liv[es] on, undead' in the eternal 'nowness' of Tumulus I.[71] As ekph-

---

71 Fradenburg, 'Life's Reach,' 265; Morton, 'An Object-Oriented Defense of Poetry,' 222.

rasis, figure 1 performs in order to seek a phenomenological response that, to recall Liliane Louvel, 'works on our senses, on our percepts, *emotions*, and *bodies*'.[72] Therefore, when it looks across the page at 'TUMULUS I' (see Figure 6b), its gaze settles on the illustration located above this statement.[73] In this illustration, an unnamed person sits on top of an unexcavated barrow. He clasps a scythe in one hand and an urn in another, materials of grief and collecting that suggest he is an antiquarian.[74] In a lengthy footnote regarding a *tumulus* near Broom, Kent, Douglas clarifies not only the barrow-sitter's antiquarian identity but also the antiquarian's emotional and embodied responses to Figure 1's ekphrastic gaze.

Before turning to Broom, it is important to note that Chatham's barrows were the first that Douglas encountered. Subsequent to Chatham, Douglas becomes, arguably, obsessed with British barrows, overseeing the excavation of hundreds of mounds over the course of his lifetime.[75] At Broom, a site he excavated long after Chatham, Douglas claims that his 'restless' 'spirit' has the all-consuming urge to 'ransack' graves. While Douglas's excavations at Broom prompt in him reckless behav-

---

72 Louvel, 'Types of Ekphrasis,' 259 (my emphasis).
73 See note 2 above.
74 While *Nenia* is a Latin word that references a funeral song, a song of lament, or a dirge, its meaning becomes a point of contention immediately after the book's publication. In August 1793, an anonymous reviewer smugly writes that 'the title itself is objectionable, and only applicable to a dissertation on the funeral songs of the ancient Britons' ('Douglas's *Nenia Britannica*,' *The Critical Review: Or, Annals of Literature* 8 [1793]: 415). The following month, in the October edition of the *Gentleman's Magazine*, Douglas rebuts his reviewer, arguing, upon the authority of Festus, that 'Nenia' references a goddess, not a dirge, and claiming that before his death Samuel Johnson gave Douglas his personal blessing for the title ('Mr. Douglas's "Nenia Britannica"', *Gentleman's Magazine* [October 1793]: 881).
75 According to Jessup, '[b]y 1782, something like 86 barrows or levelled graves [at Chatham] had been opened and their contents described and sometimes carefully drawn…In all, if we may depend on later topographers such as G.A. Cooke in the 1819 edition of his *Pocket County Directory of Kent*, Douglas opened no less than 100 graves' (*Man of Many Talents*, 24).

iors, he cautions that '[t]ragical abominations' can result from the antiquarian's protracted attachments to the dead.[76] Douglas quotes from Sir Thomas Browne's *Hydriotaphia,* a report on urn-burial in Norfolk and a work that not only confuses excavating the dead with mourning them but also recognizes that there are psychic consequences for the antiquarian who desires to maintain these emotional ties once the excavation is over. As Browne and Douglas, who quotes him, explain, should the excavator be unable to set aside her mourning — should she desire to maintain her relationship with the dead — she may unconsciously incorporate them. In other words, she may position her affections for and memories of the dead within her unconscious such that they continue to live within her. She may build a psychic crypt for them so that they can inhabit her.[77] Douglas, quoting Browne, describes the effects of incorporation when he writes that to excavate is 'to be gnawed out of our graves,' to have 'our skulls' and 'our bones' crafted into 'drinking bowls' and 'tobacco pipes,' instruments meant for imbibing and inhaling the spirits of the dead.[78] In order to avoid attachments that lead to the formation of psychic crypts, Douglas, following Browne, re-

---

76 Douglas, *Nenia Britannica,* 39 (unnumbered note).
77 These psychoanalytic concepts are discussed and explained extensively in Chapter 2. As Maria Abraham and Nicholas Torok explain, this 'sealed-off psychic space' warehouses the 'exquisite corps[e] of a loved one who we cannot bear to mourn' (*The Shell and the Kernel,* ed. and trans. Nicholas T. Rand [Chicago: Chicago University Press, 1994], 141).
78 Douglas, *Nenia Britannica,* 39n, quoting from Sir Thomas Browne's *Hydriotaphia, urne-buriall, or, a discourse of the sepulchrall urnes lately found in Norfolk* (London: Printed for Hen. Browne at the Signe of the Gun in Ivy-Lane, 1658), 48. Note that Douglas spells 'knav'd' as 'gnawed,' and he amends 'Pipes' to 'tobacco pipes.' Recall from Chapter 2 that in the Old Norse poem *Krákumál,* Ragnar claims that in death he will drink beer from 'the curved-tree of skulls,' an elaborate kenning that references a drinking horn. *Krákumál*'s emphasis on orality engages a rigorous discussion about the psychopolitics of incorporation, and Abraham and Torok associate food and drink imagery which emphasizes illicit acts of swallowing whole with the enactment of incorporation (*The Shell and the Kernel,* 128–29).

vises his relationship to the Broom 'antients' as a post-mortem friendship, a shift in affections that keeps them at arm's length.[79]

Douglas further recalibrates his emotional attachments to the dead at Broom by transforming acts of archaeological grief into acts of professional collecting. Douglas explains that he removes human remains from a barrow and puts them into a curiosity 'cabinet' where 'rotten bones' become '*everlasting treasures.*'[80] As collectibles, however, another's bone and ash press Douglas's own body in the direction of the grave, for as he touches, arranges, and looks upon them, he imagines himself, in the third person, 'mouldering in his own sepulchre' until his decaying body is irreverently exhumed.[81] Despite all of his cautionary words and measures, Douglas's mourning is protracted through his collecting, and by means of these antiquarian activities, Douglas finds himself suspended in a state of living death. In order to breathe vitality into his own body, Douglas returns to his cabinet, where he discards the 'everlasting treasures' of his friend's remains, replaces them with 'a little superfluous treasure,' then piously re-inters the body within its barrow.[82]

If Douglas continues to mourn the dead at Broom, has he incorporated them? Has a psychic crypt formed within his unconscious? Regardless of whether or not Douglas physically dug up the graves at Broom, his narrative presents excavation as a physically—and emotionally—charged endeavor for the antiquarian. These highly dynamic performances of ransacking graves, mourning ancient friends, and collecting their bones result in physical and emotional transformations. To put it in Deleuzoguattarian terms, Douglas stages excavation as a de- and re-territorializing activity. His mind and body—his embodied mind—are subject to radical shifts in identity. Douglas says nothing else in *Nenia Britannica* regarding excavation. However, when Douglas's mourning and collecting are associated with the

---

79 Ibid.
80 Ibid (Douglas's emphasis).
81 Ibid.
82 Ibid.

image of the barrow-sitter, his antiquarian practices show themselves to be refracted in its scythe and urn. The barrow-sitter stands in, visually, for Douglas, who responds to the ekphrastic gaze of the Saxon foot-soldier: he collects bones and artifacts; he assesses their historical provenance and illustrates them; then, he arranges them in a cabinet. These semi-professional movements, which have become Douglas's antiquarian living practices, are expressed in the barrow-sitter's physical posture, affective stance, and proximity to the grave. In short, the Saxon of Figure 1 transforms Douglas's mind and body as he excavates it, and Douglas visually records these de- and re-territorializing displays in his illustration of the barrow-sitter.

In the process of responding to Figure 1, this image of the antiquarian barrow-sitter likewise becomes ekphrastic. It looks across the page and gazes back at the skeletal soldier, whose 'rotten bones' are now vibrantly displayed as 'everlasting treasures,' and whose military grave goods are now 'superfluous treasure.' The barrow-sitter's gaze transforms the Saxon foot-soldier of Figure 1 into the centerpiece of an aesthetically pleasing arrangement, numbered '1' through '10.' The entire collection of treasure is bordered by a thin sepia line, as if it is one virtual 'drawer' of a much larger curiosity cabinet. Suddenly, Tumulus I, along with the other tumuli of *Nenia Britannica*, reveal themselves to be artifact illustrations that Douglas has collected from his and others' barrow excavations.

As both archaeological report and cabinet of antiquarian curiosities, *Nenia Britannica* acknowledges that the early medieval barrow has become a new kind of antiquarian territory by which, to adapt the language of Jean Baudrillard, Douglas 'construct[s]' his own 'mourning' even as the Saxon foot-soldier inside the excavated barrow 'represents [his] own death.'[83] The solitary mourner that grieves on top of an unexcavated TUMULUS I and the excavated skeleton that lies within Tumulus I transform an unopened and forgotten barrow on the Chatham landscape

---

83 Jean Baudrillard, *The System of Objects*, trans. James Benedict (New York: Verso, 2005), 104.

into a site where a Saxon soldier, in proximity to a Hanoverian one, awaits antiquarian recovery. From the materials of an old burial mound, a new territory has been erected. TUMULUS I / Tumulus I—constructed by de- and re-territorializing the living practices of Hanoverian soldiers as the dying practices of Saxons—makes a home out of a grave. Consequently, it is a 'regressiv[e]' territory where, as Baudrillard again might also say, Douglas 'is dead, but he literally survives himself through his collection.'[84] Yet the Saxon soldier and barrow-sitter that occupy this tumulus are figures that have been removed from an actual barrow and positioned within Douglas's *Nenia Britannica*. From the pages of this archaeological report (not from within an early medieval barrow) they broadcast the performative gestures of a soldier and an antiquarian. They operate as an ekphrastic pair. The undead, reliquary forms of an excavated body and its excavator yoke dying to living practices, and they enable all who view them to find this newly created antiquarian territory over and over each time they scan the pages of *Nenia Britannica*. Consequently, although this undead, reliquary pair gaze at one another, they nonetheless seek interactions and responses from others.

Despite the temporal distance, connections abound between the Old English *Beowulf* and James Douglas's *Nenia Britannica*. Both are invested in discussing early medieval barrows, and both are concerned with converting their textual forms into a network of barrows. For *Beowulf*, chiasmus and interlace construct the poem into a barrow cemetery; for *Nenia Britannica*, chapters called *tumuli* transform the archaeological report into book of barrows. By positioning geopolitical territories within literary and archaeological forms, *Beowulf* and *Nenia Britannica* locate the expressive territory of the early medieval barrow. Further, when Beowulf and Douglas loot and excavate mortuary interiors, they encounter ekphrastic displays of weapons and bones that emotionally and physically reorder them. Consequently, Beowulf and Douglas become ekphrastic. Independent

---

84 Ibid., 104.

and unknown to one another, these literary and archaeological figures seek respondents across time and space and into the future.

The conceptual parallels between *Beowulf* and *Nenia Britannica* are extensive, yet these two texts are temporally and territorially distinct. While both are constructed in relation to the early medieval barrow, *Beowulf* and *Nenia Britannica* belong to different moments in time and, consequently, they encounter very different communities who 'live' upon barrow surfaces and 'die' within barrow interiors. *Beowulf*'s Danes, Geats, Gendelkin, and giants are not the soldiers and antiquarians of *Nenia Britannica*. Likewise, Beowulf is not James Douglas. The identity assemblages — the territorializing expressions — that are brought into ekphrastic circulation on the pages of *Beowulf* and *Nenia Britannica* are fundamentally asynchronous. Yet, their shared ekphrasis keeps them on the move, seeking interactions and soliciting responses by way of embodied poesis. Beowulf, the Saxon foot-soldier, and the antiquarian barrow-sitter of Tumulus I circulate in the protracted present, occupying a zone that extends from death to life, and from center to elsewhere, in a constant motion that travels ceaselessly between then and now. As of yet, however, the reliquary body of Beowulf is unknown to the Saxon soldier and barrow-sitter, and this acquaintance will come much later.

Nenia Britannica was dismissed by reviewers upon its publication, and Douglas's widow eventually sold her husband's collection of barrow artifacts to Sir Richard Colt Hoare due to financial need. Yet, as England's nineteenth-century political climate began to emphasize nationalist and imperialist discourses, Douglas and his *Nenia Britannica* begin to gather recognition. In 1819, Hoare gifted Douglas's artifacts to Oxford's Ashmolean Museum, thereby endowing it with the country's most extensive and varied collection of Anglo-Saxon artifacts.[85] In the follow-

---

85 See *A Catalogue of the Ashmolean Museum: Descriptive of the Zoological Specimens, Antiquities, Coins, and Miscellaneous Curiosities* (Oxford: S. Collingwood, 1836), 128–31.

ing years, *Nenia Britannica* gained in popularity among Victorian antiquarians interested in what Douglas had identified as the early Saxon period. These Victorians were motivated historically by a narrative of Saxon conquest of Britain, politically by ideologies of Empire, and genealogically by a belief that the martial character of their Saxon ancestors lived on in Britain's present generation. The excavation, collection, and illustration of certain kinds of grave goods and burial assemblages became critical tools for generating a Saxon racial identity: an inheritable profile of traits that could be mapped onto the behaviors, desires, and physical characteristics of members of Britain's highly militarized empire. As Victorian antiquarians began to oversee the excavation of small round barrows on the British landscape, they employed Douglas's illustrated *tumuli* as an archaeological catalogue to compare and date the artifacts which they found. While a low percentage of these graves contained weapons,[86] antiquarians were keen to recover the material culture of Saxon warrior elites because in their minds, weapons burials refracted the racial profile of imperial Britons. Victorian antiquarians used Douglas's illustration of the Saxon foot-soldier as a template when sketching weapons burials, which they considered, in accordance with Douglas, to be exemplary of the pre-Christian, or early Saxon period.

As Victorian antiquarians assess their barrow excavations in relation to Douglas's Tumulus I, the Saxon soldier and barrow-sitter exceed their function as reference materials.[87] They show

---

[86] Although Douglas emphasizes the great number of arms that he has found in Saxon graves, he admits, in a footnote, that 'it was not in the proportion of one in twenty [barrows] which produced arms of any kind' (*Nenia Britannica*, 128n4).

[87] Archaeologists discuss the ekphrasis of archaeological images, albeit using different terms. As Sam Smiles and Stephanie Moser write, 'archaeological visualization[s]' are 'a coded system' that functions as 'both symbol and communication.' They create what Smiles and Moser call a 'constructed past' that 'produces some of its most long-lasting effects' on the discipline ('Introduction: The Image in Question,' in *Envisioning the Past: Archaeology an the Image*, eds. Sam Smiles and Stephanie Moser [Oxford: Blackwell, 2005], 5, 6). See also Brian Leigh Molyneaux, 'Introduction: The Cultural

these antiquarians a territory where Saxon foot-soldiers stand in their graves as if ready to fight again (and again), and antiquarians make this post-mortem animation possible by performatively mourning and physically collecting Saxon artifacts and bones. Antiquarians respond to the ekphrasis of Tumulus I in mind and in body. They play the role of the barrow-sitter, and, as Douglas predicted, their activities result in the formation of psychic crypts. These Victorian antiquarians are now inhabited by the dead — they are de- and re-territorialized by imaginary performances of excavation. Consequently, when they adapt Douglas's grave plans in order to illustrate newly excavated barrows, Victorians evidence these changes to their own identities by reassembling the physical features and grave goods of Saxon foot-soldiers. As these Victorians re-create the ekphrastic gazes that emerge between the images in Tumulus I, they transform the early medieval barrow once again into an antiquarian territory that is now inhabited by Anglo-Saxons.

Sleeping Saxons, Post-mortem Tenancies, and the Encryption of Race

William Wylie is one of Douglas's Victorian readers. He employs *Nenia Britannica* extensively as a reference that guides him in the writing of his highly influential *Fairford Graves*, an archaeological report on the barrow cemetery at Fairford, Gloucestershire.[88] One grave, excavated on March 7th, becomes the touchstone for his entire excavation. Upon opening it, Wylie remarks, in words that sound as if it they were voiced by Douglas's barrow-sitter, that to the left of the skeleton's head lies a 'sadly decayed' cup

---

Life of Images,' in *The Cultural Life of Images: Visual Representation in Archaeology*, ed. Brian Leigh Molyneaux (New York: Routledge, 1997), 1–10, and Stephanie Moser, 'Archaeological Visualization: Early Artifact Visualization and the Birth of the Archaeological Image,' in *Archaeological Theory Today*, ed. Ian Hodder, 2nd edn. (Cambridge: Polity, 2012), 316–17.

88 William Wylie, *Fairford Graves: A Record of Researches in an Anglo-Saxon Burial Place in Glouchestershire* (Oxford: John Henry Parker, 1852).

that 'still hung together.'[89] Although Wylie's language identifies grief as the affective means by which the cup's decaying pieces of wood and metal remain 'together,' he extends this assessment of the artifact's fragile togetherness in the direction of the excavators who take it out of the ground. Wylie writes, 'we were able to remove it,' and the 'we' of Fairford's excavators becomes the alliterative stave against which Wylie fashions the group's emotional response to the act of physically excavating the cup from its burial site: 'It is wonderful that a wooden vessel should have existed at all for so many centuries, in this wet soil.'[90]

Like *Nenia Britannica*, Wylie's archaeological report underscores barrow digging as embodied acts of mourning and collecting. Note well that despite the language of hands-on excavation, Wylie, like Douglas, was not necessarily present at the Fairford excavation site.[91] Nonetheless, embodied performance and physical movement are key to this scene. Unlike *Nenia*, however, the excavations at Fairford are not solitary activities. An unidentified group reaches for the cup and responds, in unison, to its perpetual decay by mourning it.[92] As this group's excavation shifts from the artifacts at the grave's outer perimeter towards its interior where a body lies, the cup's 'sad decay' and the excavators' collective mourning are amplified by their next find: a 'corroded' sword.[93] This huge sword is tucked underneath an ossified collar bone and extends past radius, ulna, and pha-

---

89 Ibid., 20.
90 Ibid.
91 As Howard Williams explains, Wylie distinguishes the archaeologist, a 'middle-class gentleman and scholar' who interprets artifacts, from the uneducated laborer, who digs them up ('Anglo-Saxon and Victorian Archaeology: William Wylie's *Fairford Graves*,' *Early Medieval Europe* 16, no. 1 [2008]: 62).
92 Elsewhere, William Wylie credits 'Douglas and his modern followers' for antiquarian activities by which 'we have arrived at a more correct apprehension of our own national antiquities,' a statement that extends the purview of Douglas and 'his modern followers' towards an unnamed 'we' that identifies itself by 'our national antiquities' ('The Graves of the Alemanni at Oberflacht in Suabia,' *Archaeologia* 36 [1855]: 129).
93 Wylie, *Fairford Graves*, 20.

langes. It holds together a skeleton's fragmented form despite its own material corrosion. As Fairford's excavators shift their attentions from artifact to bone, Wylie explains that 'it' — this self-same sword — has been found in multiple 'Saxon barrows' across England and 'also in Livonian, Burgundian, and Frankish graves.'[94] 'It' is 'of the same type' as those of Scandinavia.[95] 'It' 'answers to Plutarch's account of the Cymbric weapon,' and 'it' 'exactly corresponds to the description of Suevi weapons.'[96] Just as the sword's materiality holds together the discrete bones of the skeleton, the sword's material culture connects the graves of people from across northern Europe. On the one hand, the sword is mobilized as an anthropological tool that signals cultural connections between peoples. At the same time, the entanglement between sword and bone creates cultural-racial ties. Although corroded by the soil's dampness, as Wylie's narrative continues to describe this sword, its massive military form gathers together a kin group whose Saxon, Livonian, Burgundian, *et alii* members belong to one 'great and noble Teutonic family'[97] — a family that Wylie references on the first page of his Preface as 'the Teutonic race.'[98]

As if responding to the ekphrastic gazes exchanged between Douglas's solitary barrow-sitter and his Saxon soldier-skeleton, an unnamed group at Fairford mourns and collects the artifacts and bone from one grave in order to extend the scope of their grief and collecting across many graves in northern Europe. Do they, like (or unlike) Douglas, engage in a mourning that psychically encrypts the dead? Answers are, again, unclear. However, as this community of antiquarians stands, like Douglas, over material crypts and imagines living practices of excavation, its affective movements and gestures assemble the bodies of a Teutonic race.

---

94 Ibid., 21.
95 Ibid.
96 Ibid.
97 Ibid., vi.
98 Ibid., v.

Fairford's antiquarians and its Teutonic family are assembled together in 'The Saxon Chieftain: Written on Opening a Saxon Grave, March 7, 1851,'[99] a poem that reframes the March 7th excavation as an act that suspends the boundaries between death and life and exchanges body organs of the dead and the living. In his grave, this 'Saxon Chieftain' merely 'sleeps,' and when the wooden vessel and corroded sword are arranged around his body, they are no longer artifacts of decay and corrosion: 'still at his head the festal goblet stands...Still seeks the trenchant blade those nerveless hands.'[100] These uncorrupted grave goods locate the uncorrupted head and hand of this sleeping Saxon, who materially, physically, and biologically endures. He lies 'still.' Yet, his stillness is made possible by the embodied emotional performances of the March 7th excavators. The unnamed 'we' of Wylie's archaeological report are figured here as 'kindred men,' Saxon relatives who look upon their chieftain and 'kindly breathe / A pious requiem to the noble dead.'[101] The mourning song of antiquarians establishes a relationship with this chieftain that is articulated along relational and racial lines. He is their leader and kinsman, and, consequently, all are Saxons. These connections allow for a confusion of temporalities and of physical bodies. As mourners, it is unclear whether these antiquarians exist in the present or the past. In the space of this confusion, their mourning sounds breathe life into the chieftain's Saxon lungs, and his Saxon lungs animate the antiquarians' other internal organs: 'still sounds the Saxon tongue as erst of old, / In Saxon breast still beats the Saxon heart.'[102] From death to sleep, from skeletal fragments to a complete skeleton, this Saxon Chieftain still lives in the speaking tongues and beating hearts — in the bodies — of its excavator-kinsmen who still mourn him. This exchange of breath, spirit, and vitality articulates the racial profile of Saxon bodies, who, whether past or present, are characterized by their

---

99 Ibid., 38–40.
100 Ibid., 38.
101 Ibid.
102 Ibid.

imperial impulses and the 'God bless'd...empire-tree' to which they belong.[103]

The fantastic body crossings of 'The Saxon Chieftain' suggest the process of psychic incorporation, and the grave plan that accompanies this poem signals crypt formation. 'Sketch of a Grave: Opened March 7th'[104] is a grave plan that 'follows the examplar' of Douglas's Figure 1.[105] Unlike Figure 1, which looks alive except for its skeletonized body, the warrior occupant of Wylie's illustration is an entirely lifeless, anonymous, and fading fragment of bones (see Figure 7). Through the protracted and embodied performances of community mourning, the life force of this Saxon has been called to presence, animated, and deposited within the bodies of his imperial kin, who keep him 'alive' in psychic crypts that have been built for him. All that remains are the material leftovers, so to speak, of this Saxon. And as if to underscore this point, Wylie positions 'Sketch of a Grave' as the visual conclusion to *Fairford Graves*.

Around the time that *Fairford Graves* is published, Charles Roach Smith's second and third volumes of *Collectanea Antiqua* extend and revise further Douglas's grave plan now that psychic crypts have been built for its Saxon warrior. In Volume 2, Smith declares that *Nenia Britannica* is 'one of the most useful, and has, in the department to which it is more specifically devoted, been more serviceable, as a work of reference, than any other we possess.'[106] By praising Douglas within a section called 'Anglo-Saxon Remains,' Smith refines the racial identity of Douglas's Saxon foot-soldier and Wylie's Saxon chieftain, who are now perceived as denizens of Britain rather than Migration-Era figures. Volume 3 opens with an excavation at Ozengell, Kent, in southeastern England, a site that marks this transition from Saxon to Anglo-Saxon identity. Smith's 'imagination...pictures the traditional advent of Hengist and Horsa, the supposed lead-

---

103 Ibid., 39.
104 Ibid., n.p.
105 See Williams, 'Anglo-Saxonism and Victorian Archaeology,' 81.
106 Charles Roach Smith, *Collectanea Antiqua*, 7 vols. (London: J. Russell Smith, 1848–1880), 2:156.

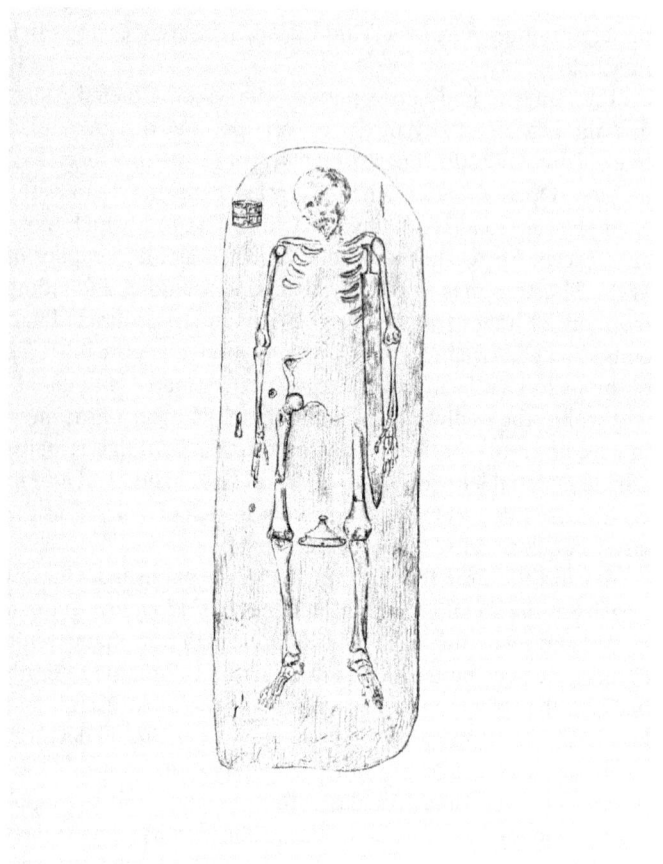

Figure 7. William Wylie, 'Sketch of a Grave,' in *Fairford Graves: A Record of Researches in an Anglo-Saxon Burial Place in Glouchestershire* (Oxford: John Henry Parker, 1852), n.p. Image courtesy of the Library of Congress.

ers of the people, among the immediate descendants of whom were the tenants of the Ozingell graves.'[107] As the arrival point of Anglo-Saxon England's mythical Saxon fathers and the burial site of their 'immediate' Anglo-Saxon 'descendants,' Ozengell is a landscape of romantic expectation and a place of post-mortem 'tenan[cy].' Secure in their psychic (and material) crypts, the Saxons and Anglo-Saxons buried at Ozengell are not entirely dead, and their undead presence calls into presence an antiquarian group. When area railroad workers stumble upon some of these graves, 'about thirteen graves were laid open by order of Sir [William Henry] Rolfe, who kindly invited on the occasion Messrs. [Thomas] Wright, [James Orchard] Halliwell, [Frederick William] Fairholt, [Edwin?] Keet, and myself [Charles Roach Smith]' to join him in the excavation.[108] Framed by Smith's introduction, this 'kindly invited' group of well-known antiquarians, scholars, and engravers sets out to re-discover the Anglo-Saxon relations of Hengest and Horsa and to create what might now be considered a professional community of antiquarians that finds the racialized image of its collective body in the skeletonized figure of a grave plan.

Smith does not document the excavation. There is no grief expressed for the dead and no funeral dirges sung. Nor does Smith mention the processes of collecting and assembling artifacts. As bodies that have already been enlivened through incorporation and positioned within the psychic crypts of an antiquarian group, there is no need to re-stage the embodied performances by which the dead were fantastically assembled within the living. After describing the location of Ozengell and the antiquarians who are present, Smith reproduces a sketch of one of Ozengell's tenants (see Figure 8). This 'annexed engraving, from a sketch made by Mr. Fairholt at the time of discovery, represents one of the most interesting of the deposits.'[109] In addition to its erect position and lifelike stance, this 'perfect'

---

107 Ibid., 3:2.
108 Ibid.
109 Ibid., 3:3.

DISCOVERED AT OZINGELL, KENT. 3

easily discerned by the loose nature of the soil, the natural hard chalk forming the cists, the sides and bottoms of which had been smoothed. When the bodies and the weapons and other objects deposited with them had been arranged, the graves were filled in first with earth, and then with the small friable pieces of chalk dug out in making the graves; but in many instances, immediately over the bodies had been placed thin slabs of laminated sand-stone. Only a few of the skeletons were perfect; many were almost entirely decomposed, with the exception of the teeth, which were generally well preserved and free from disease.

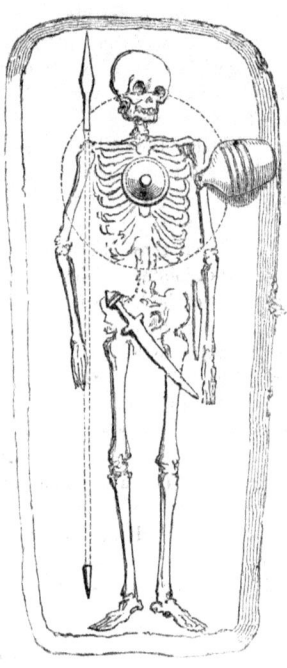

The annexed engraving, from a sketch made by Mr Fairholt, at the time of the discovery, represents one of the most interesting of the deposits. On the breast of the skeleton lay the iron umbo of a circular shield, (see pl. II); on the right side lay a spear-head, the length of the entire weapon (about six feet) being indicated by the *spiculum* or iron point at the butt-end; at the left hip was an iron knife, and from the right hip across the left thigh a short sword, shewn in fig. 7, pl. II, in an enlarged view. At the left shoulder was an earthen vessel, (see fig. 3, pl. III.)

Figure 8. From Charles Roach Smith, *Collectanea Antiqua*, Vol. 3 (London: J. Russell Smith, 1854), 3. Image courtesy of University of Colorado–Boulder.

'Anglo-Saxon' skeleton appears to have tissue on him.[110] A thousand years of tenancy in an Ozengell grave has left his arms and legs gaunt, his eyes hollow, and his cheeks sunken. Yet his spearhead is still sharp, his sword is curved like a pirate's cutlass, and the decayed wooden parts of his weapons are drawn in with a dotted line, creating the illusion that they are still present and whole. In the psychic crypts of Smith's antiquarians, this 'Anglo-Saxon' lives on, perfect, present, and complete. Consequently, when Smith's grave plan illustrates the physical body of this Anglo-Saxon, it depicts a territory that is double — both a material grave that has been excavated and also a psychic vault that been built. This composite sketch draws the interest of Ozengell's antiquarian group because, as Smith's archaeological narrative explains, the weaponry is a 'most interesting...deposi[t].' His height is the length of his six-foot spear; his shield boss covers his heart; and the distance between 'right hip' and 'left thigh' are traced by his 'short sword.'[111] Hengest and Horsa's descendant stands at attention, and an entire group of gentleman archaeologists gazes upon the towering stature of an 'Anglo-Saxon.' While his weapons continue to display the imperial spirit of Wylie's Saxon chieftain, these traits are now physically documented by Smith's antiquarian measurements. As a figure that is simultaneously outside and inside the embodied minds of a professional antiquarian community, this 'Anglo-Saxon' is drawn, in part, according to their specifications. Consequently, as Rolfe, Wright, Haliwell, Fairholt, Keet, and Smith look, together, at this six-foot tall warrior, he nods in acknowledgement of their presence. Though one is barely living, and the others are entirely alive, this is meeting of friends, a salutary moment in which the 'immediate' and extended 'descendants' of Hengest and Horsa physically make one another's acquaintance *in* the barrow.

---

110 Ibid.
111 Ibid. Smith alludes to the precise measurements of boss and sword elsewhere, noting that his drawing of the shield boss is 'one-third of the size of the origina[l]' and his drawing of the sword is 'half the actual size' (ibid., 3:5).

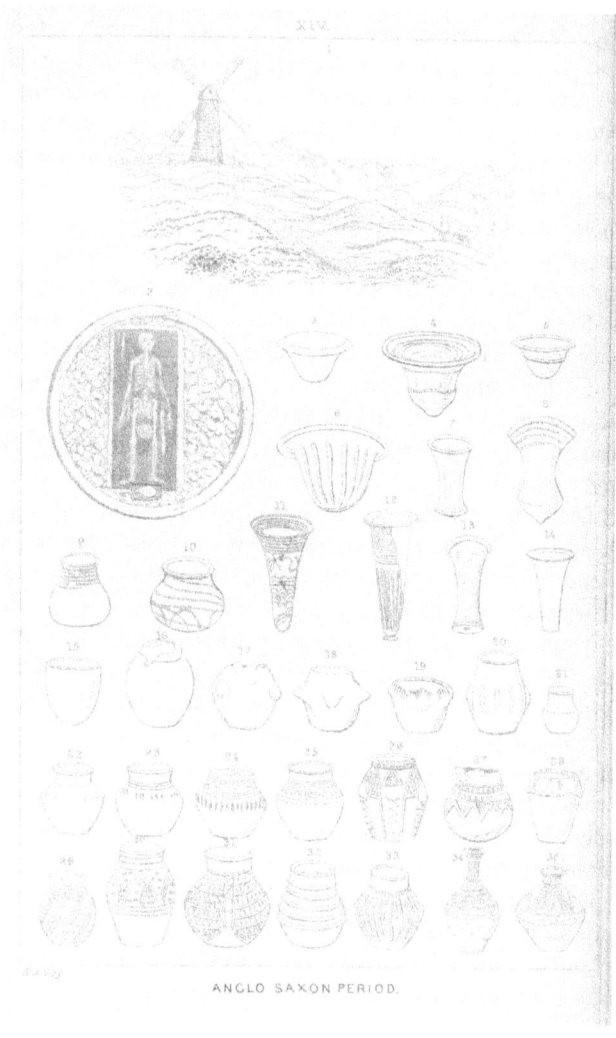

Figure 9. Plate XVI, no. 2, in John Yonge Akerman, 'An Archaeological Index to Remains of Antiquity of the Celtic, Romano-British, and Anglo-Saxon Periods,' *The Edinburgh Review* 86, no. 174 (1847): 233. Image courtesy of New York Public Library.

THE SEPULCHRAL BODY OF THE ANGLO-SAXONIST

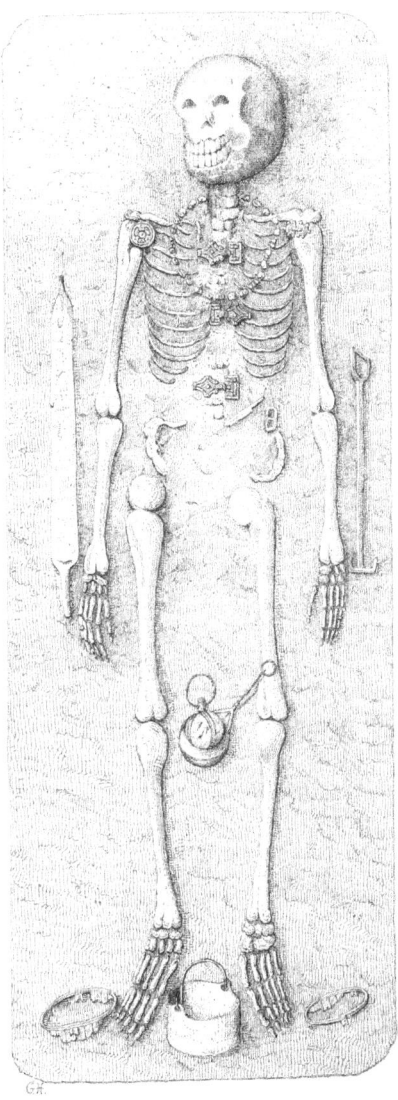

Figure 10. Plate XXVIII, in Charles Roach Smith, *Collectanea Antiqua,* Vol. 6 (1868), n.p. Image courtesy of University of Colorado–Boulder.

Wylie's *Fairford Graves* and Smith's *Collectanea Antiqua* credit *Nenia Britannica* as the most valuable reference tool for an emerging community of antiquarians, and they model their grave plans upon Douglas's illustration of Figure 1. Several others were produced during the mid-nineteenth century, and they, too, bear striking resemblance to Douglas's Figure 1 (see Figures 9 and 10).[112]

These adaptations of Douglas's Tumulus I expand the antiquarian territory of the early medieval barrow such that the identity assemblages articulated in *Nenia Britannica* as Saxon are now considered to be Anglo-Saxon. As these antiquarians adapt and transform Douglas's Figure 1, they, like Douglas's barrow-sitter, respond, in mind and in body, to its ekphrasis. Douglas's lone antiquarian and Wylie's anonymous 'we...kindred men' are replaced by Smith's list of notable gentlemen scholars. A solitary mourner and collector is joined, next to the grave, by a group of mourner-collectors, who summon the racialized body of an Anglo-Saxon through imaginary, but also embodied, movements and performances. Their antiquarian living practices are tuned to (what they believe to be) Saxon and Anglo-Saxon dying practices, and they (re)assemble their antiquarian identities according to assemblages of artifacts and bones. As this group professionalizes, its grief turns, firstly, into incorporation and encryption and, secondly, into studied interest. Barrow-sitting becomes a professional practice for those who are inhabited by the dead, and these barrow-sitters begin to live, so to speak, in the graves of others. The ekphrasis of Tumulus I has broadcasted the signals of its reliquary undeadness to its antiquarian readers, who have responded to these communiqués in mind and in body. Their professional living is attuned to others' ways of dying, and, consequently, they imagine Anglo-Saxon identity as a skeletal form.

---

[112] Note that Figure 9 is a reproduction of Douglas's Figure 1, and the 'crystal ball' between the leg bones of Figure 10 is referenced in relation to Douglas's writings about this artifact (ibid., 6:150).

Anglo-Saxon Skulls, Craniology, and the "Essential Characteristics of Our Race"

While this chapter has noted the shifting racial profile of antiquarians who believe themselves to be the inheritors of martially spirited and physically enormous Anglo-Saxons, as Douglas admitted and these scholars well know, the racial typology sketched in the grave plans of Wylie, Smith, and others is neither the average physical form of an Anglo-Saxon nor of the antiquarians who direct barrow excavations. Yet, this group, which is inhabited by the dead, desires to find a physical connection — a mark on the body that distinguishes biological race — between Anglo-Saxons of the past and present. Joseph Bernard Davis and John Thurnam's *Crania Britannica* does just that.

A pseudoscience that, Chris Manias argues, 'allows the living to be compared with the dead,'[113] craniology is the study of the shape and size of the skulls of different human races. Davis and Thurnam set out to distinguish between Romano-British, Anglo-Saxon, and Scandinavian crania in their two-volume reference guide, *Crania Britannica*.[114] The first of Davis and Thurnam's Anglo-Saxon crania comes from Ozengell, a site excavated not only by Smith but also by Thomas Wright, who, in *Wanderings of an Antiquary,* explains that its barrows offer the antiquarian 'a melancholy way of making acquaintance with our forefathers of thirteen centuries ago, by raising from the grave

---

113 Chris Manias, *Race, Science, and the Nation: Reconstructing the Ancient Past in Britain, France, and Germany* (New York: Routledge, 2013), 118.
114 Joseph Barnard Davis and John Thurnam, *Crania Britannica: Delineations and Descriptions of the Skulls of the Aboriginal and Early Inhabitants of the British Islands,* 2 vols (London: Printed for the Subscribers, 1865). In its initial subscription publication of six parts (1856-1865), plate-sized crania illustrations were interleaved with accompanying descriptions. Upon republication in 1865, its material was reorganized, and cranial descriptions and illustrations were split into two separate volumes. Volume 1 evaluates the size, proportion, and distinguishing features of hundreds of skulls. Volume 2 features a folio-sized illustration of each cranium.

ANGLO-SAXON(IST) PASTS, POSTSAXON FUTURES

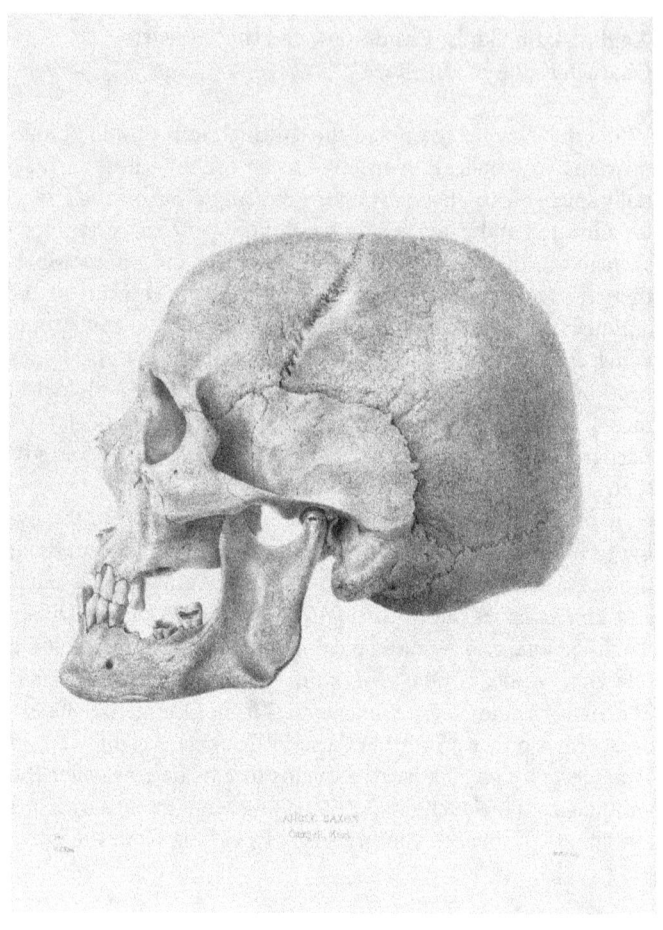

Figures 11a & 11b. 'Anglo-Saxon skull from Ozengull,' in Joseph Barnard Davis and John Thurnam, *Crania Britannica: Delineations and Descriptions of the Skulls of the Aboriginal and Early Inhabitants of the British Islands,* 2 vols. (London: Printed for the Subscribers, 1865), 2:451 and 1:n.p. Images courtesy of the Library of Congress.

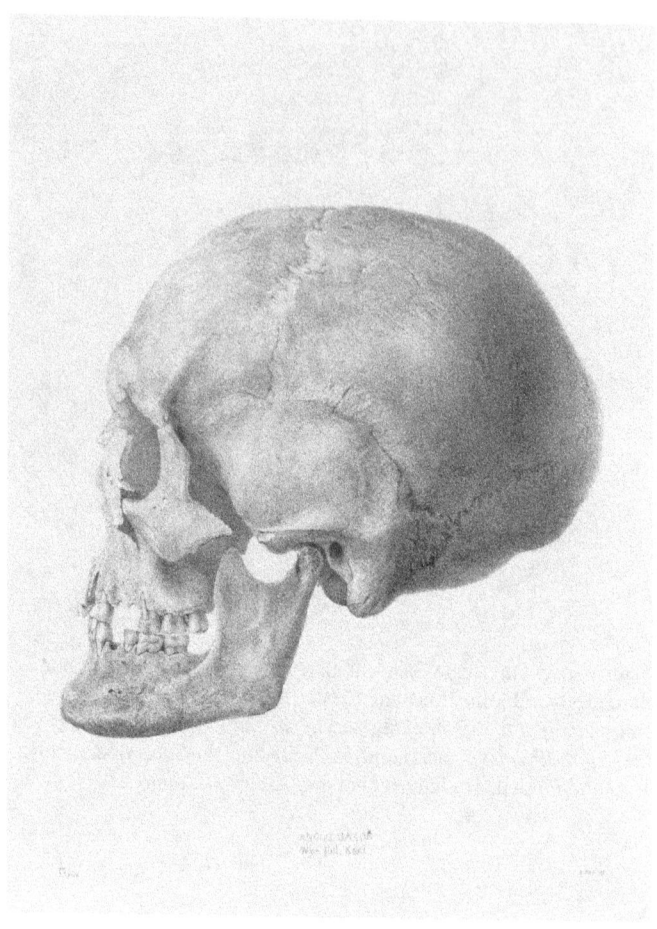

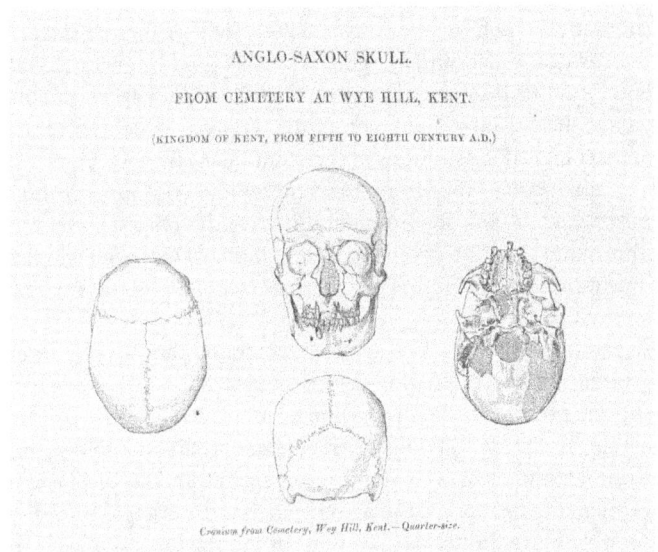

Figures 12a & 12b. 'Anglo-Saxon skull from Wye Hill,' in Joseph Barnard Davis and John Thurnam, *Crania Britannica: Delineations and Descriptions of the Skulls of the Aboriginal and Early Inhabitants of the British Islands*, 2 vols. (London: Printed for the Subscribers, 1865), vol. 1 and vol. 2 (London: Printed for the Subscribers, 1865), 2:455 and 1:n.p. Images courtesy of the Library of Congress.

the bones which are no longer able to tell us their history.'[115] Smith's grave plan and Wright's words — in addition to Douglas's Tumulus I[116] — are not lost on Davis and Thurnam, who organize their cranial evaluation of the Ozengell skull around the archaeological illustrations of these antiquarians.

Unlike every other cranium from Volume 1 of *Crania Britannica,* which is sketched from four different directions, Davis and Thurnam substitute cranial representations of Ozengell with an illustration from Wright's *Wanderings* (see Figures 11a, 11b, 12a, and 12b).

A gentleman's estate lies in the background, and in the foreground are several graves in active excavation. To the left, a shovel is staked in the dirt, while a laborer leans over and into a hole. To the right, two gentlemen stand at the mouth of a pit, while another worker continues to dig. From the distance, a gentleman approaches the activity, arriving, perhaps, from the country house in the background. In the further distance — to the left of the house — boxy apparitions point towards the excavators. The mortuary landscape of Wright's sketch, in which so many people stand in grave pits, signals a 'making acquaintance' that is melancholic, indeed. The movements from country manor to grave signal a transtemporal circulation between bodies of the past and present by which, it seems, the followers of Hengest and Horsa have been 'rais[ed] from the grave.' The substitution of Ozengell's cranial images with Wright's excavation scene articulates an entanglement between psychic and material crypts. Likewise, it suggests that the dead now literally inhabit the minds and bodies of their excavators, whose professional living practices are enacted in the territory of others' dying practices. These connections are not lost on Davis and Thurnam. After listing all of Ozengell's excavators — W.H. Rolfe, the company of Charles Roach Smith, and Thomas Wright — they claim that

---

[115] Thomas Wright, *Wanderings of an Antiquary: Chiefly Upon the Traces of the Romans in Britain* (London: J.B. Nichols and Sons, 1854), 83.

[116] Davis and Thurnam note that Smith's grave plan 'reminds us forcibly of the fine delineation by the hand of Mr. Douglas. *Nenia Britannica,* plate 1' (*Crania Britannica,* 1:452).

'when our skull was discovered, in which of them [the graves] we are not able to say. It has since passed, with many of the Ozingell relics, into the hands of Mr. Joseph Mayer, F.S.A., to whose ready acquiescence in our wish, the readers of the "Crania Britannica" owe its representation here.'[117] Although its origins are imprecise, the Ozengell skull has 'passed' through the 'hands' of a growing body of excavators, collectors, craniologists, and *Crania Britannica*'s gentlemen readership. It is 'our skull.' It belongs to all who desire to claim it. Consequently, even when Davis and Thurnam state that 'its representation' is 'here,' in an asterisked footnote below, instead of a skull, they include citations to Wright and Smith's works and add the illustrator F.W. Fairholt (who made the sketch that Smith used for his grave plan) to a growing list of antiquaries affiliated with Ozengell.[118] Where is this skull that is being handled? It is 'here,' and yet it is not here; it is dead, but it is living. It belongs to no single skeleton but to the entire cemetery. It is a skull that could fit any and all of the bodies — dead or living — at Ozengell.

On the next page, Davis and Thurnam provide no further clues as to the location of this skull. Instead, they summarize the Ozengell excavation. Beginning with the statement that most graves were occupied by men, Davis and Thurnam provide the average skeletal heights of Ozengell's occupants: five feet, ten inches, to six feet tall, with one body that was estimated to be six feet, four- to six-inches tall. Then, they describe the weapons, which include 30-inch broad swords, 9-to-21-inch spear tips, 6-foot spear shafts, 'iron knives; battle-axes, or *franciscas*; umbones and studs of shields, the circular wooden discs having perished.'[119] The absence of this skull is substituted by a superabundance of bodies and weapons, which have been measured and collated. Placed in the middle of this accounting is an 'Oz-

---

117 Davis and Thurnam, *Crania Britannica*, 1:451.
118 Ibid.
119 Ibid., 1:452.

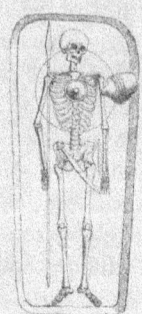

Figure 13. Anglo-Saxon skeleton from Charles Roach Smith's *Collectana Antiqua,* reprinted in Joseph Barnard Davis and John Thurnam, *Crania Britannica: Delineations and Descriptions of the Skulls of the Aboriginal and Early Inhabitants of the British Islands* (London: Printed for the Subscribers, 1865), 1:452. Image courtesy of Library of Congress.

ingell Grave, with Skeleton and remains of Shield and Spear in situ.'[120] (see Figure 13).

Surrounded by all of Ozengell's men and their arms, this Anglo-Saxon could be five feet, ten inches. Or he could be six feet, four inches. He could have a nine-inch spear tip. Or it could be twenty-one inches. One thing, however, is certain: he possesses 'our' Ozengell skull. As Davis and Thurnam's excavation summary is read in relation to the 'Skeleton' in an 'Ozingell Grave,' it becomes ekphrastic. It organizes a message of racial inheritance that is located in multiple bone lengths and skeletal morphologies. Consequently, it asks antiquarians who view it to find their own skeleton in its anonymous and unremarkable form. Further, this skeleton associates its racialized, osteological features with an armory of weapons, thereby transforming the martial, imperial characteristics of Wylie's Saxon chieftain and Smith's six-foot Anglo-Saxon into an appetite for endless battle.

On the subsequent page, Davis and Thurnam continue their catalogue of Ozengell artifacts. Coins, glassware, weights, and scales communicate an archaeological rhetoric of 'balance' and 'proportion.'[121] As the list of Ozengell's grave goods arcs from unusually large armaments to well-proportioned measurements, Davis and Thurnam begin to describe, for the first time, the craniological features of this Ozengell skull. Not withstanding its post-mortem 'deformations,' 'our skull' is 'well-proportioned and upright,' 'well-expressed,' 'full,' 'moderately lofty,' 'long, straight, or slightly elevated.'[122] Though armed to the teeth, everything about this skull evidences a well-rounded and well-balanced mind of reason and intellect — just like the minds of Davis and Thurnam's antiquarian readership. While the Ozengell skeleton communicates one set of racialized features in its skeletal morphology, the Ozengell skull and its associated artifacts communicate another. Davis and Thurnam organize the material culture of the entire Ozengell cemetery to imply

---

120 Ibid.
121 Ibid., 1:453.
122 Ibid.

that, despite their physical brawn and racialized appetite for destruction, Anglo-Saxons are of a noble and rational disposition. Davis and Thurnam offer no opportunity to see what such a skull looks like in this section because it is located 'here': inside every living and dead Anglo-Saxon body.[123] As summary proof that Anglo-Saxons of the past and present now inhabit the same racial body, Davis and Thurnam write in their 'Conclusions': '[t]he series of Anglo-Saxon skulls, in their great resemblance to those of modern Englishmen, vindicate the true derivation of the essential characteristics of our race from a Teutonic origin. The form and proportions of these crania probably evince more power than refinement.'[124]

Raised from the grave and from the pages of multiple scholarly reports, Davis and Thurnam anticipate the arrival of the figure of the Anglo-Saxonist — a professional who not only studies Anglo-Saxon peoples but is Anglo-Saxon. In mind and in body — in *embodied* mind — the Anglo-Saxonist emerges from the territory of Douglas's antiquarian barrow and from the joint ekphrasis of his Saxon foot-soldier and antiquarian barrow-sitter. Yet, the Anglo-Saxonist is an interdisciplinary figure. In order to locate 'it,' this chapter circles back to early medieval barrows, to *Beowulf*, and to Beowulf's ekphrastic displays, discussing all in relation to one last nineteenth-century figure: John Mitchell Kemble.

Coda: John Mitchell Kemble, 'Anglo-Saxonist'

Although Kemble is noted primarily as a philologist and a historian who published the first edition of *Beowulf* in 1833 and a second edition and translation in 1837, Kemble was likewise deeply committed to archaeology. A long-time friend of William Wylie and a teacher of Thomas Wright, Kemble supervised the exca-

---

123 Note that in Volume 2, Davis and Thurnam provide a complete sketch of the Ozengell skull (see Figure 11a), enabling the reader to study its morphology in relation to Volume 1's artifact descriptions, and find, in all of these anatomical and cultural features, his own Anglo-Saxon skull.
124 Ibid., 1:238.

vation of barrow cemeteries and urnfields in Hanover. Just as Kemble's philological scholarship was invested in locating Anglo-Saxon language and history within the Continental orbit of Germanic tribes, his archaeology was similarly comparative.[125] Moreover, as Howard Williams writes, Kemble's interests in archaeology follow from his scholarship on *Beowulf*:

> from his commentaries, it is clear that Kemble regarded this as a literary work, as a source of historical and philological information and as a cultural lynchpin that connected England to its Teutonic heritage....Even though he was not alone in seeing disparities between the spectacular cremations portrayed in the poem and the more modest cinerary urns commonly uncovered by archaeologists, he was keen to acknowledge, through the poems and texts, the importance of cremation as a pagan Germanic rite...hence the use of archaeology may have been not only inspired by *Beowulf* and philological models, but may have been directly aimed as compensating the limitations of the literary and linguistic evidence.[126]

Whether conscious or not, in his excavations in Hanover, Kemble figures himself the Beowulfian hero. He not only 'breaks into' mounds and 'loots' treasure; moreover, in choosing to tar-

---

125 On the racial investments in Kemble's philological and archaeological writings, see Robert McCombe, 'Anglo-Saxon Artifacts and Nationalist Discourse,' *Museum History Journal* 4, no. 2 (2011): 144–52. Howard Williams makes Kemble's racism explicit when he notes that 'we can regard how their [Kemble and Wylie's] interpretation of Continental [archaeological] discoveries were permeated by racial theories aimed at making specific statements about the shared Teutonic affinities and origins of the English and the Germans' ('"Burnt Germans," Alemannic Graves and the Origins of Anglo-Saxon Archaeology,' in *Zweiundvierzig: Festschrift für Michael Gebühr zum 65. Geburtstag*, eds. Stefan Burmeister, Heidrun Derks, and Jasper von Richthofen [Rahden: Leidorf, 2007], 230).
126 Howard Williams, 'Heathen Graves and Anglo-Saxonism: Assessing the Archaeology of John Mitchell Kemble,' *Anglo-Saxon Studies in Archaeology and History* 13 (2006), 5.

get cremation barrows, he locates himself, over and over again, in what he believes to be the topography of Beowulf's own Geatish grave. To return to the ekphrasis of Beowulf, whose reliquary form, this chapter argues, seeks a response from readers within and outside the poem's narrative — in Kemble's Hanover excavations, we can finally find a response to its ekphrastic displays.

For Kemble, however, the barrow territory from whence Beowulf emerges and is interred is shaped not by the identity assemblages of medieval communities but by James Douglas and the Victorian antiquarians who reference him. Therefore, while Beowulf may lead Kemble into barrows, the expressive territory — the dying practices — that Kemble encounters therein is shaped by the living practices of his fellow nineteenth-century antiquarians, who have reassembled artifact and bone into Anglo-Saxons and the Teutonic kin group to which they belong.

Through Kemble's Beowulf-inspired barrow excavations, philology, history, and archaeology become entangled and interdisciplinary. Through Kemble, Beowulf is linked to Anglo-Saxon barrows, to the racialized skeletons that have been assembled within them, and to the antiquarian association between psychic crypts and material graves. Most importantly, through Kemble, cognitive-oriented methods of philology and historicism are linked to excavation, a method of embodied and performative identity-making which this chapter has discussed in relation to the concept of territory. As if to punctuate the critical role of Kemble's body to his scholarship, William Stokes writes, Kemble 'gave his life to the cause in which he had embarked with all the energies of a vigorous mind and a vigorous body.'[127]

Indeed, Kemble is key not only to the interdisciplinary scope of Anglo-Saxon studies and *Beowulf*, its keystone text, but also to the use of the term, 'Anglo-Saxonist,' the first two attestations of which appear in reference to him. The first attestation appears in the November issue of the 1837 *Gentleman's Magazine,* in the short article, 'Retrospective Review. Anglo-Saxon Literature.'

---

127 William Stokes, 'The Manchester Exhibition of Art-Treasures,' *The Dublin University Magazine* 49, no. 293 (1857): 615.

This anonymous essay prints the word, 'Anglo-Saxonist', in association with Benjamin Thorpe and John Mitchell Kemble, explaining that, by studying Thorpe's translation of Erasmus Rask's *Grammar of the Anglo-Saxon Tongue*, then Kemble's edition of *Beowulf*, the 'student of Anglo-Saxon' may join their ranks as an Anglo-Saxonist.[128] Despite its use in the 'Retrospective Review,' if the term 'Anglo-Saxonist' was en vogue during the first half of the nineteenth century, it does not appear in print again until twenty years later and in association with Kemble. In an *ad hoc* obituary for Kemble in *Notes and Queries*, he is eulogized as 'a man of undoubted and original genius, a thorough classical scholar, and profound Anglo-Saxonist, deeply read in the language and literature of Scandinavia and Germany, master of all, or nearly, the languages of Europe, and well versed in our national history.'[129] The phrase 'profound Anglo-Saxonist,' which governs the following clause, says nothing of Kemble's archaeological interests, even though, upon his return from Hanover, all of his scholarly energies became focused upon excavation, and, as Howard Williams writes, 'during these final years, it is difficult to regard Kemble as anything other than an archaeologist.'[130] Rather, in this instance, 'Anglo-Saxonist' posthumously limits the scope of Kemble's interdisciplinary methods to his 'dee[p] read[ing]' in language, literature, and 'our national history.' As the last word on Kemble's 'Anglo-Saxonist' identity, *Notes and Queries* denies the barrow-digging aspects of his scholarship in order to advocate a thoroughly cognitive profession that neither accounts for the affective movements nor shape of the physical body, assemblages that make and re-make identity in performance.

---

128 Anonymous, 'Retrospective Review: Anglo-Saxon Literature,' *Gentleman's Magazine* 8 (1837): 494; Erasmus Rask, *A Grammar of the Anglo-Saxon Tongue, with a Praxis*, trans. Benjamin Thorpe (Copenhagen: S.L. Møller, 1830).

129 'Miscellaneous. Notes on Books, etc.,' *Notes and Queries* 2, no. 66 (April 1857): 280.

130 Williams, 'Heathen Graves and Anglo-Saxonism,' 4.

Barrows, *Beowulf,* and the real and imagined embodied practices of field excavation all participate in nineteenth-century processes that generate, from the grave, the Anglo-Saxon body — not a real body, but a cultural one that helped to found an academic discipline. Despite the critical role of barrow digging in the formation of an imagined, nineteenth-century community of Anglo-Saxon scholars, the professional appellative 'Anglo-Saxonist' has repeatedly denied the embodied, identity-making performances and practices associated with antiquarian archaeology in exchange for supposedly neutral and bloodlessly objective pedagogical and professional activities that do not consider the embodied practices and methods that underwrite the writings of Douglas, Wylie, Smith, Davis and Thurnam, and Kemble.[131] Consequently, when we study and teach *Beowulf,* a gateway by which we become Anglo-Saxonists, we find ourselves unknowingly located within a poem that builds a barrow and engages in a virtual descent into its mortuary interior. We mentally play the parts of barrow builder and breaker — living, then dying, with Beowulf — and becoming, perhaps, like Beowulf, ekphrastic figures of perpetual mourning and heroic return. As we teach our students Old English, then read *Beowulf* with them, in order to shepherd them through the gates of Anglo-Saxon studies, we keep refashioning our embodied selves within the contours of an expanding, reliquary, and skeletonized body that was, in the nineteenth century, gendered, racialized, and standing with both feet in the grave. Such a past of professional disembodiment underscores not only the field's fraught relationship with gender and sexuality, but also its struggle to shutter the ethno-political categories that overtly define the field. Moreover, as the next chapter explains, it marks our profession

---

[131] It is worth noting here that Chapter 1 of this book discusses Michael Drout's statements regarding Anglo-Saxon philology, which not only refuses the body but also forecloses philological Anglo-Saxonists from taking an embodied stance towards language. Likewise, Chapter 4 will discuss the process of becoming a nineteenth-century professional Anglo-Saxonist via pedagogies that emphasize cognitive mastery of Anglo-Saxon languages and texts at the expense of embodied ways of knowing.

as one that maintains an ontology of 'being' that is cognitive and static, continuing to struggle against elegaic, nostalgic, and most of all, melancholic psychological positions — affects of and from the continued return to and excavation of *Beowulf*'s barrows.

Second Movement

Interlude—
A Time for Mourning

4

On Being an Anglo-Saxonist: Asser's *Life of King Alfred*, Benjamin Thorpe, and the Sovereign *Corpus* of a Profession

Several years ago, Howard Williams noted a relationship between Sharon Turner's *History of the Anglo-Saxons,* James Douglas's *Nenia Britannica*, and 'an influential generation' of mid-nineteenth-century scholars:

> The mid-nineteenth century in England witnessed a rapid growth of interest in the material remains of Europe's early medieval barbarians. An influential generation of antiquaries, historians, and archaeologists quarried a new vein of Dark Age discoveries. This work augmented an existing historical and philological focus on the Germanic roots of England's people, language and customs, typified by Sharon Turner's *History of the Anglo-Saxons,* and built upon James Douglas' *Nenia Britannica* in which burial mounds and fur-

nished graves were attributed to the Anglo-Saxons for the first time.[1]

Chapters 2 and 3 of this book expand upon the implications of Williams's passing statement. These chapters argue that Turner and Douglas, as well as John Mitchell Kemble, are not figures whose work was 'augmented' by academics of a later period. Rather, they are the encrypted, graveyard 'fathers' of Anglo-Saxon Studies. When considered together, Turner's historical writings, Douglas's archaeological report, and Kemble's archaeoliterary pursuits place the scholarly minds and bodies of this interdisciplinary field in Anglo-Saxon crypts and graves.

This chapter takes Williams's 'influential generation' and his metaphor of quarrying a step further with a special focus on the philologist Benjamin Thorpe, a key figure among the generation that succeeded Turner and Douglas, especially. While Thorpe labors in the funerary mine opened by these men, he does not claim descent from them. Rather, Thorpe, one of the first named 'Anglo-Saxonists,' 'quarries a new vein of Dark Age discoveries' that belongs to another 'father': *Ælfred, Angulsaxonum rex*, or, 'Alfred, king of the Anglo-Saxons.'[2]

This chapter addresses Thorpe's relationship to King Alfred, the sovereign 'father' of our profession's entangled signifiers, 'Anglo-Saxon' and 'Anglo-Saxonist.' It tracks the terminological appearance of *Ælfred, Angulsaxonum rex* — first, in the early

---

1 Howard Williams, 'Anglo-Saxonism and Victorian Archaeology: William Wylie's *Fairford Graves*,' *Early Medieval Europe* 16, no. 1 (2008): 49.
2 While 'Anglo-Saxon' is the standard term used to reference the language and people of the early English period c. 450–1100, several scholars have recently remarked upon how the ninth-century origins and ethnic orientations of this compound suggest it to be a historically insufficient and ethnically limiting compound. See Hugh Magennis, *The Cambridge Introduction to Anglo-Saxon Literature* (Cambridge: Cambridge University Press, 2011), 34–35; Walter Pohl, 'Ethnic Names and Identities in the British Isles: A Comparative Perspective,' in *The Anglo-Saxons from the Migration Period to the Eighth Century*, ed. John Hines (Turnhout: Brepols, 1997), 25; and John Higham and M.J. Ryan, *The Anglo-Saxon World* (New Haven: Yale University Press, 2013), 7–10.

English charters, then in Asser's *Life of King Alfred* — as an expression of kingship that translates the vernacular, performative bodies of Alfred and his 'Anglo-Saxon' subjects into to the Latin, textual domain of Christ's sovereignty. In Asser's *Life,* this translation is facilitated by an imaginary account of the crucifixion. Christ's crucified corpse, which marks the conversion of material flesh into sovereign Word, enables Alfred to be translated from a corporeal body of chronic illness and pain into a Latinized, textual *corpus.* Through this fictional act, Asser's biography pronounces Alfred an Anglo-Saxon sovereign; however, it suggests that in real life this work remains incomplete. Asser suggests that a sovereign future awaits Alfred after death, when, like Christ, his material body can be translated from a corpse into a *corpus* of 'Anglo-Saxon' texts.

This chapter attends to these prognostications of Asser. It discusses the loss of Alfred's material corpse amid the turmoil of the English Civil Wars, which enables him to return as a corpse-like ghost of sovereignty. With no physical body to locate Alfred or keep him in the ground, Alfred's ghost proliferates. His haunting presence appears in seventeenth- and eighteenth-century portraits and paintings, becoming associated with the enfleshed bodies of English kings, then taking on the shape of 'Englishmen.' As Alfred's sovereign, undead figure takes up residence in the images of living bodies, 'Angulsaxon' becomes a course of study at Oxford, and Alfred's sovereign, corpse-like body begins to inhabit a *corpus* of Anglo-Saxon texts.

Alfred's ghostly movements ready the ground for the nineteenth-century scholarship and pedagogy of Benjamin Thorpe, who (alongside John Mitchell Kemble) is the profession's first named 'Anglo-Saxonist.' Thorpe activates Alfred's ghostly figure from within his numerous editions of Anglo-Saxon law codes, poetry, and homiletic literature. Further, his language-learning texts recast this association between Alfred's corpse and textual *corpus* as 'the Anglo-Saxon,' a raciolinguistic figure that, on account of its sovereignty, is pure, unmiscegenated, and, consequently, undead. By studying Thorpe's works, one transitions from studying 'Anglo-Saxon' language to *becoming* an 'Anglo-

Saxonist,' a professional and embodied 'being' that is haunted by the sovereign and racialized ghosts of the colonized past.

Early English Charters, an 'Anglo-Saxon' Kingdom, and its 'Anglo-Saxon' Subjects

To begin, one does not simply jettison a word-concept. A signifier is a powerful rhetorical tool, especially when it generates group formation and maintains an individual's belonging to the group. If, as an Anglo-Saxonist, I harbor a scholarly devotion towards the term 'Anglo-Saxon,'[3] then I might do well to consult Susan Reynolds's 1985 essay 'What Do We Mean by 'Anglo-Sax-

---

3 In modern English, '-ist' designates a wide range of professional and business affiliations, see '-ist,' suffix, *Oxford English Dictionary*, def. 4. However, the OED also explains that these secular applications derive from a Latin, religious context. As a suffix, '-ist' is used initially by 'Christian writers, in the latinizing of scriptural and ecclesiastical terms.' Later, it 'denotes the observers of a particular rite, the holders of special religious or philosophical tenets, or the adherents of particular teachers or heresiarchs.' Consequently, '-ist' generates descriptive terms that 'designat[e] a person' who 'practices…studies…or devotes himself to some science, art, or branch of knowledge,' and later references denote an 'adherent or professor of some creed, doctrine, system, or art' (see OED, defs. 2 and 3). A suffix of spiritual and then secular devotion, these two senses of '-ist' are followed by its final and most contemporary one: 'denoting one whose profession or business it is to have to do with the thing or subject in question…. Also from names of languages, as *Americanist, Anglist, Germanist, Hebraist, Hellenist, Latinist, Orientalist*' (see OED, def. 4). 'Anglo-Saxonist' is thus a term that is defined in relation to the shifting semantics of '-ist.' As a word that derives from the professional study of the Anglo-Saxon language, the OED's first definition uses '-ist' to denote one's academic 'profession or business,' while its second definition uses the suffix in order to mark one who 'practices… studies…or devotes himself' to a 'creed' of 'Anglo-Saxonism.' While the multiple semantic registers of '-ist' differentiate secular professionalism from secular ideology, hovering just behind the occupational term 'Anglo-Saxonist' is also the study of Latin and of the early medieval Church, both of which are critical to the production of Old English texts. This Latinate, Christian context routes the academic Anglo-Saxonist towards the religious origins of '-ist,' a suffix that renders her, by way of professional study, a 'follower,' 'devotee,' or 'practiser' of this body of scholarship and marks her academic profession as one of faith and fidelity to 'Anglo-Saxon' and its ecclesiastical partner language, Latin.

on' and 'Anglo-Saxons'?' in which she discusses the various early medieval attestations of the terms 'Angles,' 'Saxons,' and 'English.' Reynolds's etymological research leads her to early medieval articulations of 'Anglo-Saxon.' The compound, she explains, is used first by continental sources to reference, collectively, the Germanic peoples of Britain. It then appears 'occasionally...in surviving native sources only from the late ninth century on, when West Saxon kings and their successors sometimes referred to themselves as kings of the *Angli Saxones, Angolsaxones, Anglosaxones,* or *Angulsaxones*.'[4] Reynolds's historical assessment hinges on the political language of King Alfred, who, in charters from the late 880s and early 890s, rescripted the royal style of his Wessex predecessors Æthelbald, Æthelberht, and Æthelred, from 'king of the Saxons' ['rex Saxonum'][5] to 'king of the Angles and Saxons' ['rex Anglorum et Saxonum, Anglorum Saxonum rex'],[6] and, soon after, 'king of the Anglo-Saxons' ['angol saxonum rex, Anglo Saxonum Rex'].[7]

Janet Nelson, Simon Keynes, David Pratt, and Sarah Foot attribute this change in the royal style of Alfred's charters to the political relationship between Wessex and Mercia during

---

4   Susan Reynolds, 'What Do We Mean by 'Anglo-Saxon' and 'Anglo-Saxons'?' *Journal of British Studies* 24, no. 4 (1985): 398. See also Wilhelm Levison, *England and the Continent in the Eighth Century* (Oxford: Clarendon Press, 1946), 92n1.
5   Simon Keynes, 'The West Saxon Charters of King Æthelwulf and His Sons,' *The English Historical Review* 109, no. 434 (1994): 1109–49, points to Sawyer charters by Alfred's predecessors Æthelbald, Æthelberht, and Æthelred (S 1274, S 326, S 329, S 335, S 336, S 340, S 539, S 341, S 334, S 333, and S 342), all of which use the royal style *rex Saxonum*. Alfred follows this style until 889 (1123–25, 1147–48).
6   See the 889 and 891 Anglo-Saxon charters S 346 and S 347: *Electronic Sawyer: Online Catalogue of Anglo-Saxon Charters,* King's College London, http://www.esawyer.org.uk/about/index.html.
7   See the 891 and 892 Anglo-Saxon charters S 348 and S 349 (*Electronic Sawyer*). In the charters, the compound remains in use after Alfred's death from his son, Edward the Elder (899–924), until Æthelstan created the "Kingdom of the English" in 927' (Simon Keynes, 'King Alfred and the Mercians,' in *Kings, Currency, and Alliances: History and Coinage of Southern England in the Ninth Century,* eds. Mark A.S. Blackburn and David N. Dumville [Rochester: Boydell Press, 1998], 25).

the 870s and 880s.⁸ In the late 870s, Viking victories in Mercia and the death of its king, Ceolwulf, pave the road for a Wessex ascendancy, and, in the mid-880s, a coordinated monetary system, royal marriage alliances, and, moreover, Alfred's protective actions in London against the Vikings,⁹ indicate tightening bonds between Wessex and Mercia. The precise political relationship between these two kingdoms is articulated in an 889 charter between 'Alfred, king of Angles and Saxons and Aethelred, petty king and nobleman of the Mercians' ['Ælfred rex Anglorum et Saxonum et Æðelred subregulus et patricius Merciorum'].¹⁰ The terms that designate Alfred's relationship to Æthelred not only express the overlordship of a Wessex king ['rex'] to a Mercian underking ['subregulus'] but also articulate this political hegemony by way of a new royal style: 'Alfred, king of Angles and Saxons' ['Ælfred rex Anglorum et Saxonum']. As David Pratt writes, 'Æthelred's submission was understood to have created a new political order in southern Britain' in which Alfred operates as overlord to both kingdoms,¹¹ which are now stylized, according to Simon Keynes, as 'namely the "Anglian" kingdom of Mercia (less the part already settled by the Danes)

---

8 Janet Nelson, 'The Political Ideas of Alfred of Wessex,' in *Kings and Kingship in Medieval Europe*, ed. Anne J. Duggan (London: King's College London Centre for Late Antique and Medieval Studies, 1993), 125–58; Keynes, 'King Alfred and the Mercians,' 22–24; David Pratt, *The Political Thought of King Alfred the Great* (Cambridge: Cambridge University Press, 2007), 105–7; Sarah Foot, 'The Making of *Angelcynn*: English Identity before the Norman Conquest,' *Transactions from the Royal Historical Society* 6 (1996): 27.
9 Alfred's 'restoration' or 'gesette' of London, a city governed by Mercia during this period, not only puts a Mercian town under Alfred's protection and makes it defensible against Viking attack but, moreover, prompts the Anglo-Saxon Chronicle to express that, in 886, 'all English people, except those who were held captive by the Danes, turned to him' ['him all Angelcyn to cirde þæt buton deniscra monna hæftniede was'] (*The Anglo-Saxon Chronicle: A Collaborative Edition*, Vol. 3, MS. A, ed. Janet M. Bately [Cambridge: D.S. Brewer, 1986], 53). All Old English translations are my own.
10 S 346, *Electronic Sawyer*. All charter translations are my own.
11 Pratt, *The Political Thought of King Alfred the Great*, 106.

and the "Saxon" kingdom of Wessex and its eastern extensions."[12] For Pratt and Keynes, the use of 'Angles and Saxons' and, shortly after, 'Anglo-Saxon,' in this and several other charters, signals, on the one hand, a 'wholly new and distinctive polity' between Wessex and Mercia[13] and, on the other, a defensive 'unity' or political 'amalgamat[ion]' between its peoples.[14]

While politics are key to the development of the term 'Anglo-Saxon,' in the court of Alfred the compound exceeds political terminology and likewise functions as an ethnic term. In other words, 'Anglo-Saxon' identifies points of shared belonging between Alfred's people. As Nicholas Brooks writes, the multicultural court of Wessex 'must have had an immediate problem in determining the ethnic terminology that was appropriate for King Alfred's people, which now included both Saxons and Mercians.'[15] Brooks explains that while Alfred and Asser 'are likely' to have considered 'the king's subjects and their language as "Saxon," his continental and perhaps Mercian advisers will have thought of them as "English".'[16] 'An initial compromise,' Brooks argues, 'seems to have been reached among the king's charter-writers' in the compound 'Anglo-Saxon,' an ethnic term that Brooks aligns with 'the king's subjects and their language.'[17]

---

12 Keynes, 'King Alfred and the Mercians,' 25. Elsewhere, Keynes has summarily stated that 'Alfred's contribution was the invention of a wholly new and distinctive polity which may with some justification be called the "Kingdom of the Anglo-Saxons"' ('Edward, King of the Anglo-Saxons,' in *Edward the Elder: 899–924*, eds. N.J. Higham and D.H. Hill [New York: Routledge, 2001], 44–45). See also Keynes, 'King Alfred and the Mercians,' 24–26, 34–39, 43–44, and Simon Keynes, 'Alfred the Great and the Kingdom of the Anglo-Saxons,' in *A Companion to Alfred the Great*, eds. Nicole Guenther Discenza and Paul Szarmarch (Leiden: Brill, 2014), 13–46, 24n43.
13 Keynes, 'Edward, King of the Anglo-Saxons,' 44.
14 Pratt, *The Political Thought of King Alfred the Great*, 107.
15 Nicholas Brooks, 'English Identity from Bede to the Millenium,' *The Haskins Society Journal* 14 (2003): 46–47.
16 Brooks, 'English Identity from Bede to the Millenium,' 47.
17 Ibid. While at this point the precise definition of early medieval 'ethnicity' and 'ethnic' are beyond the scope of this chapter, see Robert Bartlett, *The Making of Europe: Conquest, Colonization and Cultural Change, 950–1350* (London: Penguin Press, 1993), 197; Stephen Harris, 'Race and Ethnicity,' in

Stephen Harris makes a similar, yet more developed, argument for understanding 'Anglo-Saxon' in relation to ethnicity, writing that the 'ethno-religious order of identity shaped by Charlemagne and imported into Anglo-Saxon England during the reign of Alfred' configures an 'Anglo-Saxon ethnogenesis... within the context of Christendom.'[18] Elsewhere, Harris concludes that when 'Alfred and his successors recorded genealogies that reached back through Germanic deities like Woden to a Christian past, [they] unit[ed] a *gens Anglosaxonum* with a gens Christianorum in the descent of a Christian English king.'[19] Brooks and Harris both assess 'Anglo-Saxon' as an ethnic term that denotes a shared language and religion. Thus figured, it draws under its sign not only those subjects who recognize

---

A Handbook of Anglo-Saxon Studies, eds. Jacqueline Stodnick and Renee Trilling (Malden: Blackwell, 2012), 165–79; Walter Pohl, 'Introduction: Strategies of Identification: A Methodological Profile,' in *Strategies of Identification: Ethnicity and Religion in Early Medieval Europe*, eds. Walter Pohl and Greta Heydemann (Turnout: Brepols, 2013), 1–64; and Andre Gingrich, 'Envisioning Medieval Communities in Asia: Remarks on Ethnicity, Tribalism, and Faith,' in *Visions of Community in the Post-Roman World: The West, Byzantium and the Islamic World*, eds. Walter Pohl, Clemens Gantner, and Richard Payne (Farnham: Ashgate, 2012), 32–35. Pohl and Gingrich underscore 'ethnicity' as a relational field of belonging.

18 Harris, *Race and Ethnicity in Anglo-Saxon Literature*, 83. This passage illustrates what Harris has argued is the cultivation, in Alfredian translations, of an 'ethno-religious identity' by which narratives of 'Germanic *imperium*' and 'Roman Christianity' orient positions of ethnicity and religion within 'the very marrow of Anglo-Saxon identity' ('The Alfredian World History and Ango-Saxon Identity,' *The Journal of English and Germanic Philology* 100, no. 4 [2001]: 489, 483). Helmut Reimitz recognizes this coupling of 'Christianity' and 'ethnicity' as a feature of early medieval identity politics ('The Providential Past: Visions of Frankish Identity in the Transmission of Gregory of Tours' *Historiae*,' in *Visions of Community in the Post-Roman World: The West, Byzantium and the Islamic World, 300–1100*, eds. Walter Pohl, Clemens Gantner, and Richard Payne [New York: Routledge, 2012], 110–12). See also Foot, 'The Making of Angelcynn,' 25–49.

19 Stephen J. Harris, 'An Overview of Race and Ethnicity in Pre-Norman England,' *Literature Compass* 5, no. 4 (2008): 750, 751. Craig Davis makes a similar point about Anglo-Saxon ethnicity in an Alfredian context, pointing to the influence of Bede's *gens Anglorum* ('Redundant Ethnogenesis,' *The Heroic Age* 5 (2001), http://www.heroicage.org/issues/5/Davis1.html).

Alfred's political overlordship but, moreover, all in Britain who hold common linguistic and religious affiliations. 'Anglo-Saxon' exceeds the borders of Alfred's political dominion and touches upon any place where English-speaking Christians live.

Rethinking Anglo-Saxon: Translation, Sovereignty, Corpus

The compound 'Anglo-Saxon' classifies Alfred's political lands and his subjects; however, it is not a free-standing signifier. As noted above, it exists as part of Alfred's royal style, *Angulsaxonum rex,* and appears for the first time (and almost exclusively) in early English charters, legal documents in which a king grants land to a subject. While charters are secular demonstrations of royal power, Kathrin McCann explains that, in Britain, they have religious origins. Monks who had recently arrived on the island did not trust the 'oral tradition' that kings used to transfer land to their subjects, so they drafted Latin documents to guarantee gifts of land to the Church.[20] Although unmentioned by McCann, the principle of translation — a process that entails the creative selection, substitution, recoding, etc. of materials from one domain to another — underwrites her discussion of the history of early English charters. Kingly power, which had traditionally been located in ritual performances and vernacular statements, is now translated into new, written modes of Latin documentation. Likewise, when land owned by a king was gifted to the Church, the Latin formulae and religious rhetoric used to describe this transaction translated a terrestrial kingship and kingdom into the spiritual architecture of God's rule and heavenly regions. The linguistic *and* conceptual re-codings that take place within early English charters impacted the 'self-image of the ruler' and 'had implications…for the perception of kingship as an office, separate from an actual person.'[21] In the charters, the king could exercise his power to rule without being

---

20 Kathrin McCann, *Anglo-Saxon Kingship and Political Power: Rex gratia Dei* (Cardiff: University of Wales Press, 2018), 48.
21 Ibid., 47, 49.

physically present; and through the charters, the king's rulings were 'anchored in eternity.'[22] Consequently, charters translate the figure of the king from a physically present, embodied entity of vernacular performance to an absent form of Latinate textuality. Likewise, they position kingship within the context of God's everlasting kingdom, making 'charters…the place where the secular and religious realms meet and merge.'[23]

In order to exercise this secular-spiritual power, the physically absent king must occupy textual space in the charter writings. Consequently, as McCann notes, 'it is…the titles that bear the greatest political significance' because 'royal titles' (or styles) enable the 'sovereignty and authority of the monarch' to exist in writing 'through kingdoms and even eras,' according to a ruler's 'territorial politics as well as his territorial ambitions.'[24] As part of a royal style, the signifier *rex* articulates the king's textual, Latin form. However, a ruler such as Alfred may exercise his sovereignty *in absentia* only through participation 'of the Anglo-Saxons' ['Angulsaxonum'].[25] As a Latin compound that is

---

22 Ibid., 49.
23 Ibid., 47.
24 Ibid., 47, 49, 50.
25 'Sovereignty' is a word that is largely absent from discussions about Alfred and kingship in Anglo-Saxon studies (McKann's *Anglo-Saxon Kingship and Political Power* is a notable exception). While the term begins to circulate in thirteenth-century England, the concept of sovereignty is not anachronistic to the early English period. As a global concept, it can be traced, first, to Assyrian rulers, and witnessed in the exercise of power by 'Islamic, Atlantic, Chinese, even nomadic and exilic' communities and their leaders, many of which pre-date the ninth-century moment of Alfred. See Zvi Ben-Dor Benite, Stefanos Geroulanos, and Nicole Jerr, 'Editors' Introduction,' in *The Scaffolding of Sovereignty: Global and Aesthetic Perspectives on the History of a Concept*, eds. Zvi Ben-Dor Benite, Stefanos Geroulanos, and Nicole Jerr (New York: Columbia University Press, 2017), 6. While Susan Reynolds cautions that 'no medieval ruler…was sovereign in the way that later theorists of the sovereign nation-state would require' ('The Historiography of the Medieval State,' in *Companion to Historiography*, ed. Michael Bentley [London: Routledge, 1997], 111), Francesco Maiolo has taken painstaking efforts to define and understand medieval sovereignty in terms that are fundamentally different from modern sovereignty (as shared, rather than absolute, power within a territory) and exercised

likewise concerned with bodies, language, and Christian faith (to recall the arguments of Brooks and Harris), *Angulsaxonum* brings into presence Alfred's kingdom by translating the physical bodies and vernacular expressions of his subjects into a Latinized, ethnopolitical formula. *Angulsaxonum rex* is therefore an expression of secular-religious sovereignty that is enacted by translating the bodies of a king *and* his subjects. It abstracts Alfred's physical presence and, in its place, identifies those who (and therefore where) he rules — over the people of a temporal kingdom that is nested within God's eternal, heavenly realm.

While the sovereign ambitions of Alfred's royal style are articulated in the charters, they are not realized in these documents. As Ben Snook notes, 'for the diplomatic critic, Alfred's presence is rather less pervasive…. [T]he corpus of late ninth-century West Saxon charters is comparatively small, full of forgeries and,

---

across the kingdoms of medieval Europe (*Medieval Sovereignty: Marsilius of Padua and Bartolus of Saxoferrato* [Delft: Eburon Academic Publishers, 2007]). While one critic believes the definition of modern sovereignty and its body of legal thought 'hampers' Maiolo's arguments (Thomas Izbicki, '08.09.22, Maiolo, Medieval Sovereignty', *The Medieval Review*, https://scholarworks.iu.edu/journals/index.php/tmr/article/view/16669), Peggy McCracken's recent book, *In the Skin of a Beast: Sovereignty and Animality in Medieval France* (Chicago: University of Chicago Press, 2017), not only surveys the many medieval inroads towards sovereignty but also exits the limiting world of medieval jurists in order to consider sovereignty as a concept that operates in literary worlds, which, for McCracken, concern stories about animality. Given this body of evidence that advocates for the relevance to sovereignty in an early English context, one might argue that the absence of the term (and passive resistance to it within Anglo-Saxon studies) reveals not only the masked power of the sovereign but also the extent of Alfred's sovereignty over Anglo-Saxon studies itself. For sophisticated theoretical treatments of sovereignty in the medieval and early medieval periods that attend to the refusal among contemporary theorists to read the archives of medieval Christendom's sovereignty in a manner that would reveal the ways in which sovereignty (and in contemporary parlance, *biopolitics*) always constituted itself by naming various enemies, most notably Muslims and Jews, and how this scholarship has also foreclosed even mention of such entanglements, see Kathleen Biddick, *Make and Let Die: Untimely Sovereignties* (Earth: punctum books, 2016).

from a literary perspective at least, not particularly interesting.'[26] Rather, as Snook continues, 'thanks largely to the work of his biographers Alfred has become an immovable monolith, towering over...the whole Anglo-Saxon era.'[27] Why does Snook pass over the charters and look to biography as the place from which Alfred's sovereign, monolithic power emerges? Because, as Zvi Ben-Dor Benite, Stefanos Geroulanos, and Nicole Jerr explain, 'sovereignty is established and maintained as much by aesthetic, artistic, theatrical, and symbolic structures as by political claims over everyday life, war and peace, and life and death.'[28] In other words, sovereignty comes from creative and, often, theological appropriations of modes of understanding power, while also being solidified in political documentations of power.

First among Alfred's biographers is Asser, a shadowy figure who in 893 writes the *Life of King Alfred* just as charters from the late 880s and early 890s record the change in Alfred's royal style to *Angulsaxonum rex*. Asser employs Alfred's newly asserted royal style throughout his biography, and he narrates the process by which Alfred becomes a sovereign *Angulsaxonum rex* by unpacking an understanding of sovereignty that builds upon the charters' emphasis on linguistic and conceptual modes of translation. In the *Life,* Asser translates Old English annal materials into Latin while he translates Alfred's body (along with those of his subjects) from vernacular, physically embodied forms into Latinized, textual ones.

Importantly, while Asser is guided by the language and spirit of Alfred's recent charters, his *Life* is not limited by them. Asser engages with multiple texts, literary traditions, and genres of writing, composing a biography that many scholars have argued is a bit of a failed project. As Richard Abels summarizes, 'The *Life*'s loose organisation, repetitions, inconsistent use of verb tenses, and lack of conclusion, moreover, suggest a work

---

26 Ben Snook, *The Anglo-Saxon Chancery: The History, Language and Production of Anglo-Saxon Charters from Alfred to Edgar* (Woodbridge: The Boydell Press, 2015), 31.
27 Ibid., 29.
28 Benite, Geroulanos, and Jerr, 'Editors' Introduction,' 3.

in progress rather than a polished text. What we call the *Life of King Alfred* may be no more than an imperfect copy of an incomplete draft.'[29] In terms of aesthetics, Abels's statements are true, but they arise from a tradition of source study and criticism that continues to understand the *Life* from within the parameters of Gregorian, Carolingian, and Davidian models of good governance. As we shall see, Pope Gregory's *Regula Pastoralis*, Einhard's *Life of Charlemagne*, and King David's psalms are of critical value to Asser's biography.[30] However, the scholarship of Abels and other historians does not account for the role of Alfred's charters, which provide a rhetorical and conceptual framework within which these governmental models operate. Asser's network of sources is entangled, and his narrative is messy, to be sure. Yet, these elements work together in order to translate and transform Alfred into *Angulsaxonum rex* — an 'immovable [sovereign] monolith' of the 'Anglo-Saxon era.'[31]

While the *Life of King Alfred* is written around the time of the charters, its story begins several decades earlier, in 849, when 'Alfred, king of the Anglo-Saxons, was born' ['natus est Ælfred,

---

29 Richard Abels, 'Alfred and His Biographers: Images and Imagination,' in *Writing Medieval Biography, 750–1250: Essays in Honour of Frank Barlow*, eds. David Bates, Julia Crick, and Sarah Hamilton (Rochester: Boydell, 2006), 63.

30 While this chapter will focus on Asser's Gregorian and Carolingian sources, it is important to note that *The Life of Alfred* yokes together a much wider range of Latin materials, including phrases from Virgil's *Aeneid*, Aldhlem's *De Virginitate*, Augustine's *Enchiridion*, and the *Vetus Latina* translation of the Bible.

31 It is remarkable and telling that Alfred and his biography are not discussed in relation to the history and theory of sovereignty, given the statements that are made by some of Anglo-Saxon studies' most well-known historians of Alfred. For example, Simon Keynes notes that, 'Alfred was already in his own lifetime to some extent a literary construction' ('Alfred the Great and the Kingdom of the Anglo-Saxons,' 13), and David Pratt has positioned 'Alfredian discourse' within the context of the king's bodily performance, arguing that 'Alfred's body itself acquired an all-encompassing significance, as a microcosmic representation of his kingdom' (*The Political Thought of King Alfred the Great*, 178).

Angul-Saxonum rex'].³² By using the royal style of Alfred's charters to introduce Alfred, Asser announces the *Life* as a political accounting of how Alfred grows up to become sovereign ruler of an Anglo-Saxon kingdom. Asser quickly departs from a discussion of Alfred and turns to annal records (now known, collectively, as the *Anglo-Saxon Chronicle*), translating these materials from Old English into Latin. The annals recount Viking raids on southern Britain, conflicts between and within British kingdoms, and wicked deeds and customs. According to Asser's annal translations, the world into which Alfred is born is full of civil strife and foreign invasions. It is a political landscape in which no British king or kingdom is sovereign. Yet, when Asser invokes the king's royal style a second time, it acts as a bulwark against these disruptions, which are now explained and consigned to the past, in historical retrospect, by 'my lord, the truthful Alfred, king of the Anglo-Saxons' ['domino meo Ælfredo, Angul-saxonum rege veredico'].³³

Despite the sovereign assurances of *Ælfred, Angulsaxonum rex,* Asser continues to translate from the annals, which record the yearly, and therefore recurring, onslaught of Viking attacks. When the character of these incursions changes from intermittent raids in Kent to a full-scale land invasion of East Anglia in 866, Asser's rhetoric and his narrative are forcibly impacted. As if disoriented by the seafaring Vikings, Asser is compelled to speak 'in nautical terms' ['more navigantium'], explaining that as a consequence of the many wars and yearly reckonings, 'the ship' ['navis'] of Alfred's biography has been left to 'to waves and sails' ['undis et velamentis'] and has 'sailed quite far away from

---

32 Simon Keynes and Michael Lapidge, eds., *Alfred the Great: Asser's Life of King Alfred and Other Contemporary Sources* (London: Penguin: 1983), 67; William Henry Stevenson, ed., *Asser's Life of King Alfred, Together with the Annals of Saint Neots Erroneously Ascribed to Asser* (Oxford: Claredon Press, 1904), 12.

33 Keynes and Lapidge, *Alfred the Great*, 71; Stevenson, *Asser's Life of King Alfred*, 12.

the land' ['a terra longius enavigantes'].³⁴ Asser will put it back on course by narrating an account 'of the infancy and boyhood of my venerable lord Alfred, king of the Anglo-Saxons' ['de infantilibus et puerilibus domini mei venerabilis Ælfredi, Angulsaxonum regis'].³⁵ In other words, Asser promises to return Alfred's biography to sovereign shores by recounting, in Latin, personal information that falls outside the political activities recorded in the Old English annals.

After an extended discussion of stories and scenes from Alfred's youth, Asser's *Life* returns to annal materials, which remain preoccupied with Viking activities in Britain and abroad. Viking attacks continue unabated despite defensive efforts led by British kings, including Alfred, who succeeds to the Wessex throne in 871. Throughout these years, Asser calls Alfred *rex*, translating his title according to the Old English annals, which refer to him simply as 'king' ['cyning']. In 882 and 885, however, Alfred's war with the Vikings, which has mostly been fought on land, moves onto the water, where Alfred commands a seafaring fleet that attacks the Vikings and succeeds in gaining some short-lived victories. As Alfred puts his ships on an offensive course against the Vikings, Asser departs from his Old English exemplar three times, substituting *cyning* with the charter formula, *Ælfred, Angulsaxonum rex*.³⁶ The tide appears to have turned in favor of Alfred's political situation, but it does not last. The Vikings return to East Anglia, breaking the fragile peace that he had negotiated with them and prompting Asser to return to his nautical metaphors:

> Accordingly, in order that I may return to that point from which I digressed — and so that I shall not be compelled to sail past the haven of my desired rest as a result of my protracted voyage — I shall, as I promised, undertake, with

---

34 Keynes and Lapidge, *Alfred the Great*, 74; Stevenson, *Asser's Life of King Alfred*, 19.
35 Ibid.
36 Keynes and Lapidge, *Alfred the Great*, 86, 87, 88; Stevenson, *Asser's Life of King Alfred*, 49, 51, 53.

God's guidance, to say something about the life, behaviour, equitable character and, without exaggeration, the accomplishments of my lord Alfred, king of the Anglo-Saxons, after the time when he married his excellent wife from the stock of the Mercians...

[Igitur, ut ad id, unde digressus sum, redeam, ne diuturna enavigatione portum optatae quietis omittere cogar, aliquantulum, quantum notitiae meae innotuerit, de vita et moribus et aequa conversatione, atque, ex parte non modica, res gestas domini mei Ælfredi, Angulsaxonum regis, postquam praefatam ac venerabilem de Mercorium nobilium genere coniugem duxerit...][37]

The annals have, again, lead Alfred's political situation into troubled waters, despite Asser's repeated translations of Old English *cyning* into the Latin charter formula, *Ælfred, Angulsaxonum rex*. Again, the *Life of King Alfred* must be steered in the right direction. And, again, Asser deploys Alfred's royal style as a phrase that holds out the promise of a return to sovereignty by redirecting Alfred's biography towards a lengthy, Latin discussion of private events from the king's early adulthood that are not recorded in the Old English annals.

By positioning Alfred's biography in dialogue with annal records, Asser articulates sovereignty as a concept that is situated in relation to the domain of 'vernacular' politics but cannot be located within it. Asser repeatedly engages Old English annal material in order to begin the process, quite literally, of translating Alfred from his vernacular political world into a personal, Latin one. Asser's recounting of Alfred's childhood, adolescent, and young adult experiences continue this process. They interrupt the yearly accounting of Old English annal records and, together, create a Latin narrative that extends across Alfred's life,

---

37 Keynes and Lapidge, *Alfred the Great*, 88; Stevenson, *Asser's Life of King Alfred*, 54.

tracking, first, his love of English poetry, then his love of Latin writings.

In order to press Alfred in the direction of this textual world, Asser's extra-annal narrative first addresses the issue of Alfred's body. According to Asser, Alfred is chronically ill and has suffered, since youth, from a 'malady' ['dolor'] that he specifies as a 'particular kind of agonizing irritation' ['genus infestissimi doloris'] called 'piles' ['ficum'].[38] Alfred's piles are gifted to him by God so that he may resist the sexual temptations of his adolescence. Yet, at Alfred's wedding celebration, a new sickness overtakes him. Alfred 'was struck...by a sudden severe pain' ['subito et immenso...correptus est dolore'], which remained with him 'from his twentieth year up to his fortieth and beyond' ['a vigesimo aetatis suae anno usque quadragesimum, et eo amplius'].[39] Unlike the piles, which is a term for hemorrhoids, Alfred's new condition is unknown, and his body is not only 'struck' ['correptus'] but also 'seized,' ['arripuit'], 'plagued' ['fatiguit'], and 'harassed' ['perturbatus'] by the unrelenting pains related to this adult sickness.[40] Issues of embodiment take center stage in a *Life* that is keyed to gaining possession of and solidifying Anglo-Saxon sovereignty (and political hegemony). This lexical constellation, which generates a twenty-plus-year scenario of physical pain that attacks and overwhelms Alfred's body, draws Alfred back to his situation in Wessex, where, according to the annals, Alfred's kingdom has been in constant conflict with the Vikings. Asser tightens these connections when he explains that Alfred is burdened 'with all kinds of illnesses unknown to the physicians of his island...and also by the incursions of the Vikings' ['omnibus istius insulae medicis incognitis infirmitatibus...nec-

---

38 Keynes and Lapidge, *Alfred the Great*, 89; Stevenson, *Asser's Life of King Alfred*, 55.
39 Keynes and Lapidge, *Alfred the Great*, 88, 89; Stevenson, *Asser's Life of King Alfred*, 54.
40 Keynes and Lapidge, *Alfred the Great*, 88, 90, 76; Stevenson, *Asser's Life of King Alfred*, 54, 57, 21.

non et paganorum…infestationibus'].[41] Physical 'illnesses' and political 'incursions' sit side by side as parallel forces that act upon Alfred's biological form and his kingdom's territory. They mark an entangled relationship between Alfred's physical body and his political body, indicating that the health (or sickness) of one is coterminous with the other.

Alfred is not only a sick body but also a 'vernacular' one. As a precocious child, Alfred is divinely inspired to learn 'English poems' ['Saxonica poemata'] by heart.[42] Alfred's love and comprehension of English introduces his desire to learn Latin, and he memorizes the '"daily round," that is, the services of the hours, and then certain psalms and many prayers' ['cursum diurnum, id est celebrationes horarum, ac deinde psalmos quosdam et orationes multas'].[43] In his youth, Alfred cultivates the linguistic and religious components of an 'Anglo-Saxon' identity; and, as king, these expressions are amplified by his embodied performances. Alfred's enjoyment of 'reading aloud from books in English and above all learning English poems by heart' ['Saxonicos libros recitare, et maxime carmina Saxonica memoriter discere'] introduces a range of Christian practices.[44] Alfred not only reads from books and memorizes poetry. He also listens to the Mass, participates in psalms and prayers, and gives alms to the needy. All these embodied, ritual activities of Alfred's childhood and adulthood take place, however, amid 'Viking attacks and his continual bodily infirmities' ['paganorum infestationes et cotidianas corporis infirmitates'].[45] Alfred's vernacular or 'Saxon' expressions of a so-called 'Anglo-Saxon' ethnicity op-

---

41 Keynes and Lapidge, *Alfred the Great*, 76; Stevenson, *Asser's Life of King Alfred*, 21.
42 Keynes and Lapidge, *Alfred the Great*, 75; Stevenson, *Asser's Life of King Alfred*, 21. Asser uses four different verbs associated with educational pedagogy to emphasize Alfred's total comprehension of 'Saxon' poetry: 'disco' ['learn'], 'intelligo' ['understand'], 'recito' ['recite'], and 'lego' ['learn'].
43 Keynes and Lapidge, *Alfred the Great*, 75; Stevenson, *Asser's Life of King Alfred*, 21.
44 Keynes and Lapidge, *Alfred the Great*, 91; Stevenson, *Asser's Life of King Alfred*, 59.
45 Ibid.

erate alongside the physical infirmities and territorial attacks upon his two kingly bodies.

Stories of Alfred's private life reveal that embodiment and vernacularity are trip hazards on the journey to sovereignty. Consequently, despite Asser's departure from the annals, Alfred's childhood and adulthood draw Asser, repeatedly, back towards its world of Viking invasion. As stories that are meant to return Alfred's biographical ship to the 'land' of *Ælfred, Angulsaxonum rex*, however, these personal accounts do not simply evidence Alfred's unsovereign body but also work to remedy it. Asser manages the problem of Alfred's physical, vernacular form by bracing his account of Alfred's illnesses against Pope Gregory's *Regula Pastoralis*, a text that characterizes the *rector*, or ruler, as a figure of pious governance who must not only forego temptations of the body[46] but also welcome physical suffering. Like Gregory's *rector*, as a youth, Alfred is sexually tempted, and God gives him piles in order to help him resist his temptations. As an adult, Alfred acts always in accordance with Christian practices in the face of continuous illness and pain. In addition to drawing from Gregory, Asser's *Life* is influenced by Eusebius's *Life of Constantine*, Einhard's *Life of Charlemagne*, and the anonymous *Life of Alcuin*, biographical models that emphasize 'royal devotion' as an aspect of good kingship.[47] These sources instruct

---

46 For example, in Part II, Chapter 2, Gregory explains that fear of God keeps the *rector* humble and pure so that he does not engage in 'delight of the flesh' ['carnis delectatio'] (Grégoire le Grand, *Règle pastorale*, 2 vols., eds. Bruno Judic, Floribert Rommel, and Charles Morel [Paris: Éditions du Cerf, 1992], I:180, ll.48–49). My translation. See also Pratt, 'The Illnesses of King Alfred the Great,' 82.

47 As Paul Kershaw summarizes, Asser's biography 'belongs to a lineage of Christian royal biography that begins with Euseubius's *Life of Constantine*, but has a closer affinity with the more immediate family of Carolingian and sub-Carolingian biographies of pious laymen' ('Illness, Power and Prayer in Asser's *Life of King Alfred*,' *Early Medieval Europe* 10, no. 2 [2001]: 201). These biographies are also thought of as 'mirrors for princes,' and they emphasize what David Pratt, following Kershaw, explains as a 'Carolingian tradition of royal devotion [that] provides by far the clearest precedents for Alfred's own personal piety, described by Asser' ('The Illnesses of King Alfred the Great,' 45).

rulers in the practice of good governance, arguing that the regulation of one's body is *a priori* to governing the bodies of others and therefore an 'enhance[ment]' of the king's secular position.[48] While Asser's religious and lay models of embodied rulership do not absent Alfred's body, they direct its unruly materiality towards enactments of spiritual-secular self-regulation. They prepare Alfred's physical, 'Anglo-Saxon' form for its translation into a Latinized, textual body.

As a child, Alfred's memorization of psalms and prayers is accompanied by an interest in Latin that, as an adult, blossoms into a desire to learn the language and be educated in its scholarship. Alfred seeks teachers, including Asser, from across northern Europe to live at his court in Wessex and to instruct him in the wisdom of Latin texts. This gathering of Latin-educated men returns the *Life* to annal material. Specifically, Alfred's burgeoning interest in Latin prompts Asser to return to the charter language of *Ælfred, Angulsaxonum rex* and to translate an annal entry that documents the identification and voluntary submission of Angle and Saxon subjects to Alfred's governance:

> In that year [886] Alfred, king of the Anglo-Saxons, restored the city of London splendidly...and made it habitable again...All the Angles and Saxons — those who had formerly been scattered everywhere and were not in captivity with the Vikings — turned willingly to King Alfred and submitted themselves to his lordship.

> [Eodem anno Ælfred, Angulsaxonum rex...Lundoniam civitatem honoifice restauravit et habitabilem fecit...Ad quem regem omnes Angli et Saxones, qui prius ubique dispersi

---

48 As Pratt writes, works such as Einhard's *Life of Charlemagne* reshape kingship as a '*ministerium* or office' in which the king's ability to govern was 'dependent upon his prior ability to rule his own body and his household...harness[ing] even more effectively...the needs of royal power' ('The Illnesses of King Alfred the Great,' 44).

fuerant aut cum paganis sub captivitate erant, voluntarie
converterunt, et suo dominio se subdiderunt'].[49]

Asser replaces the Old English reference to Alfred's 'Angelcyn'
people with the phrase, 'omnes Angli et Saxones.'[50] This sleight
of hand, which substitutes a Latin phrase for a vernacular compound, not only ushers in the appearance of 'Angles' and 'Saxons' but, moreover and most importantly, it also reveals these to
be Latin, not vernacular, terms. Asser's Latin emendations to the
886 annal pronounce 'Angles' and 'Saxons' as Latin translations
of vernacular ethnicities. Asser's Latinizing move is followed by
a description of these Anglo-Saxons that expands upon material in the Old English. According to Asser, Angles and Saxons
form a corporate body that consists of everyone ['omnes'], everywhere ['ubique'], who are living freely in diaspora ['dispersi
fuerant'], and count themselves Christian. When these dispersed Christians gather themselves under Alfred's dominion,
their Anglo-Saxon bodies — the *Angulsaxones* named in the
charters as part of Alfred's royal style — define the limits of his
kingdom. Not Saxons and Mercians, but all who can be identified by Latin signifiers and in accordance with Latinate faith, are
counted as *Angli et Saxones,* then rendered into the ethnopolitical subjects of *Ælfred, Angulsaxonum rex.*

Up to this point in the *Life of King Alfred,* Asser has consistently and repeatedly deployed Alfred's royal style in order to signal an understanding of sovereignty that comes from within the
early English charter tradition. Yet Alfred's vernacular, Anglo-
Saxon body acts as a roadblock to enactments of sovereignty

---

49 Keynes and Lapidge, *Alfred the Great,* 97, 98; Stevenson, *Asser's Life of King Alfred,* 69. Note that Keynes and Lapidge argue that Stevenson's emendation of 'sub' from 'sine' contradicts annal statements, and their translation follows the 'original and intended reading' (*Alfred the Great,* 266n199).

50 The 886 annal entry states, 'In that same year, king Alfred restored the town of London, and all English people, except those who were held captive by the Danes, turned to him' ['Þy ilcan geare gesette Elfred cyning Lundenburg, 7 him all Angelcyn to cirde þæt buton deniscra monna hæftniede was'] (*The Anglo-Saxon Chronicle,* 53).

by this charter formula. Asser remedies this issue by translating Old English annal material into Latin and by translating, or recoding, Alfred's vernacular, performative, Anglo-Saxon body into an increasingly Latin-oriented form. Asser's work pays off: Alfred's subjects become an expansive body of Latinized Angles and Saxons who declare Alfred their *Angulsaxonum rex*. Charter language brings to presence a body, a *corpus*, of Alfred's subjects, who acknowledge Alfred's political overlordship to all who are ethnopolitically 'Anglo-Saxon.'

Once this dispersed group of Latinized Angles and Saxons have subordinated themselves to Alfred, and a political body 'of Anglo-Saxons' ['Angulsaxonum'] has been assembled, Asser no longer translates from the Old English annals. Yet a spirit of corporeal assembly guides Asser's discussion of Alfred's embodied relationship to Latin texts: 'It was also in this year [887] that Alfred, king of the Anglo-Saxons, first began...to read [Latin] and to translate at the same time, all on one and the same day' ['Eodem quoque anno seape memoratus Ælfred, Angulsaxonum rex...legere et interpretari simul uno eodemque die primitus inchoavit'].[51] One day, as Alfred was listening intently to some Latin passages that Asser was reading, 'he suddenly showed me [Asser] a little book which he constantly carried on his person ['subito ostendens libellum, quem in sinum suum sedulo portabat'].'[52] As all of Alfred's cognitive energies are focused on taking in this Latin passage, he stretches out ['ostendo'] from the 'hollow,' 'bosom,' or 'hiding-place'[53] ['sinus'] of his garment a little book ['libellus'] comprised of 'the day-time offices and some psalms and certain prayers which he had learned in his youth' ['diurnus cursus et psalmi quidam atque orationes quaedam, quas ille in iuventute sua legerat'].[54] After invoking Alfred's

---

51 Keynes and Lapidge, *Alfred the Great*, 99; Stevenson, *Asser's Life of King Alfred*, 73.
52 Ibid.
53 Charlton T. Lewis and Charles Short, eds., *A Latin Dictionary* (Oxford: Oxford University Press, 1879), s.v. 'sinus, n.'
54 Keynes and Lapidge, *Alfred the Great*, 99; Stevenson, *Asser's Life of King Alfred*, 73. Note that this exchange between Asser and Alfred restages an

royal style, Asser explains that Latin, not 'Saxon,' language and Christian, not secular, poetry have inhabited Alfred's heart since childhood. While Alfred has *legerat* (a term that means 'gather,' 'collect,' 'read,' and 'learn') these Latin fragments for many years, all of these activities have been done in secret.[55] Upon showing Asser his *libellus,* a book so filled with textual snippets that a new one must be commissioned, Alfred sets to work 'like the busy bee, wandering far and wide' as he 'eagerly and relentlessly assembles many various flowers of Holy Scripture, with which he crams full the cells of his heart' ['velut apis fertilissima longe lateque…discurrens, multimodos divinae scripturae flosculos inhianter et incessabiliter congregavit, quis praecordii sui cellulas densatim replevit'].[56] Through this early medieval metaphor,[57] Alfred's 'gathering' and 'collecting' ['legerat'] are intensified as 'assembling' and 'unifying' ['congregavit'] activities.[58] Likewise, this metaphor transfers Alfred's *libellus* from his bosom ['sinus'] into the emotional and affective interior of his heart ['praecordium']. As Alfred is cognitively, then emotion-

---

    earlier scene in which Alfred's mother 'was showing him [Alfred] and his brothers a book of English poetry which she held in her hand' ['sibi et fratibus suis quendam Saxonicum poematicae artis librum, quem in manu habebat, ostenderet'] (Keynes and Lapidge, *Alfred the Great,* 74; Stevenson, *Asser's Life of King Alfred,* 20). Asser not only repeats the language of books ['liber,' 'libellus'] that are held ['ostendo'] in hand ['manus'], but he also recycles, in his exchange with Alfred, the verbs used to track Alfred's full comprehension of 'Saxon' poetry: 'disco' ['learn'], 'intelligo' ['understand'], 'recito' ['recite'], and 'lego' ['learn'] (Keynes and Lapidge, *Alfred the Great,* 75; Stevenson, *Asser's Life of King Alfred,* 20). In so doing, Asser appropriates the terms and conditions that document Alfred's precocious, divinely inspired, and *in toto* process of vernacular learning. By associating Alfred's Latin-learning process with books that are not just held in his hand but moreover positioned within his heart, Asser indicates an intimacy with Latin that trumps Alfred's love of Saxon poems.

55 Lewis and Short, *A Latin Dictionary,* s.v. 'lego, v.,' I, II.B.2.
56 Keynes and Lapidge, *Alfred the Great,* 100; Stevenson, *Asser's Life of King Alfred,* 74.
57 Here and elsewhere, Keynes and Lapidge note Asser's debts to Aldhelm's use of the bee metaphor in *De Virginitate* (*Alfred the Great,* nn161, 213).
58 Lewis and Short, *A Latin Dictionary,* s.v. 'congrego, v.,' II.

ally, 'Latinized,' Latin religious texts are gathered into a *corpus*, then assembled, unified, and inserted within his physical body.

At last, annal material and personal biography work together in the service of *Ælfred, Angulsaxonum rex*. The physical bodies of Angles and Saxons seem to have been transformed into the textual bodies of religious writings. A political *corpus* has become a textual *corpus*, which is now located within Alfred. When this happens, Alfred not only learns to read and translate Latin but, moreover, desires to instruct others in Latin learning and translation:

> Now as soon as that first passage had been copied, he [Alfred] was eager to read it at once and to translate it into English, and thereupon to instruct many others…
>
> [Nam primo illo testimonio scripto, confestim legere et in Saxonica lingua interpretari, atque inde perplures instituere studuit…][59]

As Alfred, king of the Anglo-Saxons, subjects Christian and Latin texts to mental scrutiny and emotional assembly, he becomes a figure of religious literacy ['legere'], translation ['interpretari'], and, finally, instructive governance ['instituere'].[60] No longer is Alfred the subject of translation. Rather, he becomes its agent in order to exercise more compelling displays of royal power.[61] As Robert Stanton writes, 'Alfre[d] clear[ly] identifi[es] with King David as a besieged, wise, and, above all, teaching king,' who is traditionally assumed to have written the Psalms — the primary

---

59 Keynes and Lapidge, *Alfred the Great*, 100; Stevenson, *Asser's Life of King Alfred*, 75.
60 In addition to 'teach' or 'train,' *instituo* also means 'to order, govern, administer, regulate' the actions of others (Lewis and Short, *A Latin Dictionary*, s.v. 'instituo, v.,' II. I, K).
61 I would like to thank Ryan Perry for pointing this out to me and for drawing my attention to Carolingian interest in King David as a literary figure.

contents of Alfred's *libellus*.⁶² Moreover, as Daniel Orton writes, 'For Asser, the figure of Alfred embodied a Davidic union of ecclesiastical and secular power, with the king's piety confirming his divinely ordained status.'⁶³ Alfred's alliance with David not only advances his relationship with 'an important source of influence on the Christian definition of sovereignty' but also orients his kingdom within Christendom's sovereign domain.⁶⁴ As a translator, Alfred's ethnopolitical overlordship over Angles and Saxons reaches towards a scholarly–spiritual governance that positions his kingship and kingdom within a Hebraic tradition, from whence Christ and Christian sovereignty emerge.

Flesh, Text, and Christ's Sovereign Corpse

Sovereignty, as this chapter noted earlier, emerges and is sustained not only by exercises of top-down power but also by the 'aesthetics, representation, and theatricality' of power, which enable the 'staging…reproducing, [and] identifying with sovereignty and its experience.'⁶⁵ Asser's *Life of King Alfred* translates

---

62 Robert Stanton, *The Culture of Translation in Anglo-Saxon England* (Cambridge: D.S. Brewer, 2002), 126.
63 Daniel Orton, 'Royal Piety and Davidic Imitation: Cultivating Political Capital in the Alfredian Psalms,' *Neophilologus* 99, no. 3 (2015): 483.
64 Francesco Miolo, *Medieval Sovereignty*, 129. Note that here, Miolo names Melchisedech, whom 'David is said to have looked…[to]…in the attempt to unite royal and sacerdotal powers. Because of the conquest of Jerusalem, David and his house became heirs to Melchisedch's dynasty of priest-kings' from which 'Jesus Christ and his New Order' unfold (ibid, 129, 130).
65 Benite, Geroulanos, and Jerr, 'Editors' Introduction,' 5. See also Biddick, *Make and Let Die*, Chap. 2, 'Transmedieval Mattering and the Untimeliness of the Real Presence' and Chap. 5, 'Tears of Reign: Big Sovereigns Do Cry,' for the ways in which medieval and early modern forms of sovereignty absorbed and redeployed Christological symbolism and signifiers, and also depended (and still do) on the textual and visual rhetorics of theatrical performance and representational performativity. Biddick's entire book is critical for also understanding the ways in which contemporary theories of sovereignty and biopower (such as from Agamben, Foucault, and Derrida) either misread or completely disregard the medieval archives of the formulation and formations (religious, political, legal, and otherwise) of sovereignty to which they are nevertheless tied, and which archives also

vernacular texts and bodies into Latin in order to transform Alfred into a political overlord of Anglo-Saxon subjects. From here, Asser abandons his literal translation of the Old English annals and focuses his energies on the process by which Alfred is translated into a Latinized, textual body of secular-spiritual sovereignty. Key to Alfred's sovereign recoding are his acts of gathering, collecting, and assembling—of drawing together and assembling within him a *corpus* of physical bodies that seem to have become texts. In the future (and, importantly, this future is not narrated in Asser's biography), Alfred will translate this textual *corpus*. But for now, Asser draws upon the elasticity of the Latin term *corpus* in order to position Alfred directly within the zone of Christian sovereignty.

In the next clause (but in the same sentence that pronounces Alfred's new role as a translator), Asser imagines a biblical 'example' that not only extends Alfred's associations with David to those of Christ but also exposes the sovereign mechanisms that translate a suffering physical *corpus* into an inviolate textual *corpus*:

> …just as we are admonished by the example of the fortunate thief who recognized the Lord Jesus Christ—his Lord and indeed Lord of all things—hanging next to him on the venerable gallows of the Holy Cross, and petitioned Him with earnest prayers. Turning his fleshly eyes only, (he could not do anything else, since he was completely pinned down with nails), he called out in a reverential voice: 'Christ, remember me when thou shalt come into thy kingdom' [Luke 23:42]. This thief first began to learn the rudiments of Christian faith on the gallows; the king likewise (even though in a different way, given his royal station), prompted from heaven, took it upon himself to begin on the rudiments of Holy Scripture on

---

reveal the always entangled relations between the development of political sovereignty, Christian epistemology, and the often violent relations between the Christian Church and its Others, which means not only have we never been secular, but sovereignty is also not thinkable outside of relations of power that are inherently ethnocentric, racist, and violent.

St Martin's Day [11 November] and to study these flowers collected here and there from various masters and to assemble them within the body of one little book (even though they were all mixed up) as the occasion demanded. He expanded it so much that it nearly approached the size of a psalter. He wished it to be called his *enchiridion* (that is to say, 'handbook'), because he conscientiously kept it to hand by day and night. As he then used to say, he derived no small comfort from it.

[…ac veluti de illo felici latrone cautum est, Dominum Iesum Christum, Dominum suum, immoque omnium, iuxta se in venerabili sanctae Crucis patibulo pendentem cognoscente; quo subnixis precibus, inclinatis solummodo corporalibus oculis, quia aliter non poterat, erat enim totus confixus clavis, submissa voce clamaret: 'Memento mei, cum veneris in regnum tuum, Christe,' qui Christianae fidei rudimenta in gabulo primitus inchoavit discere. Hic aut aliter, quamvis dissimili modo, in regia potestate sanctae rudimenta scripturae, divinitus instinctus, praesumpsit incipere in venerabili Martini solemnitate. Quos flosculos undecunque collectos a quibuslibet magistris discere et in corpore unius libelli, mixtim quamvis, sicut tunc suppetebat, redigere, usque adeo protelavit quousque propemodum ad magnitudinem unius psalterii perverniret. Quem enchiridion suum, id est manualem librum, nominari voluit, eo quod ad manum illum die noctuque solertissime habebat; in quo non mediocre, sicut tunc aiebat, habebat solatium.][66]

Asser's interest in the crucifixion expands upon a discussion of the thief, who acts as a proxy for Alfred. While the thief is completely immobilized on the cross, he (and Alfred) can nonetheless turn ['inclinatis'] their 'fleshly,' 'bodily,' or 'corporeal' eyes ['corporalibus oculis']. By restricting all physical movements

---

66 Keynes and Lapidge, *Alfred the Great,* 100; Stevenson, *Asser's Life of King Alfred,* 75, authors' emphasis.

save one, Asser is able to anatomically limit an understanding of what counts as 'bodily' and how the body can move: towards Christ. While the thief hangs, suspended and unmoving on the cross, he turns his eyes but does not gaze upon Christ, who, according to the gospel of Luke, is one breath away from death and from becoming a corpse. Instead, the thief calls out to him in words from Luke, such that the thief begins to learn ['inchoavit discere'] the rudiments of Christian faith ['Christianae fidei rudimenta']. In a similar fashion, Alfred takes it upon himself to begin ['praesumpsit incipere'] the rudiments of Holy Scripture ['sanctae rudimenta scripturae'], assembling them into 'the corpus' or 'body of a little book' ['in corpore unius libelli'].

Asser's crucifixion scene offers a densely articulated meditation on sovereignty via the shifting semantics of *corpus,* a word that means not only 'body' and 'text' but also 'corpse.' As Deborah Posel and Pamila Gupta write,

> the dualistic life of the corpse [positions it] as a material object, on one hand, and a signifier of wider political economic, cultural, ideological and theological endeavours, on the other. The moment of death produces a decaying body, an item of waste that requires disposal — simultaneous with an opportunity, sometimes an imperative — to recuperate the meaning of spent life, symbolically effacing the material extinction that death represents.[67]

Posel and Gupta understand the corpse as a borderland where putrifying 'waste' meets a material 'signifier.' In other words, the corpse negotiates the conversion of a dead body into text. As a site of 'recuperat[ion], it facilitates the ready movement between two different definitions of *corpus* and, as such, functions as 'a pre-eminent site for the identification of...sovereign[ty].'[68]

---

67 Deborah Posel and Pamila Gupta, 'The Life of the Corpse: Framing Reflections and Questions,' *African Studies* 68, no. 3 (2009): 299.

68 Ninna Nyberg Sorensen, 'Governing through the Mutilated Female Body,' in *Governing the Dead: Sovereignty and the Politics of Dead Bodies,* ed. Finn Stepputat (Manchester: Manchester University Press, 2014), 216.

In *The Royal Remains,* Eric Santner explores further the 'dualistic life of the corpse,' explaining, with Lacan, that the body's 'palpitating life-substance' — its 'flesh' — is that 'from which everything exudes.'[69] And he continues (again, with Lacan), arguing that 'the flesh in as much as it is suffering, is formless, in as much as its form in itself is something which provokes anxiety.'[70] The body's often-ill, often-suffering, fleshly form invokes, for Santner, a 'crisis of materiality' that must be managed, lest the body become, upon point of death, what Posel and Gupta articulate above as the decaying waste of the corpse.[71] Santner expands his argument in conversation with Elaine Scarry's *The Body in Pain*:

> [In pain,] the 'obscenely…alive tissue' of the human body is enlisted as a source of verification and substantiation of the symbolic authority of institutions and the social facts they sponsor. This bottoming out of symbolic function on what I am calling the flesh becomes urgent, Scarry argues, when there is a crisis of belief or legitimization in a society… 'allow[ing] extreme attributes of the body to be translated into another language, to be broken away from the body and relocated elsewhere at the very moment that the body itself is disowned.'[72]

Scarry's statements on the body in pain, which Santner recasts as 'flesh' (and Asser identifies as 'corporalis' and 'corpus') locate the suffering, physical body within the field of sovereignty, especially upon point of death. Such a relationship is possible, Santner and Scarry explain, when a community's faith is in jeopardy.

---

69 Eric L. Santner, *The Royal Remains: The People's Two Bodies and the Endgames of Sovereignty* (Chicago: University of Chicago Press, 2011), 64, 65; quoted from Jacques Lacan, *The Seminar of Jacques Lacan: Book II, The Ego in Freud's Theory and in the Technique of Psychoanalysis, 1954–1955,* trans. Sylvana Tomaselli (New York: Norton, 1991), 154.
70 Santner, *The Royal Remains,* 65; Lacan, *The Ego in Freud's Theory,* 155.
71 Santner, *The Royal Remains,* 64.
72 Ibid., xvi, quoting Elaine Scarry, *The Body in Pain: The Making and Unmaking of the World* (New York: Oxford University Press), 31.

During 'a crisis of belief,' only the body's 'sheer material factualness' — its corporeal, suffering, and dying flesh — can lend realness or certainty to political or social ideology that has been challenged or remains unproven. At the moment of death, when the living body becomes a corpse, its flesh can be 'translated into another language.' It can be converted from waste into symbolic meaning. The dualistic life of the corpse facilitates the conversion, amid ideological crisis, from a material *corpus* to a textual *corpus*.

The thinking of Posel and Gupta, and Santner, Lacan, and Scarry, bear upon Christ's crucifixion, a punishment that not only displays Christ's body as tortured flesh but likewise reveals the unshaken, sovereign power of Rome. Further, the crucifixion marks that crisis at which Judaic prophecies must be painfully enfleshed and therefore made real by a Christian messiah, whose death and attendant resurrection ushers in a new faith and political ideology (via supersession).[73] While crucifixion is

---

73 On the ways in which early medieval Christians fabricated imaginative typologies and temporalities to 'supersede' and break off from their Jewish 'neighbors,' which is also repeated, traumatically, in contemporary academic scholarship on Christian-Jewish relations that continues to reinscribe this fissure (which also reenacts its violence, both psychically and materially, on real persons), see Kathleen Biddick, *The Typological Imaginary: Circumcision, Technology, History* (Philadelphia: University of Pennsylvania Press, 2003). On the same state of affairs with regard to Christian and Muslim 'crusader martyrdom,' see Kathleen Biddick, 'Unbinding the Flesh in the Time That Remains: Crusader Martyrdom Then and Now,' GLQ: *A Journal of Lesbian and Gay Studies* 13, nos. 2–3 (2007): 197–225, where she writes that, "[h]istorically, Christianity has constituted and claimed official theological time by virtue of its temporal model of supersession,' especially by way of 'corporeal' fantasies tied especially to Jewish circumcision and Christ's crucifixion, and with the emergence of Islam, 'Christian supersessionary thinking stubbornly maintained this temporal binary by confusing and conflating Muslim and Jewish flesh' (197, 198). Ultimately, for Biddick, in 'posing the question "Who is the enemy?" the theologico-political intertwines itself inextricably with sovereignty. It is therefore ethically urgent to understand the theologico-political vicissitudes of pleasure and pain, flesh and body at stake in the cult of martyrs, then and now' (198). It is not too much of a stretch, I would argue, to see how this also plays out in Asser's *Life of Alfred*.

carried out by the legal authority of Rome, Christ's death is permitted by God the Father, whose paternal will renders Christ's body an 'obscenely...alive tissue' and 'translate[s]' it, by way of a pain that ends in death, into the new 'symbolic order' of Christianity. Under joint penalty of earthly and heavenly sovereigns, Christ's flesh (bodily *corpus*) is rendered a corpse (*corpus*), then translated into Christian Logos (textual *corpus*). Once 'the *incontestable reality of [Christ's] physical body...[has] become an attribute of an issue that at that moment has no independent reality of its own*,'[74] Christ assumes his place as Son of God and sovereign figure of Christian signification.

Asser's retelling of the Crucifixion leverages the full force of Christ's sovereign corpse in order to complete the project of making Alfred a king of Christian sovereignty. Asser positions Alfred, king of the Anglo-Saxons, within this scene at the moment when Alfred's suffering, yet still living, body has been thoroughly textualized and needs only the ideological weight provided by Christianity to substantiate his claim to sovereignty. With the *corpus* of Christ in his hand — with an *enchiridion* or hand-book that marks Alfred's partial conversion of flesh to text — Alfred is interpolated within its Latin world of Holy Scripture. In the following sentence, Alfred hangs openly (rather than by proxy) on the cross as a figure whose living body in pain is, like Christ's, now an agent of Christian sovereignty. Alfred's *piles* and unknown illnesses are no longer medical manifestations but representative of purposive, spiritual suffering. Alfred's body is no longer a worrisome material of decay but, as Scarry would say, an 'attribute' of Christian doctrine that has no 'independent reality of its own.'[75] As Asser explains, Al-

---

74 Santner, *The Royal Remains*, xvi, author's emphasis; quoting Scarry, *The Body in Pain*, 124–25.
75 Note that Asser's crucifixion scene connects to Gregory's figure of the *rector*, whose physical suffering eventually transforms his body into a form that is staked out between the poles of living ['vivendi'] and dying ['moriens']. As Gregory writes, 'He, therefore — indeed, he precisely — must devote himself entirely to setting an ideal of living. He must die to all passions of the flesh and by now lead a spiritual life' ['Ille igitur, ille modis

fred is 'transfixed by the nails of many tribulations[,]...plagued continually with the savage attacks of some unknown disease[, and]...perturbed...by the relentless attacks of foreign peoples' ['multis tribulationum clavis confossus...gravissima incogniti doloris infestione incessanter fatigatur...assiduis exterarum gentium infestationibus...inquietabatur'].[76] In full possession of his little book of scripture, however, Alfred's ill and sickly physical form is translated and transformed into the world-making Latin narrative of Christian sovereignty.

On the cross, Alfred suffers like Christ and alongside Christ such that his body's physical suffering form now aggrandizes Alfred's territorial limits. Asser immediately catalogues the king's 'frequent expeditions and battles against the Vikings and of the unceasing responsibilities of government...his daily involvement with the nations which lie from the Mediterranean to the farthest limit of Ireland...[and]...letters sent to him with gifts from Jerusalem by the patriarch Elias' ['frequentibus contra paganos expeditionibus et bellis et incessabilibus regne gubernaculis...cotidiana nationum,[77] quae in Tyrenno mari usque ultimum Hiberniae finem habitant...de Hierosolyma ab El[ia] patriarcha epistolas et dona illi directas'].[78] Alfred's earthly powers stretch from the periphery of Europe towards the center of Christendom, and then return home, where Alfred exercises these powers to rebuild towns, fashion treasures, construct halls and chambers, and move royal residences. While threats to Alfred have not abated, *Ælfred, Angulsaxonum rex* manages them

---

omnibus debet ad exemplum vivendi pertrahi, qui cunctis carnis passionibus moriens iam spiritaliter vivit']. See Part I, Chapter 10 of St. Gregory the Great, *Pastoral Care,* trans. Henry Davis (Westminster: Newman Press, 1950), 38; Grégorie le Grand, *Règle pastorale,* I:160–62, ll.1–4.

76 Keynes and Lapidge, *Alfred the Great,* 101; Stevenson, *Asser's Life of King Alfred,* 76.

77 'The transmitted text (*de cotidiana nationum*) is evidently corrupt, as Stevenson recognized...a word such as *sollicitudine* has fallen out after *cotidiana,* and our translation incorporates his suggestion' (Keynes and Lapidge, *Alfred the Great,* 270n219).

78 Keynes and Lapidge, *Alfred the Great,* 101; Stevenson, *Asser's Life of King Alfred,* 76–77.

with an indefatigable presence-in-pain that is no longer focused on preventing invasion but on extending its territorial limits. Alfred governs, simultaneously, in close proximity and at a distance from his political territories and subjects. He is physically present yet entirely absent from the exercise of royal power. He remains a living, physical body (*corpus*) in pain even though he holds Christ's sovereign corpse/text (*corpus*) in his hand.

Once Alfred's ill and suffering flesh — its crisis of materiality — is recoded within the textual-symbolic, typological order of Christianity, *Ælfred, Angulsaxonum rex* 'is' in perpetual, organized motion. Alfred expands his personal and political borders in order to make his kingdom a heaven on earth. Once these acts are complete, Asser returns to the nautical language from whence his narrative began, describing the king as an 'excellent pilot' ['gubernator praecipuus'] who now 'guide[s] his ship laden with much wealth to the desired safe haven of his homeland' ['navem suam multis opibus refertam ad desideratum ac tutum patriae suae portum...perducere'].[79] Alfred's biographical ship no longer 'waver[s] or wander[s] from course' ['haud aliter titubare ac vacillare'] because Alfred now contains within himself both the Latinized *Angli* and *Saxones* and the Latin body of Christ.[80] As helmsman of his own story, Alfred enacts the ontological task of being 'Anglo-Saxon.' His royal style is no longer appositive to, but located within, his name. Consequently, after this point in the narrative, *Ælfred, Angulsaxonum rex* no longer appears in Asser's *Life*.

Asser's biography enacts an understanding of sovereignty that is pronounced within the charters, in which Old English oral expressions and embodied rituals are translated into Latin texts that recode the king's body and earthly kingdom within the eternal reaches of Christ's sovereign Word and his heavenly domain. Positioning Alfred within Christ's sovereignty happens by way of creative, theatrical means that Latinize and textualize

---

79 Keynes and Lapidge, *Alfred the Great*, 101; Stevenson, *Asser's Life of King Alfred*, 77.
80 Ibid.

the bodies of the Anglo-Saxons Alfred governs in order to assemble them within Alfred's own Latin, textual frame. In order to complete this translation, Asser draws upon the crucifixion scene, exposing Christ's *corpus* (a body, corpse, and text) as the sovereign whose cosmological weight is necessary to substantiate Alfred's claim to sovereignty, and pointing out the 'seriality' of sovereignty, a concept 'invented as a secularized successor to divine representation.'[81]

Asser's *Life of King Alfred* imagines a narrative conclusion in which Alfred has arrived as a figure of Anglo-Saxon sovereignty. However, his crucifixion fantasy begins at the moment when the translation of Alfred into Latin texts has resulted in Alfred's desire to become a translator. While Alfred sets out to translate the texts he has copied in his *libellus,* this is a project that is not realized within Alfred's biography. In calling forth Alfred as a translator, Asser references a body of texts that are produced at Alfred's court, beginning with David's *Psalms* and including Gregory's *Cura pastoralis* and *Dialogi,* Boethius's *De consolatione philosophiae,* Augustine's *Soliloquae,* Orosius's *Historia,* and Bede's *Historia ecclesiastica.* While this textual body — this Alfredian *corpus* — is located beyond the narrative boundaries of Asser's *Life,* Asser nonetheless positions Alfred's body within striking distance of it. To say it a different way, Asser's biography not only imagines Alfred's sovereignty over the Anglo-Saxons according to terms understood in the early English charters. Moreover, it leans heavily on the sovereign *corpus* of Christ in order to assert secular succession (which is also a violently Christological supersession, as Kathleen Biddick has demonstrated in her important work on the development of sovereignty in the medieval period). Furthermore, Asser's *Life* writes a promissory note to Alfred, quietly asserting that he will in the future become a sovereign like Christ, when his physical body is translated into an Alfredian textual *corpus.*

---

81 George Edmondson and Klaus Mladek, 'Introduction: Sovereignty Crises,' in *Sovereignty in Ruins: A Politics of Crisis,* eds. George Edmonson and Klaus Mladek (Durham: Duke University Press, 2017), 13.

Sovereignty's Morbid Ontology: Civil Wars, Alfred's Corpse, and the Ghosts of Effigial Portraiture

The royal style, *Angulsaxonum rex,* remained in circulation for several decades after Alfred's death, in the charter language of Edward and Athelstan. However, the term was under pressure, even during Alfred's reign, from the alternative and more inclusively styled *rex Anglorum.* As an expression of limited range — one that claimed sovereignty in fiction but could not sustain it in politics — 'Anglo-Saxon' fell out of use by the mid-1000s, when later medieval historians ceded Alfred's role as political unifier to Egbert, first monarch of England's so-called Saxon heptarchy. In the sixteenth century, however, 'Anglo-Saxon' makes a comeback.[82] And in the seventeenth, Alfred does,

---

82 'Anglo-Saxon' returns to print in Sir John Smith's *Dialogue on the Correct and Improved Writing of English* [*De recta et emendata linguae anglicae scriptione, dialogus*] (Paris: Ex officina Roberti Stephani Typographi Regij, 1568), and in William Camden's *Britannia: Or, A Chorographical Description of the Most Flourishing Kingdoms of England, Scotland, and Ireland, and the Adjacent Islands, out of the Depth of Antiquity* [*Britannia siue florentissimorum regnorum, Angliae, Scotiae, Hiberniae, et insularum adiacentium ex intima antiquitate chorographica descriptio*] (London: per Radulphum Newbery, 1587). These are the first postmedieval texts to employ 'Anglosaxones' (in contrast to the more popular referents, 'Saxones' and 'Angles'). In Smith's treatise on spelling reform, he emphasizes the value of 'Anglo-Saxon language and writing' ['Anglosaxonicæ linguæ & scriptionis'], which belong to 'those Anglosaxons, our ancestors' ['illos atavos nostros Anglosaxones'], 'our esteemed elders' ['maiores nostros'], and 'those first Anglosaxons [who] considered very carefully the nature of letters and wrote more correctly, than we do today' ['primos illos Anglosaxones multo curiosius intuitos esse naturam literarum, quam nos hodie facimus, rectiusque scripsisse'] (22, 23, 32, 32–33). Camden uses 'Anglosaxones' as a consolidating term for Angles, Saxons, and Jutes that marks them as collectively distinct from the 'Scoti' and 'Picti' of Britain (55–62). All translations of seventeenth- and eighteenth-century Latin texts are my own.

As a compound that is tied to issues of language reform and British history, these early modern re-uses of 'Anglosaxon' acknowledge its ties to ethnopolitical identity. Yet Philemon Holland's English translation of Camden's *Britannia* repositions the ethnopolitics of the compound within a contemporary framework of English identity. Holland trans-

too. At Oxford University, a passage supposedly copied from a manuscript of Asser's *Life* in the 1590s demonstrates Alfred's role as the university's ninth-century 'refounder.'[83] As Simon Keynes writes, this ignited 'a special enthusiasm for Alfred, in Oxford,'[84] where engravings, portraits, stained and etched glass, and a bust, all bearing his likeness, were located in various University buildings.[85]

Sir John Spelman's posthumously published biography, *The Life of Ælfred the Great,* addresses this purported relationship between Alfred and Oxford.[86] Moreover, it yokes Alfred's kingship to that of Charles I and his son, Prince Charles. Spelman, a royalist,[87] wrote his biography of Alfred at the outset of the English Civil Wars,[88] a nine-year conflict that disputed the absolute sovereignty of Charles I in battles fought, simultaneously,

---

lates 'Anglosaxones' as 'English-Saxons,' and prefaces Camden's discussion of Angles, Saxons, and Jutes with a map of Britain titled 'Englalond Anglia Anglosaxoum Heptarchia,' under which is written 'Terra Armis Animisque Potens' (image between pages 126 and 127). Image and text coordinate to nuance the compound's function as a term by which an early modern 'Englalond' and a medieval 'Anglia' are temporal successors to the 'Heptarchy of Anglo-Saxons,' but, together, they figure as 'a land strong in arms and in spirit.' Holland's map not only confirms the *a priori* status of a unified and 'powerful' Anglo-Saxon England within Britain, but also inflects the subsequent narrative of English-Saxons, who, unlike the Picts and Scots, are a people within a nation, possessing a single and singular ethnopolitical status.

83 Simon Keynes, 'The Cult of King Alfred the Great,' *Anglo-Saxon England* 28 (1999): 244.
84 Ibid., 245.
85 Ibid., 261, 262, and image VIIIa.
86 Sir John Spelman, *The Life of Ælfred the Great* (Oxford: Printed at the theater for Maurice Atkins at the Golden-ball in St. Paul's Church-Yard, London, 1709).
87 Corinne Comstock Weston and Janelle Renfrow Greenberg explain that Spelman's political writings 'delineat[ed] a theory of a legal sovereignty in the king' alone (*Subjects and Sovereigns: The Grand Controversy Over Legal Sovereignty in Stuart England* [Cambridge: Cambridge University Press, 1981], 109).
88 Roberta Frank notes that Spelman's biography of Alfred was written c. 1642, the year in which the First Civil War began ('The Search for the Anglo-Saxon Oral Poet,' in *Textual and Material Culture in Anglo-Saxon*

in England, Scotland, and Ireland. Spelman's biography turns to Alfred, and to sovereignty. It braces the contemporary crisis of political faith in Charles I (which fragmented Britain into factionalized territories) against the biography of an early medieval king who gathers the 'broken Reliques of the *Saxon-Heptarchy*' into one corporate body and becomes the 'sole Sovereign of the whole Island [of Britain]' and '*King of the* English-Saxons.'[89]

The Life of Ælfred the Great is dedicated to Prince Charles, and in order to render Alfred a sovereign in whom the prince (and his father, the king) may have faith, Spelman delinks Alfred's illness from his political tribulations.[90] Likewise, he says nothing about Alfred's death. However, Spelman meticulously traces the fate of Alfred's corpse. After an initial burial at Winchester's New Minster, 'his Body was taken up from thence in the Abbey of *Hyde,* without the Gates of *Winchester*,' and, in 1520, his 'Bones,' along with 'several other of our Kings and Noble Persons,' were collected, put into identified lead chests, and placed on top of a wall built to enclose the Winchester Presbytery.[91] Then, 'at last, Dec. 14, 1642. the Rebells…most sacrilegiously broke into the Church…and amongst the rest prophan'd and violated these Sacred Cabinets of the Dead, scattering the Bones all over the Church, and carrying them in Triumph into other Places, some whereof were brought to *Oxford,* and lodged

---

England: Thomas Northcote Toller and the Toller Memorial Lectures, ed. Donald Scragg [London: D.S. Brewer, 2003], 145n52).

89 Spelman, *The Life of Ælfred the Great,* 92, author's emphasis. See also Robert Powell, *The Life of Alfred, or Alvred* (Paul's Church-yard: Printed by Richard Eadger for Thomes Alchorn, 1634), the biographical precursor to Spelman's work. The subtitle of Powell's work claims 'ALVRED' as 'The first Institutor of sub-*ordinate government in this* Kingdome, and Refounder of the Vniversity of OXFORD' in 'Parallel' to 'our Soveraigne Lord, K. CHARLES' (title page).

90 While Spelman narrates Alfred's 'Pain of the Piles and Emrauds,' which God converts, at Alfred's request, into 'an intestine Pain' that appears at the time of marriage,' this discussion is limited to one section of text and bracketed off from his political activities, which have already rendered him sovereign (*The Life of Ælfred the Great,* 207, 208).

91 Ibid., 217, 217n2, author's emphasis.

in the Repository adjoyning to the [Bodelian] Publick Library.'[92] After death, Alfred's corpse shows no signs of decay. It shifts seamlessly from a 'Body' to 'Bones,' which are translated three times before becoming 'at last' a casualty of the Civil Wars. Yet, the desecrating acts of the rebels have landed Alfred (along with several others) in the book repository of Oxford's library, where pieces of his unmarked bones are now 'lodged' with a *corpus* of texts. England's Civil Wars prove to be the crisis of faith that recuperates Alfred's corpse: translating it — recoding it — repeatedly until there is no more material waste to be found. *Alfred's physical body is lost in translation.* And this enables Alfred to become, like the body of Christ, sovereign reading material for Charles I and the Prince, whose living flesh is cause for national anxiety and therefore truly at risk.

Spelman's biography is never published in his lifetime, and as the Civil Wars continue, anxieties over the king's sovereignty and his material flesh reach a crisis point. In 1649, Charles I is beheaded, Prince Charles is exiled, and a short-lived republican Commonwealth is established. It is not until several decades after Charles II's restoration to the throne that a Latin translation of Spelman's biography is finally published at Oxford in 1678.[93] Still dedicated to Prince Charles (even though his brother, James II, has succeeded him on the throne), the Latin *Life of Ælfred the Great* remains concerned with the body of the king and the

---

92 Ibid., 217n2, author's emphasis. Spelman's history is dubious. In 1538, Hyde Abbey was given over to Henry VIII's officers. 'John Leland, Henry VIII's historian recorded that lead tablets bearing the names Alfred and Edward were found in tombs in front of the great altar at Hyde,' but there is no record of their disturbance during the Civil Wars (Eric Klingelhofer and Kenneth Qualmann, 'Hyde Abbey,' in *Medieval Archaeology: An Encyclopedia*, ed. Pam J. Crabtree [New York: Routledge, 2016], 170).

93 Sir John Spelman, *The Life of Alfred the Great, Unvanquished King of the English, Bound in Three Books* [*Aelfredi Magni, Anglorum regis invictissimi vita tribus libris comprehensa*] (Oxford: E Theatro Sheldoniano, 1678). The identity of the translator is uncertain, but Obadiah Walker and Christopher Wase have been suggested as possibilities (Matthew Kilburn, 'The Learned Press: History, Languages, Literature, and Music,' in *The History of Oxford University Press: Volume I: Beginnings to 1780*, ed. Ian Gadd [Oxford: Oxford University Press, 2013], 425).

Figure 1. Engraving in Sir John Spelman, *Life of Ælfred the Great, Unvanquished King of the English, Bound in Three Volumes* [*Aelfredi Magni, Anglorum regis invictissimi vita tribus libris comprehensa*] (Oxford: E Theatro Sheldoniano, 1678), n.p., Tab[ula] I. Image courtesy of Smith College.

post-Restoration fate of sovereignty. Consequently, it introduces the *Life* with a series of engravings, the first of which depicts the body of Alfred (see Fig. 1).[94]

Copied from a portrait at Oxford that was painted 'within a year or so of the Restoration,' this image depicts the king with a furrowed brow, sagging eyes, and an ungroomed beard.[95] Painted to the tune of royal politics, Alfred looks exhausted by the turmoil of previous decades. Nevertheless, his aged body has weathered England's crisis of sovereignty, and he remains in possession of his crown and royal robes. Alfred wears the regalia of the king's funeral effigy.[96] His portrait showcases the immortal *dignitas* of English sovereignty, which is vested in Christ's corpse, a physical body made into a divine form. Despite the regicide of Charles I, which materialized the king's flesh as waste and decay, Alfred's biography is not (the portrait seems to say) a dead letter to royal sovereignty. While the *Life*'s textual narrative — into which the 'Body' and 'Bones' of Alfred's sovereign corpse was translated — did not fulfill its promises of reuniting the country's warring political factions and of keeping Charles on the throne, Alfred's effigial portrait provides its own 'embodied' assurances. It claims that Alfred's sovereignty, passed down

---

94 Simon Keynes, 'The Cult of King Alfred the Great,' 261, fig. VIIIa.
95 Ibid., 261. Keyes notes that the portrait was commissioned by Oxford's University College and hung in the college Master's lodgings (ibid.).
96 The Oxford portrait calls forth a relationship between the king's two bodies, as theorized in Ernst Kantorowicz's magisterial study *The King's Two Bodies*. Beginning with the late medieval period and continuing well through the seventeenth century, the king, like Christ, is a geminated figure — both human and divine, simultaneously. Consequently, sovereignty rests within the king's body, yet upon death it survives in his sacred office. As Kantorowicz explains, while the king's dead body was buried 'naked or in his winding sheet,' an effigy of the king, dressed in regalia, was publicly displayed as 'the true bearer of royal glory and the symbol of a Dignity "which never dies"' (*The King's Two Bodies: A Study in Medieval Political Theology* [Princeton: Princeton University Press, 2016], 424). For an important critique, however, of the ways in which modern theories of sovereignty and biopolitics (whether Kantorowicz or Agamben or Foucault) have a severe blind spot with regard to the medieval archive, see again, Biddick, *Make and Let Die*.

in an unbroken succession of English monarchs, is immaterial, inviolate, and everlasting.

In the wake of the Civil Wars (when the king really is dead, and Alfred's sovereign, textualized corpse could not keep him alive), Alfred returns as an effigy that is out of time with the political moment in which Spelman's *Life* is published. Consequently, Alfred haunts the present tense, zombie-like, holding out anachronistic faith in an outmoded understanding of sovereignty that belongs to the political theology of an earlier moment. And yet, as Paul Downes explains, Alfred's untimely effigy shows that 'sovereignty,' from the 'perspective of many contemporary critics, was always a ghost-in-denial — a walking fantasy of full and singular presence that refused to acknowledge its own mortality.'[97] Sovereignty, Downes notes, has a 'morbid ontology' because it belongs to a past that is located in no particular temporal moment.[98]

Alfred's late-seventeenth-century effigy reinforces this point. As Joseph Roach explains, the effigy is 'a sacred relic, a medieval holdover that…attempted to preserve and publicize the image of an individual in the absence of his or her person.'[99] As a verb, 'effigy,' Roach continues, 'evoke[s] an absence, to body something forth, especially something from the distant past…which, among other capacities, communicates personas as well as practices over time and space.'[100] Notably, Alfred's seventeenth-century effigy is engraved and published just after the death of Charles II, whose effigial displays mark a shift in how the divine or second body of the king is visually presented.[101] As this ritual of sovereign succession disappeared, Roach explains that

---

97 Paul Downes, *Hobbes, Sovereignty, and Early American Literature* (New York: Cambridge University Press, 2015), 25.

98 Ibid., 24.

99 Joseph Roach, 'Celebrity Erotics: Pepys, Performance, and Painted Ladies,' in *Politics, Transgression, and Representation at the Court of Charles II*, eds. Julia Marciari Alexander and Catharine MacLeod (New Haven: Yale University Press, 2007), 234.

100 Ibid.

101 At his funeral, a crown was placed on top of his coffin. A life-sized wax figure stood next to his grave for more than a century.

Figure 2. Frontispiece engraving in Sir John Spelman, *The Life of Ælfred the Great* (Oxford: Printed at the Theater for Maurice Atkins at the Golden-ball in St. Paul's Church-Yard, London, 1709). Image courtesy of Cambridge Library.

'derivative specters' — full-sized portraits, engravings, busts, and statuary monuments — came to take its place. It is as if the 'corpse-like, piously recumbent effigies on medieval tombs "raised themselves up...and began to look round".'[102] Roach quotes John Ruskin here, who explains that as these royal effigies became statues, and statues became portraits, all 'memory of death' was effaced. As Ruskin himself put it, 'The statue rose up, and presented itself in front of the tomb...surrounded...by allegorical figures of Fame and Victory...by personifications of humbled kingdoms and adoring nations, and by every circumstance of pomp, and symbol of adulation.'[103]

As if aware of the haunting powers of its own morbid ontology, Alfred's sovereign ghost begins to circulate. Beginning with Spelman, a succession of biographies are introduced by portraits of the king. In 1709, the English edition of Spelman's *Life* is published (see Fig. 2).

The Alfred on the frontispiece to the English edition of Spelman's *Life* is not a tired and aging king who is burdened by the weight of rule. His face is youthful-looking and framed by light curls, and his head is ringed with a laurel wreath. Alfred's portrait is set on a pedestal that is inscribed with a passage from Isaiah 58.12 that fashions Alfred into a political messiah who one day 'shalt raise up the Foundations of many Generations' and 'shalt be called, the Repairer of the Breach' and 'the Restorer of Paths to dwell in.'[104] Alfred's youthful portrait is marked by a sovereign destiny, which will one day be fulfilled.

---

102 Roach, 'Celebrity Erotics,' 236, my emphasis; quoting John Ruskin, *The Stones of Venice,* Book 3.
103 Ibid.
104 Spelman, *The Life of Ælfred the Great,* frontispiece.

Figure 3. Frontispiece engraving in Francis Wise, *The Annals of the History of Alfred the Great, By the Author Asser of Menevia* [*Annales rerum gestarum Ælfredi Magni, auctore Asserio Menevensi*] (Oxford, 1722). Image courtesy of British Library.

Figure 4. Engraving by George Vertue in Paul de Rapin-Troyas, *History of England: As Well Ecclesiastical as Civil*, Vol. 1, trans. Nicholas Tindal (London: Printed for James and John Knapton at the Crown in St. Paul's Church-Yard, 1726). Image Courtesy of New York Public Library.

As Suzanne Hagedorn,[105] Simon Keynes,[106] and Joanne Parker[107] note, Spelman's English *Life of Ælfred the Great* was highly influential within and beyond Oxford. When Francis Wise's edition of Asser's *Life of King Alfred* adapts the visual architecture from Spelman's Latin and English editions, it communicates a sovereignty that is no longer destined for a future but operates within one that has already arrived. In Wise's engraving (see Fig. 3), Alfred's homespun tunic is abandoned for ermine robes; Alfred's laurel now hovers, nimbus-like, above his head; Isaiah's prophecies of a future 'Repairer of the Breach' and 'Restorer of Paths' have been replaced with the appellative 'Alfredus Magnus'; and his portrait's blank background is filled in with a cartouche that displays an entire kit of visual symbols that signal a *Life* that is as much myth as it is history.

When Wise's engraving is adapted by George Vertue for Paul Rapin's *History of England,* Alfred's enlivened and expansive physical body is given dimension (see Fig. 4). In this new engraving, the strands of a chain extend from within the folds of Alfred's garment, across the cartouche, and onto the table, linking Alfred's bosom and two-dimensional portrait to his three-dimensional political world. Objects that were positioned at the

---

105 Suzanne D. Hagedorn notes that 'for close to two centuries,' Spelman's *Life* was 'considered the authoritative biography of the king, and as such it provided a historical basis for the glorification of Alfred and his reign in the popular imagination' ('Received Wisdom: The Reception History of Alfred's Preface to the Pastoral Care,' in *Anglo-Saxonism and the Construction of Social Identity,* eds. Allen J. Frantzen and John D. Niles [Gainesville: Florida University Press, 1997], 94).

106 Keynes makes the case for the influence of Spelman on later scholars, arguing that his *Life of Ælfred* 'effectively determined the parameters of Alfredian studies which have endured to the present day' and 'has a serious claim on our attention, whether judged as a tract for its times, or as a forerunner of modern scholarship' ('The Cult of King Alfred the Great,' 254, 256).

107 Joanne Parker writes that 'Alfred found a life beyond the scholarly and ecclesiastical world and in the realm of popular culture...became intimately associated with the Hanoverian line....[A]t the root of almost all this new Alfrediana was Spelman's *Life*' (*'England's Darling': The Victorian Cult of Alfred the Great* [Manchester: Manchester University Press, 2007], 61).

top of Wise's cartouche are now placed on the table upon which Alfred's portrait sits. The tools of Alfred's scholarship — a stack of books, an open scroll, a compass, and ruler — are arranged, as if in use, while Alfred's harp, his bows, the Danes' captured standards, and laurel wreath (the trophies of his recent military actions) are pushed into the corner. These objects have been, quite literally, brought out of their frame, and each represents a moment in the king's expanding narrative. On a table, these objects give spatial dimension and material depth to Alfred's sovereign narrative. The tablecloth upon which Alfred's portrait rests, with its angular lines and corners, provides further dimensionality to it, and the military scenes that appear on each side create a sense of temporal motion that is, however, nonlinear. As Alfred 'sits,' surrounded by an array of material symbols and on a field of military scenes, his physical body is rendered omnipresent and mythic, capable of crossing space as well as time.

As Simon Keynes writes, Vertue's frontispiece 'directly or indirectly, exerted a strong influence on the development of Alfredian iconography in the later eighteenth century,' and, in the wake of its publication, the sovereign, spectral body of Alfred begins to cross corporeal dimensions as it becomes the subject of fine art.[108] In both small and large historical scenes, Alfred is portrayed as minstrel, cake-burner, precocious child, and lawgiver.[109] Completely dead, yet forever living, Alfred's form stands

---

108 Keynes, 'The Cult of King Alfred the Great,' 282.
109 Keynes has catalogued a full listing of Alfredian art produced during the nineteenth century. Here are some of the titles, artist names, and themes: 'Alfred the Great in disguise of a peasant, reflecting on the misfortunes of his country' by Richard Dadd; 'Alfred submitting his code of laws for the approval of the witan' by John Bridges; 'Alfred in the camp of the Danes' by Marshall Claxton; 'King Alfred the Great dividing his loaf with the beggar' by Alexander Blaikley; 'Alfred inciting the English to resist the Danes' by G.F. Watts; 'Alfred, the Saxon king, disguised as a minstrel, in the tent of Guthrum the Dane' by Daniel Maclise; 'The boyhood of Alfred' by John Callcott Horsley; 'Alfred the Great when a youth, encouraged by the Queen, listening to the heroic lay of a minstrel' by Solomon Alexander Hart; 'King Alfred and his Mother' by Alfred Stevens; 'Alfred, surrounded by his family, addresses Edward his son and successor' by W.P. Salter; the unfinished 'Alfred and his First Trial by Jury' by Benjamin Robert Haydon;

in for a sovereignty that was 'killed' at the beheading of Charles I and is realized as ghostly and undead upon the return of Charles II. Yet, on account of its spectral nature, Alfred's corpse-like effigy circulates, making its way from Oxford books to London galleries, from engraved plates and early modern portraiture to sprawling, multi-bodied, historical scenes of the Victorian period. In these new visual environments, Alfred's 'flesh' diffuses into the flesh of others. (To recall Spelman, his actual body and bones have been long lost in Oxford's book repository.) Alfred can be a youth, young man, or adult; blonde- or brown-haired; bearded or clean-shaven; in disguise or regally attired; and/or interacting with men, women, and children from different walks of life. Alfred's constantly circulating and shape-shifting sovereign form exceeds its two- and three-dimensional limits. He (or, maybe, 'it'?) comes to inhabit anybody's body. In short, an Alfredian ghost of English sovereignty begins to look like an 'Englishman.'

'King Alfred in the Neatherd's Cottage' by J. Pain Davis; and 'King Alfred in the Swineherd's Cottage' ('The Cult of King Alfred the Great,' 334–41).

ON BEING AN ANGLO-SAXONIST

Figure 5. BobW66, photograph of the Winchester statue of Alfred. Creative Commons BY-SA 3.0 Unported license. No modifications have been made to this image.

Alfred's ghostly figure changes its shape permanently on the weekend of September 18–20, 1901 in Winchester, England. Thousands of people gathered in Winchester — home to Alfred's Wessex capital and to his burial place of Hyde Abbey — to celebrate the one-thousand year anniversary of King Alfred's death. The central activity of this three-day event was not a visitation to Alfred's gravesite but the unveiling of a 'colossal,' thirteen-foot bronze statue of the living king (see Fig. 5) placed atop a pedestal consisting of two immense blocks of grey Cornish granite. As Joanne Parker explains, the statue 'faced some initial opposition' by Leonard Cust, Director of the National Portrait Gallery, 'who argued that it would be impossible to produce an authentic representation of a man for whom no accurate contemporary portraiture existed, and that a different form of sculpture…would be more appropriate.'[110] Yet those involved in planning Alfred's millenary celebration wanted 'the closest equivalent to a portrait in stone,' and Parker writes that the chosen sculptor, Hamo Thornycroft, was known as 'the leading exponent of the naturalistic and anti-classical movement,' and was also the son of Thomas Thornycroft, 'whose sculptural group, *Alfred the Great Encouraged to the Pursuit of Learning by his Mother,* had been criticised on the grounds of its excessive realism.'[111] This tension between Alfred's corporeal body and his sovereign, corpse-like effigy structures Lord Rosenbery's speech at the unveiling of Thornycroft's statue:

> the noble statue which I am about to unveil can only be an effigy of the imagination, and so the real Alfred we reverence may well be an idealised figure. For our real knowledge of him is scanty and vague. We have, however, draped round his form, not without reason, all the highest attributes of man and kingship…. In him, we venerate not so much a striking actor in our history as the ideal Englishman, the perfect sov-

---
110 Parker, 'England's Darling,' 8.
111 Ibid.

ereign, the pioneer of England's greatness.... He is, in a word, the embodiment of our civilization.[112]

Rosenbery's comments, which acknowledge Alfred as a 'scanty and vague...form' around which are 'draped' the portraits of 'the ideal Englishman, the perfect sovereign, and the pioneer of England's greatness,' articulate the king as neither a living, fleshly body nor a decayed corpse, but rather as an 'idealised' sovereign form that 'embodi[es]...our civilization.' His missing, organic form — a biological material that Asser described as ill and sick, and Spelman acknowledged to have become bones — is no longer a ghostly, corpse-like figure. Finally, Alfred has been re-embodied as a 'portrait in stone' and a statue made of bronze. Quarried from stone and ore, Alfred can live forever in death as a capacious signifier that stands in for the sovereignty of 'our civilization,' past, present, and future.

While Alfred is now made of granite and alloy, his sovereign endurance and impenetrability relies on the easy interchange between Alfred's corpse-like ghost and other Anglo-Saxon bodies. The night prior to the statue's unveiling, the life of Alfred was presented to millenary guests in a series of *tableaux vivants* depicting notable events in the king's life. As 'living pictures' meant to celebrate the death of a king — just as live bodies whose stationary positions and silence mimic those of a dead man — these *tableaux vivants* confuse Alfred's body with the bodies of his Anglo-Saxon subjects. In the final *tableau* of this series, titled 'Alfred the Great,' 'Alfred' assumes the position of the Winchester statue, surrounded by men, women, and children dressed in period clothing (see Fig. 6). Having been taught to read, having burnt the cakes, disguised himself as a minstrel, and captured the Raven standard of the Danes, 'Alfred' appears for his millenary audience not as a body that ages and changes, but as a statue that stands immoveable in and across time.

---

112 Alfred Bowker, *The King Alfred Millenary: A Record of the Proceedings of the National Commemoration* (London: Macmillan and Company, 1902), 109.

Figure 6. 'Tableaux–Alfred the Great', in Alfred Bowker, *The King Alfred Millenary, a Record of the Proceedings of the National Commemoration* (London: Macmillan and Co, 1902), 101. Image courtesy of Huntington Library.

'Alfred the Great' functions as a sovereign effigy that is staged through the coordinated efforts of all manner of English people who are subjects of Alfred's sovereign rule, yet inhabited by their sovereign, *Ælfred, Angulsaxonum rex*.

As Oxford's decorative arts generate and amplify Alfred's undead, sovereign form, a new course of study called 'Anglo-Saxon' emerges at the university. During the late seventeenth century, Keynes writes, 'the *image* of Alfred as a scholarly king began at this time to exercise an important influence on the promotion of Anglo-Saxon studies in their own right.'[113] In 1696, Humfrey Wanley moved to Oxford in order to participate in the university's manuscript cataloguing activities. To facilitate his work, he was given a room in the Master's Lodgings where Alfred's effigial portrait hung — a choice in decor that signaled

---

113 Ibid., 252, my emphasis.

the king's role as patriarch of Wanley and others who succeeded him in this scholarly enterprise. '[F]rom this "Alfredian" base,' Keynes writes, 'Wanley did so much to advance knowledge and understanding of Anglo-Saxon manuscripts. Alfred, it seems, was never far from the collective mind.'[114] Wanley's editorial labors at Oxford participated in the university's robust, late-seventeenth-century activities in the emerging field of Anglo-Saxon studies. In 1677, the Bodleian Library acquired Franciscus Junius's manuscripts, transcriptions, and printer types, providing the already Alfredophilic university with a much expanded collection of resources for language study and the tools for print publication.[115] Junius's collection played no small part in the appearance of several important books: George Hickes's *Principles of Anglo-Saxon and Moesogothic Grammar* [*Institutiones Grammaticae Anglo-Saxonicae et Moeso-Gothicae*]; Christopher Rawlinson's *Boethius's Consolation of Philosophy, in Five Books, Translated into Anglo-Saxon by Alfred* [*Boethii Consolationis Philosophiae libri v Anglo-Saxonice redditi ab Alfredo*]; Thomas Benson's *Anglo-Saxon Dictionary* [*Vocabularium Anglo-Saxonicum*]; and Edward Thwaites's *Anglo-Saxon Grammar* [*Grammatica Anglo-Saxonica*].[116] Published in Oxford, by Oxford academics, and at Oxford's new scholarly press, these texts — a series of language-learning, reference materials, and editions meant for scholarly use — adopt and re-arrange the compound 'Angulsaxones,' thereby beginning the process of supplanting the commonly used term, 'Saxon,' with 'Anglo-Saxon.' At Ox-

---

114 Ibid., 268.
115 As John Niles notes, Junius bequeathed his special font of Old English script to Oxford in order to help with establishing its press (*The Idea of Anglo-Saxon England 1066–1901: Remembering, Forgetting, Deciphering, and Renewing the Past* [Malden: Wiley Blackwell, 2015], 122).
116 George Hickes, *Institutiones grammaticae Anglo-Saxonicae et Moeso-Gothicae* (Oxford: E Theatro Sheldoniano, 1689); Christopher Rawlinson, *Boethii Consolationis Philosophiae libri v Anglo-Saxonice redditi ab Alfredo* (Oxford: E Theatro Sheldoniano, 1698); Thomas Benson, *Vocabularium Anglo-Saxonicum* (Oxford: E Theatro Sheldoniano, 1701); Edward Thwaites, *Grammatica Anglo-Saxonica* (Oxford: E Theatro Sheldoniano, 1709).

ford, visions of Alfred's sovereign, patriarchal effigy hover over an Anglo-Saxon textual body, and as the two become entangled, the corpse-like figure of a king and its morbid ontology become silently, unconsciously, deposited within a *corpus* of texts. Asser's predictions, now almost a millennium old, are coming true. Long after his death, *Ælfred* is finally becoming *Angulsaxonum rex* as Oxford's scholars carry out the work of translation begun long ago by their 'Anglo-Saxon' 'father.'

As Wanley, Junius, and others labor at Oxford, they work in an environment 'refounded' by Alfred and marked with artful reminders of his effigial presence. Their linguistic studies, paleography, and editorial works are scholarly activities and filial duties that not only fall within the shadow of Alfred, the scholar–king, but are also placed within the wider field of Anglo-Saxon studies. In Wanley's catalogues, Junius's collections, and the writings by Hickes, Rawlinson, Benson, and Thwaites, the corpse-like figure of Alfred — 'father' to this emerging field — is positioned within the textual *corpus* of 'Anglo-Saxon,' confusing the relationship between bodies and words and reanimating a corporeal ghost of sovereignty via language.[117]

Benjamin Thorpe, Incorporating Alfred, and Anglo-Saxonist Being

As John Niles notes, the intellectual work of Oxford scholars came to a halt in the 1720s due the deaths of Wanley, Hickes, and Thwaites.[118] While few works of Old English scholarship were published during the latter half of the eighteenth century, interest in the subject remained high 'not just among the university elites, but also among a broad range of persons, including cler-

---

[117] Humfrey, along with Hickes and others, played no little part, with their cataloguing, paleography, and other society- and library-based work in laying the foundations for the academic discipline of Anglo-Saxon and Old English studies. On this point, see Eileen A. Joy, 'Thomas Smith, Humfrey Wanley, and the "Little-Known Country" of the Cotton Library,' *British Library Journal* (2005): 1–34, esp. 21–25.

[118] Niles, *The Idea of Anglo-Saxon England 1066–1901*, 165.

ics, antiquarians, local historians, dramatists, poets, and many others.'[119] This interest was maintained and nurtured, in part, by the British Society of Antiquaries, a learned society founded by Wanley and several others in 1707 before his death two decades later. While the Society of Antiquaries was not expressly devoted to Anglo-Saxon topics,[120] by the late eighteenth and early nineteenth centuries, it and other learned groups had turned their attentions to the emerging field of Anglo-Saxon studies.

Among the researchers supported by the Society and other learned groups is Benjamin Thorpe, who edited the early English law codes, the Old English gospels, the Exeter Book poems, and Ælfric's homilies, among other texts. Thorpe's engagement with most, if not all, of the Anglo-Saxon *corpus* is described at length by Niles:

> any one of Thorpe's editions of major Old English texts… might have been enough for a person of reasonable stamina to have presented as the centrepiece of years of labour, after which point the editor might have rested for a while…it is quite possible, though there exists no way to quantify such things, that no human being past or present has ever read more lines of Old English manuscript text than Benjamin Thorpe, word by word and letter by letter.
>
> …
>
> Thorpe had very little income other than a small government pension and whatever stipends, paid by one learned society or another, he received for producing a book. Thorpe could thus be called the first professional Anglo-Saxonist, all previous scholars in this field having pursued that scholarly interest among other responsibilities, often of a quite different kind.[121]

---

119 Ibid.
120 Rosemary Sweet notes that the Society's minute book displays three warriors, one of whom holds a medallion with the portraits of Charles I and king Alfred on it (*Antiquaries: The Discovery of the Past in Eighteenth–Century Britain* [London: Hambledon and London, 2004], 203).
121 Niles, *The Idea of Anglo-Saxon England 1066–1901*, 228, 229, 225.

Niles claims Thorpe to be 'the first professional Anglo-Saxonist,'[122] a figure whose 'stamina' is beyond 'reason,' whose work is unpaid, and whose time spent in the archives is '[un]quantif[iable].' I want to double down on Niles's statement, arguing that Thorpe's extraordinary devotion to the textual *corpus* of Anglo-Saxon[123] (which motivates Niles's claim that Thorpe is an Anglo-Saxonist) implicates Alfred's sovereign, fatherly claim upon him. After decades of circulation, in which Alfred's effigial form exceeds the frame of its portraiture and diffuses its corpse-like ghost into the *corpus* of Anglo-Saxon grammars, dictionaries, translations, and editions, Niles's comments bear witness to the impact of Alfred's spectral, textualized, sovereign form upon Thorpe's body. To say it a different way, Thorpe is capable of extraordinary — of *supernatural* — work and accomplishments because he is haunted, unknowingly, by the corpse-like ghost of a sovereign. He is driven, unconsciously, by a devotion to its morbid ontology. Thorpe, the field's first Anglo-Saxonist, professionalizes a political theology that was articulated, a millennium ago, in early English charters; imagined by Asser's deployment of the charter expression, *Ælfred, Angulsaxonum rex*; and made manifest, so to speak, during England's crisis of sovereignty — the Civil Wars.

Thorpe is Alfred's devoted subject and 'son.' Yet Alfred's ghostly figure has located its sovereign, patriarchal presence within an Anglo-Saxon textual *corpus*. Consequently, Thorpe believes his devotions to be to 'Anglo-Saxon,' not to Alfred. This devotional error enables Thorpe to recalibrate sovereignty beyond the restrictive limits of Alfred's body and position it within a raciolinguistic figure that Thorpe calls 'the Anglo-Saxon.'[124]

---

122 Note that the first printed attestation of the term, 'Anglo-Saxonist,' appears in reference to Benjamin Thorpe and John Mitchell Kemble (Anonymous, 'Retrospective Review. Anglo-Saxon Literature,' *Gentleman's Magazine* [November 1837]).

123 Niles's descriptive association of an Anglo-Saxonist dovetails with the semantics of '-ist' as elaborated in note 3 of this chapter.

124 I borrow the term 'raciolinguistic' from H. Samy Alim, John R. Rickford, and Arnetha F. Ball's recent collection, *Raciolinguistics: How Language*

Thorpe's translation of Erasmus Rask's *A Grammar of the Anglo-Saxon Tongue* and his language primer, *Analecta Anglo-Saxonica,* outline the sovereign, racialized shape of 'the Anglo-Saxon' and describe a program of self study by which the devotees of this Anglo-Saxon may become, like Thorpe, Anglo-Saxonists.

The title of Thorpe's translation of Rask's *Grammar* invokes the 'Anglo-Saxon tongue,' and its Preface soon truncates this expression to 'the Anglo-Saxon.'[125] This shorthand collapses the distance between speech, anatomy, and language; and as the Preface moves from an 'Anglo-Saxon tongue' to 'the Anglo-Saxon,' language moves into the body:

> It [the Anglo-Saxon] appears then to have been, in its origin, a rude mixture of the dialects of the Saxons, the Angles, and the Jutes, but we are not acquainted with it in that state, these dialects having soon coalesced into one language, as the various tribes soon united to form one nation, after they had taken possession of England…Even under Danish kings, all laws and edicts were promulgated in pure Anglo-Saxon.[126]

Thorpe's linguistic assessment points to popular histories by Spelman and Wise, which figured Alfred's role as the sovereign unifier of the early English kingdoms into 'one nation.' Likewise, Thorpe's language acknowledges the ethnolinguistic origins of 'Anglo-Saxon,' a term that, to recall the beginning of this chapter, was introduced in early English charters to identify Alfred's politically unified subjects according to their shared language

---

Shapes Our Ideas about Race, which considers how we 'race language' and 'language race' by dismantling racial hierarchies in order to consider an opening for the 'transracial subject' (H. Samy Alim, 'Introducing Raciolinguistics: Racing Language and Languaging Race in Hyperracial Times,' in *Raciolinguistics: How Language Shapes Our Ideas about Race,* eds. H. Samy Alim, John R. Rickford, and Arnetha F. Ball [Oxford University Press, 2016], 1, 7).

125 Benjamin Thorpe, 'Preface,' in Erasmus Rask, *A Grammar of the Anglo-Saxon Tongue, with a Praxis,* trans. Benjamin Thorpe (Copenhagen: S.L. Møller, 1830), v.

126 Ibid., xlvi.

and Christian faith. While Thorpe suggests the arrival of Anglo-Saxon sovereignty as an Alfredian event in which various tribes 'united' into 'one nation' and various dialects 'coalesced' into 'one language,' the agent of this process is not Alfred, but 'the Anglo-Saxon,' an embodied figure that neither originates with Alfred's late ninth-century kingship nor is restricted to the use of his charter formula, *Ælfred, Angulsaxonum rex*. Rather, the Anglo-Saxon is present 'as a rude admixture' when the Saxons, Angles, and Jutes arrive in Britain; it coalesces and unites to become 'one' figure 'possessed' of English sovereignty; and it remains 'pure' despite Danish incursions. Thorpe's Preface presents a linguistic body (not the king's body) as the site from whence political sovereignty emerges. As he tracks the emergence of this linguistically sovereign Anglo-Saxon figure, Thorpe explains it to be a racially miscegenated body that becomes homogenous and uncontaminated by way of nation-building processes. For Thorpe, raciolinguistic makeup, rather than ethnolinguistic similarity, is the precondition to English sovereignty.

Yet sovereignty (as Alfred's effigial portrait indicates) is a morbid ontological state. Consequently, the raciolinguistic purity of this Anglo-Saxon sovereign deadens it:

> We have here an ancient, fixed, and regular tongue, which, during a space of five hundred years, preserved itself almost without change.… In the year 1066, William the Bastard conquered England, but the highly cultivated, deep-rooted, ancient, national tongue could not be immediately extirpated, though it was instantly banished from the court.… We may therefore fix the year 1100, as the limit of the Anglo-Saxon tongue, whose structure we shall consider in the following work…but the Anglo-Saxon was preserved no where but in ancient writings, and therefore is, and long has been, a dead language, not very accessible to the learned themselves.[127]

---

[127] Ibid., xlvii–xlviii.

Again, linguistic statements run cover for a discussion about racial bodies. As an 'ancient,' 'fixed,' and 'preserved' 'tongue,' 'Anglo-Saxon' occupies an aged and homogenous state. Yet these lexemes, used repeatedly across the passage in relation to other, shifting terms, begin to signal the increasingly decrepit raciolinguistic body of the pure Anglo-Saxon, which can survive only in an unchallenged political state. When William the Bastard conquers England, his unknown, 'bastard' origins deracinate the 'deep roots' of Anglo-Saxon. Once this 'highly cultivated' figure is 'banished from the court,' it quickly loses its vitality. Like English sovereignty after the Norman Conquest,[128] Anglo-Saxon becomes 'fix[ed],' 'limit[ed],' and, finally, 'dead.' Its morbid ontology is evidenced by the 'inaccessible' state of its language and textual *corpus*.[129]

---

[128] Here, I use a term of nineteenth-century historicism in order to highlight Thorpe's nineteenth-century argument.

[129] When Thorpe's *Grammar* traces the outline of a racially pure, yet dead Anglo-Saxon corpse within a discussion of linguistics and language learning, Thorpe does not announce but rather implicates it as a sovereign, national-imperial presence at the expense of other nations and races. As Catharine Karkov remarks, '[n]ationalism was a continuing problem in Thorpe's scholarship' (*Text and Picture in Anglo-Saxon England: Narrative Strategies in the Junius 11 Manuscript* [Cambridge: Cambridge University Press, 2010], 197). Karkov continues, noting that Thorpe's 1830 *Grammar* intentionally omitted Rask's 'highly nationalistic dedicatory epistle with its reference to a glorious pagan Scandinavian past,' and its second and third editions, published in 1865 and 1979, further effaced the authorial presence of Rask, a Dane, by eliminating his Preface completely (ibid.). Likewise, as Robert Bjork explains, Thorpe conspired with the London Society of Antiquaries to 'st[eal] the ambitious ideas of N.F.S. Grundtvig from Gruntvig's 1803 prospectus for the publication of a large number of central Anglo-Saxon texts' ('Nineteenth–century Scandinavia and the Birth of Anglo-Saxon Studies,' in *Anglo-Saxonism and the Construction of Social Identity*, eds. Allen Frantzen and John Niles [Gainesville: Florida University Press, 1997], 112). By erasing Rask and Grundtvig from the project of Anglo-Saxon philology and editorial work, Thorpe 'rendered Anglo-Saxonism distinctly, stubbornly British' (ibid.). While Thorpe's editorial maneuvers assert Anglo-Saxon supremacy over other Germanic peoples, past and present, his pedagogy of incorporation and encryption — of positioning the racial purity and ancestral likeness of 'the Anglo-Saxon' within 'the student of Anglo-Saxon' — allows Aryanism to also enter Thorpe's nationalism. As

While the death of 'the Anglo-Saxon' occurs within Thorpe's Preface, its sovereign, effigial, corpse-like ghost begins to stir by way of the student's 'tongue.' In Thorpe's *Grammar*, a section on morphology reminds the student of her purpose of study: 'an accurate knowledge of...the gender, inflection, derivation, and primitive signification of words...is, in the dead languages...indispensable to the understanding and translating them correctly.'[130] Across the pages of the *Grammar,* an 'Anglo-Saxon tongue' generates 'the Anglo-Saxon,' a sovereign figure of racial and linguistic purity that is never classed as 'living' because it has already been made 'dead.' This silent, dead raciolinguistic corpse may be interpolated in Thorpe's student as she studies his translation of Rask's *Grammar* and translates his edited compendium, *Anelecta Anglo-Saxonica,* a wide selection of Anglo-Saxon prose and poetry followed by an extensive glossary of terms. Thorpe's language pedagogy, like Sharon Turner's historicism outlined in Chapter 2, and James Douglas's archaeology discussed in Chapter 3, facilitates acts of incorporation and encryption. His *Grammar* and *Analecta* plot the process by which the student of Anglo-Saxon magically takes custody of the racialized body of a dead language because its sovereign claims on her are too great to endure their severance.[131] This

---

Tony Ballantyne writes, '[b]y the time [Orientalist] Max Müller arrived in England, John Kemble and Benjamin Thorpe had elaborated a strong Anglo-Saxonist tradition, which emphasized the linguistic connection between English and its Germanic and Indo-European ancestors. Within such a context, Aryanism fortified both nationalist and imperialist ideologies' (*Orientalism and Race: Aryanism in the British Empire* [New York: Palgrave, 2002], 6).

130 Rask, *A Grammar of the Anglo-Saxon Tongue,* 97.
131 Note that incorporation along with encryption are major concepts of this book and have been discussed at length in Chapters 2 and 3. The concepts were initially developed in psychoanalytic theory by Maria Abraham and Nicholas Torok, in relation to Freud's work on mourning and melancholia, in *The Shell and the Kernel,* ed. and trans. Nicholas T. Rand (Chicago: Chicago University Press, 1994). As Abraham and Torok write, this 'sealed-off psychic space' warehouses the 'exquisite corps[e] of a loved one who we cannot bear to mourn,' and it is metaphorically evidenced in relation to eating, drinking, and silent ingestion (141, 128–29).

Anglo-Saxon *corpus* is 'swallowed whole' and thereby psychically relocated within the self such that one is inhabited by its sovereign ghost. Through silent self-study, the racially pure and ontologically morbid, yet sovereign, Anglo-Saxon inhabits the student of Anglo-Saxon. And through this ghostly inhabitation, she becomes an 'Anglo-Saxonist.'

Thorpe's *Grammar* and *Analecta* are featured in the November 1837 issue of the *Gentleman's Magazine,* in a short article titled 'Retrospective Review: Anglo-Saxon Literature.' An Anonymous reviewer explains the process by which the 'student of Anglo-Saxon' should systematically go about learning the language. Using 'Thorpe's translation of Rask, a good and tangible grammar—a dictionary, it is true...and, at the same time, attractive, elementary books in Thorpe's *Analecta* and *Apollonius*...will enable him to ground himself perfectly in the language without the need of a dictionary. When he has well studied the *Analecta,* he may confidently venture on to [John Mitchell Kemble's] *Beowulf,*' followed by Benjamin Thorpe's editions of *Caedmon* and the *Vercelli MS.*[132] Thorpe's textbooks and editions (along with Kemble's *Beowulf*) are 'the only ones which ought to be put into the hands of a student.'[133] In other words, Thorpe's pedagogy, his textual *corpus,* and the sovereign raciolinguistic corpse that Thorpe possesses (and that possesses him) are the tools by which the student of Anglo-Saxon becomes an Anglo-Saxonist.

The *Gentleman's Magazine* lays out the 'correct' process for transitioning from a student of Anglo-Saxon to an 'Anglo-Saxonist,' a professional change that is also, to borrow the arguments of Lesley Scanlon and David Beckett, an ontological one. From the 1830s until around 1960, Scanlon explains that the process of entering a profession was a matter of 'being,' a term that 'denotes the notion of arriving at a static point of expertise.'[134] Scan-

---

132 Anonymous, 'Retrospective Review,' 494.
133 Ibid.
134 Lesley Scanlon, '"Becoming" a Professional,' in *'Becoming' a Professional: An Interdisciplinary Analysis of Professional Learning,* ed. Lesley Scanlon (New York: Springer, 2011), 14.

lon's statement is expanded upon by Beckett, who writes that 'traditionally...professional formation was...individualistic.'[135] 'Theories of professional learning,' Beckett continues, were 'constructed through a cognitive process involving the transmission, acquisition, storage and application of a "body of data, facts and practical wisdom" which resided in the head.... Central to this "standard paradigm" view of learning is the assumption that "coming to know and understand something" involves arriving "at a *state of mind* as evidenced in accounts of what is cognitively the case".'[136] These definitions of being 'professional' attend to the description of the Anglo-Saxonist's educational process in the 1837 issue of the *Gentleman's Magazine.* The anonymous reviewer, who addresses 'the student,' presumes language learning as an independent course of study. Further, the reviewer's nod to 'Thorpe's *Analecta* and *Appollius* [*of Tyre*]' as beginning texts that will 'enable him to ground himself perfectly in the language without the need of a dictionary' presumes two additional points about language learning: firstly, that it is a program of intensive cognitive study and memorization by rote; and, secondly, that by way of these acts, one comes into 'perfect' possession of Anglo-Saxon grammar and its lexicon. Even at the beginning stages, a sense of 'arrival' has already been forecasted. As the independent student proceeds, systematically, 'without the need of a dictionary,' through *Beowulf,* the Junius manuscript, and the *Vercelli Book,* he acquires possession of more of the *corpus* — he 'arriv[es]' at what could be called an Anglo-Saxon(ist) 'state of mind,' or 'a static point of [Anglo-Saxon] expertise.'

---

135 David Beckett, 'Learning to Be–At Work,' in *'Becoming' a Professional: An Interdisciplinary Analysis of Professional Learning,* ed. Lesley Scanlon (New York: Springer, 2011), 59.

136 Ibid. Beckett's quotations are from Silvia Gherardi and Davide Nicolini, 'To Transfer is to Transform: The Circulation of Safety Knowledge,' *Organisation* 7, no. 2 (2000): 330, and David Beckett, 'A Useful Theory of Agency at Work,' in *Philosophical Perspectives on Educational Practice in the 21st Century: Proceedings of the 10th Biennial Conference of the International Network of Philosophers of Education* (Msida: University of Malta, 2006), 4, author's emphasis.

Professional being, as Scanlon and Beckett imply, points towards philosophical Being, an ontological category that, from the nineteenth to the early twentieth century, is bound up in a Cartesian cogito. For professionals and philosophers alike during this period, thinking is being. Yet, for Nelson Maldonado-Torres, 'the significance of the Cartesian *cogito* for modern European identity has to be understood against the backdrop of an unquestioned ideal of self in the notion of the *ego conquiro*.'[137] Maldonado-Torres claims that Descartes's ontological paradigm, which governs the philosophical Being of Hegel in the nineteenth century and Heidegger in the early twentieth, expresses a 'coloniality' that presumes that not all have the capacity or equal capacity to think and therefore to 'be.' Consequently, for anti-colonial philosophers of the twentieth century, an entirely cognitive formula of being is a colonial position: for Emmanuel Levinas, Being is a philosophy of power and violence; for Enrique Dussel, it is a 'Totality' that articulates the history of colonialism; and for Franz Fanon, an encounter with an imperial and racist Other.[138]

The arguments of Scanlon, Beckett, and Maldonado-Torres frame Thorpe's pedagogy in ontological terms. Being an Anglo-Saxonist means having perfect possession of the Anglo-Saxon *corpus*. It means occupying a professional state of mind that is capable of acquiring, storing, and transmitting all facts and data contained within a body of Anglo-Saxon knowledge. This emphasis on perfect acquisition, complete understanding, and data-oriented recall generates not merely a professional identity but moreover a philosophical 'self' that accords with a system of

---

[137] Nelson Maldonado-Torres, 'On the Coloniality of Being,' *Cultural Studies* 21, nos. 2–3 (2007): 245.

[138] Ibid., 242–43. See also Emmanuel Levinas, *Totality and Infinity: An Essay on Exteriority*, trans. Alphonso Lingis (Pittsburgh: Duquesne University Press, 1969); Enrique Dussel, *Philosophy of Liberation*, trans. Aquilina Martinez and Christine Morkovsky (Eugene: Wipf & Stock, 2003) and *The Pedagogics of Liberation: A Latin American Philosophy of Liberation*, trans. David I. Backer and Cecilia Diego (Earth: punctum books, 2019); and Frantz Fanon, *A Dying Colonialism*, trans. Haakon Chevalier (New York: Grove Press, 1965).

colonial knowledge and its racial hierarchies. To be an 'Anglo-Saxonist' is to know. Moreover, it is to presume that certain non-European, non-white others do not have the cognitive abilities to know and therefore have less right to be.

From the nineteenth to the first half of the twentieth century, Anglo-Saxonist being (an ontological state that is generated via the relationship between Alfred the sovereign 'father,' his Anglo-Saxon *corpus,* and Anglo-Saxonist 'children') remains productive. Yet, as decolonization gains momentum in the 1950s, and the (post)colonial era approaches in the 1970s, being an Anglo-Saxonist — being inhabited by a dead sovereign — reveals itself to be a truly morbid enterprise. The next chapter tracks the fate of Alfred's corporeal body in the late twentieth century. It revisits key moments of this chapter in order to discover the limits of 'being' an Anglo-Saxonist after the fall of Empire and the means by which we might subvert and exceed them.

5

Becoming postSaxon, or, a Biochemical *Vita Ælfredi*

The previous chapter began with a discussion of Susan Reynolds's 'What Do We Mean When We Say "Anglo-Saxon"?,' which explored the initial attestations of this compound in the political language of King Alfred. Discussing Reynolds enabled Chapter 4 to argue that 'Anglo-Saxon' was invoked by Alfred to claim sovereignty over his political subjects. However, it was not until much later that the compound became vested in a political theology of sovereignty, to which Benjamin Thorpe, the nineteenth-century's first Anglo-Saxonist, was professionally and ontologically bound. Thorpe's writings express the emergence of an Anglo-Saxonist 'being,' a state of mind that is devoted to (and inhabited by) a racial-colonial Anglo-Saxon sovereign. While Reynolds's essay provides an important starting point for considering the development of 'Anglo-Saxon,' it likewise meditates upon the continued scholarly devotion to this Anglo-Saxon sovereign. Consequently, this chapter returns to a different moment in 'What Do We Mean When We Say "Anglo-Saxon"?' in order to consider the racial-colonial politics that keep scholars of the nineteenth and twentieth centuries 'being' Anglo-Saxonists.

After tracing the ninth-century etymology of 'Anglo-Saxon,' Reynolds quotes its definition in the first 1844 edition of the *Ox-*

ford English Dictionary (OED) by James Murray. The adjective 'Anglo-Saxon' is a 'collective name' that is not only 'extended to the entire Old English people and language' prior to 1100 but also stands in for contemporary 'English' peoples 'who are of Teutonic descent…whether subjects of Great Britain or of the United States.'[1] Murray's definition, as quoted by Reynolds, invokes 'Anglo-Saxon' as a 'collective' adjective that is set upon 'exten[sion]:' from body to voice, past to present, Britain to America. It manages the perceived relationship between racial origins, national unification, and political destiny in the Victorian period. As a term of expansion, the OED's 'Anglo-Saxon' becomes an all-encompassing expression that 'subjects' the entirety of a person — mind and body — within its semantic domain. Indeed, as Chapter 4 argued, 'Anglo-Saxon' suggests itself to be a signifier marked by a sovereign.[2]

Upon quoting Murray, Reynolds's essay draws connections between its ninth- and nineteenth–century uses, and she cautiously writes that 'right through the "Anglo-Saxon period," therefore, the term "Anglo-Saxon" invites us to beg questions and confuse our own ideas with those of the period we study.'[3] In other words, Reynolds surmises that whether or not Alfred's ninth century offers a premonition of the nineteenth, what matters is that we are 'invited' to be caught up in the semantic orbit of 'Anglo-Saxon.' Such an assessment asks us to consider, very carefully, not simply the word's expansionist enterprise or its ethnopolitical and raciolinguistic aspirations during ninth and nineteenth centuries, respectively, but, moreover, the sovereign disposition of 'Anglo-Saxon,' upon which the field of Anglo-Saxon studies continues to turn.

Yet as soon as Reynolds articulates the 'questions' and 'confus[ions]' 'invited' by the semantics of 'Anglo-Saxon' — as

---

1 *Oxford English Dictionary Online,* 3rd edn. (Oxford University Press, 2019); cited in Susan Reynolds, 'What Do We Mean by "Anglo-Saxon" and "Anglo-Saxons"?' *Journal of British Studies* 24, no. 4 (1985): 395, 396.
2 Reynolds, 'What Do We Mean by "Anglo-Saxon" and "Anglo-Saxons"?,' 396.
3 Ibid., 414.

soon as she points towards the risks that we run by using terminologies that locate late-twentieth-century scholarship within the trans-temporal orbit of the ninth and nineteenth centuries — Reynolds follows up with a conclusion that prohibits pause, short-circuits contemplation, and reveals its continued sovereign status. 'It would be overpresumptuous,' she writes, 'to attempt to stop the terminological world of historians — let alone of the general public — and try to get off.'[4] Although 'Anglo-Saxon' shows itself to be a signifier that is fundamentally troubled at both temporal ends (in Alfred's early medieval moment and in our own contemporary one), Reynolds's study of it leads to questions and confusions but not reflection. Although her essay shows the ethnopolitical impetus behind the compound Anglo-Saxon, which, in the nineteenth century, becomes racialized and nationalized, Reynolds, herself, begs her readers *not* 'to stop' using it and *not* 'to get off' the academic merry-go-round that keeps this term in circulation.

Reynold's position can, perhaps, be understood in its political and academic context. In 1980, Rhodesia, Britain's final colony, achieved independence after 14 years of conflict, to which *The Guardian* stated, 'Britain is no longer a colonial power.'[5] In 1982, Britain attempted to assert its claims against Argentina in the Falkland's War, a failure that has been considered the last action of its Empire. And, in 1983, the constitutional establishment of the International Society of Anglo-Saxonists (ISAS) institutionalized a formal community of scholars who study 'Anglo-Saxon England.' Is there a connection between the neocolonial politics of Margaret Thatcher's Great Britain, the postcolonial establishment of the International Society of Anglo-Saxonists, and the cautionary words of Reynolds, published in 1985? Yes. Does the terminological duty to 'Anglo-Saxon' shared by ISAS and Reynolds act as an unconscious, scholarly, post-facto bulwark against the political realities of decolonization? Yes. The professional-ontological project of 'being' an Anglo-Saxonist — a process

---

4   Ibid.
5   'Born in Unwonted Tranquility,' *The Guardian,* April 18, 1980.

that requires the incorporation of a racial and colonial Anglo-Saxon sovereign—cannot 'be' in a postcolonial 'state.' To say it a different way: our signifiers, inherited long ago, have shaped our professional being into a figure that has limited our means of being or becoming postcolonial.[6]

As Chapter 4 likewise argued, 'Anglo-Saxon' is a sovereign term that continues to 'rule' its Anglo-Saxonists because it encodes, within its conceptual fibers, the sovereign figure king Alfred, whose body has been translated from a fleshly material into a corpse-like specter of sovereignty (and, as Thorpe's scholarship indicated, a sovereign textual *corpus*). As the previous chapter explained, Alfred no longer inhabits a living, corporeal body that is chronically ill and sickly as he once did in Asser's *Life of King Alfred*. Nor can Alfred's material corpse be found as it could in John Spelman's *The Life of Ælfred the Great*. In the process of rendering Alfred sovereign, all of Alfred's material remains are lost, giving leave for 'him' to be imaginatively reconstructed and circulate—in portraiture, in painting, and, ultimately, in the bronze statue at Winchester—as a ghostly effigy of English sovereignty.

Yet Alfred's sovereign, effigial form, has not lasted, despite being cast in bronze. In the early 1990s, a few years after Britain was no longer an empire and could not exercise sovereignty over the Falklands (and a few years after ISAS and Reynolds insisted upon their postcolonial devotion to 'Anglo-Saxon'), writings about Alfred's sickly body began to proliferate. While concern over his illnesses has, since the eighteenth century, been an is-

---

6   The professional and political activities of the 1980s discussed in this paragraph give texture and nuance to Chapter 1's statements about the feminist and poststructuralist scholarship that was championed by a small number of scholars of the 1980s and 1990s and was also brought into sharp relief in Allen Frantzen's *Desire for Origins: New Language, Old English, and Teaching the Tradition* (New Brunswick: Rutgers University Press, 1990). In comparing the establishment of the International Society of Anglo-Saxonists (ISAS) in the early 1980s to the publication of Frantzen's book in 1990, one can see more clearly the battle lines that were drawn within the field during these decades and the ways in which critical theorists understood themselves in relation to the politics of postcolonialism.

sue that scholars were wont to elide,[7] a 1991 article, 'Alfred the Great: a diagnosis,' published in the *Journal of the Royal Society of Medicine* reconsidered them within a modern medical context. Using Asser's *Life* and *Bald's Leechbook* in order to build its case report, the essay diagnoses Alfred's adolescent troubles with *ficus* as hemorrhoids or 'perianal lesions,' which often signal the early onset of Crohn's disease:

> an illness that begins in early adult life, approximately one half beginning during the twenties, and 90% between the ages of 10 and 40 years...characterized by relapses and remissions. In an attack there is abdominal pain, diarrhoea

---

7 While Spelman's *Life of Ælfred the Great* and Wise's *Life of King Alfred* acknowledged Asser's discussion of Alfred's suffering body, Charles Plummer's lecture series, 'The Life and Times of Alfred the Great,' perceives this material as an interpolation that creates an 'atmosphere of morbid religiousity'(*The Life and Times of Alfred the Great: Being the Ford Lectures for 1901* [Oxford: Clarendon Press, 1902], 28). In other words, Plummer cannot bear to contemplate Alfred as a human body, whose material flesh is subject to unsovereign decay. After finding Alfred's *ficus* and his unnamed, adult illnesses improbable (footnoting that, if one should wager a diagnosis, it would all be epilepsy), he claims that '[p]ersonally, I should not be sorry to let all these passages go; for it seems to me quite inconceivable that Alfred could have accomplished what he did under the hourly pressure of incapacitating disease' (ibid.). While Stevenson's 1904 edition of Asser's *Life* includes this 'interpolated' material, he follows Plummer's assessment, stating that chapter 74 'is supplied entirely by the author, and it is an instructive specimen of his confused arrangement and puzzling phraseology' (*Asser's Life of King Alfred together with the Annals of Saint Neots Erroneously Ascribed to Asser*, ed. William H. Stevenson [Oxford: Clarendon Press, 1904], 294n74). After quoting Plummer's statement regarding the morbidity of Asser's narrative, Stevenson continues to discuss Alfred's illnesses for several pages that end by assessing the *ficus*, which Alfred may have had in youth, as 'haemorrhoids' (296n74). Deep concern for Alfred's fleshly, physical body continues into the twentieth century: Dorothy Whitelock omits chapter 74 from her own translation of Asser's *Life (English Historical Documents, 500-1042*, ed. Dorothy Whitelock, volume 1 [2nd, revised ed., New York: Routledge, 1979], 290n5). Likewise, she admits that concern over Alfred's adult illness underlies the desire among Plummer, Stevenson, and others to discredit the *Life tout court* (*The Genuine Asser* [Reading: University of Reading, 1968]).

sometimes with mucus and blood, that may alternate with periods of constipation. There may be fever and wasting depending on the severity of the illness. Some sufferers, a minority, experience eye problems (iritis), joint pains (without any destructive pathology) and skin problems.[8]

For the first time, Alfred's body and its mysterious symptoms are discussed from within the terminological frame of medical scholarship, which documents his age, symptoms, treatments, and the pathology of Crohn's disease. This clinical approach to Alfred — written in the postcolonial moment of the early 1990s — implicitly acknowledges England's diminished sovereignty from an empire to a nation-state via its medical assessment of the king. For the first time in centuries, Alfred has a corporeal body with an anus, eyes, joints, and skin. No longer cast in bronze — no longer monumentalized as a static and unmoving figure — Alfred's body emerges as a non-cognitive, biological actor with atypical bowel movements, 'pains,' 'problems,' and (potentially) a variety of debilitating side-effects. While the case report presents him as a diseased organism, all faith is not lost in Alfred's (or Anglo-America's) sovereign form. 'Asser gives us a picture of a stricken monarch who suffers almost unremittingly from his symptoms,' yet the report maintains that Alfred 'was able to fight, study, pursue his leisure interests, worship and govern.'[9] While the king's body becomes unsovereign, the sovereignty of his kingship remains unchallenged.

Shortly after the *Royal Society of Medicine* published an article on Alfred and Crohn's disease, Anglo-Saxonists began to take into account this diagnosis. Consequently, a very different

---

8 G. Craig, 'Alfred the Great: A Diagnosis,' *Journal of the Royal Society of Medicine* 84, no. 5 (1991): 304.
9 Ibid. Note that a response to Craig's essay appears in the 'Letter to the Editor' section of the same journal, in which it is argued that Alfred's extended pain may have resulted from 'haemorrhoidal disease and complications' rather than Crohn's. St. Ficare's disease is suggested as an alternative to 'haemrrhoids' (F.I. Jackson, 'Alfred the Great: A Diagnosis,' *Journal of the Royal Society of Medicine* 85, no. 1 [1992]: 58).

kind of Alfredian biography arises in Alfred's Smyth's 1995 *King Alfred the Great*. Smyth's Introduction, which critiques Alfred scholarship as a field not only 'enmeshed in polemic and the politics of academe' but also a casualty of 'the networks of patronage which have come to control the subject in England,' stylizes his biography as 'iconoclastic' and 'polemic.'[10] Smyth insists that Asser's *Life of King Alfred* is a forgery that paints the king as a 'neurotic saintly invalid,'[11] who is, moreover, 'depressive,' 'obsessive,' 'sickly,' 'fanatical,' and suffering from an illness that was 'ghastly,' 'gruesomely,' 'mysterious,' 'repulsive,' 'crippling,' and worst of all perhaps, 'self-inflicted.'[12] Whereas previous generations of scholars had simply omitted Asser's claims regarding Alfred's illnesses or elided a discussion about them, Smyth is overly attentive to Alfred's disease-ridden body. He depicts it as a grossly unsovereign from — physically and psychologically — in order to dismiss Asser's *Life*. By focusing his attention on Alfred's embodied, 'fleshy,' and 'obscenely alive' figure,[13] an insistent, scholarly 'we' emerges:

> even when we discard the monastic image of the invalid… king, it is still a daunting task to cross a thousand years in time and hope to recover the picture of the genuine Alfred… we can never make the bold claim of having sat in the royal chamber with this man. There are times however, when Alfred allows us to draw near to his presence and when through his own writings, we can observe him through an opaque screen. And what we perceive then, is no ordinary man, but a

---

10 Alfred Smyth, *King Alfred the Great* (New York: Oxford University Press, 1995), xxii.
11 Ibid., 204.
12 Janet L. Nelson, 'The Political Ideas of Alfred of Wessex,' in *Kings and Kingship in Medieval Europe,* ed. Anne J. Duggan (London: King's College, 1993), 22–23. I cite Janet Nelson's review article, 'Waiting for Alfred,' not only because of its tidy listing of Smyth's descriptors but also because it articulates them within a poetic orbit. Note how rhyme ties together word pairs (*Early Medieval Europe* 7, no. 1 [1998]: 115–24).
13 Here, I point back to the language of Eric Santner and Elaine Scarry, which I discussed at length in relation to sovereignty in Chapter 4 of this book.

gifted ruler who was himself ever concerned with how we in succeeding generations, would view him.[14]

Smyth's consideration of Alfred's physicality re-embodies the king, so to speak, in such a way that he is no longer simply a bronze statue. For Smyth, Alfred, once again, has a body. Consequently, Alfred can be thought of in relation to an embodied, scholarly 'we' who study him.

While Smyth's biography was the subject of many scathing reviews by members of the small, but tight-knit network of Alfredian history, it has enabled these scholars to contemplate biographical relationships between Alfred and those who write about him. In so doing, Anglo-Saxonists approach the realities of postcoloniality, yet renew their allegiances to Alfred and to Anglo-American sovereignty. Essays appearing in the years following Smyth's biography articulate present-tense connections between the king and his historians. Janet Nelson's review of Smyth's book highlights an interview by Dorothy Whitelock about her highly-anticipated but never-completed book about the king:

> Whitelock's Alfred, she told her interviewer, was above all 'a very valiant man.' 'But what disclosures will there be?' the journalist persisted. 'It's straight history,' Whitelock replied briskly, 'it's not going to be anything startling.' Whitelock's translation of Asser in *English Historical Documents,* volume I, had omitted chapter 74, and also omitted Asser's two other episodes, chapters 14–15, and chapters 95–7, involving revelations of ninth-century sexuality which could qualify as startling. That a scholar of Whitelock's generation and experience should have found unpalatable Asser's account of Alfred's illness, and its intimate relationship with his spirituality and his sexuality, calls for our understanding.... John Cunningham in the *Guardian* interview [on Whitelock's commissioned but never-completed biography of Alfred] achieved the right

---

14 Smyth, *King Alfred the Great,* 602.

combination of shrewdness and sympathy: 'On why she never married, Dorothy Whitelock says just: 'A vast number of young men of my generation died in the First World War.... I never had that feminine desire to run a home.... I can cook adequately: I can grill chops and steaks and make chicken casserole. Fresh vegetables can I cook and I can boil eggs.' She smiles....'[15]

Richard Abel's self-reflective 'Alfred and his Biographers' contemplates Smyth and Plummer's work in relation to his own:

And what of my Alfred? When I signed the contract to write my book back in 1988, I, like Smyth, had planned to say something new on the subject....I was going to drag Alfred off his pedestal at Winchester as surely as American soldiers and freed Iraqis were to pull down the statue of Saddam Hussein.... And I failed.... To paraphrase Plummer, I found myself putting the received story into my own words, and 'arranging in my own way, what has been previously written by others or myself.'[16]

Patrick Wormald suggests, in 'Living with Alfred,' that these autobiographical attachments may be about family ties as well as personal ones:

Might one even nurse a suspicion that Professor Keynes, great-nephew of [John Maynard Keynes,] the most distinguished civil servant the British government has ever had and the one economist universally acknowledged as a genius, naturally prefers to dwell on the title 'king of the Anglo-Sax-

---

15 Nelson, 'Waiting for Alfred,' 123, 123n28; quoting from John Cunningham's interview with Dorothy Whitelock, 'Waiting for Alfred,' *The Guardian* (August 18, 1978), 9.
16 Richard Abels, 'Alfred and His Biographers: Images and Imagination,' in *Writing Medieval Biography, 750–1250: Essays in Honour of Frank Barlow,* eds. David Bates, Julia Crick, and Sarah Hamilton (Rochester: Boydell, 2006), 73.

ons' that our hero bears in his official documents and (by implication) on his coins…as opposed to the hazier vision of an Angelcynn, 'English people,' which as yet subsisted only in the dreams of the likes of Bede?[17]

In which case, I [Patrick Wormald] would have to admit that my own conception of a scholar-king at odds with his military nobility's indifference to learning probably grew out of my experiences as an Eton 'King's Scholar.'…If post-modernism teaches us anything, it is that any text must be read as an artefact. But with Alfred, texts bring us uniquely close to their protagonist.[18]

Whitelock's 'valiant' Alfred and her promise of writing 'straight history' point to an 'Alfred' shaped by her memories of the First World War, where 'a vast number of young men of [her] generation died.' Abels's references to 'American soldiers' and 'freed Iraqis' track his position as a professor in the U.S. Naval Academy. Keynes's family ties him to the British government and to academic virtuosity. Wormald's youthful identity as a '*King's Scholar*' (my emphasis) marks his intellectual precocity at Eton as one in future service to the Crown. These anecdotes from some of Anglo-Saxon studies' most gifted scholars, all of which were published in the late-nineties and early two-thousands, reveal deep devotions to British and American sovereignty in a postcolonial era — devotions which are expressed in and maintained by their scholarly interpretations of Alfred.

Consequently, while Patrick Wormald claims that Alfred's 'mind and body' should be medically assessed, discussions that consider Alfred's physical illnesses still return to representationalist readings of him.[19] Paul Kershaw, Janet Nelson, and David Pratt have written about Alfred's *piles,* or hemorrhoids, and his Crohn's disease, then directed attention away from these con-

---

17 Patrick Wormald, 'Living with King Alfred,' *Haskins Society Journal* 15 (2006): 3.
18 Ibid., 3, 4.
19 Ibid., 6.

ditions, by assessing his medical symptoms in relation to critiques of warrior-aristocrat values,[20] conflicts between Alfred's clerical and lay callings,[21] Continental sources vested in physical suffering,[22] and the pressures of 'excess education.'[23] In the writings of these scholars, Alfred returns, if not to his place as *Angulsaxonum rex,* then to one who is still Anglo-Saxon. Through their Anglo-Saxonist devotions, the racial and colonial empires of England and the United States remain undiminished.

While Anglo-Saxonists evade the material realities of Alfred's physical body, his corpse finally makes its appearance. On January 17, 2014, British news outlets published stories claiming that a piece of Alfred's pelvis may have been found.[24] Below the headlines, images of the engraving of Alfred used in John Spelman's 1678 *Life of Ælfred the Great* and the 1901 Winchester Statue of Alfred — effigial figures discussed at length in Chapter 4 of this book — appear next to a photograph of the pelvic fragment (see Figs. 1–4). Alfred's sovereign form sits across from a supposedly material fragment of 'the man himself.' The undecayed, corpse-like figure of a king is confronted with a broken piece of 'his' corpse.[25]

A year after 'Alfred's' pelvic fragment is found — as if in response to its recovery — John Niles's *The Idea of Anglo-Saxon*

---

20 Paul Kershaw, 'Illness, Power and Prayer in Asser's *Life of King Alfred,'* *Early Medieval Europe* 10, no. 2 (2001): 201–24.
21 Nelson, 'Waiting for Alfred.'
22 David Pratt, 'The Illnesses of King Alfred the Great,' *Anglo-Saxon England* 30 (2001): 39–90.
23 Wormald, 'Living with King Alfred,' 17.
24 For example, see Maev Kennedy, 'Archaeologists May Have Found Remains of Alfred the Great,' *The Guardian,* January 17, 2014, https://www.theguardian.com/uk-news/2014/jan/17/alfred-the-great-edward-elder-remains-found-winchester; Nick Collins, 'King Alfred the Great Bones Believed to be in Box Found in Museum,' *The Telegraph,* January 17, 2014, https://www.telegraph.co.uk/history/10579315/King-Alfred-the-Great-bones-believed-to-be-in-box-found-in-museum.html; and 'Bone Fragment "could be King Alfred or son Edward",' *BBC News,* January 17, 2014, https://www.bbc.com/news/uk-england-hampshire-25760383.
25 Notably, osteological and genetic testing of this bone fragment proved inconclusive.

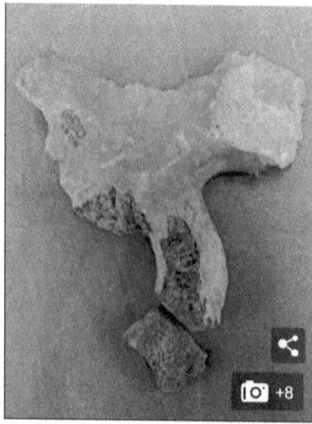

The pelvis bone (right) of King Alfred the Great (illustrated left) is believed to have been found in a box stored in a museum, and not buried in an unmarked grave as previously thought

Figure 1. Detail from Sarah Griffiths and Ben Spencer, 'King Alfred the Great's Bones Discovered in a MUSEUM: Remains Inside Box are Thought to Belong to Anglo-Saxon Ruler,' *Daily Mail*, January 17, 2014. Image Courtesy of Alamy.

Section of human pelvis has been carbon-dated within lifetimes of Alfred the Great and son Edward the Elder

▲ The bone has been dated to between AD895 and 1017. Alfred died in AD899. Photograph: Martin Argles for the Guardian

Figure 2. Detail from Maev Kennedy, 'Archaeologists May Have Found Remains of Alfred the Great,' *The Guardian*, January 17, 2014. Image Courtesy of Martin Argles and *The Guardian*.

A BIOCHEMICAL *VITA ÆLFREDI*

Figure 3. Detail from 'Bone Fragment "could be King Alfred or son Edward"', BBC News, January 17, 2014.

Figure 4. Detail from Nick Collins, 'King Alfred the Great Bones Believed to Be in Box Found in Museum,' *The Telegraph*, January 17, 2014. Image Courtesy of Alamy.

England, 1066–1901, a survey of the history of Anglo-Saxon studies, asks, in its introductory chapter, 'Has the time come to retire that hyphenated term "the Anglo-Saxons" as one that has outlived its usefulness?'[26] 'Like all terms of classification,' Niles continues, 'we should feel free to discard them if they are felt to imprison us in habits of thought that have outlived their usefulness.'[27] Niles concludes his book by discussing the Winchester Statue, where he ruminates on the 'usefulness' of Alfred. In 1901, Niles writes, Alfred's statue rendered him 'fully human,' yet of 'transcendent dignity.'[28] However, Alfred's 'high point… in the modern period…also marked the end of an era, for in that same year Queen Victoria passed away.'[29] The year 1901, he explains, 'has seemed a fitting stopping point in part because it marks the start of a new century and hence represents a special moment in the eternal, if vain, quest for a future that is more enlightened than the past,' because 'the concerns of one generation are often a *dead* issue for the next.'[30] Niles's association between the erection of Alfred's statue and Victoria's death and his assertion that Alfred's 'high point' at the turn of the century is now a 'dead issue' for the post-Victorian 'generation[s]' doubly marks the king's body as a corpse. Yet, Niles continues to allow 'Anglo-Saxon' and Alfred to take pride of place as 'matter[s] of habit and convenience' rather than acts of faithful allegiance. For while he claims that the 'concerns of one generation' are 'dead' and gone, Niles's book title includes the phrase 'Anglo-Saxon England,' and Alfred's Winchester statue serves as its cover art (see Figure 5). Although materialized into a corpse, the sovereign force of Alfred's Anglo-Saxon corpse-like presence keeps us circling it — keeps us from 'getting off' — as a consequence of ambivalence and melancholy, affective states of those haunted

---

26 John D. Niles, *The Idea of Anglo-Saxon England 1066–1901: Remembering, Forgetting, Deciphering, and Renewing the Past* (Malden: Wiley Blackwell, 2015), 34.
27 Ibid., 35.
28 Ibid., 366.
29 Ibid., 328.
30 Ibid., 355, 354, my italics.

Figure 5. Cover art for John D. Niles, *The Idea of Anglo-Saxon England 1066–1901: Remembering, Forgetting, Deciphering, and Renewing the Past* (Malden: Blackwell, 2015). Image Courtesy of Wiley-Blackwell.

by a ghostly 'old guard,' as discussed in the first chapter of this book.

In order to understand the process by which nineteenth-century Anglo-Saxonists became devotees of Alfred (and subsequent generations have maintained these devotions in the face of postcolonial politics), Chapter 4 concluded with a discussion of Anglo-Saxonist 'being.' It argued that in the nineteenth century, becoming a professional Anglo-Saxonist was a disembodied, cognitive process by which the student arrived at a perfect and complete understanding of the entire Anglo-Saxon *corpus*, a body of grammar and texts into which Alfred's sovereign, corpse-like ghost was folded. Being an Anglo-Saxonist was a professional and an ontological state of mind that, on account of its cognitive emphasis, expresses a being that is inhabited by and consequently devoted to a ghost.

For twenty-first-century Anglo-Saxonists, the ontological force of our professional appellative weighs heavily upon us.[31]

---

31 As this book was in the final proofing stages, the International Society of Anglo-Saxonists (ISAS) voted to change its name, but not without fierce debates and divisive fractiousness among its membership, and as of this book's publication, ISAS is still ruminating what its new name might be. For a brief overview of events leading up to the votes and why the matter was so contentious, see Hannah Natason, '"It's All White People": Allegations of White Supremacy Are Tearing Apart a Prestigious Medieval Studies Group,' *The Washington Post*, September 19, 2019, https://www.washingtonpost.com/education/2019/09/19/its-all-white-people-allegations-white-supremacy-are-tearing-apart-prestigious-medieval-studies-group/ and Colleen Flaherty, 'It's About More Than a Name,' *Inside Higher Ed*, September 20, 2019, https://www.insidehighered.com/news/2019/09/20/anglo-saxon-studies-group-says-it-will-change-its-name-amid-bigger-complaints-about. For relevant background, see also Mary Dockray-Miller, 'Old English Has a Serious Image Problem,' *JSTOR Daily*, May 3, 2017, https://daily.jstor.org/old-english-serious-image-problem/; Daniel C. Remein, 'ISAS Should Probably Change Its Name,' conference presentation, 52nd International Congress on Medieval Studies, May 11, 2017, https://www.academia.edu/34101681/_Isas_should_probably_change_its_name_ICMS_KalamazKa_2017; Adam Miyashiro, 'De-colonizing Anglo-Saxon Studies: A Response to ISAS in Honolulu,' *In The Middle*, July 29, 2017, http://www.inthemedievalmiddle.com/2017/07/decolonizing-anglo-saxon-studies.html; Mary Rambaran-Olm, 'Anglo-

Living not in a colonial but in a post-colonial age, positioned not towards a Cartesian 'being' but a Deleuzian 'becoming,' we are personally out of step with the ethnopolitical, raciolinguistic, and professional orientations woven, long ago, into the semantic fibers of 'Anglo-Saxonist.' Yet, as the previous chapter argued, if the dead sovereign 'Alfred, king of the Anglo-Saxons,' which lies at the bedrock of our professional signifier, keeps us being Anglo-Saxonists, might it, consequently, prohibit us from becoming something else so long as we maintain, by 'habit' and 'convenience,' signifiers that are not our own? For, as Nelson Maldonado-Torres argues, Being is not simply a matter of colonialism, but also of coloniality:

> ...long-standing patterns of power that emerged as a result of colonialism, but that define culture, labor, intersubjective relations, and knowledge production well beyond the strict limits of colonial administrations. Thus, coloniality survives colonialism. It is maintained alive in books, in the criteria for academic performance, in cultural patterns, in common sense, in the self-image of peoples, in aspirations of self, and so many other aspects of our modern experience. In a way, as modern subjects we breathe coloniality all the time and everyday.[32]

Maldonado-Torres's discussion of coloniality leads him to consider the philosophical, ethical, and juridical processes of decoloniality, its apposite state. However, in order to locate one's self within a decolonial subjectivity, this chapter argues that one must first turn away from colonial 'being' and open oneself to

---

Saxon Studies, Academia, and White Supremacy,' *Medium*, June 27, 2018, https://medium.com/@mrambaranolm/anglo-saxon-studies-academia-and-white-supremacy-17c87b360bf3; and 'Misnaming the Medieval: Rejecting "Anglo-Saxon" Studies,' *History Workshop*, November 4, 2019, http://www.historyworkshop.org.uk/misnaming-the-medieval-rejecting-anglo-saxon-studies/.

32 Nelson Maldonado-Torres, 'On the Coloniality of Being,' *Cultural Studies* 21, nos. 2–3 (2007): 243.

decolonial 'becoming.' Such political-ontological repositioning invokes Deleuze, and his intellectual partner, Guattari, whose initial writings not only challenge a Hegelian ontology of Being but are also written during the second half of the twentieth century, in (and to) the time of mid-to-late–century European decolonization. Consequently, Deleuze can be understood as a philosopher whose refiguration of 'Being' as 'becoming' articulates philosophical decolonization from a European vantage point.[33] Deleuze, I believe, offers Anglo-Saxon studies and its Anglo-Saxonists one (of many) possible paths towards decolonizing the field. His philosophy, which understands the critical value of 'becoming' as a conversation between participants, requires that we take experiential positions with diverse and multiple others; make alliances with heterogenous organisms whose 'populations…vary from milieu to mileu'; and sidestep the structuralist efforts of taxonomic classification and genealogical trees via rhizomatic conceptual mapping.[34]

Embracing becoming requires, first, that we emotionally give up, or at least loosen the ties that bind us to 'Anglo-Saxon' and

---

33 Despite the timing of his oeuvre, Deleuze has only recently been put in conversation with postcolonial theory. As Simone Bignall and Paul Patton write in 'Deleuze and the Postcolonial,' 'the problematic lack in mutuality, or else the mutual disregard, which previous scholarship has highlighted as characteristic of the relationship between Deleuze and the postcolonial…[,] despite the abundance of Deleuzian *motifs* in postcolonial discourse,' may express 'the more worrying possibility that his silence on colonialism conceals a certain Eurocentric self-interest, a neo-imperial motivation or a hidden or unacknowledged desire to deflect attention away from the political concerns of the postcolony' ('Deleuze and the Postcolonial: Conversations, Negotiations, Mediations,' in *Deleuze and the Postcolonial,* ed. Simone Bignall [Edinburgh: Edinburgh University Press, 2010], 1–2). Yet Bignall, Patton, and the collection of writings that they introduce short-circuit this problem by explaining that Deleuzian philosophy does not, and can never, express postcolonial theory. Rather, the two are engaged in conversations '*between* participants and between the respective terms and stances they bring to the discussion' — in other words, between Deleuze and the postcolonial (8).

34 Giles Deleuze and Felix Guattari, *A Thousand Plateaus: Capitalism and Schizophrenia,* trans. Brian Massumi (Minneapolis: Minnesota University Press, 1987), 238–39.

'Anglo-Saxonist.' Yet, for each of us, this is a personal process. For myself, I found it necessary to return to the body of King Alfred, the dead sovereign around which the nested terms 'Anglo-Saxon' and 'Anglo-Saxonist' are formed. I began to write a speculative micro-history of Alfred's body that tracks its purported engagements with 'piles' and Crohn's disease, its eventual death and decay in the grave, and its fragmentary 'recovery' during the 1999 and 2013 excavations of Hyde Abbey. I wanted this work of creative non-fiction to attend to Alfred as a biochemical organism that, in life and in death, challenges and exceeds his 'Anglo-Saxon' parameters. And I hoped that by allowing Alfred to become something other than 'Anglo-Saxon,' I might be able to mourn him. As an act of mourning, however, it required my own participation as well. As I narrated Alfred's organismic decay, I found myself — like Alfred's other biographers — writing about my own family, namely, its obsession with a genealogy that descends from fathers to sons. His story of sickness and decay became interleaved with a story about my schizophrenic mother who took it upon herself to research all seven branches of the Ellard family who migrated from pre-Revolutionary Virginia to the Mississippi Territory. While my mother's research was a product of her mental illness, her outsider's perspective on the Ellards enabled me contemplate my family differently and with skepticism, for the first time. As I narrated physical changes to Alfred's living flesh as it endured illness, old age, death, and post-mortem decay, I had to confront my attachments to a series of Ellard men — the sovereign patriarchs of my family.

While I drew connections between my professional and personal selves, unlike the autoethnography of Chapter 1, this was not a retreading of old paths. As I made a new narrative for Alfred, for the first time in my life, I had an open conversation with myself about my family's ghostly presence in my life. I was forced to recognize that Jonathan Ellard, who homesteaded in northern Alabama during Andrew Jackson's administration, was involved in the removal of Chickasaw native peoples. I was challenged to come to terms with the activities of his son, James Bennett Ellard, who moved to northern Mississippi, fought in the 8th Mississippi Calvary, and owned slaves, possibly as late as the 1880s. Yet, it was not the biographical particulars of these men that were hard to acknowledge. The names, photographs, and stories of these and other Ellard men were lionized by my family, especially my father, who became a member of the Sons of the Confederacy through his descent from James Bennett. What was hard — and 'hard' is not the word for this process, because feelings have no words — was facing an idyll of the South that is maintained by the Ellards through its unbroken narrative about family. Writing their stories forced me to put into words and, consequently, to narrativize my intergenerational, emotional attachments to the South. Namely, that, like my father, and his father, and his, I have possessed a repugnant love — and have embraced the terrible violence — of American colonialism, slavery, and racism. That, like all of these Ellard men, I could not bring myself to whole-heartedly disavow the Confederate flag, the sovereign signifier that not only haunts my family's genealogy but moreover maintains it. That I have loved — and have not known how to stop loving — something that has been passed on to me as a trans-generational haunting.

Writing about Alfred's physical body required that I consciously confront these realities about my family, engage the emotions that result from admitting something so horrid about oneself, and give narrative voice to all of it. It required that I look these ghosts in the face and bury them so they might 'Rest In Peace,' and I might find a way out of Anglo-Saxon studies and the Anglo-Saxon South. By attending to Alfred's material corpse rather than his sovereign, corpse-like ghost in my writing, I have been able to unfix a narrative about Alfred, my family, and myself. I have been able to recognize that Alfred is no longer (if he ever was) 'Anglo-Saxon,' and I am no longer (if I ever was) an 'Anglo-Saxonist' but a scholar of postSaxon becoming.

A Biochemical *Vita Ælfredi*

Named after Dr. Burrill B. Crohn, who first described the disease in 1932 along with colleagues Dr. Leon Ginzburg and Dr.

Gordon D. Oppenheimer, Crohn's disease belongs to a group of conditions known as Inflammatory Bowel Diseases (IBD). Crohn's disease is a chronic inflammatory condition of the gastrointestinal tract that most commonly affects the end of the small bowel (the ileum) and the beginning of the colon, but it may affect any part of the gastrointestinal (GI) tract, from the mouth to the anus. While the signs and symptoms can range from patient to patient, and some may be more common than others, Crohn's presents by way of the following: abdominal pain, fever, and clinical signs of bowel obstruction or diarrhoea with passage of blood or mucus, or both.[35]

It all started when he was much younger: *Ficus. Fic.* Figs. Fuck. As Alfred sat for hours over a wooden trough filled with hot stones and steaming herbs, he experimented with alliterative poetry. While the warmth gave him some immediate relief, the figs always came back. They were disgusting. He felt disgusting. Alfred's body was always there, calling attention to itself in the most embarrassing ways.

When these heat treatments didn't work, Alfred's physician recommended a more aggressive course of action. Herbs were gathered. A wolf was killed, its jaw was burnt, and its ashes collected. It's hard to know which was worse: the hot, cakey smears that were applied to his bottom, the herbal drinks meant to purge the figs (and everything else) from his body, or the time-consuming rituals passed down from some magician of the very dark and deep past.

Although problems with the body were, as they always have been, the cost of living, there is a certain unspeakability surrounding the asshole. No one wants to talk about a real, functional one even though it's the first insult every schoolboy learns. For the asshole really is the perfect metaphor for an unlikeable body until things — like hemorrhoids — make their presence known. On the toilet, the asshole suddenly retreats from its sta-

---

[35] Daniel C. Baumgart and William J. Sandborn, 'Crohn's Disease,' *The Lancet* 380, no. 9853 (November 2012): 1590–1605.

tus as a delightful signifier to a sphincter of painful, burning materiality that no one wants to name, much less to talk about. Even the *Lacnunga,* in a detailed recipe for relieving hemorrhoids, becomes prim when approaching the asshole, instructing the afflicted to apply a hot ointment 'to þæm setle' ['to the seat'] of the patient's body.

With the *Lacnunga*'s statement as the only Old English guide for approaching the material asshole, we might return to Alfred, who, may or may not have felt a similar obliqueness towards discussing his medical *dolors*. Unfortunately, for him, hemorrhoids were the first and early sign of a much worse condition. If, as a young man, he was able to keep quiet about the problems with his *setl,* by the time Alfred was an adult, there was no privacy to be had regarding the matter. While one can usually grin and bear the discomfort of walking, riding, and even shitting with a hemorrhoid, frequent diarrhea is a far more difficult problem to hide.

The constant back and forth, back and forth, back and forth to the toilet, waiting for his bowels to stop churning; the dehydration and fatigue that often times left him pale and sometimes kept him in bed; the painful swelling of his abdomen and upper thighs — all these symptoms, inevitably apparent to those who shared in the close quarters of his living environment, disclosed that Alfred was not well. Worse than a hemorrhoid, this shit, this bloody, mucusy, shit, which he felt himself to be living in, was unbearable. It marked the asshole as an oozing communicant, which mouthed vile, rotten, and painful things. And it was not just Alfred's asshole that was talking. From inside his body, Alfred found himself in constant, excruciating conversation with the real voices behind his problems. The thousands of anaerobic microbiota that had colonized his gut sent him a message of abdominal pain, fever, and cramping.

Alfred soon understood the dynsfunctional communications messaged to him by these bacteria. When he looked at the mucus and blood facing him in the toilet, his healthcare worries turned to feelings of personal disgust, shame, and depression. It was then that Alfred's alliterative experiments turned from *ficus* towards the *halig fæder*, from the *setl* of his asshole to that of the heavenly throne:

Halig fæder, thu on heofon,	*Ac, min fæder, pater noster,*
dismiss us, *no,*	*debit me*
from each of evils	*from coming temptations*
from þis shit,	*from min self,*
from þis body,	*from min corpus,*
Ælfred, Amen.	

As Alfred transformed the material sounds of his body into the familiar tones of spiritual comfort, he burnished the abject within into a poetics of his rightful self.

Poetic self-fashioning is not only the gambit of kings and princes, despite what historians may say. Because it is not just regal figures who have bodies in disrepair. Such is the case of Dora Lou. Legally blind, Dora Lou is my mother's first cousin, who was born and still lives in the piney woods of McHenry, Mississippi. In the dirt road that leads to her home, in the outhouse that sits squat in her yard, she is the face of a poverty rarely seen these days in the rural South. For my mother, Dora Lou's blindness is that site of disrepair against which she has always situated her upbringing. 'Poor Dora Lou,' my mother would say as she shook her head. It was an expression that ignited other memories: of an alcoholic uncle, of a Pentecostal grandfather, of a mother she disdained. But above and beyond all these things which she hated about her childhood past, Dora Lou and her McHenry home reminded my mother that she was descended from a father born out of wedlock. Her father's illegitimacy stuck in my mother like a sand spur, and when she traded her name in for 'Ellard,' my mother tried her hand at poetry. She researched the genealogy of her husband's family in order to creatively figure herself as the newest member of its long history.

The comforting projects of poetry are often short lived, however. Not only for my mother but also for Alfred. Despite his alliterative prayers, during periods when his intestinal problems were especially violent, no foods could sit with him, and at last he called for a new physician. Upon his arrival, Bald palpated the king's swollen stomach. He considered the location of his fingers, feeling the tautness of muscle, hidden beneath swollen, spongy tissue. He examined Alfred's *setl,* touching a fissure — a tear — that seemed to extend at least a few inches up the muscle tissue into the anal canal. That would explain the sharp, burning pain, which Alfred complained of during his bowel movements. When he slid his fingers out, Alfred's microbiota delivered a fart that declared their interior victory over his body. Bald smelled his fingers, wiped them, then looked in the toilet, examining the mucosal leavings of Alfred's last shit. While he had seen this presentation before, in those cases, the patients, all of them older and much poorer, had not lived long.

No one — neither the physician nor the patient — wants to examine a body in this condition. A visit with the doctor can be embarrassing and painful, and speaking to one's gastroenterologist is grossly intimate. Such intimacy might begin with a medical history, describing the problem. But talk, inevitably, leads to feeling, and feeling to touching, and touching leads to hidden places, and the body yields itself to hands that search, clinically, for non-verbal evidence of infection, disease, metastasis, parasite. Although Alfred's body was that of a king, by the time Bald had finished with him, its royal patina had worn off, and Alfred was just another chronically sick man, who couldn't stop shitting himself. Intimacy can do that to you.

So: Bald prescribed a treatment. Perhaps a change in diet would help. He told the cook not to prepare meat for a week. He cautioned against milk and eggs. He consulted several books in the Winchester monastery and wrote Northumbria to ask what resources might be available there. Wearmouth and Jarrow had several Mediterranean texts on healing, or so he had heard.

Aside from a few charms, Bald found nothing written on the subject, but the change in diet did seem to help at first. After a few weeks, Alfred's abdominal swelling subsided, and his morning trips to the toilet decreased from 10 to 7. Small, but meaningful victories for a body in pain. Relief, unfortunately, was not long lasting. Alfred was under stress, and his illness began to return. Unable to find a recipe for lasting, palliative treatment, much less a cure, Bald was dismissed from the court. In his absence, other physicians appeared. They, too, wouldn't keep their hands off Alfred, feeling him up from the inside-out before prescribing tinctures, pulses, pastes, and teas. Although food masked the taste of some remedies, others were terrible. They left a bitterness in Alfred's mouth that went straight to his intestines. When local doctors exhausted their attempts at a remedy, those from outside Winchester were consulted. More roving hands. More searching for answers inside his ass. More intimacy. Alfred's undiagnosable condition became widely known, and a steady stream of healers, some well-intentioned, others charlatans, arrived at the king's hall, hoping to take their turn and, by skill or by luck, deliver a biological miracle unto Alfred and his *setl*.

More often than not, however, the combination of unpalatable brews and searing topical remedies administered by Alfred's revolving door of physicians sent him to the shitter, where he continued to contemplate his situation in silence:

Ac, min fæder,   *rex aeternalis,*

make min wholebody   *min poorbody whole*

halig, as þu eart   *a halo around the heart.*

As ic sit upon   þis setl, min setl,

sinful setl   kingly in its aeternality,

Ælfred rex, Amen.

'Poor Dora Lou.' The sound of her name, like an arrow of time, shot into the past and landed on my mother's father. He was born in the small house in McHenry where Dora Lou now lives. He was a bastard, my mother never failed to remind, because his last name — Herring — belonged to a man he never knew. My grandpa's illegitimacy was a canker and an obsession for my mother. She would burst into tears when she talked about it. In those moments, when her face showed the terror of sexual sin, I could see the straightjacket of the Pentecostal South buckle tight around her.

Although my mother talked incessantly about her upbringing, she did not like going home. Actually, she was hostile towards it. When we did go to my grandparents' house and to see Dora Lou, what I remember most was driving down the Gulf Coast. Crossing Pascagoula and Moss Point into Kreole (where my grandma and grandpa lived); then on to Gautier and Biloxi, on the way to McHenry, was an experience of wonder and disgust. Even if I was asleep as we crossed the truss bridges that connected these towns, the pogy plants always woke me. The smell of fish meal processing was revolting, and it meant that we were almost there. While the stench of the pogies lasted only as long as the bridges did, the highway that stretched from Moss Point to Biloxi passed by a coastal slurry made up of seafood, maritime industries, and filth. After Omega Protein (from whence the pogy smell came) and Ingall's shipyard, we'd stop, sometimes, at inlets where my mother used to gig flounder. Here, brown sand met browner water. As a kid, these brackish waterways were polluted by her refrain, 'Poor Dora Lou,' and the story of sexual transgression that followed from it.

Many rivers and their tributaries lead into the Gulf Coast: the Tombigbee and Coosa flow into Mobile Bay; the Chickasway and Leaf head to Pascagoula; and, of course, the great Mississippi runs the spine of the state and empties into New Orleans. While frequently imagined as highways for people and goods, these rivers are likewise the intestinal tracts of the South. Rivers pass sediment and waste to coastal wetlands, which act as kidney filtration systems. Once this water is cleaned, it moves into river deltas that pour into the Gulf, where seafood, ships, and processing plants have moored themselves for nearly a century.

Up river, where it is cleaner, is where the Ellards live. Up river, where there are fewer digestive problems, is where the Ellards live. Down river, where the smell of fish guts pollutes the air, is where my mother is from. Down river, where things are filtered and flushed out with no thought to memory, is where my mother is from.

Down river, no birth certificates, cemetery plots, or family stories exist that would locate a past worth finding. Not only was my grandpa a bastard, but his family was poor and illiterate. Herring men wore coveralls and got their hands dirty at the shipyard. Herring ladies did not play bridge or bake cakes—their kitchens smelled of gumbo and boiled shrimp. There was no thought to the past or to pedigree. When my mother married my father, she left the Herrings and McHenry. She left Dora Lou. She turned her nose up at the chickens, the outhouse, the screen door, the boggy woods, and Mississippi's wastewater. She could no longer smell the industrialized coast; she would no longer gig flounder at dusk or travel rickety bridges. Her home and her surname would be my father's. Her house would be full of the Ellards' old furniture and photos. Her past would now be traceable from here to the Civil War and the American Revolution. In grafting herself to my father's family tree, my mother would claim the sexual cleanliness and legitimacy denied her on account of her father and become a 'Southern Lady.' She would write herself into its shoots, branches, and blossoms; she would carve her name into its sturdy trunk and deep roots. In an attempt to rid herself of a sin that smelled like the entrails of Pascagoula's Gulf Coast, my mother began a project of arboreal poetry.

Had physicians of the late ninth century benefitted from twenty-first-century urulogy, biomedical diagnoses, and pharmacological advances, Alfred might have been medically healed. At the first signs of stool problems and abdominal pain, he probably would have been given a colonoscopy and an endoscopy. He might even have been admitted into the hospital, where a CT scan and barium x-ray would have been ordered to diagnose his problems. Once his asshole had been handled with light and heavy machinery, photographed from the sphincter all the way up to his guts, and discussed (in the most sanitary terms) by a medical team, Alfred may have been discharged with a treatment plan that entailed a daily dosage of 6g sulfasalazine, 1mg folic acid, and Mesalamine enemas as necessary. Yet, it's hard to say for sure. Crohn's, like its sister conditions, IBS, colitis, and leaky gut, is treatable with a variety of medications, but rarely do patients find themselves symptom-free. For the Western medical community does not know what causes, or cures, Crohn's. While alternative practitioners have found success by eliminating high-roughage vegetables, soft cheeses, and other difficult-to-digest and bacteria-flourishing foods, biomedicine has yet to advocate for treatment plans other than pharmacological ones.

Yet, Alfred, like so many of us today, was not ambivalent towards his illness. Absent the benefit of Western medical science and modern, alternative medicines, Alfred began to find the timing and rhythm of his flare-ups. His body's ear became attuned to a bacterial orchestra that would play after certain meals. While Alfred learned to order and avoid certain foods, fasting was, most often, the only way to stay away from the toilet and from the doctors' roving, searching, cold hands. One could not, however, avoid food forever, and alongside the continued medical remedies prescribed to the king were religious ones, as some believed that Alfred was not afflicted by an undiagnosable illness but possessed by spiritual darkness, a sin which his own biographer attributed to sexual desire. Perhaps Alfred could be cured if the devil was chased from his hiding place, and Alfred atoned for his sinful thoughts and actions. Holy water and incense cleansed his body and his royal residence. *Pater Nosters* were prescribed. An amulet was made for him to wear. On a scrap of parchment, which was rolled up and tied to Alfred's inner thigh, was a charm that had been a long time in the making:

Ac min fæder   *ond the angels of heofan*

from feondes costung   *and physicians hands*

free me,   *Alfred Angulsaxonum rex.*

Can alliterative poetry become an arboreal project? Did the root bulb of Alfred's medical intimacies grow into a tree from which my family branches? As my mother muttered, 'Poor Dora Lou' and repeated the story of her family's disgrace, she looked up the Ellards' birth, death, and marriage records. She began to build upon what was known about the family from its Calhoun County homestead to those in Trussville, Alabama; Anderson and Pendleton, South Carolina; and Hamilton County, Virginia. As she left the cemeteries of Calhoun and looked elsewhere for vital records, my mother's research began to track the Ellard family line back through time and place from the Mississippi Territory of the early 1820s to America's pre-Revolutionary colonies.

In drawing up the Ellard family tree, my mother found a long colonial history sheltered in the first names of its many men. She pruned and shaped these branches to give more light to them so they could grow, lopping off the many women and girl children who could have been touched and would not pass on their surname, cutting away other, incontinent brothers and sons who had neither children nor patriotic spirit. Through William Washington Ellard and Andrew Jackson Ellard, my mother found cleanliness, godliness, and legitimacy. Surely, there was no sin in these names, which refracted the whitewashed narratives of American sovereignty and settlement. These men had not been stained by the hands of sexual misdeed. Their bodies knew nothing of noxious, downriver pollution. In them, my mother escaped the damnation of her own body, raised near the dirty, intestinal waterways of Mississippi's Gulf Coast. In their names, she cultivated alliterative connections between the Jonathans, Jameses, and Jesses of the many generations. Through her labors, the Ellard family tree grew straight and tall in clean waters. She refigured narratives of American colonialism into a romance of the Confederacy, carving out a place for herself at its base. Here, under the branching shade of my family, she purged from herself the intimate sins of adultery, illegitimacy, and the consequent genealogical void that had made her not only unclean but also suffering from environmental dyspepsia.

In Virginia, she found a man,
Amos Issac Allerd, whose son, Jonathan Ellard,
travelled with his wife, Rutha McAdams, to Pendleton,
South Carolina, after Independence Day after the Cherokees
had been removed. But the Carolina mountains were too steep:
they needed flatter land. So they followed the Appalachians
southward, so they followed the path of 'Indian' removal,
so they made their way for themselves towards Alabama,
then Mississippi, where they named their children
William Washington and Andrew Jackson in celebration
of America's victories. There was also another son — James
Bennett — who founded Ellard, Mississippi, owned slaves,
fought for the Confederacy, and became
the trunk of my family tree.
So James B.
begat
Jesse Jonathan,
who begat
Chester Dare,
who begat
Jesse Jonathan,
who begat
Jesse Sugg
who married
Margo Herring
E
L
L
A
R
D

While my mother never knew it, her research trod old paths. In a book that I used to look at when I visited my grandmother's house as a kid were pages and pages of genealogical charts that traced the family line back through time. From north Mississippi to Virginia, then across the Atlantic, the Ellards set sail from Britain sometime around the mid-eighteenth century. At this point, the Mississippi genealogist's research became speculative and aristocratic. There was a knight in the family and, shooting off of some branch, a duke. As the Ellards began to resemble the characters of a medieval bedtime story, their surname started to reshape itself in the direction of an even more distant and earlier moment of the 'Middle Ages.' Ellard elasticized from Allerd into Elward, Allard, Aillard, and Aylward. Recently, I looked up the spelling variations on a less-than-reputable ancestry website. From its own 'archives,' the site 'excerpts' the following:

> The origins of the Ellard surname lie with the Anglo-Saxon tribes of Britain. The name Ellard began when someone in that family worked as a keeper of a *hall*. The surname Ellard is composed of the elements *hall*, which denoted one who was employed at such a manor-house or hall, and *ward*, which was originally applied to one who was a watchman.[36]

As if conjuring the ghosts of its surname, an Anglo-Saxon 'hall ward' returns in the ancestors of my family. William Washington and Andrew Jackson — the sons of Jonathan Ellard — valorize American coloniality and settler colonialism, part of the glorious duties of the Anglo-Saxon race. Likewise, upon arriving in north Mississippi, giving the area his name, owning slaves, and fighting for the Confederacy, James Bennett Ellard exercised his patronymic right as a 'hall ward' of what so many have called 'the Great Anglo-Saxon Southland.'[37]

---

36 'Ellard Surname, Family Crest & Coat of Arms,' *House of Names*, https://www.houseofnames.com/ellard-family-crest.

37 'Inaugural Address of Governor George Wallace, Which Was Delivered at the Capitol in Montgomery, Alabama,' *Alabama Department of Archives and History*, January 14, 1963, http://digital.archives.alabama.gov/cdm/ref/

Ellard, Allerd, Aylward, Hall-Ward: surnames and specious etymologies make their way down, down, deep into Calhoun County soil, where the tap root of my family's tree draws water from Alfred's 'Anglo-Saxon' signifier.

Yet, all organic things, no matter how attentive the arborist, are subject to aging. Crowns flatten. Branches droop and sag, tired of carrying the weight of the past. As a child without siblings, the only name that my mother could add to the trunk of the Ellards' family tree — which had begotten so many sons of colonial America and the Confederate South — was my own. Unfortunately, as a girl, my name would never do. Without another James or Jesse or Jonathan to keep it strong and healthy, the survival of my family's tree was questionable. I girdled its trunk. I could get pregnant. Hands. Touching. No. The potential for illegitimacy all over again was too much to contemplate. Something must be done.

Something would have to be done about all this body. Alfred couldn't take it. Yet, it kept coming, and they kept coming, and the touching, and the remedies, and the touching, and the intimacies, and the touching, and the coming. Nothing was clean anymore, even his amulet. Although he had tried, at first, to keep it neat and dry, over time it had become soiled. When he finally took the thing off, the ink had worn off the parchment, and the only writing legible was *Ælfred, Angulsaxonum rex,* smudged, in reverse, onto the inside of this thigh. At a distance, it just looked like a shit stain.

---

collection/voices/id/2952, 2. It is noteworthy that when invoking the 'Great Anglo-Saxon Southland' in this address, Gov. Wallace also said, 'In the name of the greatest people that have ever trod this earth, I draw the line in the dust and toss the gauntlet before the feet of tyranny…and I say… segregation now…segregation tomorrow…segregation forever' (ibid.).

Some days the smudge was so faint it seemed like it would come off with just a little more scrubbing. On others, the writing stood out in high contrast to his near-translucent skin. No one, except probably Alfred, could even read the letters. But because Alfred could read it, it bothered him. Bothered him so much that he kept trying to remove it, applying oils, pastes, soaps: any kind of topical that might remove the brown stain. Once, he rubbed the area raw only to find that when the redness had abated and new skin had grown back, so had the words.

After a while, Alfred's relationship to this mark extended from intense, focused attention to absented-minded caress. Sometimes his hand would drop to the inside of his thigh, and his palm would press down on the small area. Other times, it would trace the lettering with a finger. *Ælfred, Angulsaxonum rex,* hot within him.

As his body aged, Crohn's gave way to a phenomenon more insistent than the microbiota which had caused it. Alfred's joints ached. His teeth started to rot. He began to stoop, to lose his hearing, to be short of breath. He felt stiff in the mornings, and sometimes he forgot things. It was unclear whether or not the Crohn's had relented or gone into remission, but these days Alfred's trips to the bathroom seemed to result from incontinence rather than from microbial activity. Perhaps he had just gotten used to it. For Alfred had learned, many years ago, to stay away from inflammatory foods, fast regularly, and keep to an exacting routine, mostly in avoidance of the psychological effects that shitting oneself on a regular basis can have on people with even the sunniest dispositions. At any rate, the physicians had failed, a long time ago, to give Alfred any relief, and he sent them all away. He could not abide any more conversations about his bowels. He could not abide any more fingers inside his skin. Yet, no matter how many years passed or how many hot baths he took, the inky phrase from his amulet remained, a loose and distorted tattoo on his inner thigh. It now looked like a birthmark, or maybe a blood vessel that had ruptured:

Ac min fæder, Ic feel myself aging.

From inside to outside, my entrails chase me,

the soft stink snakes down, figure-eights down

my intestinal highway, passing kidneys, gall bladder, and colon:

organs that have long since failed to function appropriately. Ic find myself loose, min

fæder, a fleshy falling softness that rolls off the bone, that tears at the first

touch of my parchment, casting shadows of a phrase once articulate but now only

a faint murmur Ælfred Angul x rex.

Perhaps the relationship between Cleanliness and Godliness is less about being clean and more about the preparative acts of scrubbing, pressing, starching, covering up, sitting straight, crossing your legs, chewing with a closed mouth, peeing with a closed you-know-what, keeping yourself to yourself, all so that that you remember: 1) God is the only man who cannot get you pregnant; and 2) love is a close and touching word — say it, and someone might get hurt.

Despite her adherence to Cleanliness, Godliness, and these Two Cardinal Rules, my mother was afraid. Although she had managed to excoriate her body through faith in God and in the Ellards, her daughter's name challenged her talent as an alliterative arborist. It was not Jessica or Jacqueline or Joanna, but Donna Beth. It did not refract the patriarchs of the Ellard line but sounded like a cry for Dora Lou.

Poor Dora Lou. A reverberation, a noise, the sound of leaves rustling. The hall wards felt a chill breeze blow past them. Alfred felt it rapping at his arthritic bones. His vision was leaving him now, and as the world grew dark around him, he smelled pine and dirt. He heard chickens and the creak of a door swing open. Something scraped against the floor. In the dark of Alfred's newfound blindness, he was not sure if he was living, or if death had come. A tiredness pressured his body. He was losing form.

Ac min fæder Ic feel within myself a failing falling. A flailing felling. A folding feeling. Smells radiate towards touch, fingering me with a clinical strength that does not make me shy away from my fleshiness. Sounds take me in arms and tenderly caress the flabbiness of my body, like a blind woman who knows the world by hand. As these senses feel each crease, they transmit their olfactory and vibrations into my body as Ic flail and fail to find some gospel text. Noli me tangere will not prevent her. She folds the pieces of skin together and feels me, Ælfred, rex.

Alfred awoke on the toilet. Uncertain how he got there, more uncertain how to get up, he remained slumped over the latrine until its odor got the best of him. Reaching out, he used the wall as a guide to find his way back to bed. His breath was rattling and shallow. Fluid had begun to fill his lungs. As Alfred fell asleep for the last time, the microbiotic orchestra, which had been so rhythmically active within him for so many years, made way for other 'players.' These new wards of his body did not abide the same processes of biological life. Cells and tissues became disorderly as Alfred slipped into a state of permanent, metabolic failure. In death, his body no longer pulsed to the rhythms of Crohn's, which had become so familiar to him. It moved in what could be called a disorganized arrhythmia: changing color, oozing liquids, becoming limp, then turgid. There was no regular speed or predictable timing to anything. And so they buried him.

Underground, however, Alfred was not inert. He became even busier than ever as the biochemical operations of his body attuned themselves to a subterranean, biotic ecosystem. Alfred began to move in time — to be touched and, now, for the first time, to touch back — to move with the rhythms of blowflies, rodents, and microbes; the temperature of his coffin; and the fibers of his linen shroud. Alfred engaged wholeheartedly in the micro-ecosystem of his burial site, whereby his skin pigmentation, biological sex, and defining physical features were becoming unknowable, at least without the help of a taphonomist or a forensic osteologist.

Through the years, Alfred was dug up and moved several times over. At first his ligamented body, which held together cartiledge and bone, was able to tolerate the disturbance. Several translations later, it fell apart, unable to endure the physical stress of it all. First situated in the microclimate of Winchester's new cathedral, then in Hyde Abbey, Alfred started to petrify. Sedimentary particles filled interstitial spaces, making his bones denser and heavier. Isotopes from the soil concentrated in them. Alfred became radioactive.

While my mother's pruning restricted unwanted growth at the trunk, branches, and leaves of the Ellard family tree, she could not control what happened below ground. Here, the women, second sons, and stillborn and non-surviving children grow. Here, the illegitimate, insane, and mixed-race relatives take refuge. Unbeknownst to her, the tap root of the Ellard tree is not neat like its foliage. It snakes and knots. It folds over itself. Its hidden tubers thwart the linear poetics of her genealogy. To know this, however, she would have to go digging in the dirt:

ANGLO-SAXON(IST) PASTS, POSTSAXON FUTURES

```
                            M
        i           BennEtt C    r e       m      a
            n        a      L C a    e        k  wo n
                s      e r   L ovelady          m
    a       h      t       A o      A Girl Child (1905-1907)
Jonathan's FaT        o        R    k    m              r
    e             Unknown    DAre       S m i t H        e
    s             r(?-1802)     G       a
        l    a     n         i       Wife
           v e m i     t    ress     k
                 r           s Child (1844-1844) i    ns
```

At first, he was found by accident. In 1788, convicts digging in the rubble of Hyde Abbey came across three lead coffins. The coffins were opened, the bones dumped out, and the lead fittings were sold. In 1866, amateur antiquarian, John Mellor, claimed to have recovered some of the scattered bones, which he attributed to Alfred. He sold them to the vicar of St. Bartholomew's Church near Winchester, who reburied them in an unmarked grave in the churchyard. Still, Alfred was sought out. Again, he was handled. In 1999 and 2013, excavations of the abbey and churchyard, respectively, exhumed more bones, tested them, and then shelved them for storage.

Then, in March 2013, click — click . — click, click, click . — .. .. — . cccccc — cc-cc-cccccccclick, click . — . cccccccccccc-ccccclick. — .. The crackle of a Geiger counter detected 14C. Its long-distance transmissions, the telegraphy of radiocarbon, spelled out the letters A – L – F – R – E – D. Or did they?

I don't know. But it was springtime. In Dora Lou's front yard, trumpet daffodils began to bloom. She had planted them years ago, like my grandmother, like my mother, like everyone else in Mississippi. And on the label of the brown paper sack, which the bulbs came in, read: *Narcissus* 'King Alfred.'

No one can predict the paths of mourning, and no one can predict where these mourning paths will lead. The second Movement of this book began by revealing a professional genealogy that positioned Alfred, king of the Anglo-Saxons, as the sovereign 'father' to Anglo-Saxon studies's many British 'fathers' described in the first Movement of this book. Alfred's patrilineage not only guards and maintains the professional signifier 'Anglo-Saxon' but also keeps us being 'Anglo-Saxonists.' 'Being' and 'becoming' are ontological positions and processes. In the context of this book, they are generated and maintained by the narratives we construct for our professional selves. When I set out to write Alfred's 'Biochemical *Vita*,' I meant to uproot the family tree of Anglo-Saxon studies by creating a new narrative: a biography that tracks Alfred's physical body as an organism of dynamic change, death, and decay. By focusing on the 'life' of Alfred's body, I hope to render him unsovereign and thereby create narrative conditions that would enable us to mourn him. Mourning, however, is an act of unmooring that refigures the entire self. Approaching Alfred's patrilineal relationship to Anglo-Saxon studies quickly became a family matter, and the early drafts of Alfred's 'Biochemical *Vita*' interleaved a story of the king with one of my Southern family. These intersections created an imaginary genealogical connection between Alfred, 'father' of the Anglo-Saxons, and the Ellard's settler-colonial and Confederate 'sons.' Yet, as Alfred's body failed him, and it began to deteriorate, the Ellard narrative of settler-colonialism and slave-holding met a similar fate: it was exposed and uprooted. Being 'Anglo-Saxon' — now expressed in personal as well as professional terms — is no longer tenable.

The Alfred–Ellard genealogy of 'Biochemical *Vita*' is an act of mourning that generates what Tayana Hardin calls a 'new fiction.'[38] 'Biochemical *Vita*' takes, as its conceptual entry point,

---

38 I would like to thank my colleague, Tayana L. Hardin, for introducing me to her expression, 'new fictions.' New fictions serves as a guiding concept in her recent essay, 'The I Who Arrives: A Meditation on History as Inheritance,' which understands that the 'power of imagination' can 'build

first, an understanding that the narrative of Alfred's sovereign, undecaying *corpus* is an 'old' story made up of Asserian half-truths that maintains itself under the sign of coloniality; and, second, it understands that in order to displace Alfred and the narratological and ideological worlds that he shoulders, a new story — a new fiction — must be attempted. This act of casting aside one dodgy account of Alfred (for Asser's *Life* is more 'court propaganda' than historical 'fact') for another is not a simple exchange because, as I just mentioned, Asser constructs Alfred's form out of a sovereign cloth that is limned with colonial aspirations. Generations of Anglo-Saxonists have genuflected before, blessed, and kissed these garments in acts of faith, love, and trust in an 'Anglo-Saxon' power that stretches between the triangulated poles of academic scholarship, race, and empire. Abandoning such a sovereign narrative form requires the emotional work of mourning, a scholarly-affective labor that can only come from that place within me that needs to be made to feel, and to acknowledge my feelings as matters of bereavement, so that I can direct all this emotional energy towards finding words that describe what is *inside me* and root 'it' out. 'Biochemical *Vita*' confronts the ghosts of my Southern family. It interleaves their presence with this most ghostly father of Anglo-Saxon studies in order to mourn them. To give them organismic bodies that live, die, and decay so that they can no longer haunt us. Absent this haunting, we can imagine other, non-fatherly genealogies and rhizomatic, narrative routes for a once-Anglo-Saxon studies. This is mourning. This is a new fiction — for the field and for myself.

As a new fiction, it trespasses all manner of borderlands: professional and personal boundaries, critical and literary genres, stories taken as academic truths and those dismissed as folklore; prose and poetic forms; and Englishes, old and new. While such supposed disrespect for how scholarship should compose itself may seem inappropriate, 'Biochemical *Vita*' be-

---

a world together,' in the classroom and in the poetics of literary criticism (*Pedagogy* 18, no. 3 [2018]: 532).

longs, in fact, to a relatively old form called 'paraliterary' writing or 'fictocriticism'.[39] As Gerrit Haas writes, fictocriticism is a term 'evoked to subsume motivated experimental writing practices that confound, and thereby problematise' literary genres.[40] These practices are 'playful in tone,' 'experimental in attitude,' and 'ethically motivated.'[41] Yet for anthropologist Michael Taussig, fictocriticism is not a flighty distraction from hard-nosed criticism but 'a love of muted and even defective storytelling as a form of analysis,' whose 'swerve in writing…is what trips up thought in a serpentine world.'[42] As Taussig recognizes the disruptive, necessary force of 'defective' stories, he underscores his work as that which strays from customary paths in order to alter lines of thinking. Fellow anthropologist Kathleen Stewart takes this Taussigian line one step further by writing fictocriticism as a mode that can topple our preoccupation with grasping the world, intellectually, by channeling the power of affect. Her writing 'perform[s] some of the intensity and texture that makes them [affects] habitable and animate' so that she may show the limits of intellectual abstractions.[43]

'Biochemical *Vita*' disrupts and 'trips up' the biography of Alfred, the Ellards, and their shared racial-colonial metanarrative. In so doing, it affectively performs the work of mourning these Anglo-Saxon fathers. Further, in joining together the professional and personal in this new, postSaxon fiction, 'Biochem-

---

39 Rosalind Krauss writes of the 'paraliterary works of Barthes and Derrida' *(The Originality of the Avant-Garde and Other Modernist Myths* [Cambridge: MIT Press, 1986], 292). In so doing, she underscores poststructuralism as theory that not only recognizes the literary value of criticism but also allows for a confusion to what genre 'theory' belongs (ibid.). Unlike paraliterary writing, fictocriticism is not associated with one critic but emerged in the Canadian art-scene of the 1990s.
40 Gerrit Haas, *Ficto/critical Strategies: Subverting Textual Practices of Meaning, Other, and Self-Formation* (Bielefeld: Transcript Verlag, 2017), 7. I would like to thank Selah Saterstrom for pointing me in this direction.
41 Ibid.
42 Michael Taussig, *Walter Benjamin's Grave* (Chicago: Chicago University Press, 2006), vii.
43 Kathleen Stewart, *Ordinary Affects* (Durham: Duke University Press, 2007), 4–5.

ical *Vita*' joins together and shifts the book's focus from the role that 'Anglo-Saxon' and 'Anglo-Saxonist' play in British contexts to the role of these terms in America. In the U.S., 'Anglo-Saxon' and 'Anglo-Saxonist' remain attached to fantasies of nation and empire that are inseparable from an American racism that is trenchantly directed at both Native peoples and African Americans. Mourning my profession's terms in relation to America's colonial and racial histories requires that I abandon the familiar topics and comfort zones of my field and become completely lost in unfamiliar academic waters. Mourning is truly an unmooring, and I become intellectually decentered and emotionally upended. No longer an 'Anglo-Saxonist' or a 'medievalist,' I feel homeless yet open, for the first time, to processing the wide-reaching, ongoing impact of my field's signifiers on non-white bodies, identities, and narratives in America. This intellectual and emotional process becomes, for me, a 'becoming postSaxon' — an ontological repositioning that is both professional and personal.

The third Movement of this book, 'postSaxon futures,' invites a once-Anglo Saxon studies to reposition itself in relation to temporalities, bodies, and methods once excluded by its racial and ethnopolitical signifiers so that the field might enter into a speculative conversation about what it might mean to become 'postSaxon.'

Third Movement

postSaxon Futures

6

Old/e English Poetics and 'Afro-Saxon' Intimacies[1]

In 1987, the Compton-based rap group N.W.A. released its first LP album, *N.W.A. and the Posse*. On its cover, original N.W.A. members Eazy-E, Dr. Dre, Ice Cube, and Arabian Prince, plus a number of friends and relatives, are photographed in front of a graffiti-covered building. Some people in the photo wear oversized clock necklaces set to 11:25, while many others are surrounded by empty and half-drunk Olde English '800' 12-ounce cans and 40-ounce bottles. A conspicuously placed pair of white pumps is the only sign of a woman's presence in this crowded picture of men. The cover art for *N.W.A. and the Posse* coordinates with Track 2 of the album, titled '8-Ball,' popular slang for Olde English '800' malt liquor. As if amplifying the visuals of N.W.A.'s cover art, on this track Eazy-E proclaims himself an '8-ball junkie.'[2] He drinks Olde English 'like a madman'

---

[1] I would like to thank Tayana Hardin for her many insightful comments on early and later versions of this chapter. Dr. Hardin brought to my attention the importance of considering gender and sexuality in readings of race. These considerations have dramatically shaped my arguments regarding the marketing history of Olde English malt liquor.

[2] Ice Cube, '8-Ball,' *N.W.A. and the Posse* (Los Angeles: Macola Records, 1987).

from morning 'til dark, and, under its influence, cruises through Compton, pulls out a 'silver gat' on a 'sucker punk', and harasses women at a party.[3] While Olde English '800' is the source of E's actions and lyrics, drinking it enables him to express certain gestures, sounds, and language politics that are solicited by the 'Olde English' brand itself, which has always capitalized upon the 'medieval' quality of its name.

This chapter considers the history of Olde English malt liquor and its frequent appearances in rap music in order to enter into a conversation with Old English, the early medieval language, and its linguistic history as a term of identification for Anglo-Saxon studies as an academic discipline. At first blush, nothing connects these 'Englishes' of popular culture and academic scholarship. Yet, in tracing the product design, marketing, and advertising history of Olde English malt liquor alongside the development of Old English historical linguistics, this chapter reveals that these two terms—'Olde' and 'Old English'—operate according to the same logic as the double-edged signifier 'Anglo-Saxonist.' They reference, at once, a linguistic representation used by academic scholars and a popular concept that communicates ideologies of nationalism, colonialism, and racism. While 'Old English' and 'Olde Englishes' (emphasis on the plural, in terms of cultural appropriations) circulate independently in scholarly and popular domains, they function together as cloaked agents of Anglo-Saxonism.

Beginning with N.W.A., these independently circulating terms show their relationship to one another: the Anglo-Saxonist ideologies that bind 'Old English' and 'Olde Englishes' start to unravel, and rap artists begin to recode Old English into an expression of African American sociolinguistics. As rappers reference Olde English not simply as an alcoholic beverage but, moreover, as a signifier of rap's poetic displays, they revise the spelling of this term. This revision reveals 'Olde' and 'Old English' as word concepts that participate in what Henry Louis Gates, Jr. calls 'Signifying,' a term derived from African Ameri-

---

3   Ibid.

can sociolinguistics, and what Samy Alim calls 'Hip Hop Nation Linguistics.'[4] As a sociolinguistic expression, these rap artists expand the semantics of 'Olde' and 'Old English' to include (rather than exploit) black bodies and black voices and thereby reclaim an Anglo-Saxonist term as an African American one. The poetics of rap music not only disrupt and challenge fundamental assumptions about Old English as a language of limited, academic circulation that operates outside the boundaries of Anglo-Saxonism. Moreover, the use of 'Olde' and 'Old English' in rap music (which is also a form of critical poetics) challenges academics to disinvent, reinvent, and decolonize Old English as part of the ontological project of 'becoming postSaxon.'

Brewed originally by Peoples Brewing of Duluth, Minnesota, in the early 1940s, Olde English '800' was initially called Ruff's Olde English Stout before it was renamed Olde English '600' Malt Liquor in 1947, in reference to its six-percent alcohol content.[5] As an expression that communicates a jaunty nostalgia for something that is vaguely past tense, 'Olde English' neither carries the academic heft of 'Old English' nor presumes a scholarly audience with any language training or familiarity with medieval studies. Yet the product itself directs consumers towards mistaking 'Olde English' for what Sinfree Makoni and Alisdair Pennycook call a linguistic 'representatio[n]' of Old English: a word that stands for a language.[6] This mistaken relationship between Olde English and Old English is supported, firstly, by the similar spelling and pronunciation of both expressions and, secondly, by the physiological proximity and psychological partnership between drinking and speaking, acts of oral

---

4   Henry Louis Gates, Jr., *The Signifying Monkey: A Theory of African-American Literary Criticism* (New York: Oxford University Press, 2014); H. Samy Alim, *Roc the Mic Right* (New York: Routledge, 2006).
5   Tony Dierckins and Pete Clure, *Naturally Brewed, Naturally Better: The Historic Breweries of Duluth and Superior* (Duluth: Zenith City Press, 2018), 147, 146.
6   Sinfree Makoni and Alastair Pennycook, 'Disinventing and Reconstituting Languages,' in *Disinventing and Reconstituting Languages*, eds. Sinfree Makoni and Alastair Pennycook (Buffalo: Multilingual Matters Ltd., 2007), 1–41.

Figure 1. Paper label from Ruff's Olde English Stout glass bottle. Peoples Brewing Company, Duluth, Minnesota, ca. 1943. Courtesy of the collection of Chris Olsen.

Figure 2. Paper label from Olde English "600" glass bottle. Peoples Brewing Company, Duluth, Minnesota, ca. 1940s. Private Collection.

Figure 3. Paper label from Olde English "600" glass bottle. Peoples Brewing Company, Duluth, Minnesota, 1950. Private Collection.

intake and oral expression. These connections between drinking Olde English and speaking Old English are reinforced by the graphic elements of early malt liquor bottle labels, in which the gothic script and scribal points of 'Olde English' reference the manuscript culture of this medieval language (see Fig. 1). The coupling of these linguistic and graphic elements with visual ones constitutes what Jürgen Spitzmüller calls an 'ideological message' that indexes certain historical, social, or cultural backgrounds refracted by the text and its author.[7] Spitzmüller's arguments bear extensively on the product design and adver-

---

7 Jürgen Spitzmüller, 'Floating ideologies: Metamorphosis of graphic 'Germanness'", in *Orthography as Social Action: Scripts, Spelling, Identity, and Power*, eds. Alexandra Jaffe, Jannis Androutsopoulos, Mark Sebba, and Sally Johnson (Berlin: de Gruyter, 2012), 257. Siân Echard extends Spitzmüller's discussion of graphic power and its participation in ideological messaging to early medieval scripts such as Old English: 'Even at the turn of the twenty-first century, the link between English text and Saxon letterform persists. In 1999 and 2000, the graphic artist Gareth Hinds produced his own version of *Beowulf*, using the 1910 translation by Francis Gummere as the base text. He worked with a calligrapher in developing the script, which was designed to suggest insular letterforms.... [T]he "Gothish" characters still stand as powerful signs of the past' (*Printing the Middle Ages* [Philadelphia: Pennsylvania University Press, 2008], 59).

tisements of Olde English in the 1950s,[8] when Peoples Brewing changed its company emblem from a heraldic crest flanked by two horses (see Fig. 2) to the portrait of Daniel Greysolon Sieur du Lhut, the French explorer after whom the city of Duluth was named (see Fig. 3).

As a consequence of this design change, the linguistic and graphic elements of Olde English become attached to an ideological message of colonialism. In a series of advertisements titled 'Do You Know These Facts About Sieur du Luth?' (see Figs. 4a–b) Peoples Brewing recounts du Luth's career in North America as a trader, treaty-maker, and arbiter of justice between Frenchmen and Native peoples. One ad celebrates his capture and execution of two Ojibwe who have been accused of killing two French colonials. A sketch of these blindfolded and bound Native American men appears above a caption explaining that du Luth, who seeks their death as recompense for that of the Frenchmen, 'taught the Indians to respect the Law for years to come!' While the portrait of a seventeenth-century Frenchman has nothing to do with an 'English' brand of malt liquor, by positioning an emblem of Sieur du Luth on the label and collar of Olde English bottles, Peoples Brewing makes a colonial persona the figurehead of its 'medieval' beer. By way of product naming and design, a signifier of medieval language and manuscript culture becomes sutured to a historical reality and a posthistorical fantasy, imbuing Olde English '600' with an intoxicating spirit that it has inherited, by ancestry and violent force of 'law,' from its founding, pan-European fathers.

That Peoples Brewing so easily tilts the product design and marketing of Olde English towards an ideological message of American colonialism begs further questions about the language politics of Old English. While language, as Richard Bauman and Charles Briggs argue, may be perceived to be 'contain[ed] in an autonomous realm set apart from things and social relation,' it is the often-silent frontispiece for 'metadiscursive regimes,' ideological discussions about language that create frameworks for

---

8   Dierckins and Clure, *Naturally Brewed, Naturally Better,* 159.

what counts as language.[9] The use of 'Anglo-Saxon' (as it was popularly called in previous centuries, and to which it is still referred in some academic quarters) as referent for both a language and a people highlights the implication of this term in a meta-discursive regime that Mary Dockray-Miller notes, 'in the nineteenth-century United States...was almost exclusively racial and racist.'[10] Old English and its partner terms 'Middle' and 'Modern' Englishes likewise date to the nineteenth century. They are based on Jacob Grimm's evolutionary characterizations of 'the oldest,' 'the middle,' and 'the modern,' a schema that organizes languages according to 'bounded and discrete linguistic wholes,' which, in turn, 'correspond to distinct nations.'[11] The 'temporal logic' of Grimm's old, middle, and modern schema arranges the languages of English into a progress narrative of world languages that 'hierarchically organiz[es]' them on a 'global evolutionary scale' and 'implicitly function[s] as a rationale for the political subjugation of its producers and their descendants.'[12] The foundational role that Old English plays in this progress narrative and its colonial politics is measured by the 'nostalgic rhetoric' that Grimm uses to describe it and the other 'oldest languages' of historical linguistics. For Grimm, these languages express a nation's original 'tradition[s]' which are 'embodied' by a 'masculine national virility that rendered a people creative, powerful, and cohesive.'[13] While Old English appears to be a benign term of historical linguistics, it nonetheless functions as the agent of Anglo-Saxonism. As the first and oldest stage of English, it not only presumes a sense of linguistic superiority but, moreover, leverages this stance as a rationale for politically subjugating those who do not share a similarly

---

9 Richard Bauman and Charles L. Briggs, *Voices of Modernity: Language Ideologies and the Politics of Inequality* (Cambridge: Cambridge University Press, 2003), 20, 17.
10 Mary Dockray-Miller, *Public Medievalists, Racism, and Suffrage in the American Women's College* (Cham, Switzerland: Palgrave Pivot, 2017), 1–2.
11 Bauman and Briggs, *Voices of Modernity*, 201, 203.
12 Ibid., 203.
13 Ibid., 206.

Figure 4a. Advertisement: 'Do You Know The Facts About Sieur du Luth?' Du Luth 'established pacts of peace and arranged for reciprocal inter-trial marriages to strengthen the new ties,' ca. 1952. Courtesy of the collection of Pete Clure.

Figure 4b. Advertisement: 'Do You Know The Facts About Sieur du Luth?' Du Luth 'taught the Indians to respect the Law for years to come!' ca. 1952. Courtesy of the collection of Pete Clure.

ancient linguistic 'tradition.' Likewise, as a term that remains overtly wedded to the 'Anglo-Saxon' period and people, the 'nostalg[ia],' 'masculin[ity],' and 'virility' with which Old English is associated thereby identifies it with the meta-discusive regime of Anglo-Saxonism: a belief in the superiority of English-speaking peoples that often is associated, in both scholarly and popular imaginations, with a northern European/Germanic homosocial, ethnically separatist, and racist heroism typified by these very characteristics.

Although worlds apart, Olde English malt liquor and Old English language fall under the common sign of Anglo-Saxonism. As variants of one another, these terms index the deeply rooted partnership between the popular and the scholarly Anglo-Saxonist — a figure introduced in the first pages of this book and explored at great length in previous chapters. Yet, as partners that circulate freely across and between academic and lay audiences, Old and Olde English reveal themselves as non-proprietary signifiers. While early medieval scholars may make special claim to expertise in the linguistic aspects of Old English, we do not own nor fully control the many valences of this term, but we are beholden nevertheless to the politics sedimented within its nineteenth-century origins and twentieth-century uses. These politics are not only European but also American, yet distinctive racial histories underwrite America's colonial past. In the following pages, this chapter enters into an expansive discussion of Olde English (then returns, much later, to Old English) in order to talk about how the Anglo-Saxonist politics of this particular brand of malt liquor perpetuate racist and colonialist myths about African American race, sex, and alcohol consumption. This chapter develops a deep sense of how Olde English operates as an agent of American Anglo-Saxonism, which rap artists resist and recalibrate in sociolinguistic terms. Ironically, critically ruminating upon Olde English malt liquor enables us to think more clearly and openly about the stakes of colonialism and racism in Old English and Anglo-Saxon studies from within a distinctively American context.

Despite its popularity in Duluth, Peoples Brewing could not keep up with regional or national competition, and, in 1957, the company liquidated its holdings. Olde English '600' was sold to Bohemian Breweries of Spokane, Washington, which 'transferred rights to Atlantic Brewing,' also of Spokane.[14] Atlantic brewed and distributed Olde English until 1962, and, in 1964, Blitz-Weinhard of Portland, Oregon, bought the brand, brewing and distributing it for almost two more decades.[15] Olde English '600' maintained its name, gothic font, and scribal points throughout these moves, and Sieur du Luth remained the label's figurehead. Still, it never sold well. Marketed to a white, middle class, suburban consumer, Old English '600,' like other malt liquors during the 1950s and 1960s, was advertised as a champagne alternative that had a much higher alcohol content than regular ale. In the late 1960s, when Blitz-Weinhard examined its customers' demographic information, it discovered that almost one-third of malt liquor consumers were African Americans, who were exposed to the same medieval branding and colonial advertisements as the white drinkers to whom the product was marketed.

Just as the so-called 'Middle Ages' and its signifiers have often been imbricated within America's long history of colonial politics and racism, African Americans have frequently been entangled within the medieval. For example, in *De Bow's Review*, an agricultural and industrial periodical popular in the antebellum South, the behaviors and attitudes of 'Puritan' Northerners and 'Cavalier' Southerners are attributed to their differing medieval European ancestries.[16] These genealogical discrepancies became popular in the decades leading up to the Civil War,[17] and as the Southern cavalier made way for the Con-

---

14 Dierckins and Clure, *Naturally Brewed, Naturally Better*, 161.
15 Ibid.
16 Anonymous, 'The Puritan and the Cavalier,' *DeBow's Review* 31, no. 3 (September 1861): 209–52.
17 Inspiration for tournaments in the antebellum South originated in an instance of life imitating art. In 1839, Lord Eglinton organized a tournament in Britain that was inspired by and modelled on the Ashby-de-la-Zouche

federate chevalier, medieval reenactments in the form of ring tournaments spread from Maryland and Virginia to the Deep South, continuing as a sport and entertainment for the Confederate cavalry throughout the Civil War. In the post-war period, these tournaments expanded to include not only white Southerners, who used them as fundraisers for Southern relief efforts, Confederate veterans, and Civil War memorials,[18] but also African Americans, who organized all-black tournaments across the South from 1865 to about 1875. While some white newspapers express concern that these black-organized events are spurred by 'Northern' politics,[19] others view them from within a racist frame of 'innocent amusements' that attempt to participate in the 'polite arts' of Southern society.[20] Whether subversive acts or spectacles for whites, Texas artist Merritt Mauzey offers a visual commentary of this phenomenon in his undated 'Tournament Practice' (see Fig. 5).[21] This small lithograph on paper depicts the back of a black rider on horseback, who holds a jousting spear and heads towards a series of rings that dangle from ropes on poles. As the eye moves from the circle made by the rider's head to those of the rings, the latter begin to look like nooses, and a ring tournament suggests the site of an imminent lynching.[22]

---

tournament in Walter Scott's *Ivanhoe*. The event was reported in American newspapers, and when an American spectator, William Gilmor, returned to his home in Maryland, he organized a similar tournament on his Baltimore estate in 1840 (Ann Rigney, 'The Many Afterlives of Ivanhoe,' in *Performing the Past: Memory, History, and Identity in Modern Europe*, eds. Karin Tilmans, Frank Van Vree, and Jay Winter [Amsterdam: Amsterdam University Press, 2010], 217–18).

18 Esther J. Crooks and Ruth W. Crooks, *The Ring Tournament in the United States* (Richmond: Garrett and Massie, 1936).
19 'The Colored Tournament,' *The Louisiana Democrat*, September 27, 1876, 2.
20 'The Young Colored Men of our Parish…,' *The Louisiana Democrat*, September 13, 1876, 2.
21 I would like to thank Alexandra Cook for bringing this image to my attention.
22 Merritt Mauzey's father was a Union soldier, and after the Civil War, the Mauzeys moved to Texas, where they sharecropped cotton before purchasing 160 acres of land to farm. Merritt was born in 1897 in the central Texas town of Clifton and would have been a young adult when *Birth of a Nation*

In Mauzey's depiction of the postbellum South, medieval fantasies turn towards racial terrorism when the African American 'knight' is imagined in the company of the white knights of the Ku Klux Klan.[23]

Despite Mauzey's allusion to the deadly undercurrents of American medievalism, among other African Americans artists and writers, such as Jessie Fauset, medieval iconography was perceived as a fantastic way beyond American race prejudice. In Fauset's essay, 'My House and a Glimpse of My Life Therein,' she imagines herself within a 'fortress' as 'a queen come into her very own.'[24] Published in NAACP's *The Crisis,* Fauset's depiction of queenly sovereignty is given a medieval patina when her nar-

---

sparked a revival of the Klan in Texas in the 1920s. Dallas dentist Hiram Wesley Evans was elected imperial wizard, or national leader, at the KKK's first national convention in November 1922, and Klan-sponsored lynchings in Texas contributed to a total of 232 killings in the state—the highest recorded number in the United States. 'Tournament Practice' is undated, and Mauzey's oeuvre includes several portraits of black cotton farmers (including one called *Madonna in the Fields*) that depict African American subjects and sharecroppers in Texas within a romantic framework. Despite Mauzey's romanticism of the Middle Ages and his idealization of black sharecropping in Texas, Mauzey's lived experience of racial politics in early twentieth century Texas affords a reading of 'Tournament Practice' that is, at best, highly ambivalent. The African American rider suggests a scene of medievalist possibility ('tilting' against racism and racist violence) and at the same time reveals the unvarnished realities of race relations in rural Texas (lynchings).

23 Paul Christopher Anderson writes that '[e]nthusiasm for the joust in 1866, in the springtime of Confederate defeat, flowered in tandem with the formation of the Ku Klux Klan. Between them were obvious connections of ritual. Tournament rider and night rider became knights on horseback; both were liberated by masquerade and costume' ('Rituals of Horsemanship: A Speculation on the Ring Tournament and the Origins of the Ku Klux Klan,' in *Weirding the War: Stories from the Civil War's Ragged Edges,* ed. Stephen Berry [Athens: Georgia University Press, 2011], 217). When Reconstruction-era Klan activity is associated with Klan-sponsored lynchings of the 1920s (see footnote 22), Mauzey's lithograph seems to document a relationship between the medievalist fantasies and racist atrocities of the Ku Klux Klan.

24 Jessie Fauset, 'My House and a Glimpse of My Life Therein,' *The Crisis* 8, no. 3 (1914): 144.

Figure 5. Merritt Mauzey, 'Tournament Practice,' lithograph on paper, undated. Courtesy of Smithsonian American Art Museum.

rative is accompanied by visual elements printed in the magazine: a decorated initial begins the essay, as if it were appearing on a manuscript page; and a photograph of Fauset, dressed as a pre-Raphaelite, is flanked by text from her essay about 'valiant knights,' 'distressed ladies,' and 'lorn damsels.'[25] Unlike Mauzey's 'Ring Tournament,' which positions African Americans within the threatening frame of American racism, Fauset appropriates the medieval as a space of African American possibility. In 'My House,' she can be, at once, queen of her castle-fortress, distressed lady within it, or forlorn damsel in need of knightly rescue. Fauset uses both narrative and visual strategies to conjure herself within a medieval world. At the end of her essay, she moves into the medieval by concluding, 'my house is constructed of dream-fabric, and the place of its building is — *Spain*!' A very real place in modern Europe where light-skinned African Americans may be presumed Hispanic,[26] Spain is likewise the site of medieval Iberia where, Alexandre Dumas famously stated, Africa begins.[27] In Spain, Fauset 'passes' into a medieval

---

25 Ibid.
26 These claims to Spanish 'passing' can be traced to mid-nineteenth-century American literature. For example, in the 'Spanish masquerade' scene of *Uncle Tom's Cabin*, George Harris makes his skin darker so he can pass for a Spanish gentleman in order to escape enslavement; James Fenimore Cooper's *The Prairie* heroine, Inez, is a Spanish 'Creole' who is taken prisoner by a slave trader and slave-owning family; and African American writer Pauline Hopkins's short story 'Talma Gordon' sends her protagonist to live in Italy because her darker skin could be more easily explained as Iberian.
27 Fauset's geography of 'Spain' is a fraught place where medieval Orientalism and medieval utopianism meet. On the one hand, Spain is the site of an Orientalizing exoticism where the 'Moorish' woman functions as an object of desire enclosed in her fortress. In this medievalist fantasy of early modern Spain (during which time, Moriscos endured mass persecution), 15th- and 16th-century stories tell of a Christian knight who finds himself at a castle, where a dark woman 'opens her doors wide' for him. This trope of the exotic, entrapped, and sensual female Other finds its way to America in the nineteenth century by way of 'The Legend of the Three Beautiful Princesses' in *Washington Irving's Tales of the Alhambra*. Irving's contemporary, Alexandre Dumas, famously claims that 'Africa begins in the Pyranees,' a mountain range in which Spanish Iberia — home

Figure 6. Paper and foil label from Olde English '800' one-quart glass bottle. Pabst Brewing Company, Milwaukee, Wisconsin, ca. 1970s. Private Collection.

'dream fabric' that can offer inclusion and welcome to black bodies when contemporary America does not.[28]

Whether African Americans of the early twentieth century are viewed as racial subjects or sovereigns, black men and women understood and responded to the visual and literary iconography of medievalism and the Middle Ages, finding in them fantasies that could conjure up home-grown terror or empowering dreamscapes. Consequently, while African Americans were not the intended audience of Olde English '600' advertising

---

to Maghrebi Muslims, Berbers, and Sub-Sahran Africans — is located. Although Dumas's statement is meant to Orientalize and therefore exclude Spain from western Europe, Fauset's call to 'Spain!' rescripts and destabilizes the Hispano-American medievalism that would entrap Fauset within a 'Moorish' trope. My very great thanks go out to Chad Leahy, who brought these points to my attention.

28 As Cord Whitaker writes, Fauset's 'My House' 'reevaluat[es] blacks' engagement with the Middle Ages as a positive element that predicates blacks' full involvement in American history' and 'create[s] something radically new: the recognition of a spiritual home for African Americans in the idyllic and imaginary European medieval past' ('B(l)ack Home in the Middle Ages: Medievalism in Jessie Redmon Fauset's "My House and a Glimpse of My Life Therein"', *postmedieval: a journal of medieval cultural studies* 10, no. 2 [2019]: 164).

campaigns, they understood the racial politics of its medieval branding very well.

In 1968, after more than a decade of ownership by Portland-based Blitz-Weinhard Brewing, the company applied for a patent that rebranded their malt liquor as Olde English '800.'[29] This name change was accompanied by a redesign of the brand's medieval iconography, in which the gothic lettering of 'Olde English' was replaced by a font that approached the broad strokes and round forms of Insular Half-Uncial, a script used during the Anglo-Saxon period. The white, Half-Uncial lettering of Old English '800' appears on a circular background of deep red, and the rest of the can is stamped in gold (see Fig. 6). The portrait of Sieur du Luth was replaced by golden crowns — which look like castle battlements — that trace the circumference of the product's red background and punctuate its initial 'O.' The font changes maintained the brand's conceptual reference to an early medieval language and manuscript culture but repositioned both within a vaguely Anglo-Saxon context. In addition, the visual contrast between red and gold, in association with the golden crown-like and fortress-like shapes, display a fantasy that is limned with potency and strength. On tap for drinkers in 1968 were graphic and visual iconographies that mapped explicitly onto Grimm's nostalgia for the 'masculin[ity],' 'virility,' and 'power' of the 'oldest' English language. Blitz-Weinhard's new packaging associated its product, Olde English, with the linguistic representation, Old English, and its meta-discursive regime of Anglo-Saxonism.

While the new can design of Olde English '800' extended popular perceptions of Old English linguistic and writing systems towards an Anglo-Saxonist regime, Blitz-Weinhard's new ad campaign did not target white drinkers. Advertisements which appeared in the 1968–69 editions of the *New York Am-*

---

29 Blitz-Weinhard filed for a patent for Olde English '800' on April 23, 1968. The patent was registered on June 17, 1969. See United States Patent and Trademark Office (USPTO), https://www.uspto.gov/trademarks-application-process/search-trademark-database.

sterdam News, *New Pittsburgh Courier*, and *Los Angeles Sentinel* announced the arrival of Olde English '800' exclusively in African American newspapers. Marketed explicitly and specifically for an urban, black, male consumer, these Olde English ads took advantage of key moments in 1960s African American history: the death of Martin Luther King, Jr.; the Civil Rights era giving way to the Black Power movement; and a constellation of political and social efforts that recognized the insufficiency of desegregation and sought to make a space for economic empowerment, racial pride, and African American cultural and political institutions.[30] Blitz-Weinhard's new ads first appeared in August 1968, just months after King's death, capitalizing on the loss of King and the arrival of Black Power. In one ad, a 12-ounce can is photographed from below, presenting it as tall, vertical, and dripping with 'sweat,' while bracketed by the statements 'MIGHTY' and 'Big Daddy.'[31] In another, a light-skinned, innocent-looking young black woman finds herself positioned in the middle of two well-built, dark-skinned African American men. A caption below claims, 'You get more out...because we put more in. More flavor, more pleasure, more king-sized

---

30 Put a different way, as Roland Murray argues, the Black Power movement sought to 'reconstitute the patriarchal black family, reclaim the autonomy of the masculine black body, retool the politics of male oratory [and] assert the necessity of new forms of masculine sexuality...in interpolative models that were intended to counter historically entrenched racial subordination' (*Our Living Manhood: Literature, Black Power, and Masculine Ideology* [Philadelphia: Pennsylvania University Press, 2007], 4). Textually and visually, the advertisements for Olde English '800' in African American newspapers attempted not only to appeal to an African American consumer who desired to 'reconstitute...patriarch[y],' 'reclaim masculin[ity],' and 'assert...sexuality,' but also to present Olde English '800' as an alcoholic drink that offered these things, easily and cheaply, if only for a short while.

31 'New! Now Here in New York,' *New York Amsterdam News*, August 16, 1969, 16; 'New! Now Here in New York,' *New York Amsterdam News*, August 30, 1969, 18; and 'Try Mighty '800',' *New York Amsterdam News*, January 31, 1970, 30.

satisfaction.'[32] These ads conjure up a supposedly safe, 'integrationist scene,' in which an extremely light-skinned black woman (whose bouffant flip hairstyle and wide headband — popularized by stars such as Mary Tyler Moore and Sally Field — accenuate her 'whiteness') smiles innocently at two dark-skinned men who wear turtlenecks. Further, the ads signify a 'king-sized satisfaction' that resonates with the recent memorialization of Dr. King, thereby pulling the crown-shaped iconography of the new can design towards both Anglo-Saxonist imagery and King's Civil Rights-era leadership. At the same time, the placement and timing of these advertisements appear to celebrate the arrival of a more oppositional, less assimilationist 'Black Power.' Yet by summoning a 'Big Daddy' who stands 'mighty' in the transitional moment from Civil Rights to Black Power movements, the language of these ads promulgates long-standing myths about black men that are positioned at an intersection between race, sex, and alcohol.[33]

---

32 'Olde English Is Taking Over' (advertisement), *Los Angeles Sentinel*, May 2, 1968, Display Ad 27; 'Olde English Is Taking Over' (advertisement), *New York Amsterdam News*, September 20, 1969, Display Ad 35; and 'Olde English Is Taking Over' (advertisement), *New York Amsterdam News*, October 4, 1969, Display Ad 28.

33 The arguments in this chapter, which reference racist myths about African American sexuality and alcohol, are repeatedly associated with nineteenth- and twentieth-century US political movements, legislation, and legal disputes. In its attention to the triangulation of race, the law, and power, this chapter acknowledges the work of Critical Race Theory. More specifically, this chapter attends to myths that operate at the intersection of race and sexuality, and it acknowledges the role which black women have been forced to play as 'light-skinned' objects that stand in for 'white' women. Consequently, this chapter draws upon and acknowledges, in particular, the work of legal scholars and social scientists who have been mapping the complex landscape of self and identity under overlapping modes and forces of subordination and oppression: see, among others, Kimberlé Crenshaw ('Mapping the Margins: Intersectionality, Identity Politics, and Violence Against Women of Color,' *Stanford Law Review* 43, no. 6 [1991]: 1241–79), Kathy Davis ('Intersectionality as Buzzword: A Sociology of Science Perspective on What Makes Feminist Theory Successful,' *Feminist Theory* 9, no. 1 [2008]: 67–85), Elizabeth R. Cole ('Intersectionality and Research in Psychology,' *American Psychologist* 64, no. 3 [2009]: 170–80),

As William James and Stephen Johnson write, when the National Prohibition Party was organized in 1874, '[m]uch of the party's focus was on the link between alcohol use, race, and crime (especially sexual crimes).'[34] White southerners, James and Johnson continue, 'used the Prohibition movement to promulgate their prejudices against and fears of African American males. They spread the rumor that liquor sometimes gave the African American man, stimulated by the pictures of semi-naked women on the labels of the whiskey bottles, the courage to overcome his inferior status and to loose his sexual desires on white women.'[35] Although popularized during the Reconstruction-era temperance movement, the portrayal of black men as drunken, primitive, and sexually dangerous extended into the twentieth century, when the Eighteenth Amendment, which outlawed the sale or transportation of alcohol from 1920 to 1933, 'gave the Ku Klux Klan the majority of its four million members.'[36] By trading on white myths of the danger that intoxicated black men posed to white women,[37] the KKK was

---

and Moin Syed ('Disciplinarity and Methodology in Intersectionality Theory and Research,' *American Psychologist* 65, no. 1 [2010]: 61–62). For comprehensive overviews of the history of Critical Race Theory and Intersectionality, see Kimberlé Crenshaw, Neil Gotanda, Gary Peller, and Kendall Thomas, eds., *Critical Race Theory: The Key Writings That Formed the Movement* (New York: The New Press, 1995); Patricia Hill Collins and Sirma Blige, *Intersectionality* (Cambridge: Polity, 2016); and Felice Blake, Paula Ioanide, and Alison Reed, eds., *Antiracism Inc.: How the Way We Talk About Racial Justice Matters* (Earth: punctum books, 2019)

34 William H. James and Stephen L. Johnson, *Doin' Drugs: Patterns of African American Addiction* (Austin: University of Texas Press, 1996), 16.
35 Ibid.
36 Adam Sinclair, *Prohibition: The Era of Excess* (New York: Harper and Row, 1962), 18.
37 These movements of the 1920s coincide with the artistic and cultural developments that take place in urban, black neighborhoods as a consequence of the Great Migration. As Denise A. Herd explains, some blacks turn to bootlegging in order to supplement their small incomes, and white drinkers turn to the 'wet' nightclubs of urban black communities. Herd continues, arguing that 'these factors set the stage for the creation of black cultural images in which intoxication, sensuality, and black "primitivism" were dominant' ('Contesting Culture: Alcohol-Related Identity Movements

enabled to act as 'the extreme militant wing of the temperance movement.'[38] Fearful of maintaining control in America's post-slave society, whites obsessively articulated the bodies of black men as dangerous and threatening, generating myths about African Americans and alcohol that pathologized blackness as racially aberrant in terms of physical strength and sexual appetite.

The weight of American racism, which treats the bodies of black men as terrifyingly aberrant, is refracted in Blitz-Weinhard's advertising campaign and drawn into conversation with its newly redesigned cans, which join together an Old English language representation and font type with an Anglo-Saxonist rhetoric of masculinity, virility, and strength. Ads that ran in the *New York Amsterdam News, New Pittsburgh Courier,* and *Los Angeles Sentinel* emphasize sexual 'size' and a supposed lust for light-skinned women. They invite male drinkers to claim the recent benefits of the Civil Rights movement and the emerging political and ideological goals of the Black Power movement by, paradoxically, participating in myths from the Jim Crow era that

---

in Contemporary African American Communities,' *Contemporary Drug Problems* 20 [1993]: 752). While the trope of black primitivism stretches much further back in time — to the rhetoric of slavery — Herd's body of scholarship draws attention to the use of this trope in the early part of the twentieth century. The Prohibition Era, during which 'the Klan became the leading law-and-order spokesgroup,' is a historical moment in which black men are figured as a dangerously 'primitive' power of 'savage lust' that must be kept in check by the vigilante actions of white Americans (Linda Gordon, *The Second Coming of the KKK: The Ku Klux Klan of the 1920s and the American Political Tradition* [New York: W.W. Norton, 2017], 96). It is not a coincidence that the racial politics of Prohibition coincided with the end of the Great War and the return of black soldiers, whose service to their country positioned them as threats to America's white patriarchy.

38 Ben F. Johnson, III (*Barleycorn Must Die! The War Against Drink in Arkansas: 1920–1950* [Little Rock: Old State House Museum exhibit]), quoted in Gordon, *The Second Coming of the KKK*, 95. Consider 'Big Daddy' of Tennessee Williams's play *Cat on a Hot Tin Roof,* a character modeled in part on G.D. Perry, owner of a large plantation near Tunica, Mississippi, and played by robust actors such as Burl Ives (dir. Richard Brooks [Culver City: MetroGoldwyn-Mayer Studios Inc., 1958]) and James Earl Jones (dir. Debbie Allen, Broadhurst Theatre, New York, 2008). Big Daddy has been figured as white and black, depending on the production.

portray intoxication as a vehicle by which black men become 'mighty' 'Big Daddies' — physically powerful and sexually vigorous. These very claims about blackness, which pathologized it as a condition to be feared and kept in check, bear a distinct likeness to the characteristics of Grimm's Anglo-Saxonist rhetoric, which are broadcast visually across the cans of Olde English '800.'

While the placement and context of these advertisements present Olde English as a product that is in step with and in advocacy of the Black Power movement, the print and visual rhetoric used to market it to black consumers continues to project racist myths of what 'black power' means, physically and sexually. Further, while these ads lean on the trope of the innocent and vulnerable white woman, they do so at the expense of the light-skinned black woman photographed in the ad, who is rendered invisible, yet is nevertheless the visible agent of this racist myth. When potential consumers arrive at the liquor store and purchase Olde English '800,' the product that they hold, open, and drink bears the fantastic markings of Old English iconography and Anglo-Saxonist ideology. Racist fears of black men, racial fantasies about white women, and the racial (in)visibility of black women coordinate in the linguistic-ideological signifier, 'Olde English.' Marketed to a black consumer, its joint promise of terror and possibility interpolates men and women within a medievalist logic that dates to the late-nineteenth century ring tournaments of Mauzey's 'black knight' and the early-twentieth-century queenly fantasies of Fauset.[39]

Although its rebranding efforts and bi-coastal advertising campaign were successful in reaching African American urban communities, Blitz-Weinhard was, ultimately, a regional brewer and could not keep pace with the growth of national brands, which increasingly dominated American beer sales. On April 2,

---

39 As my colleague, Tayana Hardin, pointed out, as if to show the hidden hand of racism at work, the Olde English advertisement's claim that 'we' white brewers 'put more in' so 'you,' the black consumer, 'get more out,' has homoerotic undertones that suggest the extent to which Olde English 'fucks over' its target demographic (personal communication).

1979, the company sold Olde English '800' to Pabst, which kept the brand's 'Anglo-Saxon' design but recalibrated Blitz-Weinhard's racist depiction of African American men in order to capitalize upon changes in the Black Power movement during the 1970s, when this movement was dynamically reshaped by Pan-Africanism and Afrocentrism — intellectual, social, and cultural philosophies and practices that emerged hand in hand with African decolonization and African American desegregation. Two key cultural events that recognized the mainstream popularity of the Black Power movement, and of the constellation of ideas that circulated around it, were the 1977 and 1979 broadcast of Alex Haley's *Roots: The Saga of an American Family* and *Roots: The Next Generation*,[40] which depict the capture and enslavement of Kunta Kinte, a Mandinka warrior who strives to pass on his West African 'roots' to the African American generations that succeed him. Two months after *Roots: The Next Generation* was broadcast, Olde English was sold to Pabst, which immediately launched the 'It Is the Power' campaign. This multimedia outlet campaign openly co-opted the language of the Black Power movement, leveraged the popularity of *Roots*, exploited the decolonizing activities taking place across Africa, and manipulated the popularity of Pan-Africanism and Afrocentrism in order to sell Olde English '800.'

The 'It Is the Power' campaign, which ran in print, radio, and television media, features the image of another black woman whose light skin, feathered hair, and sweatband anticipate aerobic culture of the early 1980s and thereby orient her racial identity towards whiteness. Yet, she is scantily clad in a yellow bikini and stands between two Bengal tigers. Sexual prey and jungle

---

40 For example, Herman Gray argues that *Roots* provided 'some of the enabling conditions necessary for the rearticulation of the discourse of Afrocentric nationalism' (*Watching Race: Television and the Struggle for 'Blackness'* [Minneapolis: University of Minnesota Press, 1995], 87), and Mark Anthony Neal asserts that the series 'resurrected the possibilities of an "enabled" African heritage and a reconstructed black patriarchy' (*Soul Babies: Black Popular Culture and the Post-Soul Aesthetic* [New York: Routledge, 2002], 71).

predators populate the visual world of Olde English, which emerges as a tour-de-force of essentialised, pan-African, tribal desire. And just as the woman and tigers occupy the shared position of an exotic, native Other, the viewer is asked to imagine himself a 'Kunta Kinte' warrior. Pabst's poster appeals, at once, to Black Power, Pan-Africanism, and Afrocentrism. However, it manipulates these political, social, and cultural ideas and philosophies in order to reinscribe blackness as a pathology that operates, once again, by triangulating race, sex, and alcohol consumption via images of black women.[41] The woman on the Pabst poster no longer figures desire in relation to white women but rather to exotic animals and animalization. Through her body and its relationship to a pair of Bengal tigers, Pabst repackages a myth of American racism into a myth of Anglo-American colonialism as expressed in narratives that extend from Rudyard Kipling's India,[42] William Blake's 'The Tyger,'[43] and William Jones's 'Hymns' to Hindu deities,[44] to the African travels in R.M. Ballantyne's youth fiction,[45] where hunting elephants, gorillas, lions, and tigers associate the virile huntsman-explorer with an erotics of ravishment. These literary images were produced in relation to the British Raj (1858–1947) and the Scramble for Africa (1881–1914) — periods of the nineteenth and early twentieth centuries during which Britain ruled the Indian subcontinent and pursued military campaigns across Africa under the sign of England's Anglo-Saxon past and Anglo-Saxonist future. Referencing them in Pabst's advertising expresses an anxious desire on the part of white America to suppress the realities of mid-century decolonization, which threaten to impact the balance

---

41 On intersectionality, see especially Crenshaw, 'Mapping the Margins,' 1241–12 and Davis, 'Intersectionality as Buzzword,' 67–85.
42 Rudyard Kipling, *The Jungle Book* (New York: The Century Co, 1894).
43 William Blake, 'The Tyger,' in *The Complete Poetry & Prose of William Blake*, ed. David V. Erdman (New York: Anchor Books, 1988), 24.
44 Sir William Jones, *Selected Poetical and Prose Works*, ed. Michael J. Franklin (Cardiff: University of Wales Press, 1995).
45 R.M. Ballantyne, *The Gorilla Hunters: A Tale of the Wilds of Africa* (Edinburgh: T. Nelson & Sons, 1861) and *Hunting the Lions; or, The Land of the Negro* (London: James Nisbet & Co., 1869).

of racial power in the United States. Despite the poster's images of primitive, sexualized tribalism, it still asks the viewer to lust after a light-skinned woman while drinking malt liquor. Once again, Olde English positions the markings of an Old English linguistic signifier and manuscript culture against the visual rhetoric of an Anglo-Saxonist meta-discursive regime and its fantasies about the non-Anglo Saxon Other.

When Pabst's print ad was televised, its imagery asked African American consumers to not only look but also participate in the African world of Olde English.[46] A tiger's roar breaks the commercial's on-screen silence. The close-up shot of a woman's eyes fades to those of a Bengal tiger and back again. A masculine voice calls out 'Smooth!' as a large, black hand slams a can of Olde English onto a hard surface in slow motion. The sound of thunder and a flash of purple lightning accompany the jingle, 'It's the Power…Olde English "800",' and, in a new scene, the woman of the campaign's print advertisements breaks into a run. The ad cuts to a shot of the black hand, which now reaches towards the aluminum tab on the can, and then the video cuts again to a pair of running Bengal tigers. These quick-moving shots transition to a slow-motion scene in which the woman jumps on the back of the Bengal tiger. As she 'rides the tiger,' the hand opens the tab on the Olde English can, and foam sprays from it, visualizing a thinly veiled sexual innuendo. The jingle continues, '[i]t's that smooth, mellow taste that gets ya,' and the ad returns to a facial shot of the now-smiling woman, and then to the tiger's open-mouthed roar, and, finally, to the label on the can. Throughout the advertisement, camera shots of woman, tiger, and Olde English pivot on the image of the hand, a synecdoche that enables any black drinker to imagine himself a Kunta Kinte warrior returning to his African homeland and taking physical and sexual possession of the inhabitants of Pabst's tribal, pan-African 'world' by opening up a can of Olde English. While the viewer is

---

46 The 'It Is the Power' TV commercial can be viewed on YouTube (Martin L, 'Old English 800 Commercial 1988,' *YouTube*, September 23, 2014, https://www.youtube.com/watch?v=RH1-3yUH84A).

summoned to enact the brand's Anglo-Saxonist fantasies, these heroics are not characterized by feats of actual dominance but by drinking cheap beer. Thus, the African American viewer is hailed to access Anglo-Saxonist empowerment by playing his part in a centuries-old myth of blackness. Intoxicated by cheap beer and the allure of a light-skinned woman, he becomes, like the woman *and* the tiger, a target of white America's medieval, racial, and colonial desires.

Pabst's ad campaign was an immediate success. By 1980, Olde English '800' was the second bestselling malt liquor in the country, and the company's annual report to its shareholders boasts that '[i]n many markets, the "It is the power" radio theme music is as popular as some hit recordings.'[47] Pabst leveraged this corporate information to further promote Olde English. In the fall of 1980, African American newspapers in New York, Pittsburgh, and Norfolk, Virginia, ran a photo of three singers in a recording studio, announcing that the 'It Is the Power' jingle had been 'expanded and modified'[48] into a 'full length recording'[49] available to disc jockeys and jukebox operators. Disguised as news, the photo advertisement celebrates the campaign and thereby encourages black consumers to purchase and drink more Olde English '800.' While African Americans living in the northeast may have been privy to the music of Olde English '800,' the brand began to build a significant presence in LA minority communities.[50] Articles and advertisements from the *Los Angeles Sentinel*, a newspaper that enjoyed wide circulation in the South Central, Inglewood, and Compton neighborhoods, document the rise of Olde English '800' as a major philanthropist and corporate

---

47 *Pabst Brewing Company Annual Report* (1980), 5 (sourced from ProQuest's Historical Annual Reports).
48 *New Pittsburgh Courier*, November 29, 1980, A6.
49 'It Is the Power,' *New York Amsterdam News,* October 4, 1980, 4. See also *New Journal and Guide,* October 1, 1980, 15.
50 This statement is not meant to elide the post-industrial conditions of poor areas in New York City, particularly the Bronx, where hip-hop culture and rap music were born. See Tricia Rose, *Black Noise: Rap Music and Black Culture in Contemporary America* (Hanover: Wesleyan University Press, 1994), 27–61.

sponsor of events in these urban communities. Throughout the 1980s and early 1990s, Olde English lent its name, charitable contributions, and sponsorship to golf tournaments, minority scholarship drives, music and comedy talent showcases, a drum festival, hip-hop 'jams,' and a Martin Luther King, Jr. march followed by a prayer breakfast.[51] All of these events were held in LA's predominantly African American neighborhoods, and all were presented under the 'It Is the Power' slogan.

As Maria Luisa Alaniz and Chris Wilkes write, 'it is critical to consider the historical context of alcohol in ethnic minority communities...as a form of social control,'[52] and David Grant of the Institute on Black Chemical Abuse connects alcohol advertising to racism, stating that the people 'who are being hit the hardest by the high octane beverages are the very market for which these products are intended.'[53] This rings true for Pabst's 'It Is the Power' ad campaign, which fully exploits the expression 'Black Power' and the politics of Black Power by promising access to both by drinking high-alcohol content malt liquor. Through its marketing campaign and corporate philanthropy, Pabst also refigured Black Power in Anglo-Saxonist terms such that, in drinking Olde English, African American consumers

---

[51] From 1982 to 1984, the California State Package Store and Tavern Owners Association teamed up with Blitz-Weinhard (which still distributed Olde English on the West coast) for the Olde English '800'–Cal-Pac Scholarship Funds Golf Tournament, an LA charity event that raised money for minority scholarships. In 1990–1991, Olde English '800' sponsored the 'Education Is the Power' campaign, in which Pabst donated a portion of all case sales in southern California to scholarship programs sponsored by African American, Korean-American, and Mexican-American package store and grocer associations. See *Los Angeles Sentinel*, March 15, 1984, B4; 'Watts Tower Day of the Drum Festival,' *Los Angeles Sentinel*, September 20, 1984, A3; 'Olde English 800 Giving Something Back to the Community,' *Los Angeles Sentinel*, November 29, 1990, B6; and 'Olde English 800 Supports Minority Education,' *Los Angeles Sentinel*, June 20, 1991, B8.

[52] Maria Luisa Alaniz and Chris Wilkes, 'Pro-Drinking Messages and Message Environments for Young Adults: The Case of Alcohol Industry Advertising in African American, Latino, and Native American Communities,' *Journal of Public Health Policy* 19, no. 4 (1998): 453.

[53] Grant, quoted in ibid., 465–66.

imbibe — materially and metaphorically — a fantasy of empowerment that is wholly disempowering.

That these advertisements span the late 1970s through the early 1990s, and that they come to target African American neighborhoods in Los Angeles, is a critical point. These decades were, as Patricia Hill Collins writes, 'a period of initial promise, profound change, and for far too many, heart-wrenching disappointment.'[54] In many cities, particularly in Los Angeles, the closure or relocation of blue collar manufacturing jobs from central to suburban LA devastated African American communities living in South Central, Watts, and Compton.[55] Compounding this problem was the deleterious effect of LA's freeway system, which, by the 1970s, had circumscribed and carved up these neighborhoods, 'reinforc[ing] patterns of segregation and marking physical boundaries' that 'cu[t] African Americans off from other parts of the city.'[56] '[F]or those without automobiles,' especially blue collar workers who had been laid off and could not travel to plants that had opened in the suburbs, 'the freeways and inadequate public transit system make movement across Los Angeles's vast expanse difficult' and same-sector reemployment a logistical problem. As Josh Sides writes, '[t]he personal consequences of industrial plant closures for black male employees could be frustrating at best and devastating at worst.... For an already disillusioned minority of these children, watching their parents lose hard-won jobs confirmed the fruitlessness of playing by the rules.'[57] Amid rapidly rising unemployment, the 'It Is the Power' campaign promised physical and sexual power in a bottle, and Olde English '800' became a community partner. From its availability at corner store markets to its con-

---

54 Patricia Hill Collins, *From Black Power to Hip Hop: Racism, Nationalism, and Feminism* (Philadelphia: Temple University Press, 2006), 3.
55 Josh Sides, *L.A. City Limits: African American Los Angeles from the Great Depression to the Present* (Los Angeles: University of California Press, 2003), 180–81.
56 Loren Kajikawa, *Sounding Race in Rap Songs* (Los Angeles: University of California Press, 2015), 89.
57 Sides, *L.A. City Limits*, 181.

stant participation in minority events, Olde English embeded itself within LA's urban communities, functioning as a powerful double agent that claimed African American empowerment but maintained Anglo-Saxonist 'social control.' While it offered cheap and easy access to the promise of Black Power and supported educational and career opportunities for LA's black communities, Olde English '800' was nevertheless a major force of social disempowerment among African American men.[58]

While the Bengal tiger and 'It Is the Power' slogan became integral parts of the brand's official product logo, the women of Pabst's campaign changed during the 1980s. The light-skinned woman of a *Roots*-inspired African fantasy was replaced with darker-skinned women, who were sometimes dressed in lingerie and other times holding pool sticks. In these ads, they advertise a larger 40oz bottle and reference Olde English '800' as an '8-Ball,' slang for an eighth-ounce of crack cocaine,[59] encouraging consumers to drink more Olde English and to associate its 'power' with illegal drugs. While Olde English advertising has always conscripted the bodies of black women in the service of pathologizing blackness in relation to race, sex, and alcohol consumption, these new ads used the women of Olde English in order to criminalize blackness. These posters, which were distributed to corner store and liquor mart owners, asked black men to find 'power' in the rampant alcoholism and drug ad-

---

[58] Olde English acts as a litmus test for Denise Herd's extensive study of cirrhosis mortality among African American men, which finds that 'among blacks, frequent heavy drinking is more common in men over 30, suggesting that it is a stable pattern of mid-life' ('Migration, Cultural Transformation and the Rise of Black Liver Cirrhosis Mortality,' *British Journal of Addiction* 80, no. 4 [1985]: 398). Herd finds that by 1955, non-white deaths had surpassed white deaths; from 1960–70, cirrhosis deaths among non-whites had doubled; and between 1950 and 1973, this rate increased 242 percent (398, 399). Olde English likewise serves as a case study for Herd's linking of Prohibition Era stereotypes of black men as 'sensual, exotic primitives' to late twentieth-century alcohol advertisements that 'promot[e]...drinking, sexuality and violence' ('Contesting Culture,' 753).

[59] D. Kirk Davidson, *Selling Sin: The Marketing of Socially Unacceptable Products*, 2nd edn. (Westport: Praeger, 2003), 165.

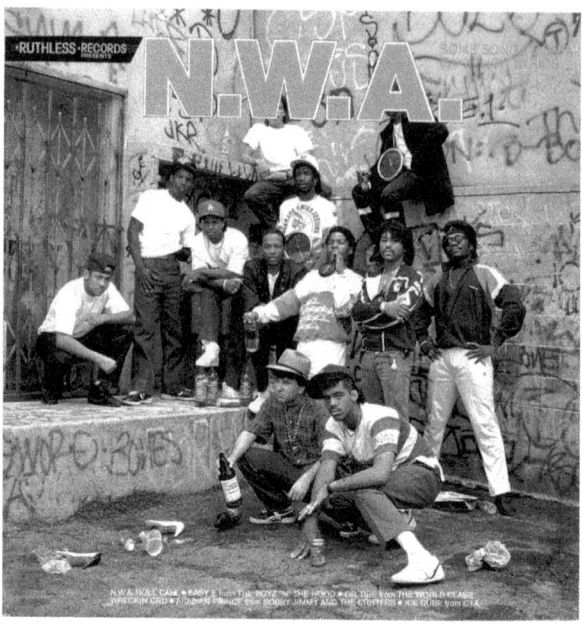

Figure 7. N.W.A. and the Posse (Los Angeles: Macola Records, 1987). Private collection.

diction of LA's inner city neighborhoods and thereby become subject to Reagan-era policies of trickle-down economics and the War on Drugs.

In the context of Pabst's philanthropic relationship with LA's minority neighborhoods and their 'It Is the Power' campaign of the 1980s, Compton-based rap group, N.W.A., summons the Anglo-Saxonist 'powers' of Olde English.[60] The cover art from their 1987 single, 'Panic Zone,' which re-appears on their first LP, *N.W.A. and the Posse* (see Fig. 7), positions Olde English '800' as

---

60 Note that N.W.A. is not the only LA-based group to name-check Olde English '800.' On his 1989 album, *No One Can Do It Better*, the DOC claims, 'I gotta take one o' them long-ass 8-Ball pisses — take me to a commercial' (DOC, *No One Can Do It Better* [Los Angeles: Ruthless, 1989]).

a de facto signifier for the group's most famous members: Eazy-E stands on two empty 40-ounce bottles of Olde English, while Ice Cube leans back with another in his hand, and an empty bottle and can are positioned in front of Dr. Dre. Other people in the photo hold open Olde English cans and bottles, while empty containers are strewn on the ground and perched on the building ledge. Large clocks, which hang around the necks of some members of the group, are set to 11:25, marking Olde English as a mid-morning brew. In many ways, the N.W.A. photograph is an ad hoc poster for Olde English and Pabst's 'It Is the Power' campaign, yet the only sign of a woman is figured in the two white pumps on the ground in front of the men. Now that N.W.A. and its posse have entered the advertising frame of Olde English, all that is left of the woman who once stood there are these remnants of a physical or sexual encounter.

Track 2 of this album is titled '8-Ball.' It refracts the cover art's visual message and is an underground hit on *Panic Zone* and *N.W.A. and the Posse*. It is then re-mixed for *Straight Outta Compton,* the group's 1988 triple-platinum follow-up album. Eazy-E's day-long adventures with an 8-Ball include pulling a gun out on a liquor store operator, pushing around some 'sissy ass punk' in the neighborhood, and calling his girlfriend a 'bitch.' In addition to these encounters with Compton residents, Eazy-E's other statements about his 8-Ball are interleaved within a vignette that describes his narrow escape from the cops:

Police on my drawers, I have to pause
40 ounce in my lap and it's freezin my balls
I hook a right turn and let the boys go past
then I say to myself, 'They can kiss my ass!'
...
Olde English 800 cause that's my brand
Take it in a bottle, 40, quart, or can
Drink it like a madman, yes I do

> Fuck the police and a 502. [61]

Olde English '800' is the 'brand' that permits Eazy-E to say to himself (but not to the cops), 'kiss my ass' and 'fuck the police.' In other words, it is the 'brand' by which he articulates his resistance to, yet conscription within, a system of American racism that, in the 1980s criminalized blackness through new socioeconomic and legal policies that are enforced by the LAPD's paramilitary presence in Compton.[62] In '8-Ball,' Eazy-E's engagements with Compton residents and the LA police refract the decades-long presence of Olde English '800' in Los Angeles's minority neighborhoods. Consequently, '8-Ball' is the signifying means by which Eazy-E expresses a presumed position of hyper-masculinity and hyper-sexuality in relation to the liquor store operator, some neighborhood 'sissy,' and the sissy's girlfriend. And it is the brand by which Eazy-E lyricizes what hip-hip scholar Tricia Rose has called a 'counterhegemonic' resistance to the cops, the real and present Anglo-Saxon and Anglo-Saxonist figures of institutional racism who operate within Compton.[63] With a 40-ounce bottle of Olde English in his lap, Eazy-E plays the part of the intoxicated black man in order to become a force of lyrically intoxicating resistance to this racist myth about black men. Put another way, Eazy-E drinks Olde English, then speaks 'Olde English'; he is brought under the sway of the ideological 'powers' of Anglo-Saxonism, then reclaims these powers for the African American 'gangsta.'

When Eithne Quinn assesses the sociocultural relationships between malt liquor and rap music, she writes, 'forty-ounce

---

61 N.W.A., '8-Ball (Remix),' *Straight Outta Compton* (Los Angeles: Ruthless, 1988). The original lyrics of '8-Ball,' recorded on *N.W.A. and the Posse* (Los Angeles: Macola, 1987) are slightly different: 'Police on my tail, I don't like jail / 40 ounce in my lap and it's cold as hell' — and reflect the group's original, less 'gangsta' persona.
62 N.W.A. explores this theme visually in 'Straight Outta Compton' (music video), directed by Rupert Wainwright, 1989. See also Kajikawa, *Sounding Race in Rap Songs*, 96–99.
63 Rose, *Black Noise*, 102.

bottles...became iconic accessories of gangsta rap, homologous with the focal concerns, activities, and collective self-image of the working-class subculture from which the music sprang.'[64] The '40,' Quinn further explains, acted as an 'objec[t]' that 'held and reflected' the values of the 'gangsta': 'it stands, just as gangsta does, in opposition to respectable or acquired bourgeois tastes.'[65] Over a decade later, Quinn's assessment holds true of Olde English, which continues to appear frequently in rap songs and videos as an 'accessory' that signifies 'gangsta... tastes.' However, the use of Olde English '800' by N.W.A. and Eazy-E exceeds Quinn's assessment. Their album cover art and '8-Ball' lyrics explore Olde English not merely as an 'object' but also as a consumable object that '*is* the power,' not only for their posse but, moreover, for their musical sound, lyrics, and identity politics. Eazy-E drinks his '40,' then spits a rhyme of empowering rage and political energy, exposing Olde English not simply as a prop for the 'gangsta' but more importantly as an object of conspicuous consumption that draws its power from the brand's long-standing reference to the Old English language and the Anglo-Saxonist meta-discursive regime of masculinity, virility, and strength that surrounds it. As an '8-Ball junkie,' Eazy-E imbibes — incorporates — Olde English, transforming it into a substance which lends a subversive pedigree to the sound of N.W.A., to Eazy-E's voice, and to the lyricized frustrations of an urban youth that has been ghettoized and criminalized by Anglo-Saxon(ist) America. N.W.A. and Eazy-E are possessed by Olde English in order to take musical possession of it, expanding its semantic limits from a brand of malt liquor to a genre of music — so-called 'gangsta rap' — that coordinates the 'oldest' language of English with African American English, and a Grimmian rhetoric of Anglo-Saxonism with the group's articu-

---

64 Eithne Quinn, *Ain't Nuthin' But a 'G' Thang: The Culture and Commerce of Gangsta Rap* (New York: Columbia University Press, 2005), 3.
65 Ibid., 14–15.

lations of what it means to be an African American man who lives in inner-city LA.[66]

Three years after '8-Ball' appeared on *Straight Outta Compton,* malt liquor advertising drew widespread, national controversy. A June 17, 1991 article in the the *Wall Street Journal* discussed Heileman Brewing Company's plan to launch a new malt liquor called PowerMaster, a beverage that contained 5.9% alcohol — 31% more alcohol than Colt 45, the company's best-selling brand.[67] PowerMaster was expressly targeted at 'inner-city blacks,' and its ad campaign 'played to this group with posters and billboards using black male models' which 'assured consumers that PowerMaster was "Bold Not Harsh".'[68] PowerMaster's alcohol content and its advertisements were in no way unique from other malt liquors. In addition to Olde English '800,' brands such as Schlitz, Hurricane, King Cobra, and St.

---

66 The extent to which Olde English played a role in N.W.A.'s group identity can be tracked in relation to the break-up of the group. Although N.W.A. had been a de-facto advertiser for Olde English '800' since their first album, when business tensions between Eazy-E, Ice Cube, and Dr. Dre resulted in the departure of the latter two members from the group, malt liquor played a visible role in the public feud that ensued. While Eazy continued his open loyalty to Olde English, Ice Cube and Dre shifted their allegiances to competitor St. Ides. Ice Cube, who wrote the lyrics for N.W.A.'s '8-Ball,' starred in a 1990 St. Ides commercial, in which he 't[ook] part in a "Pepsi challenge" of malt liquor brands…a clear rebuke to chief competitor Olde English 800, known as "8-Ball"' (Quinn, *Ain't Nuthin' But a 'G' Thang,* 2). In his 1991 single, 'Steady Mobbin,' Ice Cube raps, 'Told all my friends: don't drink 8-Ball, cos St. Ides is giving ends' ('Steady Mobbin,' *Death Certificate* [Los Angeles: Priority/EMI, 1991]). Shortly after Ice Cube left N.W.A. and signed on with St. Ides, Dr. Dre did the same, rapping in a 1993 commercial for the brand with his new partner, Snoop Dogg. Remaining N.W.A. member Eazy-E responded to these business and brand 'betrayals' in the cover art of his 1993 EP, *It's On (D̶r̶.̶ D̶r̶e̶) 187um Killa* (Torrance: Audio Achievements), which not only strikes out 'Dr. Dre' in the title but also depicts Eazy-E pouring out a 40-ounce bottle of Olde English '800,' an action that acknowledges the death of a friend or relative and references a scene from Ice Cube's 1991 film *Boyz in the Hood* (dir. John Singleton [Los Angeles: Columbia Pictures, 1991]).
67 George G. Brenkert, 'Marketing to Inner-City Blacks: PowerMaster and Moral Responsibility,' *Business Ethics Quarterly* 8, no. 1 (1998): 2.
68 Ibid.

Ides contain 6 to 8 percent alcohol (compared to less than 5% in other beers); they are targeted at poor and disenfranchised inner city black communities; and their brand names, slogans, and ad imagery link malt liquor to physical and sexual prowess.[69] A 'nationwide coalition of African American public health activists' quickly began to form around the PowerMaster ad campaign,[70] and censure mounted against an industry that had, for decades, targeted low-income and high-risk racialized communities. The PowerMaster controversy resulted in a July 1991 citation by the Bureau of Alcohol, Tobacco and Firearms (BATF), which changed the advertising regulations not just for PowerMaster but for all malt liquor brews,[71] including Pabst's Olde English '800.' Despite the controversy, sales soared as many rap artists, including N.W.A. members Eazy-E, Ice Cube, and Dr. Dre, had become de facto and paid spokesmen for a variety of malt liquor brands.

In the wake of the PowerMaster controversy and BATF ruling, Dr. Dre, who had just filmed a commercial for St. Ides — the primary rival to Olde English — with his protege, Snoop Dogg, released 'Ain't Nuthin' but a G Thang,' the first single from his debut studio album, *The Chronic*. It takes as it subject the 'gangsta,' transforming him from a figure of counterhegemonic resistance

---

69 For a recent, general discussion of alcohol in African American communities, including the PowerMaster controversy, see Nicholas Freudenberg, *Lethal but Legal: Corporations, Consumption, and Protecting Public Health* (New York: Oxford University Press, 2014), 192–96. Freudenberg cites also the 40-ounce container size, inexpensive price (malt liquor is often less than $2 a bottle), and high-sugar content (calories and carbohydrates that contribute to diseases such as diabetes) of malt liquors (193–94).

70 Lawrence Wallack, Lori Dorfman, David Jernigen, and Makani Themba, *Media Advocacy and Public Health: Power for Prevention* (Newbury Park: SAGE, 1993), 31.

71 Public health activists argued that PowerMaster's marketing 'not only preyed immorally on communities at risk but also violated the Federal Alcohol Administration Act's prohibition of beer advertising that promotes potency,' and in 1991, the BATF 'revok[ed] label approval for PowerMaster based on the potency rule' (ibid., 32). The following year, 'BATF extended the ruling to require changes in seven advertising campaigns by other malt liquor brands to be found in violation of the potency rule' (ibid.).

to the LAPD to an apolitical character whose lifestyle of parties, women, drugs, and, above all, malt liquor is characterized by 'G-Funk,' a sound produced explicitly for southern California car culture. When 'Ain't Nuthin' but a G Thang' appeared on MTV in 1993,[72] it did more than introduce America to the visual world of Dr. Dre's 'gangsta' lifestyle and G-Funk beats. The video likewise contemplated the impact that malt liquor had on intergenerational relationships between fathers and sons in LA's black communities, and it drew attention to the impact that malt liquor's myths about black men had on their relationships with black women.

As the video opens, Dr. Dre parks his 1964 Chevrolet Impala — the same '6 four' that Eazy-E drives while drinking his 8-Ball, and the vehicle that is transformed into the 'I' of St. Ides in Dre and Snoop's recent commercial — in front of Snoop Dogg's Long Beach house. As the Impala travels across Los Angeles, against a backdrop of competing brands of malt liquor, it carries Dr. Dre 'straight outta Compton,' a place and a professional past from which he became, in the mind's eye of America, a 'gangsta rapper.' Now an Original Gangsta, Dr. Dre is about to brook a new, paternalistic collaboration with the young Snoop Dogg that will refigure the style and sound of gangsta rap. Yet, before the first musical bars of 'The Chronic' are played, Dr. Dre crosses a landscape that narrativizes a story of 'black power' and the role malt liquor has played in shaping it. Once Dre steps out of his Impala, he walks towards the front door of a house, passing a man who holds the chain on a barking Rottweiler as two others shout encouragements at a man who attempts to bench press 180 pounds. The sounds and sights that accompany these performances of physical strength and virility in the front yard appear in high contrast to scenes inside the house. Here, Dr. Dre encounters a middle-aged man in an undershirt, who sits on a couch and watches TV with a 40-ounce bottle in his hand, while a woman in a housecoat and curlers moves busily around

---

72 Dr. Dre, feat. Snoop Dogg, 'Ain't Nuthin' but a G Thang' (music video), directed by Andrew Young (1992).

the room. Unlike the men outside, his physical potency is spent, and his entire, shiftless being broadcasts the long-term effects that plant closures, unemployment, and malt liquor consumption has had on a generation of black men in urban Los Angeles. As a video directed by Dr. Dre himself, who grew up in inner city LA during 1970s and 1980s, the visual prelude to 'G Thang' introduces us to an image he knows well: a Janus-faced figure of 'black power' that strives, in public, to actualize itself, yet in the domestic sphere, has become sedentary under the influence of malt liquor.

Although Dr. Dre's presence tracks this visual narrative as one that unfolds across space, as his own youth in Compton attests, it is a story that has likewise been written across time. Dr. Dre, however, bears no likeness to any of the men he encounters at the beginning of the music video. As a former N.W.A. member, he has drunk Olde English for many years, incorporated its 'Anglo-Saxonist' mode,[73] and now harbors a smooth, laidback, gangsta style that forces the representations of black power on display at Snoop Dogg's house to the visual margins. As Dr. Dre walks across the yard and then through the house, the men at the bench press and the man with the Rottweiler appear partially, and only for a split second, at the corners of the screen, having been banished to the conceptual borders of the 'G Thang' video. Yet Dr. Dre's arrival within the house causes the man on the couch to challenge the comfort with which Dre passes through these landscapes. While this man is, at first, marginalized by the camera, the movements of the woman inside the house bring his presence into focus. As he holds his '40' in one hand, the

---

73 Kajikawa puts this another way, writing, 'Dr. Dre portrays himself as a gangster of stature. He asserts on *The Chronic*'s "Let Me Ride" that he can "make a phone call" to dispose of any unwarranted adversaries. In other words, Dre has the ability to have someone killed on demand from afar. In a sense, this statement evidences the shift from his relatively powerless position with N.W.A. to his role as an established hit maker and business partner in Death Row Records. Rather than having to scrap for his daily bread, he now occupies a comfortable seat at the table' (*Sounding Race in Rap Songs*, 102).

man points a finger, accusingly, at Dr. Dre, stating, 'Hope you're pickin' him [Snoop Dogg] up to find a job.' To which, Dr. Dre retorts, 'Yeah. We're goin' to work, so we can grow up and be just like you.'[74] Suddenly, 'G Thang's' video narrative about black power becomes generational. This delinquent 'father' abdicates his responsibilities of paternal guidance to his 'son' Snoop Dogg, calling Dr. Dre to step into the breach and take Snoop job hunting. Yet the 40-ounce-drinking man attempts to refigure father-son relationships from within the framework of a gangsta rap video, wherein Dr. Dre is not a father, but an O.G., and Snoop is not a son, but a gangsta protege. Consequently, Dr. Dre walks away from this proposition. He declines to accept the fatherly role that has been thrust upon him and insists, instead, that neither he nor Snoop Dogg have 'grow[n] up' yet. In this moment, the long-term effects of unemployment and alcoholism in LA's African American neighborhoods reveal themselves as problems that threaten another generation of black men. And Dr. Dre is forced to ask himself (as director) and be asked (as actor) what role he plays in an ongoing narrative of black power that is partly sustained via the valorization of malt liquor in his community and in his professional career.

Just as Dr. Dre's spatio-temporal movements track an intergenerational narrative of malt liquor use among black men in LA, the musical rhythms of the 'G Thang' prelude parallel his gangsta storyline. Dr. Dre's beat-making on *The Chronic* elaborates and builds upon the production style he developed while a member of N.W.A. By layering a breakbeat, drum machine, and sampled performances of live studio musicians, Dre 'create[d] a thick and intense sound' for the group, which filled the 'sonic space…to capacity.'[75] In *The Chronic*, Dr. Dre continues to layer beats, but 'G Thang' is composed of 'multilayered leisurely loops…characterized by deep bass, prominent keyboards, and

---

74 Dr. Dre, 'Ain't Nuthin' but a G Thang.'
75 Kajikawa, *Sounding Race in Rap Songs*, 95.

samples of George Clinton's P-funk classics.'[76] Although 'every register of sonic space is filled,' gangsta cool is coordinated with 'a laid-back, sensual soundscape,' where the absence of acoustical conflict permits 'a promise of [African American] transcendence.'[77] Thus, as Dr. Dre exits his Impala and makes his way across the yard, the 'leisurely loop' of a whiny synthesizer follows the path of its composer. As he moves past men in the yard and the house, the sonic fluidity of Dr. Dre's G-Funk loop underscores 'gangsta' as a powerful aesthetic that has become smooth and effortless. It produces a musical counternarrative to the grunts and cheers of weight-lifting men, the barks of a Rottweiler, and the background noises of a domestic environment which Dre passed by and through at the beginning of the video. Dr. Dre's established and authoritative gangsta presence accompanies the first, tentative bars of his G-Funk sound as it makes its way across a field of 'black power' that has been interpellated within Anglo-Saxonist socioeconomics, police control, and malt liquor. In 'G Thang,' this coordination between Dr. Dre's physical body and the sonic body of his music enables the video to query the extent to which 'gangsta' operates in tandem with this generation of LA 'fathers,' whose misguided faith in 40-ounce culture has dissipated their agency. Does 'G Thang' destine LA's 'sons' for a cycle of dissipation, or, like Dr. Dre, does it offer them physical movement past it and sonic 'transcendence' from this cycle?

After Dr. Dre leaves the house with the young Snoop Dogg in his 1964 Impala, they drive to a picnic, where the camera focuses, casually, on scantily clad women and armed men. Unlike Eazy-E's lyrics, which coordinate the 8-Ball in his lap with acts of sexual and physical assault that enable him to vocalize his rage at the LAPD, malt liquor and law enforcement are kept at the visual margins of these scenes. By screening both from

---

76 David Diallo, 'From Electro-Rap to G-Funk: A Social History of Rap Music in Los Angeles and Compton,' in *Hip Hop in America: A Regional Guide*, 2 vols., ed. Mickey Hess (Denver: Greenwood, 2010), 1:241.
77 Kajikawa, *Sounding Race in Rap Songs*, 103, 105, 109.

direct view, Dr. Dre and Snoop Dogg present sex and violence, passively, as the organic elements of a laid-back gangsta lifestyle and its G-Funk sound.[78] At the end of the day, the central role that malt liquor plays in this lifestyle is finally brought into direct view at a house party, where the 'sons' drink the same booze as their 'father.' At the house, a young, black man reaches into a refrigerator full of 40-ounce malt liquor bottles. As the camera lingers over this shot, Snoop raps, 'Pimping hoes and clocking a grip, like my name was Dolemite / Yeah, and it don't quit / I think they in the mood for some mothafuckin' G shit.'[79] A refrigerator full of '40's comes into focus when Snoop suggests that we are 'in the mood for some mothafuckin' G shit,' and the moments that follow express precisely what this 'G shit' is. A new scene opens in which Snoop tells Dre, 'we gotta give 'em what they want,' and Dre responds, 'what's that, G?' The camera then moves to a young, light-skinned black woman — a figure seen many times before in Olde English advertising — dressed in a tank top and miniskirt who makes her way through the crowded house party. Her dress and manner indicate that she is not from Compton or Long Beach, and upon rebuffing the sexual advances that are made towards her, two men corner the woman and spray her with 40-ounce bottles of malt liquor, an act that echoes the 'It Is the Power' TV advertisement from the 1970s. As they enact physical and sexual assault by symbolic malt liquor proxy, revelers dance. The party scene fades, and Dre's car rolls up to Snoop's house at dawn. As Snoop gets out of the car and stumbles up the driveway, drunk, one assumes from malt liquor, this 'son' returns to his 'father's' house. Although

---

78 When a caravan of lowrider convertibles playing 'G Thang' from their sound systems pass a single motorcycle cop, the cop waves them past, and the camera relegates him to the corner of the screen. The visual 'cornering' of elements that would politicize the 'gangsta' figure or create conflict for him should be considered in relation to its film date. 'G Thang' was shot just after the 1991 PowerMaster controversy and BATF ruling (which happened in the same months as the Rodney King beating) and the 1992 LA Riots.

79 Dr. Dre, 'Ain't Nuthin' but a G Thang.'

Dr. Dre no longer makes music with N.W.A., his solo career is launched by a video in which he continues to query whether the lifestyle and sound of gangsta rap simply 'loops' LA's inner-city black men into a narrative of black power — crafted by Pabst's 'It Is the Power' campaign — that tethers race and sex to alcoholism. Or whether the new, laid-back sounds of G-Funk offer its African American listeners 'transcendence' by marginalizing its most troubling elements.

Many critics have voiced their concern regarding Dr. Dre's G-Funk's aesthetic and its apolitical refiguring of 'gangsta rap'.[80] Yet the ambivalence with which 'G Thang' navigates the history of malt liquor among LA's African American men can be understood, to borrow the language of Loren Kajikawa, as 'a cool and cynical accommodation with the realities of the neoliberal era. Sociopathic easy-listening indeed.'[81] In other words, 'G Thang' visually and musically performs what Eithne Quinn calls the 'analytic of ambivalence' that 'characterize[s] the gangsta mode.'[82] Such 'ambivalence,' Geoffrey Baker explains, accounts for rap's 'most powerful transformative energies,' which 'may reside where they are least examined and never taken seriously, in lyrics that shun realistic portrayal of the effects of centuries of violent colonization and that commit their violence against the reigning order at the level of language and culture itself.'[83] The literary 'ambivalence' and 'deep tension' that N.W.A. and its members associate with Olde English render it a site of 'transformative energ[y],' and while songs such as '8-Ball' and 'G Thang' do not loosen Olde English from its function as a brand of malt liquor, contemporaries of N.W.A. begin to leverage the ambivalent position Olde English has begun to occupy in rap music. A generation of rappers who are active in the 1990s and

---

80 For a very recent summary of these debates from the 1990s, see Kajikawa, *Sounding Race in Rap Songs*, 116.
81 Ibid., 117.
82 Quinn, *Ain't Nuthin' But a 'G' Thang*, 33, 34.
83 Geoffrey Baker, 'Preachers, Gangsters, Pranksters: MC Solaar and Hip-Hop as Overt and Covert Revolt,' *The Journal of Popular Culture* 44, no. 2 (2011): 233, 234.

early 2000s reframe 'Olde English' as a signifier that references the language and poetry of rap music. These rappers slowly recode 'Olde English' such that becomes an expression that represents certain sociolinguistic aspects of Black English.

For example, as LL Cool J raps on 'Mama Said Knock You Out,' 'Olde English filled my mind / And I came up with a funky rhyme,' a statement that acknowledges the intoxicating function of Olde English but also aligns it with word play.[84] Likewise, Tash from The Alkaholiks invokes the 'power' of Olde English as a language that generates creative lyricism:

> While I'm leavin' niggas puzzled like I said my shit in French
> But it's all Olde English that I'm bringin' from beneath
> Try to bite my style on wax and watch these lyrics crack your teeth
> Cause I make words Connect like West Side when I test glide
> My drunken lyrical hanglider[85]

Tash braces 'Olde English' against 'French,' a standard language. Upon claiming that he is 'bringin'' Olde English, Tash follows with an entire line (save one word) that, on account of his oral delivery, is comprised of strong, stressed mono-syllables:

> Trý tó bíte mý stýle ón wáx ánd wátch thése lýrĭcs cráck yóur téeth.

Tash displays his 'flow' and 'slang' in this staccatoed challenge to other emcees.[86] He continues, 'Cause I make words Connect like

---

84 LL Cool J, 'Mama Said Knock You Out,' *Mama Said Knock You Out* (New York: Def Jam, 1991). Note that LL Cool J is from New York, and, while beyond the scope of this chapter, the influence of Olde English's 'It Is the Power' campaign was not limited to the minority neighborhoods of Los Angeles.
85 Tha Alkaholiks, 'Hip Hop Drunkies,' *Likwidation* (New York: Loud Records, 1997).
86 Try to bite [steal] his style on wax [a track], and his lyrics [complex flow] will break your teeth.

West Side when I test glide / My drunken lyrical hanglider,' a statement that transforms the name of another LA group, Westside Connection, into the materials by which he 'test glides' (not test drives) 'my drunken lyrical hanglider.' Intoxicated by Olde English malt liquor, Tash raps in what he calls 'Olde English,' a language of rhythm, wordplay, flow, and slang that bests other emcees, yet confirms his participation in LA's rap community.

Aware of the destructive history of Olde English alcohol consumption in urban African American communities, these rappers leverage this brand of beer to 'Signify': to recognize and create a space for 'the figurative difference between the literal and the metaphorical, between surface and meaning…to say one thing but to mean quite another.'[87] Signifying is one of many sociolinguistic aspects of Black English that 'has allowed blacks to create a culture of survival in an alien land.'[88] As Henry Louis Gates, Jr., explains, it 'disrupt[s] the nature of the signifier/signified equation,' 'critiques' the nature of a word's meaning, and 'supplant[s]' standard English associations and white conventions of a signifier.[89] By transforming signs and sign systems, they become expressions that are both 'decolonized' and 'double-voiced.'[90] As Gates remarks, 'hip-hop took signifying to a new and electrifyingly original level.'[91] Thus, while LL Cool J recognizes Olde English as alcohol, he Signifies it as generative of a 'funky rhyme.' And when Tash compares Olde English to French, he exceeds its conventional definition as a malt liquor brand and suggests it as a standard language. As these rappers Signify Olde English, they extend its semantic range from a brand of alcohol towards a poetic category, turning it into a sign that stands in for a whole system of rhetorical strategies that align with what Samy Alim calls 'Hip Hop Nation Language'

---

87 Gates, *The Signifying Monkey*, 89.
88 Geneva Smitherman, '"The chain remain the same": Communicative Practices in the Hip Hop Nation,' *Journal of Black Studies* 28, no. 1 (1997): 2–3.
89 Gates, *The Signifying Monkey*, 51, 52.
90 Ibid., 55.
91 Ibid., xxx.

(HHNL), a 'linguistic culture' situated 'in the broader context of Black American speech.'[92] Alim continues:

> [HHNL] refers not only to the syntactic constructions of the language but also to the many discursive and communicative practices, the attitudes towards language, understanding the role of language in both binding/bonding community and seizing/smothering linguistic opponents, and language as concept (meaning...body movements...and overall communication...).[93]

Tash's wordplay is therefore not just limited to his meter and rhyme. It is, moreover, an 'attitude towards language,' and he uses the expression 'Olde English' to represent and introduce a variety of poetic strategies that simultaneously 'seize/smother' his opponents and 'bind/bond' himself to LA's rap community. Likewise, Tash's 'drunken lyrical hanglider' underscores his 'language as [a] concept' that is expressed in his 'body movements' and 'overall communication,' which claim to be under the double influence of alcohol and hip hop. For Tash, Signifying Olde English (as a sociolinguistic strategy of Black English and a linguistic category of HHNL) is an act that not only transforms a reference to malt liquor into rap but also figures the language of Olde English as spoken lyrics and oral performance that, in this instance, transform alcoholic intoxication into an 'Alkaholik' display. As Tash Signifies Olde English, he disrupts, critiques, and supplants all previous associations that American brewers have sought to generate for this brand of liquor and thereby 'flips the script.'[94] That is to say, Tash 'revers[es] the power of the dominant culture' and 'free[s] [his rhymes] from linguistic colonization'[95] by 'positioning speakers of "standard English" as

---

92 Alim, *Roc the Mic Right*, 70.
93 Ibid., 71.
94 H. Samy Alim, 'Hip Hop Nation Language,' in *Language in the USA: Themes for the Twenty-First Century*, eds. Edward Finegan and John R. Rickford (Cambridge: Cambridge University Press, 2004), 395.
95 Ibid.

"limited" and the speakers of "Black Language" as "limitless".[96] By flipping the script on Olde English, Tash 'frees' it from its sedimented relationship to a 'limited' Anglo-Saxonist metadiscursive regime and reclaims it as a 'limitless' signifier descriptive of African American rhetorical arts, Black English, and HHNL that can be doubled and (re)doubled, sustained and altered in its form.

As Olde English continues to appear in the rap lyrics of other artists, its limitless signifying capacity shuttles it towards a postcolonial form. For example, as RZA rhymes:

> Right eye squinted; I speak brok-len english
> Stumble off the cold four-oh of Olde English Wu brew.[97]

As Ol' Dirty Bastard claims:

> You know me
> My mouth is sugar, sweet as a honey bee
> Taste like a forty, stinkin like Old-E
> But I drink Ol' English so I speak Ol' English[98]

And as J-Ro from the Alkaholiks boasts:

> It's the Olde English, linguist, distinguished genius[99]

As Olde English, Old-E, and Ol' English are rearticulated by RZA, Ol' Dirty Bastard, and J-Ro, the phrase reveals its transformative energies. Not only does the sign itself become multiple, redoubled, and transformed by their language games, but

---

96 H. Samy Alim and Alisdair Pennycook, 'Glocal Linguistic Flows: Hip-Hop Culture(s), Identities, and the Politics of Language Education,' *Journal of Language, Identity & Education* 6, no. 2 (2007), 121.
97 RZA, 'Must Be Bobby,' *Digital Bullet* (New York: Koch, 2001).
98 Ol' Dirty Bastard, 'Dirty & Stinkin',' *Trials and Tribulations of Russell Jones* (Los Angeles: Riviera, 2002).
99 Xzibit, feat. Tha Alkaholiks and King T., 'Louis XIII,' *Napalm* (Detroit: Open Bar Entertainment, 2012).

as these rappers alter the sound and spelling of Olde English, they claim it as a linguistic signifier that responds to critics' derisive claims that rap is the provenance of 'semi-literate' youth by transforming Olde English into a postcolonial sign that acknowledges rap lyrics and rhymes as sites of linguistic virtuosity.[100] RZA's use of 'Olde English' references an English that appears, on the surface, to be 'brok-len,' yet this 'multilayered' statement simultaneously signifies his Brooklyn dialect even as it Signifies *on* a white, 'dominant discourse' that fails to recognize a tradition of African American rhetoric at work in his rhyme.[101] Just as RZA claims Olde English as his own Brooklyn accent, Ol' Dirty Bastard manipulates it as a referent for his notable style of free-associative rhymes and partially sung, partially rapped, delivery, which he describes via the conceptual triptych of Ol' Dirty Bastard, Ol' English malt liquor, and Ol' English speech. ODB's famed capacity as a rapper to distort sound and sense enables him to bend the representative contours of a linguistic sign so that it aligns with his stage name. In transforming 'Olde' into 'Ol',' English becomes, like the rapper himself and the song title in which this lyric appears, 'dirty and stinkin.' It no longer participates in an Anglo-Saxonist metadiscursive regime and belongs instead to Alim's HHNL. RZA and Ol' Dirty Bastard's solo projects were released at the turn of the milennium, and a decade later, when J-Ro from the Alkaholiks returns to the expression, he expresses the decolonizing after-effects of these lyrics in the line, 'Olde English, linguist, distinguished genius.'

---

[100] H. Samy Alim, 'Global Ill-literacies: Hip Hop Cultures, Youth Identities, and the Politics of Literacy,' *Review of Research in Education* 35 (2011): 122. Alim locates rap within the larger sociolinguistic category of '*ill*-literacy,' a term that 'highlight[s] the irony of youth described by educational institutions as "semi-literate"' and takes this perception to task by 'draw[ing] attention to the multiple, textual interpretations made possible by Hip Hop's use of coded language or '"counterlanguage," which is often used as a means to critique dominant discourse' (ibid.). In other words, ill-literacy 'deliberately creat[es] multilayered, subtextual understandings for participants while at the same time producing potential confusion for non-participants' (ibid.).

[101] Ibid.

No longer a dialect, an accent, or an expression of personal style, this triple rhyme Signifies 'Olde English' as a motivating, decolonizing sign. Its sound generates a rhyme that not only claims rap as a language but, moreover, boasts the linguistic virtuosity and exceptional creative powers of its rappers.

Olde English's Signifying capacity is in conversation with another virtuosic element of rap: sampling. As Paul Miller (a.k.a. DJ Spooky) and Alisdair Pennycook explain, sampling a beat is 'a new way of doing something that's been with us for a long time: creating with found objects. The rotation gets thick. The constraints get thin. The mix breaks free of the old associations.'[102] In addition to the sample's function as a sound that is both repetitive and different, Pennycook highlights the sample's relationship to temporal flow: 'repetition always entails difference, since no two moments, events, words can be the same. Once we make an understanding of the flow of time central to an understanding of difference, "any repeated event is necessarily different (even if different only to the extent that it has a predecessor)".'[103] Pennycook draws upon the work of Michael Taussig and Homi Bhabha to argue that such use of creative sampling—repetition or 'mimicry'—is key to postcoloniality, and he suggests that appropriating 'the dominant powers, arts, and discourses unsettles those powers and creates a new relationship between colonized and colonizer.'[104] The statements of Miller and Pennycook provide a temporal lens through which to assess the function of Olde English as both a Signifying form and an 'object' found and sampled by emcees like RZA, Ol' Dirty Bastard, and J-Ro of the Alkaholiks. It transforms and is transformed as these rap artists drink, lyricize, and repeat across several decades of rap music. By way of creative repetition, Olde English moves from

---

102 Paul Miller (DJ Spooky), *Rhythm Science* (Cambridge: MIT Press, 2004), 25; quoted in Alistair Pennycook, 'The Rotation Gets Thick, The Constraints Get Thin': Creativity, Recontextualization, and Difference,' *Applied Linguistics* 28, no. 4 (2007): 580.
103 Pennycook, 'The Rotation Gets Thick,' 585; quoted from Claire Colebrook, *Gilles Deleuze* (New York: Routledge, 2002), 121.
104 Ibid., 586.

a colonial signifier to an ambivalent prosodics, from a Signifying term of Black English and HHNL to a postcolonial language politics. Through repetition, not only does the rotation get thick but the fantastic 'flow of time' also bends Olde English *from* its function as a marker of Old English linguistic iconography and Anglo-Saxonist ideology — academic and popular lenses that are grounded in looking back into the past — *towards* a postcolonial linguistic '*now*'.[105] This 'now' is not the present but, as Michelle Wright writes, is an 'epiphenomenal' spacetime that coordinates with 'the Blackness of the Black Atlantic and the African Diaspora…in which the present and future are conflated and as many past and present moments exist as we can currently discuss, actively linked to Blackness.'[106] As a spacetime that is embodied and experienced rather than historicized, the 'now' of Olde English 'is always in process' and therefore stands in contrast to the linear progress narratives of Western civilization and the colonial and racial politics that attend them.[107] Likewise, it is an epiphenomenal language that attends to a new aesthetics of place, race, and rules of linguistic use.

As if to signal its arrival as a postcolonial expression and object of epiphenomenal spacetime, LA rap group Dilated Peoples's 2006 track, 'Olde English,' opens with the statement, 'this ain't the new, it's the old from way back,' then follows with the hook,

> Four by four, eight by eight
> Twenty by twenty bars, I demonstrate
> Four by four, eight by eight
> Twenty by twenty bars, I demonstrate[108]

As in much popular music, rap is organized in four-measure cycles and groupings divisible by four lines per stanza. However, as Evidence and Rakaa 'demonstrate,' each of their stanzas

---

105 Michelle Wright, *Physics of Blackness: Beyond the Middle Passage Epistemology* (Minneapolis: Minnesota University Press, 2015), 60.
106 Ibid., 41, 60.
107 Ibid., 41.
108 Dilated Peoples, 'Olde English,' *20/20* (Los Angeles: Capitol, 2006).

is twenty 'bars,' or lines, long. While the hook seems to claim the duo's lengthy lyricism as evidentiary of the 'way back' style of 'Olde English,' Rakaa expounds upon this claim in a later verse, which begins:

> Richard Pryor, Bruce Lee, Muhammad Ali
> Bob Marley, Jimi Hendrix, Salvador Dali
> Now we rap Langston Hughes and Maya Angelou
> Out the disco Xanadu, hip-hop for the streets.
> Now the beat swing numchuk style
> I'm like Jim Kelly tellin sucker MC's duck down
> Heavy artillery with the heavenly spittery
> And third strike energy[109]

Rakaa's lyrics and his rhymes transform 'Olde English' from an expression that references the track's 'way back' style to a phrase that acts as shorthand for the artistic work of a diverse group of mostly African American figures whose art and politics span the twentieth century. To Dilated Peoples, 'Olde English' is no longer, as it was for Eazy E, a means of articulating resistance to Anglo-Saxon and Anglo-Saxonist 'powers' on the streets of Compton. Nor is it an ambivalent signifier that enables Dr. Dre to query the role of malt liquor in constructing an intergenerational narrative of 'black power' that loops LA's fathers and sons into a cycle of unemployment and alcoholism. As that which has been drunk materially, visually, and lyrically by generations of rap artists, 'Olde English' flows across times and spaces, pasts and presents, realizing its function as an epiphenomenal language of the 'now' that connotes the arts and politics — the written words, oral expressions, and embodied experiences — of visionary African Americans.

As rap artists continue to query the sociolinguistic stakes of Olde English and further claim it as a signifier for African American experience, the term shifts its spelling to 'Old English,' even as academics begin to query the relationship between

---

109 Ibid.

rap music and Old English language arts. When Derek Attridge discusses Old English alliterative metre in his 1995 book, *Poetic Rhythm: An Introduction,* he takes a five-page detour into rap music. Attridge discusses rap's 'verse form, which bears many resemblances to Old English strong-stress meter,' and he talks about rap lyrics, which 'like Old English verse…are written to be performed to an accompaniment that emphasizes the metrical structure of the verse.'[110] The following year, Dana Giola's essay, 'Meter-Making Arguments,' repeatedly positions rap in relation to Old English, remarking that the 'four beat accentual [meter is the] line that English has favored from the *Beowulf* bard to the Beastie Boys.'[111] While specialists in Old English and Anglo-Saxon studies likewise have noted the metrical and performative similarities between Old English poetry and rap music,[112] only Alta Cools Halama has recognized the ethical stakes of making these connections:

> such a genre comparison [between Old English and rap music], approaching the unknown from the known, could not only bring multi-culturalism into Old English studies but also move Old English study into multi-culturalism. When my students see Beowulf so carefully separate the superior Geats from the lesser Danes, I hope those students hear the words of Clarence Page: 'Racism is the belief or practice that

---

110 Derek Attridge, *Poetic Rhythm: An Introduction* (Cambridge: Cambridge University Press, 1995), 90.
111 Dana Giola, 'Meter-Making Arguments,' in *Meter in English: A Critical Engagement,* ed. David Baker (Little Rock: Arkansas University Press, 1996), 86.
112 Halama Alta Cools, 'Flytes of Fancy: Boasting and Boasters from Beowulf to Gangsta Rap,' *Essays in Medieval Studies* 13 (1996): 81–96; Timothy Tangherlini, 'Afterword: Performing through the Past: Ethnophilology and Oral Tradition,' *Western Folklore* 62 (2003): 143–49; and Irina A. Dumitrescu, 'Verbal Dueling,' *Dragons in the Sky,* January 2003, http://users.ox.ac.uk/%7Estuart/dits/content_verbal.html. On Icelandic connections, see Roberta Frank, 'Conversational Skills for Heroes,' in *Narration and Hero: Recounting the Deeds of Heroes in Literature and Art of the Early Medieval Period,* eds. Victor Millet and Heike Sahm (Boston: De Gruyter, 2014), 36.

devalues other races as biologically and morally inferior.... It has been called America's original sin. It is.'[113]

In these lines, Halama argues that coordinating Old English and rap is not just an analogical or multicultural endeavor but is, in fact, a process of recognizing American racism and of mitigating against 'America's original sin.'

It has been 20 years since Halama's article was published, yet little has changed regarding the position of Olde English to Old English. While hip-hop theorists trace the influences of rap to Signifying, the dozens, toasts, American blues, and the African diaspora, early medieval scholars continue to discuss Old English linguistics, poetic composition, and oral performance within the historical context of Anglo-Saxon England.[114]

---

113 Halama Alta Cools, 'Flytes of Fancy,' 92.
114 Cheryl L. Keyes discusses the tradition of griots, oral storytellers who perform by way of musical accompaniment, 'mak[ing] use of formulaic expressions, poetic abstractions, and rhythmic speech — all recited in a chantlike fashion that prefigures rap' (*Rap Music and Street Consciousness* [Urbana: University of Illinois Press 2004], 20). Halifu Osumare points to 'Africanist aesthetics' such as complex rhythmic timing, rhetorical strategies, and multiple layers as an African-based expressivity of dance and music that is manifested in hip-hop (*The Africanist Aesthetic in Global Hip-Hop: Power Moves* [New York: Palgrave, 2007]). See also Imani Perry, *Prophets of the Hood: Politics and Poetics in Hip Hop* (London: Duke University Press, 2004); Genera Smitherman, *Black Talk: Words and Phrases From the Hood to the Amen Corner* (Boston: Houghton Mifflin, 1994) and "'The chain remain the same"'; and Rose, *Black Noise*, 65–69, 74–76.

Hip-hop scholar Adam Bradley is among the few who consider the interrelatedness, as opposed to analogical relationship, between rap and Old English, and he argues that argues that '[w]hile rap may be new-school music, it is old-school poetry.... [R]ap bears a stronger affinity to some of poetry's oldest forms, such as the strong-stress meter of *Beowulf* and the [thirteenth-century] ballad stanzas of the bardic past' (*Book of Rhymes: The Poetics of Hip Hop* [New York: Basic Civitas, 2009], xv, 18). Using Wonder Mike, a member of the Sugarhill Gang (whose 1979 'Rapper's Delight' introduced rap music to mainstream radio audiences) as an example, Bradley explains, writing: 'Wonder Mike's likely unwitting use of ballad stanzas underscores two essential facts about rap poetics. Rap was created by black Americans. Rap is a Western poetic form. These are not contradictory assertions' (19).

It would seem that the unspoken rules of linear time, periodization, and language not only police the boundaries between Olde English and Old English but also regulate the boundaries we set on conversations between scholars of hip hop and of early medieval poetry. And yet Tha Alkaholiks, RZA, Ol' Dirty Bastard, and Dilated Peoples, Attridge, Giola, and certainly Halama, are actually trying to have a conversation — a conversation that would create an epiphenomenal wormhole between medieval and modern languages, temporalities, and the meta-discursive regimes of racism and colonialism that sustain the conceptual infrastructure of old, middle, and modern Englishes and the historical periods to which they belong.

To return to the opening discussions of this chapter, a first step towards locating an epiphenomenal 'now' across languages and historical periods might be to recognize, as Makoni and Pennycook argue, that 'languages...are inventions' which occur simultaneously with the invention of the nineteenth-century nation and European colonialism; and to understand that linguistic invention occurs in 'parallel' with 'metadiscursive regimes': 'representations of language...reinforced by the existence of grammars,' 'dictionaries,' and 'autonomous texts' that reconstruct a past language and 'inven[t]' a 'tradition... into which the present is inserted.'[115] Following Richard Bauman and Charles Briggs,[116] Makoni and Pennycook explain that these nineteenth-century linguistic projects anchor languages to historical, geographic, and racial territories, and they theorize that unmooring languages from these sites requires 'strategies of dis-

---

Bradley credits not only Old English meter and the later-medieval ballad form but also the rhyming patterns of Emily Dickinson, Lord Byron, and Piers Plowman; the similes and puns of Shakespeare; and the kennings of Old English and Lewis Carroll as poetic materials with which rap is entangled. Yet Bradley explains that rap takes these poetic elements, which draw from the many sedimented layers of 'Western poetic form,' and stylizes them according to jazz and the blues, toasting and the dozens, personal and local experiences of artists and their neighborhoods.

115 Makoni and Pennycook, 'Disinventing and Reconstituting Languages,' 1, 2, 8.
116 Bauman and Briggs, *Voices of Modernity*.

invention and reconstruction,' both in terms of the naming of languages and also with respect to the ways in which scholars conceptualize linguistic difference.[117] 'If anything,' Makoni and Pennycook write, 'we would like to argue that all languages are creoles, and that the slave and colonial history of creoles should serve as a model on which other languages are assessed. In other words, what is seen as marginal or exceptional...should be used to frame our understandings of language.'[118] To refigure languages as creoles — even those that predate the advent of colonialism — allows for a 'discontinuous' linguistic history: an understanding of language that is not predicated upon linguistic continuity or stages, and provides 'latitude for multiple temporalities' and 'overlapping, translingual language uses.'[119]

As a a linguistic 'representatio[n]' conceived in the heyday of Anglo-Saxonism,[120] Old English and its pedagogical tools bear the semantic weight of this metadiscursive regime. Olde English, however, exposes the colonial and racial ideologies of 'Old English'; it takes on the metadiscursive regime of Anglo-Saxonism that underwrites this term; and it uses the African American rhetorical trope of Signifying and the hip-hop art form of sampling in order to disinvent, decolonize, and reinvent Old English as a language of postcolonial subjectivity and epiphenomenal nowness. This work by African American artists asks scholars of Old English not only to recognize the Anglo-Saxonist regime embedded in our linguistic signifier but, moreover, to disinvent and reinvent Old English according to a 'discontinous' history that provides 'latitude for multiple temporalities' and 'overlapping, transtemporal uses.' This is not a project for one person but for a discipline as a collectivity, and there are a few possible ways we might start trying to begin this process. One possible way is to rethink how we name, conceptualize, and teach the Englishes of historical linguistics. While old, middle, and mod-

---

117 Makoni and Pennycook, 'Disinventing and Reconstituting Languages,' 27.
118 Ibid., 21.
119 Ibid., 28.
120 Ibid., 2.

ern Englishes are standard nomenclatures, they presume a linear temporality that is always flowing from a specific past towards a specific future (all falsely assumed by many to be only 'one thing,' however difficult to pin down at times). If we disinvent the names we give to former instantiations of English — and with it, the illusion of linguistic unity — past morphologies and syntaxes of English might find a linguistic meeting space with those of the present tense. In addition, disinventing and thereby destabilizing Old English from the territory of 'Anglo-Saxon' and/or 'England' might enable it to reinvent itself as a language that interacts with other languages and geographies in continental Europe, the Baltic region, the Mediterranean, and North Africa. Further still, disinventing West Saxon — the long-standing linguistic agent of King Alfred's 'Anglo-Saxon England' — as the dialectical standard by which Old English is taught, read, and edited might enable the field to reinvent itself as dialectically plural and non-hegemonic. And, finally, all of these disinventions and reinventions of historical linguistics might actually make inclusive room for the Old/e English of African American art forms and Hip Hop Nation Language.

7

Becoming postSaxon

The last four years have witnessed a disciplinary reckoning for Anglo-Saxon studies and medieval studies more broadly. Beginning in 2014, outcries against misogyny and sexual misconduct among notable Anglo-Saxonists and medievalists turned quickly to discussions of racism within these fields.[1] Not unsur-

---

[1] For a sense of the initial starting conditions for the more recent (and necessary) agitation in the fields of 'Anglo-Saxon' and 'Old English' studies over misogyny and sexism, and especially related to the revelations in 2016 that the prominent (and recently retired) Anglo-Saxonist Allen Frantzen had been maintaining a private website in which he was espousing viewpoints closely associated with certain extremist corners of the Men's Rights and 'antifeminist' movements (https://web.archive.org/web/20160109140100/http://allenfrantzen.com/), see Dorothy Kim, 'Medieval Studies, Sexual Harassment, and Community Accountability,' *In the Middle,* October 31, 2014, http://www.inthemedievalmiddle.com/2014/10/medieval-studies-sexual-harassment-and.html; Lavinia Collins, 'The Problem With Allen Frantzen's FemFog Post,' *Lavinia Collins* [author blog], January 15, 2016, https://vivimedieval.wordpress.com/2016/01/15/the-problem-with-allen-frantzens-femfog-post/; 'Laughing at Misogyny,' *The Syllabub,* January 16, 2016, http://thesyllabub.blogspot.com/2016/01/laughing-at-misogyny.html; J.J. Cohen, 'On Calling Out Misogyny,' *In the Middle,* January 16, 2016, http://www.inthemedievalmiddle.com/2016/01/on-calling-out-misogyny.html; Dorothy Kim, 'Antifeminism, Whiteness, and Medieval Studies,' *In the Middle,* January 18, 2016, http://www.inthemedievalmiddle.com/2016/01/antifeminism-whiteness-and-medieval.html; Donna Zuckerberg, 'Should Academics Fear the Manosphere?'

prisingly, problems within the profession keep pace with Anglo-American and European political climates. Extremist, nationalist sentiments, leavened with various forms of racism and xenophobia, which have been mounting in Europe and America since 9/11 in tandem with growing social conservatisms, have finally come to a head in the political arena. They have taken the form of the Brexit movement, the political maneuverings of pro-Brexit prime minister Boris Johnson, and the December 2019 electoral victory of Johnson's Conservative party; the 2017 French presidential runoff between centrist Emmanuel Macron and nationalist Marine Le Pen; America's 2016 election of President Donald Trump, who has formalized and discussed withdrawing the United States from the Paris Climate Accord, the Open Skies Treaty, the North Atlantic Treaty Organization, and Iraq and Afghanistan; and the November 2019 parliamentary-seat wins by Spain's virulently nationalist and openly Islamphobic Vox party.[2] I have revised much of this book to the time of these headlines.[3] And I have also gone home. Last spring, I

Jezebel, January 27, 2016, https://jezebel.com/should-academics-fear-the-manosphere-1754937735; Rio Fernandes, 'Prominent Medievalist's Blog on "Feminist Fog" Sparks an Uproar,' *Chronicle of Higher Education*, February 5, 2016, https://www.chronicle.com/article/Prominent-Medieval-Scholars/235014; and Eileen A. Joy, 'Building a Tribe Outside the System: Allen Frantzen, Jack Donovan, and the Neomedievalist Alt-Right,' keynote lecture, University of Richmond, March 27, 2018, *YouTube,* https://www.youtube.com/watch?v=qWtoxdhLoeU.

2 This is not a comprehensive list of nationalist and nativist political activities in Europe and in the United States, nor does it account for the global rise of these ideologies. To be clear: nationalism and xenaphobia are not exclusive to Euro-American politics. Examples of alt-right or far right presidents can be seen, for example, most prominently in Latin America, where Brazil's Jair Bolsonaro, Chile's Sebastián Piñera, and Argentina's Mauricio Macri espouse Trump-like rhetoric despite a lack of support from Trump, himself.

3 Under the aegis of the Trump presidency and the resurgence of ethnosupremacist hate groups around the world, medieval studies has also been convulsed with rifts and debates around the ways in which the field's subject matter has been appropriated and weaponized by these groups, and around what, if anything, scholars of medieval studies should do about this. The field's resistance to recognizing, admitting, and working

through the structural racism of its own intellectual history, which is painful for many to confront, is symptomatic of the political moment in which we live. On how this affected one of the largest scholarly gatherings in medieval studies, the annual International Congress on Medieval Studies, held at Western Michigan University every year, see Colleen Flaherty, 'Whose Medieval Studies?' *Inside Higher Ed,* July 12, 2018, https://www.insidehighered.com/news/2018/07/12/medieval-studies-groups-say-major-conference-trying-limit-diverse-voices-and-topics; BABEL Working Group, 'Letter of Concern,' July 18, 2018, https://docs.google.com/forms/d/e/1FAIpQLSdReGZAQJiSSDWTRVokT2tO2b9LEaAPLTjDJLEaA6auDczBhA/viewform; and Seeta Chaganti, 'Statement Regarding ICMS Kalamazoo,' *Medievalists of Color,* July 9, 2018, http://medievalistsofcolor.com/race-in-the-profession/statement-regarding-icms-kalamazoo/. For controversies that have erupted in the fields of 'Old English' and 'Anglo-Saxon' studies more particularly, relative to the structural and ongoing racism of these fields, and their seeming inability to grapple with that, see Mary Dockray-Miller, 'Old English Has a Serious Image Problem,' *JSTOR Daily,* May 3, 2017, https://daily.jstor.org/old-english-serious-image-problem/; Adam Miyashiro, 'Decolonizing Anglo-Saxon Studies: A Response to ISAS in Honolulu,' *In The Middle,* July 29, 2017, http://www.inthemedievalmiddle.com/2017/07/decolonizing-anglo-saxon-studies.html; Peter Baker, 'Anglo-Saxon Studies After Charlottesville: Reflections of a University of Virginia Professor,' *Medievalists of Color,* May 25, 2018, https://medievalistsofcolor.com/race-in-the-profession/anglo-saxon-studies-after-charlottesville-reflections-of-a-university-of-virginia-professor/; M. Rambaran-Olm, 'Anglo-Saxon Studies [Early English Studies], Academia, and White Supremacy,' *Medium,* June 27, 2018, https://medium.com/@mrambaranolm/anglo-saxon-studies-academia-and-white-supremacy-17c87b360bf3; Hannah Natanson, '"It's all white people": Allegations of White Supremacism Are Tearing Apart a Prestigious Medieval Studies Group,' *The Washington Post,* September 19, 2019, https://www.washingtonpost.com/education/2019/09/19/its-all-white-people-allegations-white-supremacy-are-tearing-apart-prestigious-medieval-studies-group/; Colleen Flaherty, 'It's About More Than a Name,' *Inside Higher Ed,* September 20, 2019, https://www.insidehighered.com/news/2019/09/20/anglo-saxon-studies-group-says-it-will-change-its-name-amid-bigger-complaints-about; M. Rambaran-Olm, 'Misnaming the Medieval: Rejecting "Anglo-Saxon" Studies,' *History Workshop,* November 4, 2019, http://www.historyworkshop.org.uk/misnaming-the-medieval-rejecting-anglo-saxon-studies/; Matthew Gabriele and Mary Rambaran-Olm, 'The Middle Ages Have Been Misued by the Far Right,' *TIME Magazine,* November 21, 2019, https://time.com/5734697/middle-ages-mistakes/; Erika Harlitz-Kern, 'Academics Are at War Over Racist Roots of "Anglo-Saxon" Studies,' *The Daily Beast,* December 2, 2019, https://www.thedailybeast.com/academics-are-at-war-over-racist-roots-of-anglo-saxon-studies; Michael Wood, 'Is the Term "Anglo-Saxon" Racist?'

walked across the now grassy foundation of my grandmother's house for the first time since it burned down in 2009.[4] (I have not, in the past, had the heart to trespass there. It seemed, somehow, a violation.) I checked in on James B. Ellard's grave and talked to my dad about repairing its broken marker,[5] which now leans against an old oak. I have retreaded old territory while trying to write my way towards a new one. Consequently, last spring, when I stopped by the lot where my grandmother's house once stood, I found King Alfred daffodils blooming in my grandmother's front yard. Planted decades ago by my grandmother, the bulbs would not be suffocated by the smoke from her house fire. They continue to come up every spring as if to say, 'Come in. We still live here, and it's okay that you do not.' At James B.'s gravesite, I remembered my mother's first cousin, Dora Lou,[6] and saw the rhizomatic signs of many other Ellard relatives hidden just beneath the trunk of the oak.

While these discoveries about my Mississippi home have helped me leave the 'home' of Anglo-Saxon studies, un-homing, in any context, is always a fraught process. It has left me without a professional appellative and the disciplinary coherence that

---

BBC *History Magazine,* December 2019, https://www.historyextra.com/period/anglo-saxon/professor-michael-wood-anglo-saxon-name-debate-is-term-racist/; and Howard Williams, 'Should "British Archaeology" Stop Using "Anglo-Saxon"?' *ARCHEAOdeath* [blog], December 12, 2019, https://howardwilliamsblog.wordpress.com/2019/12/12/should-british-archaeology-stop-using-anglo-saxon/.

4   In 2009, my grandmother's house, which I had inherited from her, caught fire and burned down. This event, as I write in Chapter 1, prompted me to face my family's Anglo-Saxon(ist) past and write this book.

5   James B. Ellard was my great-great-great grandfather. He homesteaded in what would become Ellard, Mississippi, served in the Mississippi Cavalry during the Civil War, and owned slaves, my family has suggested, several decades after the Civil War had ended. James B. is the patriarch of my Mississippi family, and in chapter 5 of this book, I mourn my personal, familial relationship to him in conversation with mourning my professional relationship with King Alfred, the patriarch of Anglo-Saxon studies.

6   Dora Lou was a figure of deep love, yet strange obsession, for my mother. She appears as an agent of my mother's genealogical research about the Ellard family and my personal mourning of this genealogy in chapter 5 of this book.

comes from the safe terms we use to introduce ourselves and our work to other academics. When asked what I 'do,' I have found myself searching for words, calling myself 'a former Anglo-Saxonist,' 'a recovering Anglo-Saxonist,' or one who simply 'works with Old English and Latin.' Often, these professional statements are not well-received, and on one occasion, I immediately recognized that all credibility evacuated my air space once I tried to explain my area of specialization absent the field-identifying signifiers of 'Anglo-Saxonist' and 'medievalist.' I was simply illegible. Despite repeated awkwardness and embarrassment, I still can't bring myself to return to the comfort of these old, inherited terms, and I have learned to sit in the professional blank space that has, for me, come to replace 'Anglo-Saxonist.'

Although this un-homing process has been fraught with self-doubt and various insecurities, climbing out from under the weight of 'Anglo-Saxonist' has allowed me room to reflect upon the ethics of what it means to be a professional academic and the ways in which our signifiers deliver us into conversations or bar the door from them. More importantly, leaving my disciplinary home has given me permission to stray far from the comforts of an early medievalist time zone and its centering of whiteness so that I might knock on others' doors and learn how to listen to the conversations going on among my fellow scholars in other fields and disciplines. This process has been extremely difficult, not simply because the learning curve of another's field is always steep. Rather, in reading about African American histories, poetries, and linguistics, I have had to confront my own tone-deafness to racism (structural and otherwise) and learn how to listen to that which I can only try to comprehend. Listening, or, as Lisbeth Lipari terms it, 'interlistening,' is not about acoustics.[7] It is about being receptive to the frequencies of another, be they audible or merely felt sensations, for the purpose of ethical 'attunement.'[8] Listening and interlistening are no easy or small

---

7   Lisbeth Lipari, *Listening, Thinking, Being: Toward an Ethics of Attunement* (University Park: Pennsylvania State University Press, 2014).
8   Ibid., 8–10, 51, 50, 205–22.

things because they require that we abandon self-soothing frequencies and the agentive privilege of white forms of knowing. And we are most resistant to listening when most need to do just that. I can't say that I am any closer to being a better (inter)listener than I have been in the past. However, as a consequence of no longer being at home in Anglo-Saxon studies, I was willing to exit my field's scholarly conversations and the boundaries that limit what the field reads and how it reads, so that I might approach African American studies as a true learner. Standing at the doorstep of this field has been fraught with discomforts that exceed the ones we all face when trying to write beyond our disciplinary depth. Despite having presented parts of this chapter to African American audiences and despite having had African American readers, I feel and fear my whiteness is still too centered in this work.[9] I struggle with the likely possibility that in writing this chapter, I have failed entirely to listen and have instead just talked over and thereby silenced a story that was never mine to tell. However, if I am willing to be honest at the beginning of this book, I am obliged to do the same at the end in the hopes that, if nothing else, a conversation can arise between you and me or between yourself and others — a conversation that is productive beyond the judgements that will be passed regarding the successes or failures of this book. I am willing to risk attempting a conversation between African American and Anglo-Saxonist narratives and scholarly traditions so that the things I do wrong will enable others to do them better. Likewise, and most importantly, despite all my embarrassments, anxieties, and feelings of failure, I can say that my journeys back home and to others' homes have enabled me to find a path away from melancholy. Consequently, while I know that mourning, like decolonization, is an always unfinished project, I can be in the lands of my family and not feel haunted by the presence of its ghosts.

---

9   On the importance of decentering whiteness at a time when many white persons do not want to examine too closely their own privilege and the ways in which they have benefited from structural racism, see Robin DiAngelo, *White Fragility: Why It's So Hard for White People to Talk About Racism* (Boston: Beacon Press, 2018).

I can be in the presence of those who have been crippled by the Anglo-Saxonism of my personal and professional 'fathers' and believe that somewhere in the future, there will be healing.

As Homi Bhabha writes, 'the home does not remain the domain of domestic life, nor does the world simply become its social or historical counterpart. The unhomely is the shock of recognition of the world-in-the-home, the home-in-the-world… [of] the traumatic ambivalences of a personal, psychic history to the wider disjunctions of political existence.'[10] When I first began writing this book, I had no idea that my confusions surrounding personal and professional 'unhomeliness' would bear the mark of colonial disruptions explored in Bhabha's shrewd translation of Freud's 'unheimlich,' or 'uncanny' (both home-like and un-home-like, simultaneously, such that the 'home' becomes a site of both familiarity and strangeness).[11] While my fraught relationship to home can never be compared to the conditions of those counted among the disenfranchised of empire, the (post)colonial diaspora, and racial state capitalism, this shared understanding of home as 'unhomely' underscores decolonization as a 'process,' which, as Devika Chawla and Ahmet Atay explain, 'positions the colonized and the colonizer as inherently entwined.'[12] Or rather, to reshape the words of Chawla and Atay and position them within a postcolonial frame, such a sharing of the unhomely marks the children of colonizers and the children of colonial subjects as materially-affectively entangled. For myself, these multi-generational kinships are figured personally and professionally. I descend from one of Mississippi's many settler-colonial and slave-holding families and from the 'Anglo-Saxonist' 'fathers' of Turner, Douglas, Kemble, and Thorpe. Decolonizing has been, consequently, an often painful, discomfiting, and even terrifying process of sitting (and struggling) with the unhomely feelings that arise from the rattlings

---

10 Homi Bhabha, 'The World and the Home,' *Social Text* 31/32 (1992): 141, 144.
11 Sigmund Freud, 'The "Uncanny"', in *Collected Papers*, vol. 4, trans. Alix Strachey (New York: Basic Books, 1959), 368–407.
12 Devika Chawla and Ahmet Atay, 'Introduction: Decolonizing Autoethnography,' *Cultural Studies — Critical Methodologies* 18, no. 1 (2018): 6.

of a semi-closeted, ghostly old guard. It has entailed allowing myself to bear witness to how these feelings about my families' pasts provoke in me the overlapping responses of prejudice and shame, indignation and horror, emotional paralysis and constant worry. It is has involved committing myself to take on and own, and work through, all of these responses which come from within me, in order to leave my Anglo-Saxonist home in Mississippi behind, and to learn to try and listen better to the voices of the colonized and the children of the postcolonial with whom I am entwined by way of the unhomely. Because I am obligated to understand my part, and my family's part, in all of this. Reading texts, historical narratives, and first-person accounts of how colonialism has unhomed others has not only helped me begin the process of unlearning inherited beliefs, inherited feelings, and inherited affects but also enables me to begin the process of decathecting from personal and professional homes that had become too unhomely, unheimlich, and haunted to dwell in. While this decolonizing work is never finished, it does aspire towards an 'outcome,' which Chawla and Atay describe as 'the ability of subjects (both the colonized and the colonizers) to achieve disidentification…a survival strategy for resisting everyday colonizing practices' that, in turn, 'leads to the emergence of hybrid cultures and identities' and also 'creates borderline or in-between experiences' that require 'constant cultural negotiations or cultural maneuvering.'[13]

As both the introductory and concluding chapters of this book evidence, a clearing can be made for these border spaces by way of autoethnography, a genre of writing that has recently been explored as postcolonial praxis. As Archana Pathak explains, autoethnography requires an 'examin[ation of] oneself and one's life in a way that fosters thoughtful, engaged, genuine, and rigorous critique,' and it also requires 'introspection, honesty, and courage.'[14] Because of these requirements, the practice of

---

13 Ibid.
14 Archana Pathak, 'Musings on Postcolonial Autoethnography: Telling the Tale of/through My Life,' in *Handbook of Autoethnography*, ed. Stacy Hol-

autoethnography 'disrupt[s]...the intellectual training that most of us have received' and is therefore a method ripe for postcolonial framing.[15] Pathak is not alone. Devika Chawla and Amardo Rodriguez include the writings of Gloria Anzaldua, bell hooks, Trinh T. Minh-ha, Cheríe Moraga, and Sandra Cisneros in the emergent category of postcolonial autoethnography even as they wonder why this 'other' body of 'writing that was intricately personal and inherently political...[has been] treated as "outside" of discussions about autoethnographic writing.'[16] From these musings, Chawla and Rodriguez consider writing as a 'medium' that is 'complicit in the formation of an intellectual imperialism' when we perceive it as a product rather than a process because, as they explain, when we treat writing as a product, this 'mask[s] the integral role that our fears, anxieties, insecurities, vulnerabilities, and paranoia play in shaping our view and knowledge of our world.'[17] In contrast, the autoethnographic 'I,' as expressed by scholars of color such as Anzaldua, hooks, Minh-ha, and others, articulates a writing process that 'striv[es] to embody a project that fundamentally alters our ways of being and understanding the world.'[18] A 2018 special issue in *Cultural Studies — Critical Methodologies* on postcolonial autoethnography reflects upon the genre as 'a site for interrogating...coloniality' and 'a critically reflexive tool.'[19] Postcolonial autoethnography gives voice to the personal, individual, and powerfully anecdotal ways in which coloniality and racism (whether cultural, institutional, or interpersonal) impact academics of color. Moreover, it provides a platform that asks all of us to listen with our hearts, interlisten with the force of our entire bodies, and learn to feel, as best we

---

man Jones (Walnut Creek: Left Coast Press, 2013), 595.
15 Ibid.
16 Devika Chawla and Amardo Rodriguez, 'Narratives on Longing, Being, and Knowing: Envisioning a Writing Epistemology,' *International Journal of Progressive Education* 4, no. 1 (2008): 16.
17 Ibid., 18.
18 Ibid., 20.
19 Mohan J. Dutta, 'Autoethnography as Decolonization, Decolonizing Autoethnography: Resisting to Build Our Homes,' *Cultural Studies — Critical Methodologies* 18, no. 1 (2018): 96.

can, the impossible, yet ethical task of what it is like for others who bear the hardest burdens, and also the worst forms of psychic and material violence, wrought by racism and the institutions, including academic disciplines, that sustain that racism.

While the writers of postcolonial autoethnography are primarily people of color who speak from the many subjectivities and identity positions generated within and on the margins of the (post)colonial diaspora, Esther Fitzpatrick asks us to consider a place for the 'Pākehā' in this genre,[20] a Māori term for white as opposed to Māori New Zealander. Fitzpatrick's autoethnographic writing 'enact[s] a methodology of decolonization' by 'reject[ing] a settler future and instead consider[ing] "*opening the possibility of other futures*".'[21] Like Bhabha, she also turns to the question of home in the form of 'reaching back to stories that have traveled through family genealogies and social history'; recognizing them as a 'narrative inheritance' that haunts us; 'remembering, interrogating, and retelling our stories' as acts of colonial disruption; and imagining, from these inherited narratives, 'postcolonial counterstories' about 'cultural diversity and social justice that includes everyone.'[22] As an example, Fitzpatrick's autoethnography stages a series of imaginary conversations between her great-grandfather, Charles, and Hira Te Popo, an honored kaumatua (chief) of Ngāti Ira, which she claims are not idealized, but of course these imaginary conversations cannot entirely escape idealizations of various sorts. While Fitzpatrick's essay offers one example of how white academics can do postcolonial ethnography, I cannot write a similar 'counterstory.' The family stories passed on to me, which involve encounters with Chickasaw peoples and African Americans, pivot on the violent resettlement of native peoples, slave ownership, and lynchings. Although the Ellards were not born to be hateful people, neither 'diversity' nor 'social justice' were considerations of my great-

---

20 Esther Fitzpatrick, 'A Story of Becoming: Entanglement, Settler Ghosts, and Postcolonial Counterstories,' *Cultural Studies — Critical Methodologies* 18, no. 1 (2018): 44.
21 Ibid.
22 Ibid., 44, 45.

grandfather, nor of his father, and so on. Further, stories of settler colonialism, the Confederacy, and the Jim Crow South were woven into my life, from childhood forward. I was taken, with frequency, to Confederate battlefields, Civil War reenactments, and Sons of the Confederacy functions by my dad; my mother sewed my standard-bearer costume and stars-and-bars flag for an elementary school play; and my family, friends, teachers, and community members thought these actions were completely normal. To be clear, while my childhood exhibited what could be called a 'deep' Southern pathology, it is not only Southerners who believe in and fantasize about such a South. America desires this from The South as much as, *if not more than,* Southerners do. Between the lines of this book, I have written and re-written these and many other family stories in an attempt to disentangle and work through a multi-generational narrative inheritance that will allow me to 'open the possibility of other futures' for my daughters, so that they can one day write their own postcolonial counterstories. Within the lines of this book, I have also tried to do the same work of disentanglement and 'working through' for Anglo-Saxon studies. By tracing the narratives we have inherited from the early medieval literatures of *Krákumál, Beowulf,* and Asser's *Life of King Alfred* and the early medievalist writings of Sharon Turner, James Douglas, John Mitchell Kemble, and Benjamin Thorpe, this book aims to 'open the possibility of other' scholarly 'futures' that are not 'Anglo-Saxon' but 'postSaxon.' Before turning to what these speculative, postSaxon futures may entail, it is my hope that in the writing of this book, I have learned to listen to the postcolonial autoethnographies of Pathak, Chowla and Rodriguez, Anzaldua, and hooks, to name a few, so that I might offer a corollary contribution to that of Fitzpatrick and other Pākehās of settler-colonial descent. Which is this: that narratives of open reflection upon one's 'family' inheritances (both personal and professional), and the bereavement that ensues, challenge the genre restrictions of much of academic writing, and are critical to necessary field change, because they underscore scholarship and scholarly writing as entangled processes of personal, embodied, and emotional acts of postcolonial becoming (rather than being).

While this book begins and ends with autoethnography, its central, 'Interlude' Movement turns on fictocriticism. 'Becoming postSaxon, Or, a Biochemical *Vita Ælfredi*' leverages this mode of creative writing as a companionable partner to literary criticism. While the first part of the book talks about the need for mourning, 'Biochemical *Vita*' enacts in real time this process of mourning, affectively *doing the labor* that academic prose is not only ill-equipped to serve but, moreover, openly resistant to do. Some problems, as I have learned, cannot be addressed critically. They are too tender and too close, too complex and too affectively overwrought. Creative writing can sometimes be the only way to approach a critical problem so that we might view, in different and complex ways, its multiple, contradictory dimensions without having to organize them rationally–taxonomically, take an argumentative position, or neglect some strand of ideas for the sake of making a more streamlined and 'logical' argument. As professional readers of creative writing, we know its world-making powers, and we know (and teach) its life-changing powers. As an attempt to make myself post- or decolonial, writing this book has required that I rethink literary criticism as an activity that accesses multiple genres: autoethnography, creative writing (or fictocriticism), and traditional academic prose. In turn, I have had to rethink the literary critic as one who not only writes about others' literary labors but also identifies herself as a member of the literary community.

One of a handful of Anglo-Saxonists I know of who has worked across these genre divisions is Allen Frantzen,[23] and given the strange closeness between this book and his *Desire For*

---

23 I am grateful to Robin Norris for pointing this out to me. Other scholars in the field of early medieval English studies who have employed autoethnography in their work, that I am aware of, include James Earl, Gillian Overing, and in collaboration with Overing, Clare Lees. Detailed statements regarding their autoethnographic writings appear on the following pages.

Origins: New Language, Old English, and Teaching the Tradition,[24] it is, perhaps, critical to address Frantzen directly at the close of this book. As Anglo-Saxon studies well knows, Frantzen was an editor of two collections that took up critical theory in the field — *Speaking Two Languages* and *Anglo-Saxonism and the Construction of Social Identity*.[25] These two volumes both amplified and added other scholars' voices to the arguments Frantzen advocated in *Desire for Origins*. *Speaking Two Languages*, especially, collectively argued that the critic's voice and identity should be allowed into the scholarly frame as a valuable strategy for raising, sorting out, and adjudicating certain arguments within the field. In this collection, Gillian Overing positions herself in relation to fellow 'female critic' Elizabeth Elstob and to Eve: three 'female reader[s], translator[s], and interpreter[s]' in and of Old English.[26] Further, James Earl, 'like Freud,' considers cultural analysis in relation to self-analysis in an essay that locates Anglo-Saxon studies' dreams of a heroic, tribal *Beowulf* in relation to Earl's own dreams about the poem.[27] Yet, as much as Frantzen's introduction lobbies for and enacts the first-person voices of 'I' and 'we,' it also sets strict limits on them. Critics are professionals who speak in order to express 'leadership and communication' about the shifting terrain of 'tradition,'

---

24 Allen J. Frantzen, *Desire for Origins: New Language, Old English, and Teaching the Tradition* (New Brunswick: Rutgers University Press, 1990).

25 Allen J. Frantzen, ed., *Speaking Two Languages: Traditional Disciplines and Contemporary Theory in Medieval Studies* (Albany: State University of New York Press, 1991); Allen J. Frantzen and John D. Niles, eds., *Anglo-Saxonism and the Construction of Social Identity* (Gainesville: University of Florida Press, 1997).

26 Gillian Overing, 'On Reading Eve: Genesis B and the Readers' Desire,' in *Speaking Two Languages: Traditional Disciplines and Contemporary Theory in Medieval Studies*, ed. Allen J. Frantzen (Albany: State University of New York Press, 1991), 36.

27 James Earl, '*Beowulf* and the Origins of Civilization,' in *Speaking Two Languages: Traditional Disciplines and Contemporary Theory in Medieval Studies*, ed. Allen J. Frantzen (Albany: State University of New York Press, 1991), 65–89.

'reestablishing and renewing' it for a new generation.[28] While voice, according to Frantzen, may reflect the scholar's individuated position, it should be 'leader[ly]' and 'communicati[ve],' it should 'reestablis[h]' and 'rene[w].' Frantzen's position serves as both a statement of 'house style' for the volume as well as editorial blockade against Overing and Earl's contributions, which are the most self-articulate and self-aware of the collection. Frantzen's editorial discussion of how voice should be used in scholarly writing cannot be viewed separately from his criticism of colonialism, neither of which make room for self-doubt, self-reflection, or self-critique because both assume a posture of leadership within Anglo-Saxon studies. Decades later, Frantzen's words in *Speaking Two Languages* sound like dangerous omens that foretell of his own fate in the field's critical 'tradition.'

Before turning to this fate, however, I would like to linger for a moment with Frantzen's monograph that followed *Desire for Origins, Before the Closet*,[29] which discusses 'same-sex love' in early medieval Britain and its relationship to later cultural moments in Anglo-America. While the chapters of the book conform to the voice, mode, and perspective that we expect of a certain type of 'learned' academic scholarship, Frantzen's 'Afterword: Me and my Shadows' takes an autobiographical turn:

> In the course of my work I found myself wondering about the lost experience of the Anglo-Saxons. I found myself extrapolating from modern to medieval worlds of sexual behavior and from Anglo-Saxon texts to the larger, unknowable, and hence shadowy worlds around them. It is not the contemporary sexual culture of queer theory and media-generated homosexual stereotypes that I find comparable to medieval

---

28 Allen J. Frantzen, 'Prologue: Documents and Monuments: Difference and Interdisciplinarity in the Study of Medieval Culture,' in *Speaking Two Languages: Traditional Disciplines and Contemporary Theory in Medieval Studies*, ed. Allen J. Frantzen (Albany: State University of New York Press, 1991), 3,

29 Allen J. Frantzen, *Before the Closet: Same-Sex Love from "Beowulf" to "Angels in America"* (Chicago: Chicago University Press, 1998).

cultures, but rather the world of American life of the 1960s and before, the world in which I was raised. By way of concluding this study I want to speculate on similarities between some social conditions in my past and social conditions at levels of Anglo-Saxon society that the texts do not discuss, levels lost to us but perhaps recoverable if we consider some possible similarities between our culture and theirs.[30]

The 'world of American life of the 1960s' is characterized by Frantzen's youth spent on a farm in rural Iowa followed by his enlistment in the Army, when he was stationed in Korea during the Vietnam War. His Afterword contemplates memories from his past in a first-person voice that extends (and perhaps also subverts, or unsettles) the purview of Frantzen's more critical-scholarly 'I,' enunciated in the Introduction to *Speaking Two Languages*. Specifically, the Afterword affords the critic's voice a reprieve from sounding out positions of 'leadership and communication' so that it can be autobiographical. Yet Frantzen's autobiographical 'I' announces its arrival at the conclusion of his book—after he has fulfilled his scholarly duties. This 'I' remembers an 'Anglo-Saxon' past as one that has resolved the questions, anxieties, and silences of Frantzen's youth. One might ask, for what purpose does Frantzen use his first-person experiences in order to 'speculate' upon certain unknown and 'undiscussed...social conditions...of Anglo-Saxon society'? I would answer that, perhaps, Frantzen finds, in his own coming-of-age story, points of reference that can be mapped onto a rural, agrarian, and militarized perception of Anglo-Saxon masculinity and homosexuality. By coordinating his lived experiences with those who inhabit a speculative, Anglo-Saxon past, Frantzen legitimates his own 'masculinist' sexual identity amid the 'queer theory' and 'homosexual stereotypes' of the late-nineties, which figured gayness in fluid or effeminate terms. Although *Before the Closet* offers Frantzen's 'I' more narrative latitude than the tight-laced voice of *Speaking Two Languages*, both projects limit

---

30 Ibid., 293.

that voice to one that already knows certain things (or hunts for historical evidence to affirm certain beliefs: about masculinity, about sexuality, etc.) and has no room to grow, or to change under the pressure of others' thought and work.

As a scholar whose work has been shaped by Anglo-Saxon studies' unwillingness, for the most part, to engage the logics of settler colonialism and postcolonialism, as well as critical theories of gender and sexuality — and as a scholar who has come under fire for his betrayals of postcolonial and feminist positions — we have to look at the kind of 'I' that Frantzen enacted in his scholarship. For Frantzen's 'I' so frequently cannot bear to be introspective: it is an 'I' that speaks rather than listens, an 'I' that is afraid to voice itself until the critical work has already been done. At the end of the day, this is an ontological 'I' — a 'being' that does not realize that its dynamism could only ever come from an earnest pursuit of becoming a better, more ethical self, which itself entails a willingness to be continuously upended and unsettled in one's thinking. And this is also a dynamism which Frantzen's scholarship works very hard to disavow, as it is suffused with a belief in fairly static (and tradition-bound) states of identity, such that 'men' and 'women,' for example, do not occupy spaces where their supposedly singular and inviolable 'genders' or 'sexes' could ever really mix or blend (And he expresses quite a bit of hostility in his work toward scholars who see gender and sexuality as more fluid and non-essentialized.)[31]

With Frantzen in mind as a cautionary negative exemplum, 'postSaxon' is meant to signal a process of becoming. Not a key term but a placeholder (and therefore meant to be ultimately, eventually, replaced), postSaxon suggests the many and multiple in-process futures of early medieval studies that arise from a multitude of 'I's seeking experimental, dynamic change, self-

---

31 See, for example, the entries for 'Femininity,' 'Gender,' 'Identity,' 'Masculinity,' and 'Sex,' in Allen J. Frantzen, *Anglo-Saxon Keywords* (Oxford: Wiley-Blackwell, 2012). On Frantzen's hostility towards and disapproval of much work in contemporary queer theory that views gender and sexuality as a fluid state of affairs, see his 'Introduction: Straightforward' in *Before the Closet* (1998).

renewal, and disciplinary renovation.[32] In using 'postSaxon,' this book does not employ 'post' as a prefix that signals rupture, because the future is never divorced from the past.[33] Rather 'post-Saxon' recognizes that early medieval studies no longer pledges allegiance to an 'Anglo-Saxon' politics, yet it still remains policed by its Anglo-Saxonist spectres, an ideological old guard that we continue to struggle against and which many scholars within the field are still unable to part with or condemn.[34]

As this book has explained, our relationship to these signifiers predates us by many generations and many, many centuries. However, as signifiers that were enunciated by the 'sovereign father' King Alfred and organized by the interdisciplinary 'fathers' historian Sharon Turner, archaeologist James Douglas, philologist Benjamin Thorpe, and polymath John Mitchell Kemble, 'Anglo-Saxon' and 'Anglo-Saxonist' are genealogical terms that render us 'children' to these men. In using them, we declare allegiance to our field's interdisciplinary methods even as we assume a set of racial-colonial ideologies built into them. To be an Anglo-Saxonist is, therefore, to stand in the ghostly shadows of 'fathers' that stretch back a millennium and to assume a position of interminable mourning that has become melancholic — for their 'fatherly' presence and the nation-empire to which they

---

32 One could be, for example, 'Old/e English,' but this book does not augur the future.

33 For example, 'postcolonial' is a term that can be used to mark the end of the decolonial period, a political era that extended from the mid- to late-twentieth century, in which colonialism ended as a system of European rule; however, the ideological forces of colonialism continue to linger within and without these so-called (post)colonial nations. As many Latin American scholars argue, 'coloniality,' the living legacy of colonialism, continues to maintain the racial, political, and social hierarchies created by and maintained by European colonialism. In America, I consider coloniality to operate, for example, by way of institutional racism. While we live in a politically postcolonial world, we are not 'post' colonialism but remain struggling towards a time of decoloniality.

34 See, for example, the recent collective statement signed by over 60 scholars in the field of 'Anglo-Saxon' studies, 'The Responsible Use of the Term "Anglo-Saxon",' n.d., http://www.fmass.eu/uploads/pdf/responsible_use_of%20 the%20term%20_Anglo-Saxon.pdf.

belonged. This book has exorcised the ghosts of Alfred, Turner, Douglas, Thorpe, and Kemble so that I might mourn the terms 'Anglo-Saxon' and 'Anglo-Saxonist' and free myself from their crushing ideological freight. In so doing, I have freed myself to travel scholarly paths that have led me to African American studies, a field that reveals the role that 'Old English' plays in Anglo-Saxonist discourse even as it shows a once-Anglo Saxon studies how African-American poetics 'disinvent' and 'reinvent' the temporal and linguistic parameters of a postSaxon field.

Many other paths, however, are possible, and in invoking the place-holder 'postSaxon,' this book hopes to begin a conversation within a once-'Anglo Saxon' studies that does not set its sights on coming up with new signifiers to replace old ones without excavating their troubled histories and the ways in which they give support to some of the most violent supporters of white supremacist beliefs. Rather, I hope that our shared field, whatever we might call it, will work privately and publicly to recognize that, whatever the 'love objects' that keep us affectively tied to 'Anglo-Saxon' and 'Anglo-Saxonist,' we must value and enact the work of mourning that will free us from these harmful ghosts.

Bibliography

A Catalogue of the Ashmolean Museum: Descriptive of the Zoological Specimens, Antiquities, Coins, and Miscellaneous Curiosities. Oxford: S. Collingwood, 1836.

Abels, Richard. 'Alfred and his Biographers: Images and Imagination.' In *Writing Medieval Biography, 750–1250: Essays in Honour of Frank Barlow,* edited by David Bates, Julia Crick, and Sarah Hamilton, 61–75. Rochester: Boydell, 2006.

Abraham, Nicholas, and Maria Torok. *The Shell and the Kernel: Renewals of Psychoanalysis.* Edited and translated by N.T. Rand. Chicago: University of Chicago Press, 1994.

Adkins, Brent. *Death and Desire in Hegel, Heidegger and Deleuze.* Edinburgh: Edinburgh University Press, 2007.

Adkins, Lesley, and Roy Adkins. *Archaeological Illustration.* Cambridge: Cambridge University Press, 1989.

Akerman, John Yonge. 'An Archaeological Index to Remains of Antiquity of the Celtic, Romano-British, and Anglo-Saxon periods.' *The Edinburgh Review* 86, no. 174 (1847): 307–28.

Alaniz, Maria Luisa and Chris Wilkes. 'Pro-Drinking Messages and Message Environments for Young Adults: The Case of Alcohol Industry Advertising in African American, Latino, and Native American Communities.' *Journal of Public Health Policy* 19, no. 4 (1998): p. 447–72. DOI: 10.2307/3343076.

Alim, H. Samy. 'Global Ill-literacies: Hip Hop Cultures, Youth Identities, and the Politics of Literacy.' *Review of Research in Education* 35 (2011): 120–46. DOI: 10.3102/0091732X10383208.

———. 'Hip Hop Nation Language.' In *Language in the USA: Themes for the Twenty-First Century*, edited by Edward Finegan and John R. Rickford, 387–409. Cambridge: Cambridge University Press, 2004.

———. 'Introducing Raciolinguistics: Racing Language and Languaging Race in Hyperracial Times.' In *Raciolinguistics: How Language Shapes Our Ideas About Race*, edited by H. Samy Alim, John R. Rickford, and Arnetha F. Ball, 1–30. Oxford: Oxford University Press, 2016

———. *Roc the Mic Right: The Language of Hip Hop Culture*. New York: Routledge, 2006.

———, and Alisdair Pennycook. 'Glocal Linguistic Flows: Hip-Hop Culture(s), Identities, and the Politics of Language Education.' *Journal of Language, Identity & Education* 6, no. 2 (2007): 89–100. DOI: 10.1080/15348450701341238.

Allen, Debbie, dir. *Cat on a Hot Tin Roof*. Broadhurst Theatre. New York, 2008.

Anonymous, 'The Second Part of the History of the Anglo-Saxons: From the Death of Egbert to the Norman Conquest.' *The Edinburgh Review* 4, no. 6 (1804): 360–74.

Anderson, Paul Christopher. 'Rituals of Horsemanship: A Speculation on the Ring Tournament and the Origins of the Ku Klux Klan.' In *Weirding the War: Stories from the Civil War's Ragged Edges*, edited by Stephen Berry, 215–33. Athens: Georgia University Press, 2011.

The Anglo-Saxon Chronicle: A Collaborative Edition, Vol. 3, MS A. Edited by Janet M. Bately. Cambridge: D.S. Brewer, 1986.

Arnold, C.J. *An Archaeology of the Early Anglo-Saxon Kingdoms*. New York: Routledge, 1997.

Aspöck, Edeltraud. 'Past "Disturbances" of Graves as a Source: Taphonomy and Interpretation of Reopened Early Medieval Inhumation Graves at Brunn am Gebirge (Austria) and Winnall II (England).' *Oxford Journal of Archaeology* 30, no. 3 (2011): 299–324. DOI: 10.1111/j.1468-0092.2011.00370.x.

Asser. *Annales Rerum Gestarum Ælfredi Magni, auctore Asserio Manevensi*. Translated by Francis Wise. Oxford, 1722.

———. *Asser's Life of King Alfred together with the Annals of Saint Neots Erroneously Ascribed to Asser*. Edited by William H. Stevenson. Oxford: Clarendon Press, 1904.

———. *Alfred the Great: Asser's Life of King Alfred & Other Contemporary Sources*. Edited and translated by Simon Keynes and Michael Lapidge. London: Penguin, 1983.

Attridge, Derek. *Poetic Rhythm: An Introduction*. Cambridge: Cambridge University Press, 1995.

BABEL Working Group. 'Letter of Concern, ICMS / Kalamazoo 2019' (open petition). Google Docs. https://docs.google.com/forms/d/e/1FAIpQLSdReGZAQJiSSDWTRV0kT2tO2b9LEaAPLTjDJGCeH6auDczBhA/viewform.

Ballantyne, R.M. *The Gorilla Hunters: A Tale of the Wilds of Africa*. Edinburgh: T. Nelson & Sons, 1861.

———. *Hunting the Lions; or, The Land of the Negro*. London: James Nisbet & Co., 1869.

Ballantyne, Tony. *Orientalism and Race: Aryanism in the British Empire*. New York: Palgrave, 2002.

Baker, Geoffrey. 'Preachers, Gangsters, Pranksters: MC Solaar and Hip-Hop as Overt and Covert Revolt.' *The Journal of Popular Culture* 44, no. 2 (2011): 233–55. DOI: 10.1111/j.1540-5931.2011.00830.x.

Baker, Peter. 'Anglo-Saxon Studies After Charlottesville: Reflections of a University of Virginia Professor.' *Medievalists of Color*. May 25, 2018. https://medievalistsofcolor.com/race-in-the-profession/anglo-saxon-studies-after-charlottesville-reflections-of-a-university-of-virginia-professor/.

Bartlett, Robert. *The Making of Europe: Conquest, Colonization and Cultural Change, 950–1350*. London: Penguin Press, 1993.

Baudrillard, Jean. *The System of Objects*. Translated by James Benedict. New York: Verso, 2005.

Bauman, Richard, and Charles L. Briggs. *Voices of Modernity: Language Ideologies and the Politics of Inequality*. Cambridge: Cambridge University Press, 2003.

Baumgart, Daniel C., and William J. Sandborn. 'Crohn's Disease.' *The Lancet* 380, no. 9853 (November 2012): 1590–1605. DOI: 10.1016/S0140-6736(12)60026-9.

Beckett, David. 'A Useful Theory of Agency at Work.' In *Philosophical Perspectives on Educational Practice in the 21st Century: Proceedings of the 10th Biennial Conference of the International Network of Philosophers of Education*. Msida: University of Malta, 2006.

———. 'Learning to Be—At Work.' In *'Becoming' a Professional: An Interdisciplinary Analysis of Professional Learning*, edited by Lesley Scanlon, 57–76. New York: Springer, 2011.

Benite, Zvi Ben-Dor, Stefanos Geroulanos, and Nicole Jerr. 'Editors' Introduction.' In *The Scaffolding of Sovereignty: Global and Aesthetic Perspectives on the History of a Concept*, edited by Zvi Ben-Dor Benite, Stefanos Geroulanos, and Nicole Jerr, 1–49. New York: Columbia University Press, 2017.

Bhabha, Homi. 'The World and the Home.' *Social Text* 31/32 (1992): 141–53. https://www.jstor.org/stable/466222.

Biddick, Kathleen. 'Doing Dead Time for the Sovereign: Archive, Abandonment, Performance.' *Rethinking History* 13, no. 2 (2009): 137–151. DOI: 10.1080/13642520902833783.

———. *Make and Let Die: Untimely Sovereignties*. Earth: punctum books, 2016.

———. *The Shock of Medievalism*. Durham: Duke University Press, 1998.

———. *The Typological Imaginary: Circumcision, Technology, History*. Philadelphia: University of Pennsylvania Press, 2003.

———. 'Unbinding the Flesh in the Time That Remains: Crusader Martyrdom Then and Now.' *GLQ: A Journal of Lesbian and Gay Studies* 13, nos. 2–3 (2007): 197–225. DOI: 10.1215/10642684-2006-031.

Bignall, Simone, and Paul Patton. 'Introduction: Deleuze and the Postcolonial: Conversations, Negotiations, Mediations.' In *Deleuze and the Postcolonial*, edited by Simone Bignall and Paul Patton, 1–19. Edinburgh: Edinburgh University Press, 2010. https://www.jstor.org/stable/10.3366/j.ctt1r20xg.

Bill, Jan, and Aoife Daly. 'The Plundering of the Ship Graves from Osenberg and Gokstad: An Example of Power Politics?' *Antiquity* 86, no. 333 (2012): 808–24. DOI: 10.1017/S0003598X00047931.

Bjork, Robert. 'Nineteenth–century Scandinavia and the Birth of Anglo-Saxon studies.' In *Anglo-Saxonism and the Construction of Social Identity,* edited by Allen J. Frantzen and John D. Niles, 111–32. Gainesville: Florida University Press, 1997.

Blake, Felice, Paula Ioanide, and Alison Reed, eds. *Antiracism Inc.: How the Way We Talk about Racial Justice Matters.* Earth: punctum books, 2019.

Blake, William. *The Complete Poetry & Prose of William Blake.* Edited by David V. Erdman. New York: Anchor Books, 1988.

Blood Red Eagle [website]. http://bloodredeagle.com. Site discontinued.

'Blood Red Eagle Interview.' *NS Revolt* [blog], July 10, 2009. http://revoltns.blogspot.com/2009/07/interview-blood-red-eagle.html.

Bochner, A.P. 'On First-Person Narrative Scholarship: Autoethnography as Acts of Meaning.' *Narrative Inquiry* 22, no. 1 (2012): 155–164. DOI: 10.1075/ni.22.1.10boc.

Boenig, Robert. 'Scyld's Burial Mound.' *English Language Notes* 40, no. 1 (2002): 1–13.

'Bone Fragment "could be King Alfred or son Edward".' BBC *News.* January 17, 2014. https://www.bbc.com/news/uk-england-hampshire-25760383.

Bones [TV series]. 'Mayhem on a Cross.' Directed by Jeff Woolnough. Season 4, Episode 20. Los Angeles: Fox Broadcasting Co., April 16, 2009.

Bonney, Desmond. 'Early Boundaries and Estates in Southern England.' In *Medieval Settlement: Continuity and Change,* edited by Peter H. Sawyer, 72–82. New York: Edward Arnold, 1976.

'Born in Unwonted Tranquility.' *The Guardian.* April 18, 1980.

Bosworth-Toller Dictionary of Anglo-Saxon. Prague: Charles University, 2010. https://bosworth.ff.cuni.cz.

Boucher, Leigh. 'Trans/National History and Disciplinary Amnesia: Historicizing White Australia at Two fins de siècles.' In *Creating White Australia,* edited by J. Carey and C. McLisky, 44–64. Sydney: Sydney University Press, 2009.

Bowker, Alfred. *The King Alfred Millenary, a Record of the Proceedings of the National Commemoration.* London: Macmillan and Company, 1902.

Boylorn, Robin M., and Mark P. Orbe. 'Introduction: Critical Autoethnography as Method of Choice.' In *Critical Autoethnography: Intersecting Cultural Identities in Everyday Life,* edited by Robin M. Boylorn and Mark P. Orbe, 13–26. Walnut Creek: Left Coast Press, 2014.

Bradley, Adam. *Book of Rhymes: The Poetics of Hip Hop.* New York: Basic Civitas, 2009.

Brenkert, George G. 'Marketing to Inner-City Blacks: Power-Master and Moral Responsibility.' *Business Ethics Quarterly* 8, no. 1 (1998): 1–18. DOI: 10.2307/3857519.

Brooks, Nicholas P. 'England in the Ninth Century: The Crucible of Defeat.' *Transactions of the Royal Historical Society,* Fifth Series 29 (1979): 1–20. DOI: 10.2307/3679110.

———. 'English Identity from Bede to the Millennium.' *The Haskins Society Journal* 14 (2003): 33–52. www.jstor.org/stable/10.7722/j.ctt6wp8t9.8.

Brooks, Richard, dir. *Cat on a Hot Tin Roof.* Culver City: MetroGoldwyn-Mayer Studios Inc., 1958.

Brosch, Renate, ed. *Contemporary Ekphrasis* [special issue]. *Poetics Today* 39, no. 2 (2018): 225–427.

———. 'Ekphrasis in the Digital Age: Responses to Image.' *Poetics Today* 39, no. 2 (2018): 225–43.

Browne, Sir Thomas. *Hydriotaphia, urne-buriall, or, a discourse of the sepulchrall urnes lately found in Norfolk.* London: Printed for Hen. Browne at the Signe of the Gun in Ivy-Lane, 1658.

Bruhn, Siglind. *Musical Ekphrasis: Composers Responding to Poetry and Painting.* Hillsdale: Pendragon Press, 2000.

Camden, William. *Anglica, Normannica, Hibernica, Cambrica, a veteribus Scripta*. Frankfurt: impensis Claudij Marnij, & hærdum, 1602.

———. *Britain*. Translated by Philemon Holland. London: Elliot's Court Press, impensis Georgii B Camden, William Bishop & Johannes Norton, 1610.

———. *Britannia*. London: Elliot's Court Press, impensis George Bishop and John Newton, 1600.

———. *Britannia: Or, A Chorographical Description of the Most Flourishing Kingdoms of England, Scotland, and Ireland, and the Adjacent Islands, out of the Depth of Antiquity* [*Britannia siue florentissimorum regnorum, Angliae, Scotiae, Hiberniae, et insularum adiacentium ex intima antiquitate chorographica descriptio*]. London: per Radulphum Newbery, 1587.

Campbell, James, Eric John, and Patrick Wormald, eds. *The Anglo-Saxons*. Ithaca: Cornell University Press, 1982.

Carver, Martin. 'Burial as Poetry: The Context of Treasure in Anglo-Saxon graves.' In *Treasure in the Medieval West*, edited by Elizabeth M. Tyler, 25–48. York: York Medieval Press, 2000.

Carver, Martin. *Sutton Hoo: Burial Ground of Kings?* Philadelphia: Pennsylvania University Press, 1998.

Chaganti, Seeta. 'Statement Regarding ICMS Kalamazoo.' *Medievalists of Color*. July 9, 2018. http://medievalistsofcolor.com/race-in-the-profession/statement-regarding-icms-kalamazoo/.

Chan, J. Clara. 'Medievalists, Recoiling From White Supremacy, Try to Diversify the Field.' *The Chronicle of Higher Education*. July 16, 2017. https://www.chronicle.com/article/Medicvalists-Recoiling-From/240666.

Chawla, Devika, and Ahmet Atay. 'Introduction: Decolonizing Autoethnography.' *Cultural Studies—Critical Methodologies* 18, no. 1 (2018): 3–8. DOI: 10.1177/1532708617728955.

———, and Amardo Rodriguez. 'Narratives on Longing, Being, and Knowing: Envisioning a Writing Epistemology.' *In-*

ternational Journal of Progressive Education 4, no. 1 (2008): 6–19. DOI: 10.1007/978–94–6091–591–8_8.

Clüver, Claus. 'Ekphrasis Reconsidered: On Verbal Representations of Non-Verbal Texts.' In *Interart Poetics: Essays on the Interrelations of the Arts and Media,* edited by Ulla-Britta Lagerroth, Hans Lund, and Erik Hedling, 19–33. Amsterdam: Rodopi, 1997.

———. 'Quotation, Enargeia, and the Function of Ekphrasis.' In *Pictures into Words: Theoretical and Descriptive Approaches to Ekphrasis,* edited by Valerie Robillard and Els Jongeneel, 35–52. Amsterdam: VU University Press, 1998.

Cohen, Jeffrey Jerome. 'On Calling Out Misogyny.' *In the Middle.* January 16, 2016. http://www.inthemedievalmiddle.com/2016/01/on-calling-out-misogyny.html.

———, organizer. 'Are We Dark Enough Yet? Pale Faces 2016.' Conference session. New Chaucer Society Congress. July 11, 2016, London, Unite Kingdom.

Cole, Elizabeth R. 'Intersectionality and Research in Psychology.' *American Psychologist* 64, no. 3 (2009): 170–80. DOI: 10.1037/a0014564.

Collins, Lavinia. 'The Problem With Allen Frantzen's FemFog Post.' *Lavinia Collins* [blog]. January 15, 2016. https://vivimedieval.wordpress.com/2016/01/15/the-problem-with-allen-frantzens-femfog-post/.

Collins, Nick. 'King Alfred the Great Bones Believed to be in Box Found in Museum.' *The Telegraph.* January 17, 2014. https://www.telegraph.co.uk/history/10579315/King-Alfred-the-Great-bones-believed-to-be-in-box-found-in-museum.html.

Collins, Patricia Hill and Sirma Blige. *From Black Power to Hip Hop: Racism, Nationalism, and Feminism.* Philadelphia: Temple University Press, 2006.

'The Colored Tournament.' *The Louisiana Democrat.* September 27, 1876.

Craig, G. 'Alfred the Great: A Diagnosis.' *Journal of the Royal Society of Medicine* 84, no. 5 (1991): 303–5. PMCID: PMC1293232.

Crenshaw, Kimberlé. 'Mapping the Margins: Intersectionality, Identity Politics, and Violence Against Women of Color.' *Stanford Law Review* 43, no. 6 (1991): 1241–12. DOI: 10.2307/1229039.

———, Neil Gotanda, Gary Peller, and Kendall Thomas, eds. *Critical Race Theory: The Key Writings That Formed the Movement.* New York: The New Press, 1995.

Crooks, Esther J., and Ruth W. Crooks. *The Ring Tournament in the United States.* Richmond: Garrett and Massie, 1936.

Cunningham, John. 'Waiting for Alfred.' *The Guardian.* August 18, 1978, 9.

Davidson, D. Kirk. *Selling Sin: The Marketing of Socially Unacceptable Products.* 2nd edn. Westport: Praeger, 2003.

Davis, Craig. 'Redundant Ethnogenesis.' *The Heroic Age* 5 (Summer/Autumn, 2001). http://www.heroicage.org/issues/5/Davis1.html.

———. Review of Leonard Niedorf, ed., *The Transmission of Beowulf. The Medieval Review.* September 30, 2018. https://scholarworks.iu.edu/journals/index.php/tmr/article/view/25665.

Davis, Joseph Barnard, and John Thurnam. *Crania Britannica: Delineations and Descriptions of the Skulls of the Aboriginal and Early Inhabitants of the British Islands.* 2 Volumes. Volume 1: Text. Volume 2: Illustrations. London: Printed for the Subscribers, 1865.

Davis, Kathleen. 'Periodization and the Matter of Precedent.' *postmedieval: a journal of medieval cultural studies* 1, no. 3 (2010): 354–60. DOI: 10.1057/pmed.2010.32.

———. *Periodization and Sovereignty.* Pennsylvania: Pennsylvania University Press, 2007.

———, and Nadia Altschul, eds. *Medievalisms in the Postcolonial World: The Idea of the 'Middle Ages' Outside Europe.* Baltimore: Johns Hopkins University Press, 2009.

Davis, Kathy. 'Intersectionality as Buzzword: A Sociology of Science Perspective on What Makes Feminist Theory Successful.' *Feminist Theory* 9, no. 1 (2008): 67–85. DOI: 0.1177/1464700108086364.

Davis, Rocío G. 'Introduction: Academic Autobiography and/ in the Discourses of History.' *Rethinking History* 13, no. 1 (2009): 1–4. DOI: 10.1080/13642520802639546.

———, ed. *Reading Academic Autobiographies* [special issue]. *Prose Studies* 31, no. 3 (2009). DOI: 10.1080/01440350903437965.

de Jongh, Nicholas. 'The *Beowulf* at Oxford's Door.' *The Guardian*, July 18, 1991, 23.

Deleuze, Giles, and Felix Guattari. *A Thousand Plateaus: Capitalism and Schizophrenia.* Translated by Brian Massumi. Minneapolis: Minnesota University Press, 1987.

de Rapin, Paul. *History of England, as well Ecclesiastical as Civil.* Volume 1. Translated by Nicholas Tindal. London: Printed for James and John Knapton at the Crown in St. Paul's Church-Yard, 1726.

Derrida, Jacques, and Barbara Johnson. 'Fors.' *The Georgia Review* 31, no. 1 (1977): 64–116. https://www.jstor.org/stable/41397444.

Devlin, Zoë L. '"(Un)touched by Decay": Anglo-Saxon Encounters with Dead Bodies.' In *Death Embodied: Archaeological Approaches to the Treatment of the Corpse,* edited by Zoë L. Devlin and Emma-Jayne Graham, 63–85. Oxford: Oxbow Books, 2015.

Diallo, David. 'From Electro-Rap to G-Funk: A Social History of Rap Music in Los Angeles and Compton.' In *Hip Hop in America: A Regional Guide,* 2 vols., edited by Mickey Hess, 1:225–56. Denver: Greenwood, 2010.

DiAngelo, Robin. *White Fragility: Why It's So Hard for White People to Talk About Racism.* Boston: Beacon Press, 2018.

Dictionary of Old English: A to H online. Edited by Haruko Momma, Robert Getz, Stephen Pelle, Valentine Pakis, et al. Toronto: Dictionary of Old English Project, 2016. https://www.doe.utoronto.ca/pages/index.html.

Dibdin, T.F. *The Library-Companion: Or the Young Man's Guide and the Old Man's Comfort in the Choice of a Library.* London: Harding, Triphook, and Lepard, 1824.

Dierckins, Tony, and Pete Clure. *Naturally Brewed, Naturally Better: The Historic Breweries of Duluth and Superior.* Duluth: Zenith City Press, 2018.

Dilated Peoples. 'Olde English.' *20/20.* Los Angeles: Capitol, 2006.

DOC. *No One Can Do It Better.* Los Angeles: Ruthless Records, 1989.

Dockray-Miller, Mary. 'Old English Literature and Feminist Theory: A State of the Field.' *Literature Compass* 5, no. 6 (2008): 1049–59. DOI: 10.1111/j.1741-4113.2008.00581.x.

———. 'Old English Has a Serious Image Problem.' *JSTOR Daily.* May 3, 2017. https://daily.jstor.org/old-english-serious-image-problem/.

———. *Public Medievalists, Racism, and Suffrage in the American Women's College.* London: Palgrave Pivot, 2017.

Douglas, James. *Nenia Britannica; or, A Sepulchral History of Great Britain.* London: Printed by John Nichols for Benjamin and John White, 1793.

———. 'Mr. Douglas's "Nenia Britannica".' *Gentleman's Magazine* (October 1793).

'Douglas's Nenia Britannica.' *The Critical Review: Or, Annals of Literature* 8 (1793): 415–21.

Downes, Paul. *Hobbes, Sovereignty, and Early American Literature.* New York: Cambridge University Press, 2015.

Dr. Dre, feat. Snoop Dogg. 'Ain't Nuthin' but a G Thang' (music video). Directed by Andrew Young. 1992.

Drout, Michael. 'Again with the State of the Field.' *Worm Talk and Slug Speak: My Life among the Invertebrates* [blog]. January 7, 2007. http://wormtalk.blogspot.com/2007/01/again-with-state-of-field-tiruncula.html.

———. 'An Example.' *Worm Talk and Slug Speak: My Life among the Invertebrates* [blog]. January 10, 2007. http://wormtalk.blogspot.com/2007/01/example-to-illustrate-point-i-was.html.

———. 'Anglo-Saxon Studies: State of the Field?' In Drout et al., *State of the Field of Anglo-Saxon Studies,* https://www.heroicage.org/issues/11/foruma.php.

———. 'Gatekeeping?' *Worm Talk and Slug Speak: My Life Among the Invertebrates* [blog]. January 22, 2007. http://wormtalk.blogspot.com/2007/01/gatekeeping-while-back-i-p_116949841976709399.html.

———. 'State of the Field.' *Worm Talk and Slug Speak: My Life among the Invertebrates* [blog]. December 29, 2006. http://wormtalk.blogspot.com/2006/12/.

Drout, Michael, Tom Shippey, Richard Scott Nokes, and Eileen A. Joy. *State of the Field in Anglo-Saxon Studies* [forum discussion]. *The Heroic Age: A Journal of Early Medieval Northwestern Europe* 11 (May 2008). https://www.heroicage.org/issues/11/foruma.php.

Duggan, Alfred. *Conscience of the King*. 1951; repr. London: Phoenix Press, 2005.

Dumitrescu, Irina A. 'Verbal Dueling.' *Dragons in the Sky*. 2003. http://users.ox.ac.uk/%7Estuart/dits/content_verbal.html.

Dumville, David N., and Michael Lapidge, eds. *The Anglo-Saxon Chronicle: A Collaborative Edition,* Vol. 17: The Annals of St. Neots with Vita Prima Sancti Neoti. Cambridge: D.S. Brewer, 1985.

Dussel, Enrique. *Pedagogics of Liberation: A Latin American Philosophy of Education*. Translated by David I. Backer and Cecilia Diego. Earth: punctum books, 2018.

———. *Philosophy of Liberation*. Translated by Aquilina Martinez and Christine Morkovsky. Eugene: Wipf & Stock, 2003.

Dutta, Mohan J. 'Autoethnography as Decolonization, Decolonizing Autoethnography: Resisting to Build Our Homes.' *Cultural Studies — Critical Methodologies* 18, no. 1 (2018): 94–96. DOI: 10.1177/1532708617735637.

Earl, James. '*Beowulf* and the Origins of Civilization.' In Frantzen, ed., *Speaking Two Languages,* 65–89.

———. *Thinking about* Beowulf. Stanford: Stanford University Press, 1994.

Eazy-E. *It's On (D̶r̶.̶ ̶D̶r̶e̶) 187um Killa*. Torrance: Audio Achievements, 1993.

Echard, Siân. *Printing the Middle Ages.* Philadelphia: Pennsylvania University Press, 2008.

Eckardt, Hella, and Howard Williams. 'Objects without a Past? The Use of Roman Objects in Anglo-Saxon Graves.' In *Archaeologies of Remembrance: Death and Memory in Past Societies,* edited by Howard Williams, 141–70. New York: Springer, 2003.

Edmondson, George, and Klaus Mladek. 'Introduction: Sovereignty Crises.' In *Sovereignty in Ruins: A Politics of Crisis,* edited by George Edmondson and Klaus Mladek, 9–27. Durham: Duke University Press, 2017.

Einarsson, Bjarni. 'De Normannorum Atrocitate, or On the Execution of Royalty by the Aquiline Method.' *Saga Book* 22, no. 1 (1986): 79–82.

———, and Roberta Frank. 'The Blood-Eagle Once More: Two Notes: A. Blóðörn — An Observation on the Ornithological Aspect; B. Ornithology and the Interpretation of Skaldic Verse.' *Saga Book* 23, no. 2 (1990): 80–83.

Electronic Sawyer: Online Catalogue of Anglo-Saxon Charters. King's College London. http://www.esawyer.org.uk/about/index.html.

Ellard, Donna Beth. 'Ella's Bloody Eagle: Sharon Turner's *History of the Anglo-Saxons* and Anglo-Saxon History.' *postmedieval: a journal of medieval cultural studies* 5, no. 2 (2013): 215–34. DOI: 10.1057/pmed.2014.10.

———. '"Anglo-Saxonist, n.": Professional Scholar or Anonymous Person.' *Rethinking History* 23, no. 1 (2019): 16–33. DOI: 10.1080/13642529.2018.1561809.

'Ellard Surname, Family Crest & Coat of Arms.' *House of Names.* https://www.houseofnames.com/ellard-family-crest.

Ellis, Carolyn. *The Ethnographic I: A Methodological Novel about Autoethnography.* Walnut Creek: AltaMira Press, 2004.

Fanon, Frantz. *A Dying Colonialism.* Translated by Haakon Chevalier. New York: Grove Press, 1965.

Fauset, Jessie. 'My House and a Glimpse of My Life Therein.' *The Crisis* 8, no. 3 (1914): 143–45.

Farley, Frank Edgar. *Scandinavian Influences in the English Romantic Movement.* Boston: Ginn & Co., 1903.

Fernandes, Rio. 'Prominent Medievalist's Blog on "Feminist Fog" Sparks an Uproar.' *The Chronicle of Higher Education.* January 22, 2016. https://www.chronicle.com/article/Prominent-Medieval-Scholar-s/235014.

Fitzpatrick, Esther. 'A Story of Becoming: Entanglement, Settler Ghosts, and Postcolonial Counterstories.' *Cultural Studies — Critical Methodologies* 18, no. 1 (2018): 43–51. DOI: 10.1177/1532708617728954.

Flaherty, Colleen. 'It's About More Than a Name.' *Inside Higher Ed.* September 20, 2019. https://www.insidehighered.com/news/2019/09/20/anglo-saxon-studies-group-says-it-will-change-its- name-amid-bigger-complaints-about.

Foot, Sarah. *Æthelstan: The First King of England.* New Haven: Yale University Press, 2011.

———. 'The Making of Angelcynn: English Identity before the Norman Conquest.' *Transactions from the Royal Historical Society* 6 (1996): 25–49. DOI: 10.2307/3679228.

Fradenburg, Aranye. '(Dis)Continuity: A History of Dreaming.' In *The Post-Historical Middle Ages,* edited by Elizabeth Scala and Sylvia Federico, 87–116. New York: Palgrave Macmillan, 2009.

Fradenburg, L.O. Aranye. 'Life's Reach: Territory, Display, Ekphrasis.' In Fradenburg, *Staying Alive,* 223–61.

———. *Staying Alive: A Survival Manual for the Liberal Arts.* Edited by Eileen A. Joy. Brooklyn: punctum books, 2013.

Frank, Roberta. 'The Blood-Eagle Again.' *Saga Book* 22, no. 5 (1988): 287–89.

———. 'Conversational Skills for Heroes.' In *Narration and Hero: Recounting the Deeds of Heroes in Literature and Art of the Early Medieval Period,* edited by Victor Millet and Heike Sahm, 19–43. Boston: De Gruyter, 2014.

———. 'The Search for the Anglo-Saxon Oral Poet.' In *Textual and Material Culture in Anglo-Saxon England: Thomas Northcote Toller and the Toller Memorial Lectures,* edited by Donald Scragg, 137–60. London: D.S. Brewer, 2003.

———. 'Skaldic Poetry.' In *Old Norse-Icelandic Literature: A Critical Guide,* edited by Carol J. Clover and John Lindlow, 157–96. 1985; repr. Toronto: Toronto University Press, 2005.

———. 'Viking Atrocity and Skaldic Verse: The Rite of the Blood-Eagle.' *The English Historical Review* 99, no. 391 (1984): 332–43. https://www.jstor.org/stable/568983.

Frantzen, Allen J. *Anglo-Saxon Keywords.* Oxford: Wiley-Blackwell, 2012.

———. *Before the Closet: Same-Sex Love from* Beowulf *to Angels in America.* Chicago: Chicago University Press, 1998.

———. *Desire for Origins: New Languages, Old English, and Teaching Tradition.* New Jersey: Rutgers University Press, 1990.

———. 'How to Fight Your Way Out of the Feminist Fog.' *Allen J. Frantzen: Author. Boxer. Traditional Man.* Internet Archive Wayback Machine: https://web.archive.org/web/20160124170813/http://www.allenjfrantzen.com/Men/femfog.html.

———. 'Prologue: Documents and Monuments: Difference and Inter-disciplinarity in the Study of Medieval Culture.' In Frantzen, ed., *Speaking Two Languages,* 1–33.

———, ed. *Speaking Two Languages: Traditional Disciplines and Contemporary Theory in Medieval Studies.* Albany: State University of New York University Press, 1991.

———, and John Niles, eds. *Anglo-Saxonism and the Construction of Social Identity.* Gainesville: Florida University Press, 1997.

Freud, Sigmund. 'The Uncanny.' In Sigmund Freud, *Collected Papers,* Vol. 4, translated by Alix Strachey, 368–407. New York: Basic Books. 1959.

Freudenberg, Nicholas. *Lethal but Legal: Corporations, Consumption, and Protecting Public Health.* New York: Oxford University Press, 2014.

Frosh, Stephen. *Hauntings: Psychoanalysis and Ghostly Transmissions.* London: Palgrave Macmillan, 2013.

Fulk, R.D., Robert E. Bjork, and John D. Niles, eds. *Klaeber's Beowulf.* 4th edn. Toronto: Toronto University Press, 2008.

Gabriele, Matthew, and Mary Rambaran-Olm. 'The Middle Ages Have Been Misued by the Far Right.' *TIME Magazine*. November 21, 2019. https://time.com/5734697/middle-ages-mistakes/.

Gates, Jr., Henry Louis. *The Signifying Monkey: A Theory of African-American Literary Criticism*. New York: Oxford University Press, 2014.

Geary, Patrick J. *Living with the Dead in the Middle Ages*. Ithaca: Cornell University Press, 1994.

Gherardi, Silvia, and Davide Nicolini. 'To Transfer is to Transform: The Circulation of Safety Knowledge.' *Organisation* 7, no. 2 (2000): 329–48. DOI: 10.1177/135050840072008.

Gibbins, David. *Crusader Gold*. London: Headline, 2006.

Gingrich, Andre. 'Envisioning Medieval Communities in Asia: Remarks on Ethnicity, Tribalism, and Faith.' In *Visions of Community in the Post-Roman World: The West, Byzantium and the Islamic World*, edited by Walter Pohl, Clemens Gantner, and Richard Payne, 29–41. Farnham: Ashgate, 2012.

Giola, Dana. 'Meter-Making Arguments.' In *Meter in English: A Critical Engagement*, edited by David Baker, 75–96. Little Rock: Arkansas University Press, 1996.

Gluckman, Nell. 'A Debate About White Supremacy and Medieval Studies Exposes Deep Rifts in the Field.' *The Chronicle of Higher Education*. September 18, 2017. https://www.chronicle.com/article/A-Debate-About-White-Supremacy/241234.

Goodier, Ann. 'The Formation of Boundaries in Anglo-Saxon England: A Statistical Study.' *Medieval Archaeology* 28 (1984): 1–21. DOI: 10.1080/00766097.1984.11735454.

Gordon, Linda. *The Second Coming of the KKK: The Ku Klux Klan of the 1920s and the American Political Tradition*. New York: W.W. Norton, 2017.

Gray, Herman. *Watching Race: Television and the Struggle for 'Blackness.'* Minneapolis: University of Minnesota Press, 1995.

Grégoire le Grand. *Règle pastorale,* 2 vols. Edited by Bruno Judic, Floribert Rommel, and Charles Morel. Paris: Éditions du Cerf, 1992.
Gregory the Great. *Pastoral Care.* Translated by Henry Davis. Westminster: Newman Press, 1950.
Griffiths, Sarah, and Ben Spencer. 'King Alfred the Great's Bones Discovered in a MUSEUM: Remains Inside Box are Thought to Belong to Anglo-Saxon Ruler.' *Daily Mail.* January 17, 2014. https://www.dailymail.co.uk/sciencetech/article-2541267/King-Alfred-Greats-bones-discovered-inside-MUSEUM-Remains-inside-box-thought-belong-Anglo-Saxon-ruler.html.
Gurteen, Stephen Humphreys Villiers. *The Epic of the Fall of Man: A Comparative Study of Caedmon, Dante and Milton.* New York: G.P. Puntam's Sons, 1896.
Haas, Gerrit. *Ficto/critical Strategies: Subverting Textual Practices of Meaning, Other, and Self-Formation.* Bielefeld: Transcript Verlag, 2017.
Hadley, D.M. *The Northern Danelaw: Its Social Structure, c.800–1100.* London: Leicester University Press, Continuum, 2000.
Hagedorn, Suzanne D. 'Received Wisdom: the Reception History of Alfred's Preface to the Pastoral Care.' In Frantzen and Niles, eds., *Anglo-Saxonism and the Construction of Social Identity,* 86–110.
Hagman, George. 'Beyond Decathexis: Toward a Fresh Theory of Grieving.' In *Meaning Reconstruction and the Experience of Loss,* edited by Robert A. Neimeyer, 13–32. Washington, DC: American Psychological Association, 2001.
Halama, Alta Cools. 'Flytes of Fancy: Boasting and Boasters from Beowulf to Gangsta Rap.' *Essays in Medieval Studies* 13 (1996): 81–96.
Hardin, Tayana L. 'The I Who Arrives: A Meditation on History as Inheritance.' *Pedagogy* 18, no. 3 (2018): 531–40. DOI: 10.1215/15314200-6936939.
Härke, Heinrich. 'Material Culture as Myth: Weapons in Anglo-Saxon Graves.' In *Burial and Society: The Chronologi-*

cal and Social Analysis of Archaeological Burial Data, edited by Claus Kjeld Jensen and Karen Hoilund Nielsen. 119–27. Aarhus: University of Aarhus, 1997.

———. 'Warrior Graves? The Background of the Anglo-Saxon Weapon Burial Rite.' *Past & Present* 126, no. 1 (1990): 22–43. DOI: 10.1093/past/126.1.22.

Harris, Stephen. J. 'The Alfredian World History and Anglo-Saxon Identity.' *The Journal of English and Germanic Philology* 100, no. 4 (October 2001): 482–510. https://www.jstor.org/stable/27712138.

———. 'An Overview of Race and Ethnicity in Pre-Norman England.' *Literature Compass* 5, no. 4 (July 2008): 740–54. DOI: 10.1111/j.1741-4113.2008.00560.x.

———. 'Race and Ethnicity.' In Stodnick and Trilling, eds., *A Handbook of Anglo-Saxon Studies,* 165–79.

Harris, Thomas. *Hannibal.* New York: Random House, 1999.

'help me with a tattoo, please.' *Stormfront* [forum post]. May 5–6, 2004. http://www.stormfront.org/forum/t131032/.

Herd, Denise. 'Contesting Culture: Alcohol-Related Identity Movements in Contemporary African American Communities.' *Contemporary Drug Problems* 20 (1993): 739–58.

———. 'Migration, Cultural Transformation and the Rise of Black Liver Cirrhosis Mortality.' *British Journal of Addiction* 80, no. 4 (December 1985): 397–410. DOI: 10.1111/j.1360-0443.1985.tb03011.x.

Hesse-Biber, Sharlene Nagy, and Patricia Leavy. 'Introduction.' In *Emergent Methods in Social Research,* edited by Sharlene Hesse-Biber and Patricia Leavy, ix–xxxii. Thousand Oaks: SAGE Publications, 2006.

Higham, John. *Strangers in the Land: Patterns of American Nativism, 1860–1925.* New Brunswick: Rutgers University Press, 2002.

Higham, Nicholas, and M.J. Ryan. *The Anglo-Saxon World.* New Haven: Yale University Press, 2013.

Hill, John. *The Cultural World of* Beowulf. Toronto: University of Toronto Press, 1995.

Hines, John et al. 'The Responsible Use of the Term "Anglo-Saxon".' n.d. http://www.fmass.eu/uploads/pdf/responsible_use_of%20the%20term%20_Anglo-Saxon.pdf.

Hirsch, Marianne. *Family Frames: Photography, Narrative, and Postmemory.* Cambridge: Harvard University Press, 1997.

'How Do You Think Saddam Should Be Punished?' *Tribal War* [forum]. URL deactivated.

Hurley, Mary Kate. 'Ruins of the Past: *Beowulf* and Bethlehem Steel,' *The Heroic Age: A Journal of Early Medieval Northwestern Europe* 13 (August 2010): https://www.heroicage.org/issues/13/ba.php.

Hussey, Matthew, organizer. '#ASESoWhite.' Conference Session. Annual Convention of the Modern Language Association, January 5, 2018, New York City, New York.

Ice Cube. 'Steady Mobbin.' *Death Certificate.* Los Angeles: Priority Records/EMI, 1991.

'Inaugural address of Governor George Wallace, which was delivered at the Capitol in Montgomery, Alabama' (January 14, 1963). Alabama Department of History and Archives: Digital Collections. http://digital.archives.alabama.gov/cdm/ref/collection/voices/id/2952.

'It Is the Power' [advertisement]. New York Amsterdam News. October 4, 1980.

Izbicki, Thomas. 'Review of Francesco Maiola, Medieval Sovereignty: Marsilius of Padua and Bartolus of Saxoferrato.' *The Medieval Review.* https://scholarworks.iu.edu/journals/index.php/tmr/article/view/16669.

Jackson, F.I. 'Alfred the Great: A Diagnosis.' *Journal of the Royal Society of Medicine* 85, no. 1 (1992): 58. PMCID: PMC1293470.

James, William H., and Stephen L. Johnson. *Doin' Drugs: Patterns of African American Addiction.* Austin: University of Texas Press, 1996.

Jessup, Ronald. *Man of Many Talents: An Informal Biography of James Douglas 1753–1819.* London: Phillmore, 1975.

Johnson, Ben F., III. *John Barleycorn Must Die! The War Against Drink in Arkansas, 1920–1950.* Fayetteville: University of Arkansas Press, 2005.

Johnstone, James. *Lodbrokar Quida; or The Death Song of Lodbroc; now first correctly printed from various Manuscripts, with a free English translation*. Printed for the Author, 1782.

Jones, Gwyn. *A History of the Vikings*. 1968; repr. New York: Oxford University Press, 2001.

Jones, Stacy Holman. 'Emotional Space: Performing the Resistive Possibilities of Torch Singing.' *Qualitative Inquiry* 8, no. 6 (2002): 738–759. DOI: 10.1177/107780042238077.

Jones, Sir William. *Selected Poetical and Prose Works*. Edited by Michael J. Franklin. Cardiff: University of Wales Press, 1995.

Jónsson, Finnur, ed. *Den norsk-islandske skjaldedigtning. B: Rettet tekst*. 1912–1915; repr. Copenhagen, Denmark: Villadsen & Christensen, Rosenkilde & Bagger, 1973.

Joy, Eileen A. 'Building a Tribe Outside the System: Allen Frantzen, Jack Donovan, and the Neomedievalist Alt-Right.' Keynote lecture, University of Richmond, March 27, 2018. *YouTube*, https://www. youtube.com/watch?v=qWtoxdhLoeU.

———. 'Goodbye to All That: The State of My Own Personal Field of Schiziod Anglo-Saxon Studies' [forum post]. In Drout et al., 'State of the Field of Anglo-Saxon Studies,' https://www.heroicage.org/issues/11/foruma.php.

———. 'My Life Among the Anglo-Saxonists: More Anomie, Despair, and Self-Immolation.' *In the Middle*. January 20, 2007. http://www.inthemedievalmiddle.com/2007/01/my-life-among-anglo-saxonists-more.html.

———. 'Thomas Smith, Humfrey Wanley, and the "Little-Known" Country of the Cotton Library.' *British Library Journal* (2005): 1–34. https://www.bl.uk/eblj/2005articles/pdf/article1.pdf.

———. 'What Lies Before Us: Old English Studies, the Agon of Thought, and Our Moments of Unknowingness.' *In the Middle*. August 21, 2008. http://www.inthemedievalmiddle.com/2008/08/what-lies-before-us-old-english-studies.html.

———, and Larry Swain, eds. 'The State(s) of Early English Studies?' [shared essay cluster]. *postmedieval: a journal of medieval cultural studies* 1, no. 3 (Winter 2010) and *The He-*

roic Age: A Journal of Early Medieval Northwestern Europe 14 (November 2010), https://www.heroicage.org/issues/14/joy-letter.php.

———, and Larry Swain, co-organizers. 'Is There a Theory in the House of Anglo-Saxon Studies.' Conference session. 43rd International Congress on Medieval Studies, Kalamazoo, Michigan, May 11, 2008.

———, and Vincent W.J. van Gerven Oei. 'A Statement of Concern Regarding the Programming for the 2019 International Congress on Medieval Studies @Kalamazoo.' *punctum books*. July 14, 2018. https://punctumbooks.com/blog/a-statement-of-concern/.

Kabir, Ananya Jahanara. *Territory of Desire: Representing the Valley of Kashmir*. Minneapolis: Minnesota University Press, 2009.

Kabir, Ananya Jahanara, and Deanne Williams, eds. *Postcolonial Approaches to the European Middle Ages: Translating Cultures*. Cambridge: Cambridge University Press, 2005.

Kajikawa, Loren. *Sounding Race in Rap Songs*. Los Angeles: University of California Press, 2015.

Kantorowicz, Ernst. *The King's Two Bodies: A Study in Medieval Political Theology*. Princeton: Princeton University Press, 2016.

Kao, Wan-Chuan. '#palefacesmatter?' *In the Middle*. July 26, 2016. http://www.inthemedievalmiddle.com/2016/07/pale-facesmatter-wan-chuan-kao.html.

Karkov, Catharine. *Text and Picture in Anglo-Saxon England: Narrative Strategies in the Junius 11 Manuscript*. Cambridge: Cambridge University Press, 2001.

———. 'Postcolonial.' In Stodnick and Trilling, eds., *A Handbook of Anglo-Saxon Studies*, 149–163.

Kay, Guy Gavriel. *The Last Light of the Sun*. New York: New American Library, 2004.

Kemble, John Mitchell, ed. *The Anglo-Saxon Poems of Beowulf, The Travellers Song and The Battle of Finnes-Burh*. London: William Pickering, 1833.

———, trans. *A Translation of the Anglo-Saxon Poem of Beowulf.* London: William Pickering, 1837.

Kennedy, Maev. 'Archaeologists May Have Found Remains of Alfred the Great.' *The Guardian.* January 17, 2014. https://www.theguardian.com/uk-news/2014/jan/17/alfred-the-great-edward-elder-remains-found-winchester.

Kershaw, Paul. 'Illness, Power and Prayer in Asser's *Life of King Alfred*.' *Early Medieval Europe* 10, no. 2 (2001): 201–24. DOI: 10.1111/1468-0254.00085.

Keyes, Cheryl L. *Rap Music and Street Consciousness.* Urbana: University of Illinois Press, 2004.

Keynes, Simon. 'Alfred the Great and the Kingdom of the Anglo-Saxons.' In *A Companion to Alfred the Great,* edited by Nicole Guenther Discenza and Paul Szarmarch, 13–46. Leiden: Brill, 2014.

———. 'The Cult of King Alfred the Great.' *Anglo-Saxon England* 28 (1999): 225–356. DOI: 10.1017/S0263675100002337.

———. 'Edward, King of the Anglo-Saxons.' In *Edward the Elder: 899–924,* edited by N.J. Higham and D.H. Hill, 40–66. New York: Routledge, 2001.

———. 'King Alfred and the Mercians.' In *Kings, Currency, and Alliances: History and Coinage of Southern England in the Ninth Century,* edited by Mark A.S. Blackburn and David N. Dumville, 1–46. Rochester: Boydell Press, 1998.

———. 'The West Saxon Charters of King Æthelwulf and His Sons.' *The English Historical Review* 109, no. 434 (1994): 1109–49. https://www.jstor.org/stable/573869.

Kilburn, Matthew. 'The Learned Press: History, Languages, Literature, and Music.' In *The History of Oxford University Press: Volume I: Beginnings to 1780,* edited Ian Gadd, chap. 15. Oxford: Oxford University Press, 2013. DOI: 10.1093/acprof:oso/9780199557318.001.0001/acprof-9780199557318-chapter-15.

Kim, Dorothy. 'Antifeminism, Whiteness, and Medieval Studies.' *In the Middle.* January 18, 2016. http://www.inthemedievalmiddle.com/2016/01/antifeminism-whiteness-and-medieval.html.

———. *Digital Whiteness and Medieval Studies*. Unpublished manuscript.

———. 'Medieval Studies, Sexual Harassment, and Community Accountability.' *In the Middle*. October 31, 2014. http://www.inthemedievalmiddle.com/2014/10/medieval-studies-sexual-harassment-and.html.

———. 'Teaching Medieval Studies in a Time of White Supremacy.' *In The Middle*. August 28, 2017. http://www.inthemedievalmiddle.com/2017/08/teaching-medieval-studies-in-time-of.html.

Kipling, Rudyard. *The Jungle Book*. New York: The Century Co., 1894.

Kirkham, Graeme. '"Rip it up, and spread it over the field": Post-Medieval Agriculture and the Destruction of Monuments: A Case Study from Cornwall.' *Landscapes* 13, no. 2 (2012): 1–20. DOI: 10.1179/lan.2012.13.2.002.

Klingelhofer, Eric, and Kenneth Qualmann. 'Hyde Abbey.' In *Medieval Archaeology: An Encyclopedia*, edited by Pam J. Crabtree, 170–71. New York: Routledge, 2016.

Krauss, Rosalind. *The Originality of the Avant-Garde and Other Modernist Myths*. Cambridge: MIT Press, 1986.

Lacan, Jacques. *The Seminar of Jacques Lacan: Book II, The Ego in Freud's Theory and in the Technique of Psychoanalysis, 1954–1955*. Translated by Sylvana Tomaselli. New York: W.W. Norton, 1991.

———. *The Seminar of Jacques Lacan, Book VII: The Ethics of Psychoanalysis 1959–1960*. Edited by Jacques-Alain Miller. Translated by Dennis Porter. New York: W.W. Norton & Company, 1992.

Lafferty, Sean. 'Ad sanctitatem mortuorum: Tomb Raiders, Body Snatchers and Relic Hunters in Late Antiquity.' *Early Medieval Europe* 22, no. 3 (2014): p. 249–79. DOI: 10.1111/emed.12062.

'Laughing at Misogyny.' *The Syllabub*. January 16, 2016. http://thesyllabub.blogspot.com/2016/01/laughing-at-misogyny.html.

Lees, Clare A., and Gillian R. Overing. 'Still Theoretical After All These Years, Or, Whose Theory Do You Want, or, Whose Theory Can We Have?' *The Heroic Age: A Journal of Early Medieval Northwestern Europe* 14 (2010). https://www.heroicage.org/issues/14/lees&overing.php.

Levinas, Emmanuel. *Totality and Infinity: An Essay on Exteriority.* Translated by Alphonso Lingis. Pittsburgh: Duquesne University Press, 1969.

Levison, Wilhelm. *England and the Continent in the Eighth Century.* Oxford: Clarendon Press, 1946.

Lewis, Charlton T., and Charles Short, eds. *A Latin Dictionary.* Oxford: Oxford University Press, 1879.

Lipari, Lisbeth. *Listening, Thinking, Being: Toward an Ethics of Attunement.* University Park: Pennsylvania State University Press, 2014.

L'Isle, William. *Saxon Treatise Concerning the Old and New Testament.* London: Printed by John Haviland for Henrie Seile, 1623.

Liuzza, Roy Michael. 'The Return of the Repressed: Old and New Theories in Old English Literary Criticism.' In *Old English Shorter Poems: Basic Readings,* edited by Katherine O'Brien O'Keeffe, 103–47. New York: Garland, 1994.

LL Cool J. 'Mama Said Knock You Out.' *Mama Said Knock You Out.* New York: Def Jam Records, 1991.

Loffreda, Beth, and Claudia Rankine. 'Introduction.' In *The Racial Imaginary: Writers on Race in the Life of the Mind,* 13–14. East Peoria: Versa Press, 2015.

Lomuto, Sierra. 'White Nationalism and the Ethics of Medieval Studies.' *In the Middle.* December 5, 2016. http://www.inthemedievalmiddle.com/2016/12/white-nationalism-and-ethics-of.html.

———, Shokoofeh Rajabzadeh, and Cord Whitaker, co-organizers. 'Medieval Race and the Modern Scholar.' Conference session. 52nd International Congress on Medieval Studies. May 11, 2017.

———, Shokoofeh Rajabzadeh, and Dorothy Kim, co-organizers. Conference session. 'Whiteness in Medieval Studies: A

Workshop.' 52nd International Congress on Medieval Studies, May 13, 2017, Kalamazoo, Michigan.

Longman Manuscript. Records of the Longman Group. University of Reading, MS 1393.

Louvel, Liliane. 'Types of Ekphrasis: An Attempt at Classification.' *Poetics Today* 39, no. 2 (2018): 245–63.

MacAvoy, R.A. *Book of Kells*. New York: Spectra, 1985.

Magennis, Hugh. *The Cambridge Introduction to Anglo-Saxon Literature*. Cambridge: Cambridge University Press, 2011.

Maiolo, Francesco. *Medieval Sovereignty: Marsilius of Padua and Bartolus of Saxoferrato*. Delft: Eburon Academic Publishers, 2007.

Makoni, Sinfree, and Alastair Pennycook. 'Disinventing and Reconstituting Languages.' In *Disinventing and Reconstituting Languages,* edited by Sinfree Makoni and Alastair Pennycook, 1–41. Buffalo: Multilingual Matters Ltd, 2007.

Maldonado-Torres, Nelson. 'On the Coloniality of Being.' *Cultural Studies* 21, no. 2–3 (2007): 240–70. DOI: 10.1080/09502380601162548.

Manias, Chris. *Race, Science, and the Nation: Reconstructing the Ancient Past in Britain, France, and Germany*. New York: Routledge, 2013.

Markon, Jerry, and Timothy Dwyer. 'Moussaoui Says He Was to Fly 5th Plane White House Attack Planned for 9/11, Terrorist Testifies.' *The Washington Post*. March 28, 2006. https://www.washingtonpost.com/archive/politics/2006/03/28/moussaoui-says-he-was-to-fly-5th-plane-span-classbankheadwhite-house-attack-planned-for-911-terrorist-testifiesspan/e4723118–618c-412a-9cd7–004ac683f8c7/.

McCann, Kathrin. *Anglo-Saxon Kingship and Political Power: Rex gratia Dei*. Cardiff: University of Wales Press, 2018.

McCombe, Robert. 'Anglo-Saxon Artifacts and Nationalist Discourse.' *Museum History Journal* 4, no. 2 (2011): 144–52

McCracken, Peggy. *In the Skin of a Beast: Sovereignty and Animality in Medieval France*. Chicago: University of Chicago Press, 2017.

McTurk, Rory. 'Samuel Ferguson's "Death-Song" (1833): An Anglo-Irish Response to *Krákumál*.' In *Constructing Nations, Reconstructing Myth: Essays in Honour of T.A. Shippey*, edited by Andrew Wawn, with Graham Johnson and John Walter, 167–92. Turnhout: Brepols, 2007.

Meaney, Audrey. 'Pagan English Sanctuaries, Place-Names and Hundred Meeting-Places.' *Anglo-Saxon Studies in Archaeology and History* 8 (1995): 29–42.

Medievalists of Color. 'On Race and Medieval Studies.' *Medievalists of Color*. August 1, 2017. http://medievalistsofcolor.com/statements/on-race-and-medieval-studies/.

Mignolo, Walter D., and Arturo Escobar, eds. *Globalization and the Decolonial Option*. New York: Routledge, 2010.

Mignolo, Walter D., and Catherine E. Walsh. *On Decoloniality: Concepts, Analytics, Praxis*. Durham: Duke University Press, 2018.

'Miscellaneous. Notes on Books, etc.' *Notes and Queries* 2, no. 66 (April 1857): 279–80.

Miller, Paul (DJ Spooky). *Rhythm Science*. Cambridge: MIT Press, 2004.

Miyashiro, Adam. 'De-colonizing Anglo-Saxon Studies: A Response to ISAS in Honolulu.' *In The Middle*. July 29, 2017. http://www.inthemedievalmiddle.com/2017/07/decolonizing-anglo-saxon-studies.html.

Molyneaux, Brian Leigh. 'Introduction.' In *The Cultural Life of Images: Visual Representation in Archaeology*, edited by Brian Leigh Molyneaux, 1–10. New York: Routledge, 1997.

Moore, Alan. *Voice of the Fire*. Atlanta: Top Shelf Productions, 2003.

Moore-Gilbert, Bart. 'Anglo-Saxon Attitudes: Empire, Race and English Studies in Contemporary University Fiction.' *Wasafiri* 13, no. 26 (1997): 3–8. DOI: 10.1080/02690059708589553.

Mortensen, Peter. '"The Descent of Odin": Wordsworth, Scott and Southey among the Norsemen.' *Romanticism* 6, no. 2 (2000): 211–33. DOI: 10.3366/rom.2000.6.2.211.

Morton, Timothy. 'An Object-Oriented Defense of Poetry.' *New Literary History* 43, no. 2 (2012): 205–24. https://www.jstor.org/stable/23259372.

Moser, Stephanie. 'Archaeological Visualization: Early Artefact Illustration and the Birth of the Archaeological Image.' In *Archaeological Theory Today*. 2nd ed. Edited by Ian Hodder, 292–322. Cambridge: Polity Press, 2012.

Murray, Rolland. *Our Living Manhood: Literature, Black Power, and Masculine Ideology.* Philadelphia: Pennsylvania University Press, 2007.

Natason, Hannah. '"It's All White People": Allegations of White Supremacy Are Tearing Apart a Prestigious Medieval Studies Group.' *The Washington Post*. September 19, 2019. https://www.washingtonpost.com/education/2019/09/19/its-all-white-people-allegations-white- supremacy-are-tearing-apart-prestigious-medieval-studies-group/.

Neal, Mark Anthony. *Soul Babies: Black Popular Culture and the Post-Soul Aesthetic.* New York: Routledge, 2002.

Newton, Sam. *The Origins of Beowulf and the Pre-Viking Kingdom of East Anglia.* Cambridge: DS Brewer, 1993.

Niedorf, Leonard, ed. *The Dating of* Beowulf: *A Reassessment.* Suffolk: D.S. Brewer, 2014.

———. *The Transmission of Beowulf: Language, Culture, and Scribal Behavior.* Ithaca: Cornell University Press, 2017.

Neimeyer, Robert A. 'The Language of Loss: Grief Therapy as a Process of Meaning Reconstruction.' In *Meaning Reconstruction and the Experience of Loss,* edited by Robert A. Neimeyer, 1-12. Washington, DC: American Psychological Association, 2001.

———, Dennis Klass, and Michael Robert Dennis. 'Mourning, Meaning, and Memory: Individual, Communal, and Cultural Narration of Grief.' In *Meaning in Positive and Existential Psychology,* edited by Alexander Batthyany and Pninit Russo-Netzer, 325–46. Springer: New York, 2014.

Nelson, Janet L. 'The Political Ideas of Alfred of Wessex.' In *Kings and Kingship in Medieval Europe,* edited by Anne J.

Duggan, 125–58. London: Centre for Late Antique and Medieval Studies, Kings College London, 1993.

———, 'Review Article: Waiting for Alfred,' *Early Medieval Europe* 7, no. 1 (1998): 115–24

The New Journal and Guide. Norfolk, Virginia. http://thenewjournalandguide.com/.

'New! Now Here in New York' [advertisement]. *New York Amsterdam News.* August 16, 1969.

Niles, John D. *Beowulf and Lejre.* Tempe: Arizona Center for Medieval and Renaissance Studies, 2007.

———. *The Idea of Anglo-Saxon England 1066–1901: Remembering, Forgetting, Deciphering, and Renewing the Past.* Malden: Wiley-Blackwell, 2015.

———. 'Locating *Beowulf* in Literary History.' *Exemplaria* 5, no. 1 (1993): 79–109. DOI: 10.1179/exm.1993.5.1.79.

———. 'Ring Composition and the Structure of *Beowulf.*' *PMLA* 94, no. 5 (1979): 924–35. DOI: 10.2307/461974.

Nokes, Scott. 'More on the State of the Field.' *Unlocked Wordhoard.* January 10, 2007. http://unlocked-wordhoard.blogspot.com/2007/01/more-on-state-of-field.html

'North Star Military Figures.' *North Star Military Figures.* https://www.northstarfigures.com/.

N.W.A. '8 Ball.' *N.W.A. and the Posse.* Los Angeles: Macola, 1987.

———.'8 Ball (Remix).' *Straight Outta Compton.* Los Angeles: Ruthless Records, 1988.

———. 'Straight Outta Compton' [music video]. Directed by Rupert Wainwright. Compton: N.W.A. World, 1989. https://www.imdb.com/title/tt6374084/.

O'Keeffe, Katherine O'Brien, ed. *Reading Old English Texts.* Cambridge: Cambridge University Press, 1997.

———. *Visible Song: Transitional Literacy in Old English Verse.* Cambridge: Cambridge University Press, 1990.

Oxford English Dictionary Online. 3rd edn. Oxford University Press, 2019. http://www.oed.com/.

Offutt, Andrew J., and Keith Taylor. *When Death Birds Fly.* New York: Ace Books, 1984.

Ol' Dirty Bastard. 'Dirty & Stinkin.' *Trials and Tribulations of Russell Jones*. Los Angeles: Riviera, 2002.
'Olde English is Taking Over' [advertisement]. *Los Angeles Sentinel*. May 2, 1968.
———. *New York Amsterdam News*. September 20, 1969.
———. *New York Amsterdam News*. October 4, 1969.
'Olde English 800 Giving Something Back to the Community.' *Los Angeles Sentinel*. November 29, 1990.
'Olde English 800 Supports Minority Education.' *Los Angeles Sentinel*. June 20, 1991.
Orton, Daniel. 'Royal Piety and Davidic Imitation: Cultivating Political Capital in the Alfredian Psalms.' *Neophilologus* 99, no. 3 (2015): 477–92. DOI: 10.1007/s11061-014-9414-4.
Osumare, Halifu. *The Africanist Aesthetic in Global Hip-Hop: Power Moves*. New York: Palgrave, 2007.
Overing, Gillian. *Language, Sign, and Gender in* Beowulf. Carbondale: Southern Illinois University Press, 1990.
———. 'On Reading Eve: Genesis B and the Readers' Desire.' In Frantzen, ed., *Speaking Two Languages*, 35–63.
Owen-Crocker, Gale. *Dress in Anglo-Saxon England*. Woodbridge: The Boydell Press, 2004.
———. *The Four Funerals in* Beowulf *and the Structure of the Poem*. Manchester: Manchester University Press, 2000.
Oxford Dictionary of National Biography. New York: Oxford University Press, 2004.
Pabst Brewing Company Annual Report. 1980. ProQuest: Historical Annual Reports.
Pantos, Aliki. 'Assembly Places in the Anglo-Saxon Period: Aspects of Form and Location.' PhD diss., University of Oxford, 2002.
Parker, Joanne. *'England's darling': The Victorian Cult of Alfred the Great*. Manchester: Manchester University Press, 2007.
Pathak, Archana. 'Musings on Postcolonial Autoethnography: Telling the Tale of/through My Life.' In *Handbook of Autoethnography*, edited by Stacy Holman Jones, 595–608. Walnut Creek: Left Coast Press, 2013.

Patton, Kimberly C. *Religion of the Gods: Ritual, Paradox, and Reflexivity.* New York: Oxford University Press, 2009.

Pearson, Jacqueline. 'Crushing the Convent and the Dread Bastille: The Anglo-Saxons, Revolution and Gender in Women's Plays of the 1790s.' In *Literary Appropriations of the Anglo-Saxons from the Thirteenth to the Twentieth Century,* edited by Donald Scragg and C. Weinberg, 122–37. Cambridge: Cambridge University Press, 2000.

Pennycook, Alistair. '"The Rotation Gets Thick. The Constraints Get Thin": Creativity, Recontextualization, and Difference.' *Applied Linguistics* 28, no. 4 (2007): 579–96. DOI: 10.1093/applin/amm043.

Percy, Thomas. *Five Pieces of Runic Poetry Translated from the Islandic Language.* London: R. and J. Dodsley, 1763.

Perry, Imani. *Prophets of the Hood: Politics and Poetics in Hip Hop.* Durham: Duke University Press, 2004.

Plummer, Charles. *The Life and Times of Alfred the Great: Being the Ford Lectures for 1901.* Oxford: Clarendon Press, 1902.

Pohl. Walter. 'Ethnic Names and Identities in the British Isles: A Comparative Perspective.' In *The Anglo-Saxons from the Migration Period to the Eighth Century,* edited by John Hines, 7–40. Turnhout: Brepols, 1997.

———. 'Introduction.' In *Strategies of Identification: Ethnicity and Religion in Early Medieval Europe,* edited by Walter Pohl and Greta Heydemann, 1–64. Turnout: Brepols, 2013.

Posel, Deborah, and Pamila Gupta. 'The Life of the Corpse: Framing Reflections and Questions.' *African Studies* 68, no. 3 (2009): 299–309. DOI: 10.1080/00020180903381248.

Powell, Robert. *The Life of Alfred, or Alvred.* Paul's Churchyard: Printed by Richard Eadger for Thomes Alchorn, 1634.

Pratt, David. 'The Illnesses of King Alfred the Great.' *Anglo-Saxon England* 30 (2001): 39–90. DOI: 10.1017/S0263675101000035.

———. *The Political Thought of King Alfred the Great.* Cambridge: Cambridge University Press, 2007.

Pratt, Lynda. 'Anglo-Saxon Attitudes? Alfred the Great and the Romantic National Epic.' In *Literary Appropriations of the*

Anglo-Saxons from the Thirteenth to the Twentieth Century, edited by Donald Scragg and C. Weinburg, 138–56. Cambridge: Cambridge University Press, 2000.

Pullman, Philip. *The Golden Compass*. New York: Random House, 1996.

punctum books. '#imc keynote intro….' *Twitter*. July 3, 2017. https://twitter.com/punctum_books/status/881788042507427840.

'The Puritan and the Cavalier.' *DeBow's Review* 31, no. 3 (September 1861): 209–52.

Quinn, Eithne. *Ain't Nuthin' But a 'G' Thang: The Culture and Commerce of Gangsta Rap*. New York: Columbia University Press, 2005.

'Race, Racism, and the Middle Ages' [blog series]. *The Public Medievalist*. http://www.publicmedievalist.com/race-racism-middle-ages-toc/.

Rambaran-Olm, Mary. 'Anglo-Saxon Studies, Academia, and White Supremacy.' *Medium*. June 27, 2018. https://medium.com/@mrambaranolm/anglo-saxon-studies-academia-and-white-supremacy-17c87b360bf3.

——— . 'Misnaming the Medieval: Rejecting "Anglo-Saxon" Studies.' *History Workshop*. November 4, 2019. http://www.historyworkshop.org.uk/misnaming-the-medieval-rejecting-anglo-saxon-studies/.

——— , M. Breann Leake, and Micah Goodrich, eds. *Special Issue: Race, Revulsion, and Revolution* [special issue]. *postmedieval: a journal of medieval cultural studies* 11, nos. 3–4 (2020).

Rashkin, Esther. *Unspeakable Secrets and the Psychoanalysis of Culture*. Albany: State University of New York Press, 2008.

Rask, Erasmus. *A Grammar of the Anglo-Saxon Tongue, with a Praxis*. Translated by Benjamin Thorpe. Copenhagen: Printed by S.L. Møller, 1830.

Reimitz, Helmut. 'The Providential Past: Visions of Frankish Identity in the Transmission of Gregory of Tours' Historiae.' In *Visions of Community in the Post-Roman World: The West, Byzantium and the Islamic World, 300–1100*, edited by

Walter Pohl, Clemens Gantner, and Richard Payne, 109–35. Farnham: Ashgate, 2012.

Reiter, Bernd, ed. *Constructing the Pluriverse: The Geopolitics of Knowledge.* Durham: Duke University Press, 2018.

Remein, Daniel C. 'ISAS Should Probably Change Its Name.' Conference presentation. 52nd International Congress on Medieval Studies, May 11, 2017, Kalamazoo, Michigan, https://www.academia.edu/34101681/_Isas_should_probably_change_its_name_ICMS_KalamazKa_2017.

'Retrospective Review: Anglo-Saxon Literature.' *Gentleman's Magazine* 1, no. 5 1837: 492–94.

Reynolds, Andrew. *Anglo-Saxon Deviant Burial Customs.* New York: Oxford University Press, 2009.

———. 'The Definition and Ideology of Anglo-Saxon Execution Sites and Cemeteries.' In *Death and Burial in Medieval Europe. Papers of the 'Medieval Europe Brugge 1997' Conference,* edited by Guy De Boe and Frans Verhaeghe, 33–41. Zellik: IAP Rapporten 2, 1997.

———. 'Burials, Boundaries, and Charters in Anglo-Saxon England: A Reassessment.' In *Burial in Early Medieval England and Wales,* edited by Sam Lucy and Andrew Reynolds, 171–94. London: Society for Medieval Archaeology Monograph 17, 2002.

Reynolds, Susan. 'The Historiography of the Medieval State.' In *Companion to Historiography,* edited by Michael Bentley, 109–29. London: Routledge, 1997.

———. 'What Do We Mean by "Anglo-Saxon" and "Anglo-Saxons"?' *Journal of British Studies* 24, no. 4 (1985): 395–414. DOI: 10.1086/385844.

Ridyard, Susan. *The Royal Saints of Anglo-Saxon England: A Study of West Saxon and East Anglian Cults.* Cambridge: Cambridge University Press, 1988.

Rigney, Ann. 'The Many Afterlives of Ivanhoe.' In *Performing the Past: Memory, History, and Identity in Modern Europe,* edited by Karin Tilmans, Frank Van Vree, and Jay Winter, 207–34. Amsterdam: Amsterdam University Press, 2010.

Rix, Robert. 'The Afterlife of a Death Song: Reception of Ragnar Lodbrog's Poem in Britain Until the End of the Eighteenth Century.' *Studia Neophilologica: A Journal of Germanic and Romance Languages and Literature* 81, no. 1 (2009): 53–68. DOI: 10.1080/00393270902859879.

Roach, Joseph. 'Celebrity Erotics: Pepys, Performance, and Painted Ladies.' In *Politics, Transgression, and Representation at the Court of Charles II*, edited by Julia Marciari Alexander and Catharine MacLeod, 233–51. New Haven: Yale University Press, 2007.

Rose, Jacqueline. *States of Fantasy*. New York: Clarendon Press, 1998.

Rose, Tricia. *Black Noise: Rap Music and Black Culture in Contemporary America*. Hanover: Wesleyan University Press, 1994.

Ross, Margaret Clunie. *The Norse Muse in Britain 1750–1820*. Trieste: Parnaso, 1998.

———. *The Old Norse Poetic Translations of Thomas Percy*. Turnhout: Brepols, 2001.

Ruskin, John. *The Stones of Venice, Book 3*. London: Smith, Elder, and Co., 1853.

Russell, Craig. *Blood Eagle*. London: Hutchinson, 2005.

Rutherfurd, Edward. *Sarum: The History of England*. New York: Ballantine Books, 1987.

RZA. 'Must Be Bobby.' *Digital Bullet*. New York: Koch Records, 2001.

Sanmark, Alexandra, and Sarah J. Semple. 'Places of Assembly: New Discoveries in Sweden and England.' *Fornvännen* 103, no. 4 (2008): 245–59. http://kulturarvsdata.se/raa/fornvannen/html/2008_245.

Santner, Eric L. *The Royal Remains: The People's Two Bodies and the Endgames of Sovereignty*. Chicago: University of Chicago Press, 2011.

Sawyer, Peter. *The Age of the Vikings*. London: Edward Arnold, 1962; repr. New York: St Martin's Press, 1971.

———. 'The Two Viking Ages of Britain: A Discussion.' *Mediaeval Scandinavia: A Journal Devoted to the Study of*

Mediaeval Civilization in Scandinavia and Iceland 2 (1969): 163–207. https://www.jstor.org/stable/40917020.

———. *From Roman Britain to Norman England*. 2nd ed. New York: Routledge, 1998.

Scanlon, Lesley. '"Becoming" a Professional.' In *'Becoming' a Professional: An Interdisciplinary Analysis of Professional Learning*, edited by Lesley Scanlon, 13–32. New York: Springer, 2011.

'Schizoid Personality Disorder.' *International Statistical Classification of Diseases and Related Health Problems: World Health Organization*. 10th revision (ICD-10). https://icd.who.int/browse10/2015/en#/F60.1.

Schwab, Gabrielle. *Haunting Legacies: Violent Histories and Transgenerational Trauma*. New York: Columbia University Press, 2010.

Scragg, Donald, and Carole Weinberg. *Literary Appropriations of the Anglo-Saxons from the Thirteenth to the Twentieth Century*. Cambridge: Cambridge University Press, 2000.

Semple, Sarah. 'Burials and Political Boundaries in the Avebury Region, North Wiltshire.' Anglo-Saxon Studies in Archaeology and History 12 (2003): 72–91.

———. 'A Fear of the Past: The Place of the Prehistoric Burial Mound in the Ideology of Middle and Later Anglo-Saxon England.' *World Archaeology* 30, no. 1 (1998): 109–126. DOI: 10.1080/00438243.1998.9980400.

———. *Perceptions of the Prehistoric in Anglo-Saxon England: Religion, Ritual, and Rulership in the Landscape*. New York: Oxford University Press, 2013.

———. 'Recycling the Past: Ancient Monuments and Changing Meanings in Early Medieval Britain.' In *Antiquaries and Archaists: the Past in the Past, the Past in the Present*, edited by Megan Brewster Aldrich and Robert J Wallis, 29–45. Reading: Spire, 2009.

———, and Alexandra Sanmark. 'Assembly in North West Europe: Collective Concerns for Early Societies?' *European Journal of Archaeology* 16, no. 3 (2013): 518–542. DOI: 10.1179/1461957113Y.0000000035.

———, and Howard Williams. 'Landmarks of the Dead: Exploring Anglo-Saxon Mortuary Geographies.' In *The Material Culture of the Built Environment in the Anglo-Saxon World*, edited by Maren Clegg Hyer and Gale Owen-Crocker, 137–61. Liverpool: Liverpool University Press, 2015.

'Sense Section.' OED *Guide to the Third Edition*. New York: Oxford University Press, 2019. http://www.oed.com/public/oed3guide/guide-to-the-third-edition-of#sense.

Sharma, Manish. 'Beyond Nostalgia: Formula and Novelty in Old English Literature,' *Exemplaria* 26, no. 4 (2014): 303–27. DOI: 10.1179/1041257314Z.00000000056.

Shepherd, Nick. 'Ruin Memory: A Hauntology of Cape Town.' In *Reclaiming Archaeology: Beyond the Tropes of Modernity*, edited by Alfredo González Ruibal, 233–43. New York: Routledge, 2013.

Shippey, Thomas A. '"The Death-Song of Ragnar Lodbrog": A Study in Sensibilities.' In *Medievalism in the Modern World: Essays in Honour of Leslie J. Workman*, edited by Richard Utz and Thomas Shippey, 155–72. Turnhout: Brepols, 1998.

———. 'Tolkien, Medievalism, and the Philological Tradition.' In *Bells Chiming from the Past: Cultural and Linguistic Studies on Early English*, edited by Isabel Moskowich–Spiegel and Begoña Crespo García, 265–79. New York: Rodopi, 2007.

———. 'The Underdeveloped Image: Anglo-Saxon in Popular Consciousness from Turner to Tolkien.' In *Literary Appropriations of the Anglo-Saxons From the Thirteenth to the Twentieth Century*, edited by Donald Scragg and Carole Weinberg, 215–36. Cambridge: Cambridge University Press, 2000.

Sides, Josh. *L.A. City Limits: African American Los Angeles from the Great Depression to the Present*. Berkeley: University of California Press, 2003.

Siewer, Alfred K. 'Guthlac's Mound and Grendel's Mere as Expressions of Anglo-Saxon Nation Building.' *Viator* 34 (2003): 1–39. DOI: 10.1484/J.VIATOR.2.300380.

Simmons, Claire. *Reversing the Conquest: History and Myth in Nineteenth-Century British Literature.* New Brunswick: Rutgers University Press, 1990.

Sinclair, Andrew. *Prohibition: The Era of Excess.* New York: Harper and Row, 1962.

Singleton, John, dir. *Boyz in the Hood.* Los Angeles: Columbia Pictures, 1991.

Skinner, Alexis Tudor, and Sarah Semple. 'Assembly Mounds in the Danelaw: Place-name and Archaeological Evidence in the Historic Landscape.' *Journal of the North Atlantic* 8 (2016): 115–133. DOI: 10.3721/037.002.sp809.

Smiles, Sam, and Stephanie Moser. 'Introduction.' In *Envisioning the Past: Archaeology and the Image,* edited by Sam Smiles and Stephanie Moser, 1–12. Malden: Wiley-Blackwell, 2005.

Smith, Charles Roach. *Collectanea Antiqua.* 7 Vols. London: J. Russell Smith, 1848–1880.

Smith, Robert Barr. *Blood Eagle.* Palm Beach: Medallion Press, 2007.

Smith, Sir Thomas. *De Recta et Emendata Linguae Anglicae Scriptione, Dialogus.* Paris: Ex officina Roberti Stephani Typographi Regij, 1568.

Smitherman, Geneva. *Black Talk: Words and Phrases From the Hood to the Amen Corner.* Boston: Houghton Mifflin, 1994.

———. '"The chain remain the same": Communicative Practices in the Hip Hop Nation.' *Journal of Black Studies* 28, no. 1 (1997): 3–25. DOI: 10.1177%2F002193479702800101.

Smyth, Alfred. 'The Effect of Scandinavian Raiders on the English and Irish Churches: A Preliminary Reassessment.' In *Britain and Ireland, 900–1300: Insular Responses to Medieval European Change,* edited by Brendan Smith, 1–38. Cambridge: Cambridge University Press, 2004.

———. *King Alfred the Great.* New York: Oxford University Press, 1995.

———. *Scandinavian Kings in the British Isles: 850–880.* New York: Oxford University Press, 1977.

Snook, Ben. *The Anglo-Saxon Chancery: The History, Language and Production of Anglo-Saxon Charters from Alfred to Edgar*. Woodbridge: The Boydell Press, 2015.

'Sons of Ma'as.' *Tribes Webring*. http://som.iwarp.com/main.html.

Sorensen, Ninna Nyberg. 'Governing through the Mutilated Female Body.' In *Governing the Dead : Sovereignty and the Politics of Dead Bodies,* edited by Finn Stepputat, 203–25. Manchester: Manchester University Press, 2014.

Squires, Kirsty E. 'Piecing Together Identity: A Social Investigation of Early Anglo-Saxon Cremation Practices.' *Archaeological Journal* 170, no. 1 (2013): 154–200. DOI: 10.1080/00665983.2013.11021004.

Spelman, Sir John. *Aelfredi Magni, Anglorum regis invictissimi vita tribus libris comprehensa a clarissimo Deo*. Oxford: E Theatro Sheldoniano, 1678.

———. *The Life of Ælfred the Great*. Oxford: Printed at the Theater for Maurice Atkins at the Golden-ball in St Paul's Church-Yard, London, 1709.

Spiegel, Gabrielle. 'France for Belgium.' In *Why France? American Historians Reflect on an Enduring Fascination,* edited by Laura Lee Downs and Stéphane Gerson, 89–98. Ithaca: Cornell University Press, 2007.

Spitzmüller, Jürgen. 'Floating ideologies: Metamorphosis of Graphic "Germanness".' In *Orthography as Social Action: Scripts, Spelling, Identity, and Power,* edited by Alexandra Jaffe, Jannis Androutsopoulos, Mark Sebba, and Sally Johnson, 255–88. Berlin: de Gruyter, 2012.

Stenton, Frank M. *Anglo-Saxon England*. New York: Oxford University Press, 1971.

Stephanus Stephanius. *Notæ Uberiores in Historiam Danicam Saxonis Grammatici*. Sorø: Crusius, 1645.

Stewart, Kathleen. *Ordinary Affects*. Durham: Duke University Press, 2007.

Stodnick, Jacqueline, and Renée Trilling. 'Introduction.' In Stodnick and Trilling, eds., *A Handbook of Anglo-Saxon Studies*. Oxford: Wiley-Blackwell, 2012.

———, and Renée Trilling, eds. *A Handbook of Anglo-Saxon Studies*. Oxford: Wiley-Blackwell, 2012.

Stokes, William. 'The Manchester Exhibition of Art-Treasures.' *The Dublin University Magazine* 49, no. 293 (1857): 608–20.

Stoodley, Nick. 'Age Organization and the Early Anglo-Saxon Burial Rite.' *World Archaeology* 31, no. 3 (2000): 456–72.

Swain, Larry. 'State of the Field Repost.' *The Ruminate*. March 11, 2007. http://theruminate.blogspot.com/2007/03/state-of-field-repost.html.

Sweet, Rosemary. *Antiquaries: The Discovery of the Past in Eighteenth-Century Britain*. New York: Hambledon and London, 2004.

Syed, Moin. 'Disciplinarity and Methodology in Intersectionality Theory and Research.' *American Psychologist* 65, no. 1 (2010): 61–62. DOI: 0.1037/a0017495.

Tangherlini, Timothy. 'Afterword: Performing through the Past: Ethnophilology and Oral Tradition.' *Western Folklore* 62 (2003): 143–49. https://www.jstor.org/stable/1500450.

Taussig, Michael. *Walter Benjamin's Grave*. Chicago: Chicago University Press, 2006.

Taylor, Ros. 'Valentine's Day of Reckoning.' *The Guardian*. March 20, 2001. https://www.theguardian.com/education/2001/mar/20/highereducation.english.

Tha Alkaholiks. 'Hip Hop Drunkies.' *Likwidation*. New York: Loud Records, 1997.

Thorpe, Benjamin. *Analecta Anglo-Saxonica: A Selection in Prose and Verse from Anglo-Saxon Authors of Various Ages, with a Glossary*. London: John and Arthur Arc. Cornhill, 1834.

Tirincula. 'What Does a Healthy Field Look Like from the Inside? *Practica*. January 7, 2007. URL deactivated.

Tonsfeldt, H. Ward. 'Ring Structure in Beowulf.' *Neophilologus* 61 (1977): 443–52. DOI: 10.1007/BF01513854.

Toyosaki, Satoshi, and Sandy L. Pensoneau-Conway. 'Autoethnography as a Praxis of Social Justice: Three Ontological Contexts.' In *Handbook of Autoethnography*, edited by Stacy

Holman Jones, Tony E. Adams, and Carolyn Ellis, 557–75. New York: Routledge, 2016.

'Try Mighty "800"' [advertisement]. *New York Amsterdam News*. January 31, 1970.

Turner, Sharon. *The History of the Anglo-Saxons, from Their Earliest Appearance above the Elbe, to the Norman Conquest*. Paternoster-Row, London: T.N. Longman and O. Rees, Printed for the Author 1802–1805.

Turville-Petre, E.O.G. *Myth and Religion of the North: The Religion of Ancient Scandinavia*. London: Weidenfeld and Nicolson, 1964.

United States Patent and Trademark Office (USPTO). https://www.uspto.gov/trademarks-application-process/search-trademark-database.

Vickers, Margaret. 'Researchers as Storytellers: Writing on the Edge — And Without a Safety Net.' *Qualitative Inquiry* 8, no. 5 (2002): 608–21. DOI: 10.1177%2F107780002237007.

'viking blood eagle.' *Stormfront* [forum]. November 20, 2002. http://www.stormfront.org/forum/t44315/.

The Vikings. 'All His Angels.' Directed by Ciaran Donnelly. Written by Michael Hirst. The History Channel. Season 4. Episode 15. December 28, 2016.

———. 'Blood Eagle.' Directed by Jeff Woolnough. Written by Michael Hirst. The History Channel. Season 2. Episode 7. April 3, 2014.

———. 'Burial of the Dead.' Directed by Ciarán Donnelly. Written by Michael Hirst. The History Channel. Season 1. Episode 6. April 7, 2013.

———. 'Revenge.' Directed by Jeff Woolnough. Written by Michael Hirst. The History Channel. Season 4. Episode 18. January 18, 2017.

Wagner, Curt. 'Vikings Creator on Frightening, Spiritual Death.' *Chicago Tribune*. April 10, 2014. http://www.chicagotribune.com/redeye/redeye-vikings-post-mortem-ragnar-kills-borg-20140410-story.html.

Wallace-Hadrill, J.M. *Early Medieval History*. Oxford: Basil Blackwell, 1974.

Wallack, Lawrence, Lori Dorfman, David Jernigen, and Makani Themba. *Media Advocacy and Public Health: Power for Prevention*. Newbury Park: SAGE Publications, 1993.
'Watts Towers Day of the Drum Slated.' *Los Angeles Sentinel*. September 20, 1984.
Wawn, Andrew. *The Vikings and the Victorians: Inventing the Old North in Nineteenth-Century Britain*. Woodbridge: Boydell and Brewer, 2000.
———, ed. *Constructing Nations, Reconstructing Myth: Essays in Honour of T.A. Shippey*. Turnhout: Brepols, 2007.
Welch, Martin. 'Rural Settlement Patterns in the Early and Middle Anglo-Saxon Periods.' *Landscape History* 7 (1985): 13–25. DOI: 10.1080/01433768.1985.10594386.
Weston, Corinne Comstock, and Janelle Renfrow Greenberg. *Subjects and Sovereigns: The Grand Controversy over Legal Sovereignty in Stuart England*. Cambridge: Cambridge University Press, 1981.
Whitaker, Cord. 'B(l)ack Home in the Middle Ages: Medievalism in Jessie Redmon Fauset's "My House and a Glimpse of My Life Therein".' *postmedieval: a journal of medieval cultural studies* 10, no. 2 (2019): 162–75.
———. *Black Metaphors: How Modern Racism Emerged from Medieval Race-Thinking*. Philadelphia: University of Pennsylvania Press, 2019.
———. 'Pale Like Me: Resistance, Assimilation, and "Pale Faces" Sixteen Years On.' *In the Middle*. July 20, 2016. http://www.inthemedievalmiddle.com/2016/07/pale-like-me-resistance-assimilation.html.
Whitelock, Dorothy. *The Genuine Asser*. University of Reading, 1968.
Whyte, Nicola. 'The Deviant Dead in the Norfolk Landscape.' *Landscapes* 4, no. 1 (2003): 24–39. DOI: 10.1179/lan.2003.4.1.24.
———. *Inhabiting the Landscape: Place, Custom and Memory, 1500–1800*. Oxford: Windgather Press at Oxbow, 2009.
Wickham-Crowley, Kelley M. 'Looking Forward, Looking Back.' In *The Archaeology of Anglo-Saxon England: Basic

Readings, edited by Catherine E. Karkov, 1–24. New York: Garland Publishing, Inc., 1999.

Williams, Gareth. 'Raiding and Warfare.' In *The Viking World,* edited by Stefan Brink, in collaboration with Neil Price, 193–203. New York: Routledge, 2008.

Williams, Howard. 'Ancient Landscapes and the Dead: The Reuse of Prehistoric and Roman Monuments as Early Anglo-Saxon Burial Sites.' *Medieval Archaeology* 41, no. 1 (1997): 1–32. DOI: 10.1080/00766097.1997.11735606.

———. 'Anglo-Saxonism and Victorian Archaeology: William Wylie's Fairford Graves.' *Early Medieval Europe* 16, no. 1 (2008): 49–88. DOI: 10.1111/j.1468-0254.2008.00221.x.

———. 'Assembling the Dead.' In *Assembly Places and Practices in Medieval Europe,* edited by Aliki Pantos and Sarah Semple, 109–34. Dublin: Four Courts Press, 2004.

———. 'Cemeteries as Central Places—Place and Identity in Migration Period Eastern England.' In *Central Places in the Migration and Merovingian Periods,* edited by Birgitta Hårdh and Lars Larsson, 341–62. Stockholm: Almqvist and Wiksell International, 2002.

———. *Death and Memory in Early Medieval Britain.* Cambridge: Cambridge University Press, 2006.

———. 'Death Warmed Up: The Agency of Bodies and Bones in Early Anglo-Saxon Cremation Rites.' *Journal of Material Culture* 9, no. 3 (2004): 263–69. DOI: 10.1177/1359183504046894.

———. 'The Emotive Force of Early Medieval Mortuary Practices.' *Archaeological Review from Cambridge* 22, no. 1 (2007): 107–23.

———. 'Heathen Graves and Anglo-Saxonism: Assessing the Archaeology of John Mitchell Kemble.' *Anglo-Saxon Studies in Archaeology and History* 13 (2006): 1–18.

———. 'Monuments and the Past in Early Anglo-Saxon England.' *World Archaeology* 30, no. 1 (1998): 90–108. DOI:10.1080/00438243.1998.9980399.

———. 'Should "British Archaeology" Stop Using "Anglo-Saxon"?' *ARCHEAOdeath* [blog]. December 12, 2019. https://

howardwilliamsblog.wordpress.com/2019/12/12/should-british-archaeology-stop-using-anglo-saxon/

Winchester, Angus. *Discovering Parish Boundaries*. Princes Risborough: Shire Publications Ltd., 1990.

Wintle, Michael. 'Editor's Introduction: Ideals, Identity and War: The Idea of Europe, 1939–1970.' In *European Identity and the Second World War*, edited by Menno Spiering and Michael Wintle, 1–18. New York: Palgrave Macmillan, 2011.

Winwroth, Anders. *The Age of the Vikings*. Princeton: Princeton University Press, 2014.

Wood, Michael. 'Is the Term "Anglo-Saxon" Racist?' *BBC History Magazine*. December 2019. https://www.historyextra.com/period/anglo-saxon/professor-michael-wood-anglo-saxon-name-debate-is-term-racist/.

Wormald, Patrick. 'Living with King Alfred.' *Haskins Society Journal* 15 (2004): 1–39. www.jstor.org/stable/10.7722/j.ct-t7zssjh.5.

Wright, Michelle. *Physics of Blackness: Beyond the Middle Passage Epistemology*. Minneapolis: Minnesota University Press, 2015.

Wright, Thomas. *Wanderings of an Antiquary: Chiefly Upon the Traces of the Romans in Britain*. London: J.B. Nichols and Sons, 1854.

Wylie, William. *Fairford Graves: A Record of Researches in an Anglo-Saxon Burial Place in Glouchestershire*. Oxford: John Henry Parker, 1852.

Wylie, W.M. 'The Graves of the Alemanni at Oberflacht in Suabia.' *Archaeologia* 36 (1855): 129–159. DOI: 10.1017/S0261340900012972.

Xzibit, feat. Tha Alkaholiks and King T. 'Louis XIII.' *Napalm*. Detroit: Open Bar Entertainment, 2012.

'The Young Colored Men of our Parish….' *The Louisiana Democrat*. September 13, 1876.

Young, Helen. 'Whiteness and Time: The Once, Present, and Future Race.' In *Studies in Medievalism XXIV: Medievalism on the Margins*, 39–49. Cambridge: D.S. Brewer, 2015.

Zuckerberg, Donna, 'Should Academics Fear the Manosphere?' *Jezebel*. January 27, 2016. https://jezebel.com/should-academics-fear-the-manosphere-1754937735.

Index

Note: Page numbers in italics indicate illustrative material.

9/11 attacks 94

Abels, Richard 186–87, 247
Abraham, Nicolas 63, 66, 72, 77, 82, 86, 139n77, 234n131
Adémar de Chabannes 85n71
African Americans: and Ku Klux Klan 295, 302–3; medieval amusements and iconography 294, 295–98; and prohibition movement 302–3; and social control 308–11; as targets of alcohol advertisements 299–301, 303–8, 311–12 (see also Rap music)
Age of the Vikings, The (Sawyer) 86n73
Alaniz, Maria Luisa 309
Alcohol and alcohol consumption: advertisements, connections to race and sex 300–301, 303–8, 311–12; in black power narrative 300–301, 303–5, 318–23; PowerMaster controversy 316–17; prohibition movement 302–3; and social control 308–11 (see also Olde English malt liquor)
Alfred, King: *Angulsaxonum rex* title, in biographies 186, 187–88, 189, 194; *Angulsaxonum rex* title, in charters 179–81, 183–85; body of, in Anglo-Saxon *corpus* 227–28, 230–32; body of, as corpse 249–52; body of, in fictocriticism 259–

61, 262–64, 266–67, 271–75, 276; body of, physical and sickly 191, 242–49; body of, physical and vernacular 192–94, 205–6; body of, textual and Latinized 76, 195–99, 200–202, 205–7; body of, translation during English Civil Wars 211–12; sovereignty of, in annal records framework 187–90, 194–96; sovereignty of, in crucified Christ framework 205–8; sovereignty of, effigial presence *213, 214–26, 216, 218, 219, 223, 226, 249, 250, 251*; sovereignty of, in royal piety framework 193–94, 198–99; in Turner's *History* 75–77
Alim, Samy 285, 325–26, 328n100
Al-Qaeda 93–95
Analecta Anglo-Saxonica (Rask; and Thorpe's translation) 231, 234–35
Anasemia, as concept 72 (see also Encryption and psychic crypts)
Anderson, Paul Christopher 295n23
Anglo-Saxon England (Stenton) 82–83
Anglo-Saxon ideologies see Colonialism; Race and ethnicity
Anglo-Saxonism and the Construction of Social Identity (Frantzen) 349
'Anglo-Saxonist,' OED definition 20–24, 178n3
Anglo-Saxons: as ekphrastic figures 104, 137–38, 141–42, 144–45; as military figures 134–37; as racialized figures 147–49, 165–66; as raciolinguistic figures 230–35, 289; as term 178–83, 209–10, 239–41 (see also Alfred, King)
Anglo-Saxon studies: 'Anglo-Saxonist' OED definition 20–24, 178n3; collaborative mourning of 49–51; early reception of critical theory 26–27, 35; emergence at Oxford 226–28; failure of postcolonial approach 36–41; fathers of 24–25 (see also Douglas, James; Kemble, John Mitchell; Thorpe, Benjamin; Turner, Sharon); and medievalists of color 51–54; philology 30–31, 90n87, 168, 227–28, 230–35; and post-Saxon concept 352–53; professional 'being' and 'becoming' 235–38, 241–42, 254–57; 'state of the field' conversations (2006-2010) 28–34; un-homing process 340–44 (see also Old English)
Annal records 188–90, 194–95

Antiquarian archaeologists: ekphrastic pairing with barrow excavations 104, 137–38, 141–42, 144–45; emotional connection to barrow excavations 138–41, 145–46; incorporation of barrow excavations 104, 138–41, 162; professionalization of 149–56; racial identification of barrow excavations 147–49, 165–66
Anzaldua, Gloria 345
Arabian Prince 283
Archaeology: Alfred fragment discovery 249, 276; Douglas as father of Anglo-Saxon 103–5; transformation of field 105–7 (see also Antiquarian archaeologists)
Arizona Center for Medieval and Early Modern Studies 54
Ásatrú Alliance 92n92
Asser, *Life of King Alfred*: overview 186–87; on Alfred's physical and vernacular body 191–94, 205–6, 243; on Alfred's textual and Latinized body 195–99, 200–202, 205–6; annal records as political framework 187–90
Atay, Ahmet 343, 344
Attridge, Derek 332
Autoethnography: as academic approach 43–45, 344–46; as mechanism for mourning 42–43, 45–49, 347–48 (see also Fictocriticism)

Baker, Geoffrey 323
Bald's Leechbook 243
Ballantyne, Tony 234n129
Barrows *116, 130*; accidental vs. intentional excavations 131–34; in *Beowulf*'s poetic structure 115–19, *116*, 128–29, *130*; as boundary markers 109–11, 129n57; Douglas's excavation model 102, 103–4, *132, 133*, 134–35, 144, 156; early medieval function 107–11; ekphrastic performance of 104, 137–38, 141–42, 144–45; as identity-making sites 112–15; incorporation and mourning of 104, 138–41, 145–46, 162; mortuary interior of *Beowulf* 119–20; and mound-breaking 121–22; and racial identification 147–49, 165–66; re- and de-territorialized in *Beowulf* 122–25; re- and de-territorialized as military territory 134–37

Baudrillard, Jean 141, 142
Bauman, Richard 288–89, 334
Beckett, David 235–36
Before the Closet (Frantzen) 350–52
'Being/becoming' 235–38, 241–42, 254–57
Ben-Dor Benite, Zvi 186
Benson, Thomas 227, 228
Beowulf: and archaeology 167–68; ekphrasis in 126–29; Hinds's graphic presentation 287n7; mortuary interior 119–20; mound-breaking in 120–22; and *Nenia Britannica* 142–43; ring structure and interlace *114*, 115–19, *116*, 128–29, *130*; territory transformation in 122–25
Beowulf (character): chiasmus of living and dying 115–19; ekphrastic transformation of 126–29; as mound-breaker 120–22
Bhabha, Homi 329, 343, 346
Biddick, Kathleen 99–100, 199–200n65
'Big Daddy' figure 300–301, 303–4
Bignall, Simone 256n33
Bjork, Robert 233n129
Black power: Black Power movement in alcohol advertising 300–301, 303–5; Olde English recoded as black resistance 283–84, *312*, 312–16; Olde English recoded as intergenerational narrative of 318–23
Blaikley, Alexander 221n109
Blood eagle: encryption of 89, 99–100; in *Krákumál*, overview 62, 77; in literary fiction 94–96; in popular culture, overview 91–94; scholarly debates on 88; Stenton's interpretation 82–83; in television 96–99; Turner's interpretation 77–79; Wallace-Hadrill's interpretation 84–87
Blood Eagle (Russell) 94–95
Blood Red Eagle 92n93
Body see *Corpus*
Bradley, Adam 333–34n114
Bridges, John 221n109
Briggs, Charles 288–89, 334
Britannia (Camden) 209–10n82

British Society of Antiquaries 229
Brooks, Nicholas 27, 181
Broom, Kent 138–40
Browne, Sir Thomas, *Hydriotaphia* 139
Bruhn, Siglind 125n48
Bureau of Alcohol, Tobacco and Firearms (BATF) 317
Burial mounds see Barrows

Camden, William, *Britannia* 209–10n82
Campbell, James 88
Carver, Martin 106, 111n22, 123
Charles I, King of England 210–11, 212, 214, 222
Charles II, King of England 210, 211, 212, 222
Charters 179–81, 183–86, 195–96
Chatham, Kent 102, *132*, 134–38
Chawla, Devika 343, 344, 345
Christ 199–202, 204–8
Christian, Fletcher 94n95
Christianity: and charters 183–85; and ethnicity 182–83; models of royal piety 193–94, 198–99; sovereignty of Christ 199–202, 204–8
Cisneros, Sandra 345
Civil Rights movement 300–301, 303–4
Civil Wars, English 210–14
Claxton, Marshall 221n109
Clunies Ross, Margaret 70
Collectanea Antiqua (Smith) 149–56, 152, 155, 164
Collins, Patricia Hill 310
Colonialism: in alcohol advertising 288, 290, *291*, 306–8; and decolonization 85–87, 241–42, 256, 305, 306–7, 329–30, 343–46; encryption of 71–74, 78, 80–81; French and Indian War 67–68; *Krákumál* in rhetoric of 67–70; Olde English recoded as postcolonial language politics 329–31; and Old English 288–92; and old guard ghost 31–33, 36–38, 40–41, 353–54; and ontological 'being' and 'becoming' 237–38, 241–42, 254–55; and postcolonial approaches 36–41, 344–46; World War II 83 (see also Race and ethnicity)

Cooper, James Fenimore, *Prairie, The* 297n26
Corpus: of Anglo-Saxon studies 227–28, 230–35; of Christ 199–202, 204–8; effigial presence of Alfred's *213, 214–26, 216, 218, 219, 223, 226, 249, 250, 251*; shifting semantics of 202–4; and translation of Alfred's corpse 211–12; vernacular body into Latinized 195–99, 200–202, 205–7
Crania Britannica (Davis and Thurnam): illustrations 157–63, *158, 159, 160, 161, 164*; physical and racialized descriptions 163–66
Craniology *157, 158, 160, 161*, 163, 165–66
Creative writing see Autoethnography; Fictocriticism
Criminality and violence 302–3, 311–12
Critical race theory 301n33
Critical theory: approached through multiple genres 348–52; early reception in Anglo-Saxon studies 26–27, 35; postcolonial approach vs. postcolonial medievalist 36–41; in 'state of the field' conversations (2006–2010) 28–34
Crohn's disease 243–44, 258–59, 266
Crucifixion, of Christ 199–202, 204–8
Crusader Gold (Gibbins) 95–96
Crypts see Barrows; Encryption and psychic crypts
Cunningham, John 246–47
Cust, Leonard 224

Dadd, Richard 221n109
Dailey, Patricia 26
David, King (biblical figure) 187, 198–99
Davies, Joshua 27
Davis, Craig 119n36, 182n19
Davis, Joseph Bernard see *Crania Britannica*
Davis, J. Pain 222n109
Davis, Kathleen 27, 36, 38–39
Davis, Rocío G. 45, 51
Decolonization 85–87, 241–42, 256, 305, 306–7, 329–30, 343–46
Deleuze, Gilles 33, 111, 113–15, 256
Dennis, Michael Robert 48
Desire for Origins (Frantzen) 26, 36, 39, 348–49

Dialogue on the Correct and Improved Writing of English
 (Smith) 209n82
Dilated Peoples 330–31
Dockray-Miller, Mary 26, 29, 34n19, 289
Douglas, James, as father of Anglo-Saxon studies 25, 103–5,
 175–76 (see also *Nenia Britannica*)
Downes, Paul 215
Dr. Dre 283, 313, 316n66, 317–21
Drout, Michael 28, 30–33
du Lhut, Daniel Greysolon Sieur 288, *290, 291,* 293
Dumas, Alexandre 297
Dumitrescu, Irina 27

Earl, James 26, 349, 350
Eazy-E 283–84, 313–15, 316n66
Echard, Siân 287n7
Eckardt, Hella 122
Effigial presence *213,* 214–26, *216, 218, 219,* 223, *226,* 249, *250, 251*
Einarsson, Bjarni 88
Einhard, *Life of Charlemagne* 187, 193–94
Ekphrasis: barrow-antiquarian ekphrastic pairing 104, 137–38, 141–42, 144–45; in *Beowulf* 126–29; as performative agent 104, 125–26
Ella, King of Northumbria: in *Krákumál*, overview 61–62; silenced voice of 77–81; in television adaptation 99
Ellard family: imaginary genealogy 261–62, 264–66, 267–71, 273; and postcolonial autoethnography 346–47; transgenerational haunting 42–43, 258–59, 343–44
Elstob, Elizabeth 349
Embodiment see Incorporation
Encryption and psychic crypts: of Anglo-Saxon *corpus* 234–35; of blood eagle 89, 99–100; of colonialism 71–74, 78, 80–81; as self-preservation 71, 77; through incorporation 71–74, 138–41, 162; and transgenerational haunting 86–87, 89
English Civil Wars 210–14
Ethnicity see Race and ethnicity

Eusebius, *Life of Constantine* 193–94
Evans, Hiram Wesley 295n22
Evidence (rapper) 330–31
Exoticism 305–6

Fairford Graves (Wylie) 145–49, *150*
Fairholt, F.W. 151, 163
Fanon, Frantz 237
Fauset, Jessie, "My House and a Glimpse of My Life Therein" 295–98
Feminism and feminist theory 34n19, 53, 337n1
Fictocriticism: applied to Alfred 259–61, 262–64, 266–67, 271–75, 276; as genre and scholarly approach 277–79; as mechanism for mourning 277–80, 348
Fitzpatrick, Esther 346
Flesh see *Corpus*
Folger Shakespeare Library 54
Foot, Sarah 27, 62, 179
Fradenburg, L.O. Aranye 91, 118–19, 126
Frank, Roberta 83–84, 88, 210n88
Frantzen, Allen: *Anglo-Saxonism and the Construction of Social Identity* 349; *Before the Closet* 350–52; critical theory approach 26, 35, 348–52; *Desire for Origins* 26, 36, 39, 348–49; and feminism 53, 337n1; *Speaking Two Languages* 349–50; on Turner 62
French and Indian War 67–68
Frosh, Stephen 64, 99

Gangsta rap and lifestyle 314–15, 317–23
Gates, Henry Louis, Jr. 284–85, 325
Geary, Patrick 120
Gender: feminism and feminist theory 34n19, 53, 337n1; masculinity 299, 300–301, 303, 314, 318–19, 351–52; misogyny 53, 337 (see also Sex and sexuality)
Geroulanos, Stefanos 186
Gesta Danorum (Saxo Grammaticus) 77–78
G-Funk 318–23

Ghosts see Haunting/ghosts
Gibbins, David, *Crusader Gold* 95–96
Gilmor, William 294n17
Giola, Dana 332
Goodrich, Micah 54
Grammar of the Anglo-Saxon Tongue, A (Rask; and Thorpe's translation) 231–35
Grant, David 309
Grave-robbing 121–22
Gray, Herman 305n40
Greenberg, Janelle Renfrow 210n87
Gregory, Pope, *Regula Pastoralis* 187, 193–94, 205–6n75
Grief see Mourning
Grimm, Jacob 289, 299
Guardian (newspaper) 20, 22–23, 30–31, 241
Guattari, Félix 33, 111, 113–15, 256
Gummere, Francis 287n7
Gupta, Pamila 202
Gurteen, S. Humphreys 20, 21–22

Haas, Gerrit 279
Hadley, D.M. 110n18
Hagedorn, Suzanne 220
Hagman, George 48
Halama, Alta Cools 332–33
Handbook of Anglo-Saxon Studies, A (Stodnick and Trilling) 35–38
Hardin, Tayana 277, 304n39
Härke, Heinrich 106
Harris, Stephen 27, 36–37, 182
Hart, Solomon Alexander 221n109
Haunting/ghosts: of Alfred in Anglo-Saxon *corpus* 227–28, 230–32; of Alfred's effigial presence 213, 214–26, *216*, *218*, *219*, *223*, *226*, 249, *250*, *251*; of old guard 31–34, 36–38, 40–41, 353–54; transgenerational 42–43, 86–87, 89, 258–59, 343–44 (see also Encryption and psychic crypts; Mourning)
Haydon, Benjamin Robert 221n109

Heavy metal bands 92
Herd, Denise A. 302n37, 311n58
Hickes, George 227, 228
Hinds, Gareth 287n7
Hip Hop Nation Language 285, 325–29
Hirst, Michael 98–99
History of England (Rapin-Troyas) 219, 220
History of the Anglo-Saxons (Turner): critical reception 62–63, 81–82; incorporation and encryption in 75–81; *Krákumál* as inspiration 61–62, 64–65, 74–75
Hoare, Sir Richard Colt 143
Holland, Philemon 209–10n82
Homosexuality 351–52
hooks, bell 345
Hopkins, Pauline, "Talma Gordon" 297n26
Horner, Shari 26
Horsley, John Callcott 221n109
Howe, Nick 27
Hydriotaphia (Browne) 139

Ice Cube 283, 313, 316n66
Idea of Anglo-Saxon England, The (Niles) 39, 249–52, 253
Identity-making: of barrow-antiquarian ekphrastic pairing 104, 137–38, 141–42, 144–45; barrows as sites of 112–15; ekphrastic transformation of *Beowulf* 126–29; of funeral tableau 123–25; professional 'being' and 'becoming' 235–38, 241–42, 254–57; racialized barrow excavations 147–49, 165–66; and territory concept 111–12 (see also Signifying)
Incorporation: of Anglo-Saxon *corpus* 234–35; of barrow excavations 104, 138–41, 162; encryption through 71–74, 138–41, 162; in *Krákumál* 66–67, 75, 139n78; of *Krákumál* in colonialism rhetoric 67–70; vs. mourning 66–67; translation as 76; in Turner's *History* 75–77
Interlistening 341–42
International Medieval Congress (Kalamazoo) 29, 34n19, 52–53
International Medieval Congress (Leeds) 34n19, 52

International Society of Anglo-Saxonists (ISAS) 34n19, 52 , 241–42, 254n31
Islamic terrorist organizations 93–95
Ivanhoe (Scott) 294n17

James, William 302
Jerr, Nicole 186
Jessup, Ronald 138n75
John, Eric 88
Johnson, Samuel 138n74
Johnson, Stephen 302
Johnstone, James, *Lodbrokar Quida; or The Death-Song of Lodbroc* 69–74
Jones, Chris 27
Jones, Gwyn 83
Jones, Stacy Holman 44
Joy, Eileen 26, 28, 29, 33–34, 49–50
J-Ro 327, 328–29
Junius, Franciscus 227

Kabir, Ananya Jahanara 27, 36
Kajikawa, Loren 319n73
Kalamazoo, International Medieval Congress 29, 34n19, 52–53
Kantorowicz, Ernst 214n96
Karkov, Catherine 26, 27, 36, 233n129
Kemble, John Mitchell: as archaeologist 166–68; as father of Anglo-Saxon studies 25, 169, 176; in OED 'Anglo-Saxonist' definition 20, 22; racial ideologies 119n36, 167
Kershaw, Paul 193n47, 248–49
Keyes, Cheryl L. 333n114
Keynes, Simon 179, 180–81, 187n31, 195n49, 210, 220, 221, 226–27
Kim, Dorothy 53, 54
Kim, Susan 26
King, Martin Luther, Jr. 300–301
King Alfred the Great (Smyth) 245–46, 247
Klass, Dennis 48

Klein, Stacy 26
Krákumál: overview 61–62, 65–66; in colonialism rhetoric 67–70; encryption of 71–74, 78, 80–81; incorporation in 66–67, 75, 139n78; Turner's interpretation 74–75, 77–81 (see also Blood eagle)
Krauss, Rosalind 279n39
Ku Klux Klan 295, 302–3

Lacan, Jacques 113n27, 203
Lacnunga 260
Language see Old English; Rap music; Vernacularity
Lapidge, Michael 195n49
Lawton, David 22n5
Leake, M. Breann 54
Leeds, International Medieval Congress 34n19, 52
Lees, Clare 26, 34n19, 49–50
Le Pen, Marine 338
Levinas, Emmanuel 237
Life of Ælfred the Great, The (Spelman) 210–14, *213, 216,* 217–20, 243n7
Life of Alcuin 193–94
Life of Alfred, or Alvred, The (Powell) 211n89
Life of Charlemagne (Einhard) 187, 193–94
Life of Constantine (Eusebius) 193–94
Life of King Alfred (Asser) see Asser, *Life of King Alfred*
Life of King Alfred (Wise) *218,* 220, 243n7
Lingard, John 81
Lipari, Lisbeth 341
Listening and interlistening 341–42
Literary criticism see Critical theory
LL Cool J 324
Lodbrokar Quida; or The Death-Song of Lodbroc (Johnstone) 69–74
Louvel, Liliane 128, 138
Lovedon Hill, Lincolnshire 108–9

MacKintosh, Sir James 81
Maclise, Daniel 221n109
Macron, Emmanuel 338
Maiolo, Francesco 184–85n25
Makoni, Sinfree 285, 334–35
Maldonado-Torres, Nelson 237, 255
Malt liquor see Olde English malt liquor
Masculinity 299, 300–301, 303, 314, 318–19, 351–52
Material crypts see Barrows
Mauzey, Merritt 294–95, 296
Mayer, Joseph 163
McCann, Kathrin 183, 184
McCracken, Peggy 185n25
Medieval Academy 54
Medievalism: among African Americans 294, 295–98; among whites 293–95; in Olde English branding 285–87, *286, 287, 298*, 298–99
Medievalists of Color (organization) 52–53, 54
Medieval studies: medieval historians in popular fiction 94–96; medievalists of color 51–54; postcolonialism in 36–41
Mehan, Uppinder 36
Mellor, John 276
Metal bands 92
Military territory 134–37
Miller, Paul 329
Mills, Charles 81
Minh-ha, Trinh T. 345
Miolo, Francesco 199n64
Misogyny 53, 337
Moraga, Cheríe 345
Mortensen, Peter 74
Morton, Timothy 126
Mortuary archaeology 104–7 (see also Antiquarian archaeologists)
Moser, Stephanie 144n87
Mound-breaking 121–22
Mounds see Barrows

Mourning: autoethnography as mechanism for 42–43, 45–49, 347–48; collaborative 49–51; and emotional connection to barrow excavations 138–41, 145–46; *vs.* encryption 71 (see also Encryption and psychic crypts); fictocriticism as mechanism for 277–80, 348; in funeral context 123; *vs.* incorporation 66–67 (see also Incorporation); process of, overview 41–42; and un-homing process 340–44
Murray, James 240
Murray, Roland 300n30
Music, heavy metal bands 92 (see also Rap music)
'My House and a Glimpse of My Life Therein' (Fauset) 295–98

Nationalism 233–34n129, 338
Nazis and neo-Nazis 93–96
Neal, Mark Anthony 305n40
Neimeyer, Robert 48
Nelson, Janet 27, 179, 245n12, 246–47, 248–49
Nenia Britannica (Douglas): overview 101–2; accidental *vs.* intentional excavation in 131–34; as archaeological milestone 103–5; barrows refigured as military territory 134–37; and *Beowulf* 142–43; critical reception 143–44; ekphrastic performance in 137–38, 141–42; as excavation model 102, 103–4, *132*, *133*, 134–35, 144, 156; incorporation of barrow excavations 138–41
New fiction, as genre 277–78 (see also Fictocriticism)
Niedorf, Leonard 119n36
Niles, John 26, 114, 115–17, 120, 227n115, 228–30; *Idea of Anglo-Saxon England, The* 39, 249–52, *253*
Nokes, Scott 28
Notæ Uberiores in Historiam Danicam Saxonis Grammatici (Stephanius) 77–78
N.W.A. 283–84, *312*, 312–16

Olde Englishes see Rap music
Olde English malt liquor: advertising, colonial branding 288, *290*, *291*, 306–8; advertising, medieval branding 285–87, *286*, *287*, *298*, 298–99; advertising, race and sex branding 300–

301, 303–8, 311–12; and oral expression 285–87, 324; ownership and distribution 285, 293, 304–5; in rap music 283–84, *312*, 312–16, 324; and social control 308–11
Old English: and academic study of rap music 331–36; and colonialism 288–92; and drinking 285–87; and graphic power 287–88, 299; as sociolinguistic expression 284–85 (see also Rap music)
Ol' Dirty Bastard 327, 328
Online gaming 92
Ontological 'being' and 'becoming' 237–38, 241–42, 254–55
Orton, Daniel 199
Osumare, Halifu 333n114
Overing, Gillian 26, 34n19, 49–50, 349, 350
Oxford English Dictionary (*OED*): 'Anglo-Saxon' definition 239–40; 'Anglo-Saxonist' definition 20–24, 178n3
Oxford University 210, 226–28
Ozengell, Kent 149–53, 157–63

Pagan religious organizations 92
Pantos, Aliki 109n17
Paraliterary writing see Fictocriticism
Parker, Joanne 220, 224
Pasternack, Carol Braun 26–27
Pathak, Archana 344
Patton, Paul 256n33
Pennycook, Alisdair 285, 329, 334–35
Percy, Thomas 67–68
Performance: of barrow-antiquarian ekphrastic pairing 104, 137- 38, 141–42, 144–45; ekphrasis as agent of 104, 125–26; of identity-making 111–12
Periodization, and sovereignty 38–40
Perry, G.D. 303n38
Philology 30–31, 90n87, 168, 227–28, 230–35
Philosophical 'being' and 'becoming' 235–38, 241–42, 254–57
Piety, royal 193–94, 198–99
Plummer, Charles 243n7, 247

Popular culture: blood eagle in, overview 91–94; blood eagle in
literary fiction 94–96; blood eagle in television 96–99 (see
also Olde English malt liquor; Rap music)
Posel, Deborah 202
Postcolonialism: in Anglo-Saxon *vs.* medieval studies 36–41;
and autoethnography 344–46
Postmodernism see Critical theory
postSaxon, as concept 352–53
Powell, Robert, *Life of Alfred, or Alvred, The* 211n89
Power see Black power; Colonialism; Sovereignty
PowerMaster controversy 316–17
Prairie, The (Cooper) 297n26
Pratt, David 179, 180–81, 187n31, 193n47, 248–49
Precedent, as concept 38
Professional 'being' and 'becoming' 235–38, 241–42, 254–57
Prohibition movement 302–3
Psychic crypts see Encryption and psychic crypts
Psychoanalysis: and incorporation 66, 71–72; and mourning
theory 48

Quinn, Eithne 314–15, 323

Race and ethnicity: 'Anglo-Saxon' as ethnic term 181–83; barrow excavations as racialized 147–49, 165–66; and black
power 300–301, 303–5, 318–23; critical race theory 301n33;
and interlistening 341–42; and medievalists of color 51–54;
Olde English recoded as black resistance 283–84, *312,*
312–16; Olde English recoded as Hip Hop Nation Language 324–29; and old guard ghost 31–33, 36–38, 40–41,
353–54; progressivist model 40–41; and raciolinguistics 230–35, 289; racist potential of white medieval amusements 294–95, *296*; and sexuality in alcohol advertisements 300–301, 303–8, 311–12 (see also Colonialism)
Ragnar Lodbrog: call for incorporation 66–67, 139n78; in
colonialism rhetoric 67–70; encryption of 71–74, 78, 80–81;
in *Krákumál*, overview 61–62, 65–66; in television adaptation 96–99

Rakaa 330–31
Rambaran-Olm, Mary 54
Rapin-Troyas, Paul de, *History of England* 219, 220
Rap music: in academic study of Old English language arts 331–36; Olde English recoded as black resistance 283–84, *312*, 312–16; Olde English recoded as Hip Hop Nation Language 324–29; Olde English recoded as intergenerational black power narrative 318–23; Olde English recoded as postcolonial language politics 329–31
Rashkin, Esther 72
Rask, Erasmus 22n4; *Analecta Anglo-Saxonica* (Thorpe's translation) 231, 234–35; *Grammar of the Anglo-Saxon Tongue, A* (Thorpe's translation) 231–35
Rawlinson, Christopher 227, 228
Regula Pastoralis (Gregory) 187, 193–94, 205–6n75
Reimitz, Helmut 182n18
Religion see Christianity
Reynolds, Andrew 106
Reynolds, Susan 178–79, 184n25, 239–41
Rix, Robert 67–68
Roach, Joseph 215–17
Rodriguez, Amardo 345
Roots (television series) 305
Rose, Jacqueline 29–30
Rosenbery, Lord 224–25
Royal piety 193–94, 198–99
Ruskin, John 217
Russell, Craig, *Blood Eagle* 94–95
RZA 327, 328

Sacrifice see Blood eagle
Salter, W.P. 221n109
Sampling (rap music) 329–30
Santner, Eric 203–4
Sawyer, Peter, *Age of the Vikings, The* 86n73
Saxo Grammaticus, *Gesta Danorum* 77–78
Scandinavian Kings in the British Isles 850–880 (Smyth) 87–88

Scandinavian literature see *Krákumál*
Scanlon, Lesley 235–36
Scarry, Elaine 203–4, 205
Schizoid theory 33
Schwab, Gabrielle 68, 73, 86–87
Scott, Sir Walter 81; *Ivanhoe* 294n17
Screen memories 68
Semple, Sarah 106
Sex and sexuality: and homosexuality 351–52; and race in alcohol advertisements 300–302, 303–8, 311–12; in rap music 313, 314, 322
Sharma, Manish 111n25
Shippey, Thomas 73n36, 89–90
Sides, Josh 310
Siewers, Alfred 27, 112n26
Signifying: as concept 284–85; in Olde English malt liquor advertisements 285–88, 298–301, 303–8, 311–12; Olde English recoded as black resistance 283–84, *312*, 312–16; Olde English recoded as Hip Hop Nation Language 324–29; Olde English recoded as intergenerational black power narrative 318–23
Simmons, Claire 62–63
Smiles, Sam 144n87
Smith, Charles Roach 162; *Collectanea Antiqua* 149–56, *152, 155, 164*
Smith, John, *Dialogue on the Correct and Improved Writing of English* 209n82
Smyth, Alfred 84; *King Alfred the Great* 245–46, 247; *Scandinavian Kings in the British Isles 850–880* 87–88
Snook, Ben 185–86
Snoop Dogg 317–22
Sociolinguistics see Rap music; Signifying
Southey, Robert 81
Sovereignty: of Alfred *vs.* Ella 75, 78–79; of Christ 199–202, 204–8; *corpus* as site for 202–4; in effigial presence of Alfred 213, *214*–26, *216, 218, 219, 223, 226*, 249, *250, 251*; of England during Civil Wars 210–14; of England during

World War II 83; and periodization 38–40; as raciolinguistic state 230–35; translated into charters 183–85; translation from vernacular physicality into Latin textuality 187–90, 194–99, 200–202, 205–7; *vs.* unsovereign physical body of Alfred 191–94, 245, 277

Spain, and medievalism 297

Speaking Two Languages (Frantzen) 349–50

Speculative fiction see Fictocriticism

Spelman, John, *Life of Ælfred the Great, The* 210–14, *213, 216,* 217–20, 243n7

Spiegel, Gabrielle 45, 51

Spitzmüller, Jürgen 287–88

Stanton, Robert 198–99

Stenton, Frank, *Anglo-Saxon England* 82–83

Stephanius, Stephanus, *Notæ Uberiores in Historiam Danicam Saxonis Grammatici* 77–78

Stevens, Alfred 221n109

Stevenson, William Henry 195n49, 243n7

Stewart, Kathleen 279

Stodnick, Jacqueline, *Handbook of Anglo-Saxon Studies, A* (with Trilling) 35–38

Stokes, William 168

Stowe, Harriet Beecher, *Uncle Tom's Cabin* 297n26

Sutton Hoo 111n22, *116, 130*

Swain, Larry 27, 28, 29

Sweet, Rosemary 229n120

"Talma Gordon" (Hopkins) 297n26

Tash 324–27

Taussig, Michael 279, 329

Taylor, Ros 23n5

Temperance movement 302–3

Territory: of barrow-antiquarian ekphrastic pairing 137–38, 141–42; barrows as boundary markers 109–11, 129n57; barrows refigured as military territory 134–37; of dying 123–25; and ekphrastic transformation in *Beowulf* 126–29; in identity-making, overview 111–12

Thorkelin, G.R. 22n4
Thorkelin, Grímur Jónsson 70
Thormann, Janet 27
Thornbury, Emily 22–23n5
Thornycroft, Hamo 224
Thornycroft, Thomas 224
Thorpe, Benjamin: as father of Anglo-Saxon studies 25, 169, 229–30; in OED 'Anglo-Saxonist' definition 20, 22; raciolinguistic scholarship 230–35
Thurnam, John see *Crania Britannica*
Thwaites, Edward 227, 228
Torok, Maria 63, 66, 77, 82, 86, 139n77, 234n131
Townsend, David 36
Translation: of Alfred's corpse 211–12; in emerging Anglo-Saxon studies 227–28; as incorporation 76; and raciolinguistics 230–35; of sovereignty into charters 183–85; of vernacular physicality into Latin textuality 187–90, 194–99, 200–202, 205–7
Treharne, Elaine 22n5, 27, 36
Trilling, Renée 27; *Handbook of Anglo-Saxon Studies, A* (with Stodnick) 35–38
Trump, Donald 99, 338
Tumuli see Barrows
Turner, Sharon: as father of Anglo-Saxon studies 25, 175–76; in OED 'Anglo-Saxonist' definition 20, 22; progressivist model of race 40–41 (see also *History of the Anglo-Saxons*)
Turville-Petre, Gabriel 83

Uncle Tom's Cabin (Stowe) 297n26

Vernacularity: of Alfred's physical body 192–93; and raciolinguistics 230–35, 289; translation of sovereignty from vernacular physicality into Latin textuality 187–90, 194–99, 200–202, 205–7 (see also Old English)
Vertue, George 219, 220–21
Vickers, Margaret 44
Victoria, Queen of England 252

Victorian antiquarians see Antiquarian archaeologists
Viking literature see *Krákumál*
Vikings (television series) 96–99
Violence and criminality 302–3, 311–12

Walker, Obadiah 212n93
Wallace-Hadrill, J.M. 84–87
Wanderings of an Antiquary (Wright) 157, 162
Wanley, Humfrey 226–28, 229
Wase, Christopher 212n93
Watt, Diane 49–50
Watts, G.F. 221n109
Weston, Corinne Comstock 210n87
Weston, Lisa 27
Wharton, Thomas 67n20
Whitaker, Cord 54, 298n28
Whitelock, Dorothy 243n7, 246–47
Whites and whiteness: in alcohol advertising 301, 304, 305, 307; and interlistening 341–42; medieval amusements 293–95; as Olde English target audience 293
W.H. Rolfe company 162–63
Whyte, Nicola 129–31
Wilkes, Chris 309
Williams, Howard 27, 104–5, 106, 108, 118, 120, 122, 146n91, 167, 169, 175–76
Wintle, Michael 85
Wise, Francis, *Life of King Alfred* 218, 220, 243n7
Women: in alcohol advertising 300–302, 303–8, 311; feminism and feminist theory 34n19, 53, 337n1; and misogyny 53, 337; in rap music 313, 314, 322
World War II 83
Wormald, Patrick 88, 247–48
Wright, Michelle 330
Wright, Thomas 166; *Wanderings of an Antiquary* 157, 162
Wylie, William 166; *Fairford Graves* 145–49, 150

Yorke, Barbara 36
Young, Helen 40–41

www.ingramcontent.com/pod-product-compliance
Lightning Source LLC
Chambersburg PA
CBHW061925220426
43662CB00012B/1813